HEROIC COMMITMENT IN RICHARDSON, ELIOT

AND JAMES

PATRICIA McKEE

HEROIC COMMITMENT

IN

RICHARDSON, ELIOT

AND

JAMES

PRINCETON UNIVERSITY PRESS

LIBRARY OF CONGRESS CATALOGING IN PUBLICATION DATA WILL BE
FOUND ON THE LAST PRINTED PAGE OF THIS BOOK

ISBN 0-691-06666-3

THIS BOOK HAS BEEN COMPOSED IN LINOTRON SABON

CLOTHBOUND EDITIONS OF PRINCETON UNIVERSITY PRESS
BOOKS ARE PRINTED ON ACID-FREE PAPER, AND BINDING
MATERIALS ARE CHOSEN FOR STRENGTH AND DURABILITY

PRINTED IN THE UNITED STATES OF AMERICA
BY PRINCETON UNIVERSITY PRESS
PRINCETON, NEW JERSEY

For Donald Pease

CONTENTS

Acknowledgments, *ix*

CHAPTER ONE   An Introduction of Critical Issues, *3*

CHAPTER TWO   Corresponding Freedoms: Language and the Self in *Pamela*, *51*

CHAPTER THREE   Richardson's *Clarissa*: Authority in Excess, *97*

CHAPTER FOUR   Power as Partiality in *Middlemarch*, *150*

CHAPTER FIVE   George Eliot's Redemption of Meaning: *Daniel Deronda*, *208*

CHAPTER SIX   The Gift of Acceptance: *The Golden Bowl*, *270*

Afterword, *347*

Index, *351*

ACKNOWLEDGMENTS

I am concerned in this book with human relations and narrative relations which work as relations of committed alienation. To say so is not to clarify those relations, perhaps, but
it is to clarify that such relations are not subject to clear
formulation. Commitment and alienation are among many
differences in this book that are, in themselves, contradictory
and that for clarity ought to be kept distinct. I have put them
together in order to insist on relations of differences that exceed distinction—not only in language but in society. I have
found such relations in the novels of Richardson, Eliot, and
James, and it is more acceptable, according to the tenets of
New Criticism, for example, to identify such excesses in fiction
than to find them in nonfiction. Fiction does not have to make
sense, though nonfiction is supposed to. I am particularly
indebted, therefore, to writers who have written in recent years
about social relations and about literature in ways that make
more than sense. Gilles Deleuze and Felix Guattari do so, for
example, in *Anti-Oedipus*, their radical and energetic critique
of psychoanalysis. So does Leo Bersani, considering both psychoanalysis and literature in *A Future for Astyanax*. Such
works of theory and criticism have made a great difference,
though often more an implicit than an explicit difference, to
my thinking and writing.

I want to thank the members of the faculty and adminis-
tration at Dartmouth College who awarded me a Faculty Fel-
lowship while I was working on this book. And I want particularly to thank James Cox, who has been especially helpful
to me with Henry James; Sharon Cameron, who read an early
version of the chapter on *Pamela* and made many helpful
suggestions; and Susan Wadsworth, who gave me her interest
and encouragement as I worked through the manuscript.

Most of all, I want to thank two friends who, even more
than they know, have contributed to my understanding of
human relations and to the writing of this book. Cary Perry
listened to its ideas, read much of it, even typed parts of it.

Donald Pease read and reread all of it, at every stage. Their responses and their responsiveness are in this book. The difference they have made is incalculable.

Acknowledgment is made to the journal *ELH* for permission to reprint the author's essay "Corresponding Freedoms: Language and the Self in *Pamela*," as published in the Spring 1985 issue, copyright 1985 The Johns Hopkins University Press. Acknowledgment is also made to the journal *boundary 2* for permission to reprint the author's essay "Unmastered Exchanges in Richardson and Freud," as published in the Winter 1984 issue. Copyright 1984 *boundary 2*.

Hanover, New Hampshire
April 1985

HEROIC COMMITMENT IN RICHARDSON, ELIOT

AND JAMES

CHAPTER ONE

AN INTRODUCTION OF CRITICAL ISSUES

In the chapters that follow, I offer readings of novels by Samuel Richardson, George Eliot, and Henry James in which human identity and representation exceed the bounds of conventional forms of identity and narrative. The excesses of these novels—both excesses of human behavior and excesses of narrative form—mean, on the one hand, that in content and form they function in terms at odds with prevalent critical and theoretical assumptions about both human relations and literary representation. I am interested, however, not only in identifying how emphatically these works exceed conventions of social and literary meaning but in elaborating the fullness of experience that inheres in their excesses. Yet traditional concepts of human identity and literary meaning make acceptance and appreciation of such experience difficult; for the wealth of these novels depends on the inclusion within meaning of elements of experience that traditionally are excluded from our sense of what is meaningful.

The critical work of this book, therefore, is an elaboration that struggles with prior assumptions about life and art. It is an elaboration *of* struggle, both because I am concerned with how ideas in the fiction of Richardson, Eliot, and James differ from more conventional ideas, and because the novels themselves are engaged in such a struggle. These authors' vision of experience is a vision of struggle: the struggle to redeem meaning itself from the losses entailed in conventional forms of thought and behavior, and a struggle that is clarified in the novels by careful representations of alternative attitudes and the friction between such alternatives. Such struggle occurs, however, not so much because other ideas get in the way or in order to get the conflict of ideas out of the way but because struggle itself is meaningful. It is crucial to my sense of meaningful experience that meaning in these novels is always at issue. They insist that meaningful experience entails a commitment to struggle and a commitment to relations among differences rather than a distinction of or settlement of differences.

The particular novels on which I have chosen to focus— *Pamela, Clarissa, Middlemarch, Daniel Deronda*, and *The Golden Bowl*—are different in many ways. But they share a commitment to struggles of meaning and in that commitment exceed the bounds of meaning that hold in other novels of their periods. As I will be arguing throughout this book, critical reactions to these narratives have tended to neutralize their differences and in part this is due to the assumptions inherent in conventional critical practices, which always tend to have that effect. But these particular novels also have more to lose by such readings; they are, in ways I will try to elucidate, more vital than many other fictions.

In order briefly to mark their difference from other major novels, I would suggest that there is more at issue in these narratives, more at stake in their struggles. Whereas Jane Austen, for example, represents struggles of individual characters with their own conflicting feelings and with the difficulty of seeing what others mean, her novels rest on certain social conventions and orders, which are challenged during the course of her narratives only insofar as they are also finally validated. Thackeray's *Vanity Fair*, on the other hand, can be said to undermine any conventional ideals about human behavior. But here, too, a particular conception of human behavior can be depended on to account for events: all human relations are equally vain. And the narrator knows this as surely as Austen's narrators know their material. Such novels reduce the dimensions of uncertainty, therefore, by asking fewer questions than the novels I am considering. Though much of Dickens' work shares the concern of these novels to transform relations, in Dickens' novels, too, less is at issue. Characters are, for one thing, usually finally right or wrong, whereas in the five novels I am considering, characters tend to be increasingly *implicated* in events to the extent that whether they are right or wrong is rendered undecidable.

There is, then, both more at issue and less that is resolved in these novels than seems to me evident in most other novels of the eighteenth and nineteenth centuries. Yet in their refusal to settle issues they also refuse to represent irresolution in terms of indifference or nonchalance. *Tristram Shandy* is a novel which, one might say, even more clearly exceeds the bounds of determinate and conventional meaning in its constant irresolution. But such a narrative differs from works of Richardson, Eliot, and James in its narrator's lack of commitment to conflict: a lack of commitment that makes *Tristram Shandy* less intense and less meaningful, in the sense of committed meaning that I will be considering in this book.

My concern in this introductory chapter is to locate this concept of meaning in relation to other concepts of meaning, both literary and social, in order to provide theoretical contexts for the discussions of the novels that follow. As my earlier description of struggle suggests, the concept of meaning elaborated here verges closely on poststructuralist theories of meaning and on concepts of meaning underlying deconstructive critical practices. My consideration of the indeterminate and conflicting nature of meaning is largely dependent on the work of Jacques Derrida and critics who share his sense of meaning as a differential, relative, and infinite process. On the other hand, it would be fair to say that certain of the assumptions underlying American New Criticism are recognizable in the argument of this book. My readings make little reference to authorial intention, for example, and argue in fact that the meaning of words gets carried away from intention, that words always mean something different from what they are intended to mean. Moreover, particularly in the novels of Richardson and James, artistic or artful representation is recognized as a peculiar mode of representation, one that is freer to exceed the bounds of clarity and determination than are other kinds of expression in society; though my argument is that what have been considered privileges of art are put to common and practical use in these novels. Particularly because

both New Critics and poststructuralists recognize an excess
of meaning in language, I want to begin by considering the
differences between their concepts of meaning and the meaning I find in Richardson, Eliot, and James.

Though New Critics find meaning in excess, their sense of
meaningful excesses is limited to the experience of aesthetic
language. "It is the scientist whose truth requires a language
purged of every trace of paradox," Cleanth Brooks writes;
whereas "apparently the truth which the poet utters can be
approached only in terms of paradox."[1] Robert Penn Warren
argues that the "impurity" of contradiction and irony is necessary to poetry because poetry must represent a struggle:
"the poet wishes to indicate that his vision has been earned,
that it can survive reference to the complexities and contra-
dictions of experience. And irony is one such device of reference." Yet the struggle for meaning in poetry is a struggle
toward an end of struggle, "a movement through action toward rest."[2] And not only is impurity overcome; it is overcome
in an imaginative representation that distinguishes both poetic
impurity and purity from nonpoetic experience. The New
Critics' separation of poetry from other kinds of writing occurs in part in their insistence that the poem's struggle is both
contained and resolved in the poem. Paul Bové therefore sees
that

> The structure of Brooks's criticism rests upon a foun-
> dation which may best be described as a "spiritual mo-
> nism" reinforced by an almost visionary belief in the
> existence of an Ideal Absolute order in a separated world
> or Spirit. The ironic poet "re-discovers" and "represents"
> this order and returns man to these lost "origins," where

[1] Cleanth Brooks, "The Language of Paradox," *The Well-Wrought Urn:
Studies in the Structure of Poetry* (New York: Harcourt, Brace and World,
1947), p. 3.
[2] Robert Penn Warren, "Pure and Impure Poetry," in *The Kenyon Critics:
Studies in Modern Literature from the Kenyon Review*, ed. and intro. John
Crowe Ransom (Cleveland: World Publishing Co., 1951), pp. 40, 39.

he may be refreshed by the creative source of unity and wholeness.[3]

Thus it is that Brooks and Warren together insist on the special nature of poetic excess, a specialness that privileges poetic experience, leaving criticism a secondary process, a mere means to an end. In their introduction to *Understanding Poetry*, they conclude that "criticism and analysis" are "ultimately of value *only insofar as [they] can return readers to the poem itself*—return them, that is, better prepared to experience it more immediately, fully, and, shall we say, innocently."[4] The "poem itself," then, somehow retains its independent unity, while the mediating critical relation or the critical struggle—somewhat like the struggle that is resolved in the poem itself—gives way to an immediate, full, innocent relation with the poem, arriving at purity after all.

Here most emphatically a difference is signaled from the poststructuralist treatment of both poetry and criticism, since poststructuralist theory insists that language, whether of poetry, science, or criticism, is a means which never reaches an end and thus never provides any sense of fullness. For Derrida, struggle is endless and impurity inescapable, because meaning is never immediate or present.

The economic character of differance in no way implies that the deferred presence can always be recovered, that it simply amounts to an investment that only temporarily and without loss delays the presentation of presence, that is, the preception of gain or the gain of perception. Contrary to the metaphysical, dialectical, and "Hegelian" interpretation of the economic movement of differance, we must admit a game where whoever loses wins and where one wins and loses each time. If the diverted presentation continues to be somehow definitely and irreducibly withheld, this is not because a particular present

[3] Paul A. Bové, *Destructive Poetics: Heidegger and Modern American Poetry* (New York: Columbia University Press, 1980), pp. 104-105.

[4] Cleanth Brooks and Robert Penn Warren, *Understanding Poetry* (4th ed.; New York: Holt, Rinehart and Winston, 1976), p. 16.

remains hidden or absent, but because differance holds us in a relation with what exceeds (though we necessarily fail to recognize this) the alternative of presence or absence.[5]

Since a process of differing rather than a determination of differences occurs in language, the struggle for meaning is never won but is both won and lost in the perpetual struggle *of* meaning. Differance replaces difference, then, and always exceeds any distinction that would tell differences.

But Derrida also limits excesses of meaning: not because he limits them, as New Critics do, to aesthetic language but because he limits them to language itself. The role of the reader or critic or any participant in language is effectively demeaned, as is the role of the critic in *Understanding Poetry*, since meaning is limited to language on the one hand and limited to poetry on the other. Derrida insists that "the subject . . . is inscribed in the language, that he is a 'function' of the language. He becomes a *speaking* subject only by conforming his speech . . . to the system of linguistic prescriptions taken as the system of differences, or at least to the general law of differance."[6] Thus the proposition that "the signified is originally and essentially . . . trace, that it is always already in the position of the signifier" means that, whatever the excesses of language, there is no meaning that exceeds language itself.[7] As Barbara Johnson says of Derrida's reading of Rousseau's *Confessions*, "Rousseau's life does not *become* a text through his writing: it always already *was* one. Nothing, indeed, can be said to be *not* a text."[8]

There is, however, the unsaid, by which I do not mean a

[5] Jacques Derrida, "Differance," in *Speech and Phenomena: And Other Essays on Husserl's Theory of Signs*, trans. David B. Allison (Evanston: Northwestern University Press, 1973), p. 151.

[6] Ibid., pp. 145-46.

[7] Jacques Derrida, *Of Grammatology*, trans. Gayatri Chakravorty Spivak (Baltimore: The Johns Hopkins University Press, 1976), p. 73.

[8] Barbara Johnson, "Translator's Introduction" to *Dissemination* by Jacques Derrida, trans. Barbara Johnson (Chicago: University of Chicago Press, 1981), p. xiv.

void of meaning. The sense of meaning for which I am arguing depends on unsaid excesses, both in that it depends on social rather than merely linguistic excess and in that it depends on language to leave room for more meaning than language can express. Language does not represent or mean human experience so much as it repeats the experience of social relations, which exceed language just as they exceed any form. Language, then, just because of its gaps of meaning, leaves room for more meaning than it formulates; and in this excessiveness it can be said to work as human relations work when they are meaningful.

To argue that the crucial excess of meaning lies in social relations may seem to move my sense of meaning right out of any context shared with New Critical or poststructuralist notions of meaning. But if we consider the implications of those theories of literary and linguistic meaning, we can see that there is indeed implicit in them a human relation. Though it is a relation of a human being to a text, it is a relation that in fact displaces human relations per se with the relation of human being and text, which is privileged *as* the most meaningful, or the only meaningful, kind of relation. At the same time, it is given as a relation in which the human being has less meaning than the text or no meaning at all that differs from texts. The very complexity of struggle which is crucial to these writers' sense of meaning is a struggle in which human beings do not seem to take part. The reader or subject does not participate in meaning, which occurs in the text, or participation is limited to the discovery that the self makes no difference to the meaning the text has in itself. This is to say not only that such critical writers give us a human relation but that in their sense of human relations the human being is, at best, of secondary significance. The text takes over in such a relation, both because it is put into a position that is claimed to contain meaning within its own terms and because this meaning, whether complete or incomplete, has priority over, or already has expressed, any subjective interpretation. This is a relation of strictly separate parts, then, unless we accept that we do not exist outside of language, and a relation of mastery and privilege as well as of exclusion.

The sense of meaning in which the novels I am considering themselves take part is a sense of meaning that exceeds these concepts of meaning nowhere more pointedly than in the inclusion of social, nonlinguistic relations within meaning. Most of my attention in this book is given to the relations of human beings in the novels: relations that render the individual self a dependent, relative, and indeterminate phenomenon, whose meaning is inseparable from the meaning of others. Self and other become implicated in each other, both because the meaning of one implies the meaning of the other and because each is responsive to and responsible for the meaning of the other. The meaning of the self thus exceeds the bounds of separate and independent individuality, and the relations of self and other exceed the bounds of any economical or mastered exchange.

This suggests a concept of human relations that resembles the complicating and implicating struggle of meaning that both New Critics and Derrida identify in texts. But it constitutes a wealth of meaning that is clearest in the refusal to privilege any form or end of meaning and the refusal to acknowledge any mastery or predominance among the parts and means of meaning. The heroic characters of these novels, insistent on identifying themselves in indeterminate relations with others, thereby preclude any distinction or mastery of individuals. One effect of this is that social privileges are demeaned or precluded: the privileges of the master in *Pamela*, for example, or the privileges of Christian gentlemen in *Daniel Deronda*. Moreover, characters and narrators alike perceive and represent experience in terms that do not limit meaning either to art or language. Relations of human beings and of concepts, too, are clearly more meaningful in these novels than are their mere representations, and language is employed in order to leave room for meaning that exceeds it. One effect of this is that the privileges New Critics afford to art and those the poststructuralists afford to language are put to common, or excessive, use.

In all of the novels I am considering here, one crucial insistence is that there is no clear or necessary distinction between "real" and fictitious representations and that human life becomes more meaningful as the special privileges of representation—particularly the privilege of leaving meaning indeterminate and open to interpretation—are employed for practical, though uneconomical, effect. The concept of meaning at work in these novels thus revises aesthetic and social conventions of meaning in part by its refusal to separate aesthetic and social meaning. Richardson's Pamela, for one, is a character whose "artful" behavior, which is already to indicate behavior that conflates art and politics, has political effects in everyday life; and Richardson's narrative makes it difficult to tell the difference between artful and political effects. Artistic and practical modes of representation become inseparable in all these novels as characters as well as narrators exercise the privileges of the artist and thereby refuse to privilege art itself. And the interpretations of experience by characters and narrators, in these novels in which any representation is acknowledged to be mere interpretation, similarly conflate the practices of creator and critic.

Thus the sense of meaning that emerges in these novels differs from assumptions and implications of both New Criticism and deconstruction just at the point at which they can be said to have most in common. For what is crucial to meaning in these novels is the engagement of multiple subjects in meaning, which because of such engagement exceeds the terms of representation. Meaning is never, therefore, independent of interpretation and thus implicates differing subjects in differing meaning. The very conception of the self as a part and a means of the relations that constitute meaning, which is the very commitment of the self to meaning, necessitates that meaning is always a human relation. Thus the meaning of any representation is dependent on some self, who makes a difference, though an indeterminate difference, to its meaning. Whereas both New Critical and deconstructive practices insist on the disengagement of the interpreter from the meaning of a text, on the assumption that meaning is limited to the terms of the text itself, meaning in these novels depends on the participation of human beings who, because of their own excessive differences, keep meaning in the process of indeterminate differing. Thus excesses or indistinctions of meaning occur as they occur in human relations: because there is no precise or economical division of functions in the relations of art and life, or of representation and reality, as there is none in the relations of self and other.

All of these excesses of meaning may be seen to resemble the excesses critics have assigned to the meaning of literary language. Geoffrey Hartman has written most pertinently about such excesses, identifying them as uneconomical but identifying them too with the very power of literature:

> There are many ways of describing the force of literature. The priority of language to meaning is only one of these. . . . It expresses what we all feel about figurative language, its excess over any assigned meaning. . . . Literary language foregrounds language itself as something not reducible to meaning: it opens as well as closes the disparity between symbol and idea, between written sign and assigned meaning.[9]

Language, then, may seem to exceed meaning. Or, on the other hand, meaning may seem to exceed language. For example, Hartman goes on to say that there always remains a "difference between a text and the commentaries that elucidate it, and which accumulate as a variorum of readings that cannot all be reconciled."[10] Thus, given the multiplicity of meanings for any given text, we may feel an excess in the meaning, which seems irreducible to the language of the text.

That language does not coincide with meaning, then, opens up excesses on two sides of the exchange we assume to occur if we assume that language is exchangeable with meaning. Literary language either says too much or says too little to

---

[9] Geoffrey H. Hartman, "Preface" to *Deconstruction and Criticism* by Harold Bloom et al. (New York: Continuum, 1979), pp. vii-viii.
[10] Ibid., p. viii.

have a clearly equivalent, definite meaning. When we are given such language and take it to mean something else, then, the exchange is not an even exchange. Given the language, we do not "get" exactly what it represents. This indeterminate exchange can be differentiated from unambiguous or determinate kinds of exchange that offer us complete meaning, Hartman says:

> Naming, like counting, is a strong mode of specification. It disambiguates the relation of sign to signified, making the proper term one end and the thing that is meant the other. Two terms complete the act; signification itself is elided, or treated as transparent. . . . Naming of this kind does not draw attention to itself. Literary speech does, however; and not by an occult quality (a secret third term), but rather by structures like periphrasis which under- and overspecify at the same time.[11]

Whereas proper naming masters meaning by ignoring the process of meaning, literary language calls attention to that process as something that makes a difference to meaning: a difference that cannot itself be determined or settled. For such language characteristically evades rather than comes to "the point," in forms that are ambiguously related to meaning and that give us either too much or too little to give us determinate meaning.

But the pertinence of Hartman's description of literary language lies not only in its acknowledgment of the excesses of figurative signs and meaning but in the relation in which he sees the reader to those excesses. If "what we all feel about figurative language" is "its excess over any assigned meaning," then at the same time that we provide signs for its meaning, we feel meaning exceeding our signs too. Thus in our relation to the signs of literature we sense a meaning in literature beyond its representations; and our response to literature is

---

[11] Geoffrey H. Hartman, "The Voice of the Shuttle: Language from the Point of View of Literature," in *Beyond Formalism: Literary Essays 1958-1970* (New Haven: Yale University Press, 1970), p. 352.

also an experience unrepresentable by the signs we can use. This is the kind of relation, a *relation* in excess of terms of representation, that I am identifying throughout this book. It is a relation in which the self's experience exceeds language as the self responds to another's excessive meaning. The exchange between reader and text here entails a powerful excess, but it is not an overpowering excess of meaning in literature; it is rather an *em*powering excess, for the reader responds to that excess by experiencing an unrepresentable excess in the self too. In this, not only is mastery precluded by a mutually empowering relation, but power itself becomes an uneconomical relation precisely because it is recognizable on both sides of the exchange of reader and text, just as an excess is recognizable on both sides of the exchange of language and meaning described above.

Such relations are characteristic of the novels I consider in this book. The indeterminate relations of language and meaning, that is, are inseparably implicated in indeterminate human relations which are as unsettled and excessive as those relations. Formally, then, circumlocution is characteristic of the language of these narratives; we find in reading them more words than we need in order to get a clear sense of what is going on. In addition, it is not possible to identify structures in the novels themselves, such as clearly delineated and unifying plots, that will contain their meaning by providing explicit, determinate relations among their parts. And such formal excesses are repeated in the content of the novels; human relations proceed similarly, to the extent, in fact, of rendering form and content somewhat indistinct. It is not possible to identify the heroic characters of the novels making exchanges with others that enable us to determine the relation between, or the difference between, self and other.

This overlap of form and content is perhaps most obvious in Richardson's novels. The letters that make up his narratives and the characters that make up the letters "correspond" with each other in much the same way. The letters themselves often overlap and overtake each other, so that they do not fit together to form a continuous development in which each part is distinct from other parts. Shifting from one point in time to another, the parts of the narrative go back and forth among characters as well as backward and forward in time, remaining in circulation and covering and recovering the same ground. And yet in this the form of the novels is not more elusive and evasive than the behavior of the heroines, who are themselves intent on evading the efforts of B and Lovelace to "get" them. Like the narratives that bear their names, Pamela and Clarissa evade plots. At the same time, in their inability to separate themselves from B and Lovelace, these characters remain implicated in those others' behavior.

George Eliot's *Middlemarch* and *Daniel Deronda* are also excessive in the amount of language and experience they include. In both novels there are too many characters and too many plots for readers to be sure which have priority, and the relations among those parts of the novels remain indeterminate though binding. A sense of the various parts exceeds a sense of singular whole, and with such excesses Eliot insists that signification cannot be completed or unified. Eliot's narratives repeatedly emphasize, moreover, the ambiguous relations of forms of representation and what is represented. For she recognizes that any sense of determination or completion necessitates a reduction of meaning:

> The driest argument has its hallucinations, too hastily concluding that its net will now at last be large enough to hold the universe. Men may dream in demonstrations, and cut an illusory world in the shape of axioms, definitions, and propositions, with a final exclusion of fact signed Q.E.D. No formulas for thinking will save us mortals from mistake in our imperfect apprehension of the matter to be thought about.[12]

There is always an excess of meaning, Eliot insists: more meaning than our forms of representation can hold, whether those forms be fictive or nonfictive. To assume that a repre-

---

[12] George Eliot, *Daniel Deronda*, ed. Barbara Hardy (Harmondsworth, Mx.: Penguin, 1967), p. 572.

sentation can contain complete meaning is to exclude or "cut out" something from meaning: reductions occur both in the terms of representation and in the matter represented. Unwilling to exclude anything from meaning because it does not fit the terms of something else, Eliot uses language that emphasizes an excess in both the terms of representation and the represented meaning. The language of this passage is characteristic of such excesses, and characteristic of Eliot's persistent indistinction of imaginative and practical representation, as it combines argument with hallucination, dreams with demonstrations, illusions with axioms. Such terms do not logically fit together, but Eliot puts them together anyway and thereby renders the meaning of each term ambiguous and indeterminate, as the words are put into an inclusive rather than exclusive relation with each other. She is telling us that apprehension is always imperfect, and she is giving us language that insists on imperfect apprehension.

With Henry James, we are probably even more aware of the excess of meaning and language that Hartman identifies in literature; and James also puts increasing pressure on the distinction of artistic excess and practical economics, rendering the one indistinct from the other. One must often sense that James would not have used his language if he had wanted to get to the point or wanted his readers to get a clear sense of meaning; for either his language or his meaning exceeds an exact exchange. And *The Golden Bowl* is redundant both in the excess of its language and in the excess of its "plot." It keeps repeating itself, reconsidering the same events and re-enacting the same scenes. But if we get more than we need— more, perhaps, than many readers want—this is because James does not, any more than does his hero, Adam Verver, believe in even exchanges. Mr. Verver "taxed to such small purpose . . . the principle of reciprocity" in his dealings with others that it is difficult for other characters to know where they stand with him.[13] But it is such indeterminate relations, among characters as among words, that James insists are meaningful.

[13] Henry James, *The Golden Bowl* (Harmondsworth, Mx.: Penguin, 1973), p. 30.

This is to say that in all of these novels the indeterminacy of meaning is not simply a condition of literary language. It is actively generated, by both narrators and characters, with emphatically uneven exchanges among self and others; and the determination of meaning is actively resisted. These narrators and heroic characters assume indeterminate meaning as an empowering condition, identifying indeterminacy with the freedom of human beings and human relations to mean more than determination allows. Thus something like the peculiar force of literature that Hartman identifies with its indeterminate meaning and language is the power experienced by characters in these novels as they both increase and unsettle the meaning of experience. They insist on identifying themselves and their relations with others in terms that preclude any determination of meaning and instead enable conflicting elements of experience—their own differing impulses and feelings, for example, and the differing desires of self and others—to be meaningful.

To extend the critical context or critical implications of such practices, we can look at them in relation to theories of narrative and human meaning that explicitly identify such meaning with forms of mastery and determination. One such form is literary realism; another is Freud's reality principle. The novels of James, Richardson, and Eliot that I am considering here do not present us with such forms of representation and behavior except as practices that work against meaningful experience. And in these novels' resistance to forms of mastery, they can be seen to exceed governing principles of narrative form and human behavior in much literary and psychological theory.

Just at the point where characters in the novels break down the boundary between aesthetic or indeterminate meaning and realistic or determinate meaning they are of course subject to being called unrealistic; and they are called unrealistic by other characters in the novels. They are unrealistic to the extent that realistic behavior is considered to consist of mastery or the desire for mastery. To the same extent, the novels themselves can be considered unrealistic, as they exceed the terms of a "commanding structure of significance,"[14] which Leo Bersani identifies with realistic fiction. The "realistic" novel may be considered a form of human experience that limits experience to stable terms, then, and on several counts the novels I am considering reject the conventions of realism. One such convention is that language refers to some reality outside of language that provides real grounds for significance, grounds that are not indeterminate. Thus George Levine, even as he redefines realism in *The Realistic Imagination*, maintains that Victorian realists, though they wrote "with the awareness of the possibilities of indeterminate meaning and of solipsism, . . . wrote *against* the very indeterminacy they tended to reveal."[15] Bersani also identifies the tendency of realistic novels both to reveal and to work against indeterminacy in his considerations of another convention of realistic narratives: the plot that functions to limit meaning to more secure terms than poetic structure, for example, provides. Bersani sees that

> The realistic novel, for all its apparent looseness, is an extremely tight and coherent structure: it encourages us to believe in the temporal myth of real beginnings and definitive endings, it portrays a world in which events always have a significance which can be articulated, and it encourages a view of the self as organized (if also ravaged) by dominant passions or faculties.[16]

This is to suggest that the realistic novel orders meaning as it limits meaning to the terms of its representation. It is also to suggest that the organization of a self-controlled human being is implied in the organization of realistic novels.

In fact, insofar as the determination of individual identity is itself constituted as a narrative, the meaning of the realistic individual self and the realistic narrative plot may come to

[14] Leo Bersani, *A Future for Astyanax: Character and Desire in Literature* (Boston: Little, Brown, 1976), p. 53.

[15] George Levine, *The Realistic Imagination: English Fiction from Frankenstein to Lady Chatterley* (Chicago: University of Chicago Press, 1981), p. 4.

[16] Leo Bersani, "The Subject of Power," *Diacritics*, 7, no. 3 (1977), 7.

much the same thing. This is what Peter Brooks has suggested by identifying narrative plot with the "masterplot made necessary by the structural demands of Freud's thought."[17] Brooks clarifies how both conventions of narrative and conventions of selfhood discount or repress indeterminate meaning and instead find meaning in determination and resolution. Although final "recognition cannot abolish textuality, does not annul the middle which, in its oscillation between blindness and recognition, between origin and endings, is the truth of the narrative text," yet "the desire of the text is ultimately the desire for the end," and "we have repetitions serving to bind the energy of the text in order to make its final discharge more effective."[18] The indeterminate midst of experience is discounted, and the end is what counts as the end of tension. This plot, as a structure that is mobilized by the very tensions of differences it is determined to resolve, is a plot alienated from its own core or middle, working against its own energy. Such a plot is clear not only in Freud's *Beyond the Pleasure Principle*, as Brooks suggests, but in most traditional readings of the Freudian history of the ego. I want briefly to consider here how this history is read as a plot and how the plot depends on exchanges that make mastery possible and alienation inevitable. For the plotted narrative, the plotted self, mastery, and alienation are all phenomena to which the novels of Richardson, Eliot, and James create alternatives.

Freudian theory assumes an original, "primary anxiety" in human beings, "an overwhelming state of stimulation with a minimum of protection from stimuli."[19] This state of excitement is a state of tension because the infant has no way of knowing whether the stimulation—hunger, for instance—will be relieved. Because the need for relief is experienced separately from the relief, in that there is no way of knowing that relief will follow need, the need is always experienced in excess

[17] Peter Brooks, "Freud's Masterplot: Questions of Narrative," *Yale French Studies*, no. 55/56 (1977), 285.

[18] Ibid., p. 296.

[19] Otto Fenichel, *The Psychoanalytic Theory of Neurosis* (New York: W. W. Norton, 1945), p. 34.

of means of satisfaction. The precariousness of this situation is relieved by mastering the uncertainty of satisfaction. And mastery means

> a gradual substituting of actions for mere discharge re-actions. This is achieved through the interposing of a time period between stimulus and reaction, by the acquisition of a certain tension tolerance, that is, of an ability to bind primitive reaction impulses by countercathexes. The pre-requisite for an action is, besides mastery of the bodily apparatus, the development of the function of judgment. This means the ability to anticipate the future in the imag-ination by "testing" reality, by trying in an active manner and in a small dosage what might happen to one passively and in an unknown dosage. This type of functioning is in general characteristic of the ego.[20]

This is an economy in which certain exchanges occur to make mastery possible. One kind of exchange substitutes a reduced "dosage" for the larger reality that exceeds manageable pro-portions. Other exchanges work to bind together, or make connections between, previously disconnected elements of ex-perience. A stimulus and reaction to it, a need and its satis-faction, are seen as parts of equations: reaction answers stim-ulus, and satisfaction answers need. And so these elements are tied together, made parts of a unit as beginnings and ends of experience. The differences between them are repressed by such equations: the tension of waiting that occurs between a need and its satisfaction, for example, no longer has signifi-cance equal to the need and the response to it once these are seen as the two parts of a whole.

This is also how a narrative plot is said to work. " 'The king died and then the queen died' is a story," E. M. Forster says in *Aspects of the Novel.* " 'The king died, and then the queen died of grief' is a plot." The latter event is bound to the former by causality, which insists that the latter event is given its meaning in terms of the former event. "Or again,"

[20] Ibid., pp. 41-42.

Forster writes, " 'The queen died, no one knew why, until it was discovered that it was through grief at the death of the king.' This is a plot with a mystery in it, a form capable of high development."[21] This plot suspends much more meaning than the simpler plot and limits much more meaning in the end. When the cause of the queen's death is discovered, all that has been suspended between his death and hers seems unimportant; the end gives significance. When events are plotted, then, they are bound together in a way that limits their meaning to what they have in common; how they differ is discounted. The ability to equate two elements so that despite their differences they balance each other out is necessary to the construction of a plot. The "minimal complete plot" defined by Tzvetan Todorov develops by identifying equivalents for elements of experience and so balancing imbalances and resolving tension. The plot

> consists in the passage from one equilibrium to another. An "ideal" narrative begins with a stable situation which is disturbed by some power or force. There results a state of disequilibrium; by the action of a force directed in the opposite direction, the equilibrium is re-established. . . .[22]

The "ideal" here is the balance or equivalence of differences in order to relieve the tension between them.

The individual self actively plots experience, then, if it learns that its own activity can bring about the resolution of tension through the resolution of differences. By making up and resolving substitute situations in the imagination, the self is able to take active control of them. As in most other plots, the end becomes predictable even though the middle of the experience remains uncertain. Mastering differences by acting out for itself, in games and imagination, the situations that are suspenseful if dependent on others, the ego creates masterful fictions that enable independence and self-control in the face

[21] E. M. Forster, *Aspects of the Novel* (New York: Harcourt, Brace, 1927), p. 130.

[22] Tzvetan Todorov, *The Poetics of Prose*, trans. Richard Howard (Ithaca: Cornell University Press, 1977), p. 111.

of uncertain reality. In doing so, the self can be said to behave like novelists who, in Edward Said's words, "do work that compensates us for the tumbling disorder of brute reality."[23] Making up the difference between a reality we cannot control and the security we desire, the creation of fiction becomes a means of giving order to experience and securing the relation between self and world.

Moreover, the ego makes up the difference between self and world in another sense as it learns to behave in terms of the outside world. For to become realistic, Freud suggests, is to repress parts of the self as we learn the difference between what we want and what we can realistically have:

> The ego learns that it must inevitably go without immediate satisfaction, postpone gratification, learn to endure a degree of pain, and altogether renounce certain sources of pleasure. Thus trained, the ego becomes "reasonable," is no longer controlled by the pleasure-principle, but follows the REALITY-PRINCIPLE, which at bottom also seeks pleasure—although a delayed and diminished pleasure, one which is assured by its realization of fact, its relation to reality.[24]

As in the realistic plot, gratification is both deferred and guaranteed, though the security is gained, as the emphasis in this passage on various losses suggests, at the cost of other pleasure. Thus to compensate for the difference between self and world always seems to entail losses. Both in masterful fictions and in adjustments in accord with the reality principle, the ego represses part of the experience of the self in order to gain some security.

The internalization of others' values in the super-ego is another process in which such a trade-off occurs. "In classical theory, the super-ego is described as the heir of the Oedipus complex in that it is constituted through the internalisation

[23] Edward W. Said, *Beginnings: Intention and Method* (Baltimore: The Johns Hopkins University Press, 1975), p. 50.
[24] Sigmund Freud, *A General Introduction to Psychoanalysis*, trans. Joan Riviere (New York: Pocket Books, 1973), p. 365.

of parental prohibitions and demands." Once "the child stops trying to satisfy his Oedipal wishes, which become prohibited, he transforms his cathexis of his parents into an identification with them—he internalises the prohibition."[25] What is thereby made possible is not only an adjustment to others' demands but an increased sense of self-possession. For, having internalized those demands, the self is able to assume the role of others in making such demands and controlling the self. Here the distinction of the self-possessed individual seems to resemble the confusion of self and world that characterizes the archaic or narcissistic self, which is unclear about what is self and what is other. But this later identification is achieved at the cost of the earlier instinctual self, which is repressed.[26]

Yet what is striking about the development I have outlined here is that elements of experience do not in fact change very much. The difference between the primitive self and the developed self is said to be an adjustment to reality: the later ego has accommodated itself to the real difference between instinctual needs and available satisfaction. But reality does not seem to be the issue: the issue is control. For this development of self is a development of power over the tension of differences between self and world, a power that attempts to overcome such differences. Yet if the developed ego does not experience the constant tension that the archaic self experiences in relations of self and other, tension itself is not eliminated, it is internalized. The "plotted" self puts the experience of differences inside the bounds of the self, defines those differences, and experiences them independently of the outside world. But it protects itself from the tension between self and

[25] J. Laplanche and J.-B. Pontalis, *The Language of Psycho-Analysis*, trans. Donald Nicholson-Smith (New York: W. W. Norton, 1973), p. 436.

[26] The fact that both archaic and mature selves identify themselves with what lies outside them suggests the resemblance of narcissistic behavior and the behavior of the ego and suggests thereby that the various stages or parts of the Freudian self are not distinct. Nicholas Duruz stresses the structural similarities of narcissism and the ego in "The Psychoanalytic Concept of Narcissism," *Psychoanalysis and Contemporary Thought*, 4, no. 1 (1981), 3-68.

world only by assuming alienation within its own bounds and actively participating in its own frustration.

In order to posit and possess the self, whatever aspects of the world and the self exceed or differ from the posited meaning must be negated. Self-possession thereby entails the division of self from world and the division of self from self; and self-possession is achieved at the cost of losses. Thus the economy of the self-possessed and masterful self is a matter of definitive exchanges which determine gains and losses in order to determine and secure the meaning of the self. The compensatory exchange is one in which differences are reduced to the terms of substitution. Such an exchange assumes that one thing can make up for another, as when the self makes up a fiction in order to make up *for* the insecure relation of self and world. But in order to maintain such an equation of differences, the differences themselves must be cut down to common terms and so, at least in part, lost.

The novels of Richardson, Eliot, and James that I am considering here seek to avoid such losses. And one mark of this is that their language represents experience in uneconomical terms: terms that exceed the bounds of determination and resist the reductions of meaning necessary to masterful plots and masterful selves. In these indeterminate terms, a self may not be able to tell the difference between self and others; for the representation of self leaves that relation ambiguous. We might say that the heroic selves of these novels do not want to be selves. For the sense of self as an independent and sufficient being is something they want to get rid of rather than reach. " 'There is no end to these debatings,' " Clarissa says to Lovelace; " 'each *so* faultless, each *so* full of self.' "[27] Recognizing that to be full of self is to be separate from and opposed to others, Richardson's heroines wish to identify themselves as parts of their relations with others. And Eliot's and James's heroic characters also insist that selves are bound

[27] Samuel Richardson, *Clarissa*, intro. John Butt (London: Dent, 1976), II, 301.

to others for their meaning rather than being distinct or distinguished from others.

The self thereby becomes as redundant and difficult to "plot" as are these narratives themselves. The boundaries of the self become unclear, as the self is identified in its relation to others rather than in itself. To move the location of the self into the relation of self and others is to move the self into an archaic or narcissistic identity according to the Freudian scheme of development.[28] It is, moreover, to move the self closer to a feminine self according to feminist theorists. As women and men develop, Nancy Chodorow says, their personalities are

affected by different boundary experiences and differently constructed and experienced inner object-worlds, and [they] are preoccupied with different relational issues. Feminine personality comes to be based less on repression of inner objects, and fixed and firm splits in the ego, and

[28] I do not mean to suggest here that Freud's work either maintains consistently or can be contained by this scheme of development but to emphasize the traditional and prevailing interpretation of his work. What more recent readings of Freud suggest is that such an emplotment of his concept of the self chooses to read completeness and security into his concepts only while denying the real conflict and inconclusiveness of his writings. See, for example, Leo Bersani, *Baudelaire and Freud* (Berkeley: University of California Press, 1977); Jean Laplanche, *Life and Death in Psychoanalysis*, trans. and intro. Jeffrey Mehlman (Baltimore: The Johns Hopkins University Press, 1976); and François Roustang, *Psychoanalysis Never Lets Go*, trans. Ned Lukacher (Baltimore: The Johns Hopkins University Press, 1983).

In fact, Freud's work provides a "model" for the kind of relations of self and other that I am identifying in the works of Richardson, Eliot, and James. In the relation of analyst and patient, the role that Freud assigns to the analyst is a role in transference: the analyst, that is, never plays a role of his or her own but always assumes roles in response to the needs of the particular subject being analyzed. The notion of countertransference, moreover, suggests that the same thing is happening on both sides of the exchange, as the patient assumes for the analyst an identity responsive to the needs of the analyst. Freud's own most productive relationships, this suggests, would occur as engagements with others from whom he was not distinct and as relations in which neither participant determined his or her own meaning but had meaning in relation to the other.

more on retention and continuity of external relationships. From the retention of preoedipal attachments to
their mother, growing girls come to define and experience
themselves as continuous with others; their experience of
self contains more flexible or permeable ego boundaries.
Boys come to define themselves as more separate and
distinct, with a greater sense of rigid ego boundaries and
differentiation. The basic feminine sense of self is connected to the world, the basic masculine sense of self is
separate.[29]

The essential difference between feminist theories of human
selves and the conception of self I am elaborating is that I am
not distinguishing the indefinite self as feminine. It occurs in
both male and female characters and in novels written by both
men and women. The sexual differences of women and men
in these novels are differences that remain as indeterminate
as other differences: always differing but seldom subject to
necessary distinctions.[30] It is in part because these narratives
remain as uncertain about the boundary that separates women
from men as they are about the boundaries of the self that

[29] Nancy Chodorow, *The Reproduction of Mothering: Psychoanalysis and
the Sociology of Gender* (Berkeley: University of California Press, 1978), p.
169. Judith Kegan Gardiner, extending part of Chodorow's argument, says
that "female identity is a process" and a process that has a particular effect
on narratives written by women. See "On Female Identity and Writing by
Women," *Critical Inquiry*, 8, no. 2 (1981), 349.

[30] This is not to say that there are not clear distinctions made between the
roles of women and men by the conventions of meaning that prevail in the
societies of the novels. Richardson and Eliot particularly are attentive to the
fact that many more limits are placed on women than on men by conventional
codes of behavior. But Richardson's B and Lovelace are characters as essentially indeterminate as Pamela and Clarissa. Their assumption of mastery is
presented more as their choice of a conventional identity than as a form of
behavior necessary to their selves. Eliot's Daniel Deronda is a male character
who is far more a related than a separate self, as in her later novels Eliot
exceeds the sexual distinctions of *The Mill on the Floss*. The reason I do not
consider conventional distinctions more is that I see these novels as working
to exceed those conventions. My emphasis is on the potential power of the
indefinite and relative self, a power whose potential, I am arguing, exceeds
the power of distinction and mastery.

their heroic characters do not develop toward resolution or determination but remain in suspense, suspended between self and others.

The relations of such characters therefore exceed the determinate terms of exchange that define the differences of self and other and define what they have in common. The exchanges that occur among such characters tend to render characters inseparable, or bind them together, rather than distinguish them or extricate them from one another. Exchanges tend, moreover, to occur for the sake of the relation itself rather than in order to get anything by means of exchange for the sake of the individual self. The economy at work is thus closer to the primitive economies described by Marcel Mauss in *The Gift* than it is to more sophisticated social economies.

Mauss studied tribal societies, finding in them just the sort of confusions and indistinctions that prevail in the hypothesized world of the narcissistic self: indistinctions of self and other, gain and loss, interest and disinterestedness, freedom and obligation, person and thing (not in the sense that persons are objectified, as Marx saw occurring in modern Western society, but in the sense that things are animate and personal). Mauss writes, for example, of Melanesia and Polynesia:

Material and moral life, as exemplified in gift-exchange, functions there in a manner at once interested and obligatory. Furthermore, the obligation is expressed in myth and imagery, symbolically and collectively; it takes the form of interest in the objects exchanged; the objects are never completely separated from the men who exchange them; the communion and alliance they establish are wellnigh indissoluble. The lasting influence of the objects exchanged is a direct expression of the manner in which sub-groups within segmentary societies of an archaic type are constantly embroiled with and feel themselves in debt to each other.[31]

[31] Marcel Mauss, *The Gift: Forms and Functions of Exchange in Archaic Societies*, trans. Ian Cunnison (New York: W. W. Norton, 1967), p. 31.

The exchanges that go on in such societies occur not to distinguish individuals but to bind them together by obligation, not for utilitarian or individual purposes but apparently for the sake of the binding relations themselves.[32] The very indistinction of different elements in these social exchanges is in fact clearly necessary to the "indissoluble" human relations in these cultures. Mauss sees such indissoluble "alliances," moreover, not only among human beings but among various social functions that modern society separates into independent institutions. "The facts we have studied are all 'total' social phenomena," he writes. They are "at once legal, economic, religious, aesthetic, morphological and so on."[33] Such indistinctions are also evidently necessary to the priority of human relations over any other kind of relation. For the binding social relations that occur in these cultures precede and exceed any form or formulation. They simply cannot be adequately explained or exactly represented, remaining "embroiled" rather than separable into parts with clear relations to each other or to the whole economy. Mauss is particularly aware of this unrepresentability as he acknowledges that he has no words that fit what he has seen:

> Our terms "present" and "gift" do not have precise meanings, but we could find no others. Concepts which we like to put in opposition—freedom and obligation; generosity, liberality, luxury on the one hand and saving, interest, austerity on the other—are not exact and it would be well to put them to the test.[34]

[32] Georges Bataille also argues against the utilitarian concept of exchange, asserting that human beings are not interested primarily in utilitarian exchange or in profit. But Bataille identifies another primary human need and interest, and one that does not, any more than profit, contribute to indissoluble community. This is loss, or expenditure. Whereas Mauss emphasizes the indistinction of individuals in the reciprocal and binding relations of social exchanges, Bataille interprets Mauss's work as suggesting a radical means of revolt against society. He is interested in unbinding what may appear as indissoluble connections of human beings. See "The Notion of Expenditure," trans. Allan Stoekl, *Raritan*, III, no. 3 (1984), 62-79.

[33] Mauss, *The Gift*, p. 76.

[34] Ibid., p. 70.

Such oppositions may hold in theory, Mauss suggests, but in practice they may not hold at all.

It is in the excesses of social relations that ally rather than distinguish various human beings and various human interests that Karl Marx also identified an escape from the experience of alienation. In Marx's writing, alienation is inescapable to the extent that private property is the primary goal of human life, just as, in Freudian theory, alienation is inescapable to the extent that self-possession is the goal of human development. For Marx, alienation occurs as it occurs in such theories of the self, when human beings experience a separation from part of their existence; though Marx identifies this process occurring between human beings and institutions as well as within the self and between self and others. Bertrell Ollman writes that

> Three end products of this development are property, industry and religion, which Marx calls man's "alienated life elements. . . ." In each instance, the other half of a severed relation, carried by a social dynamic of it own, progresses through a series of forms in a direction away from its beginning in man. Eventually, it attains an independent life, that is, takes on "needs" which the individual is then forced to satisfy, and the original connection is all but obliterated. . . .
>
> . . . The whole has broken up into numerous parts whose interrelation in whole can no longer be ascertained. This is the essence of alienation, whether the part under examination is man, his activity, his product or his ideas.[35]

Identifying the alienated institution as if it were an alienated human subject, with an "independent life" but with " 'needs,' " in a conflation which represents Marx's insistence that institutions are essentially human, Ollman identifies Marxist alienation in terms that render subjects and objects

[35] Bertrell Ollman, *Alienation: Marx's Concept of Man in Capitalist Society* (Cambridge: Cambridge University Press, 1976), p. 135.

indistinct. And it is just such indistinctions that Marx insists actually prevail in human experience.

For Marx, then, the replacement of property relations by human relations depends on practice rather than theory. Practice is privileged over theory because it is only in practice that human beings exceed the distinctions that logical thought requires.

> It is only in a social context that subjectivism and objectivism, spiritualism and materialism, activity and passivity, cease to be antimonies and thus cease to exist as such antimonies. The resolution of the theoretical contradictions is possible only through *practical* means, only through the practical energy of man. Their resolution is not by any means, therefore, only a problem of knowledge, but is a *real* problem of life which philosophy was unable to solve precisely because it saw there a purely theoretical problem.[36]

Alienation is thus to some extent inherent in knowledge, as it attempts to determine differences in clear-cut oppositions of difference. But the terms of knowledge are exceeded in social practice for Marx, as they are for Mauss.

Concerned—as I am arguing Richardson, Eliot, and James are concerned—with differences that cannot be told, with human experience that exceeds forms of representation, with "embroiled" relations rather than forms of relation, Marx recognizes, as does Mauss in his study of archaic and "uneconomical" economies, real experience that exceeds the realistic relations with which our culture is most familiar. Unlike the Freudian Jacques Lacan, then, for whom alienation occurs as an ineradicable loss of part of the self and as an inevitable component of social relations because it occurs when the self acquires language, these social economists insist that human experience is not limited to the terms of representation but

---

[36] Karl Marx, "Economic and Philosophical Manuscripts [of 1844]," trans. T. B. Bottomore, in *Marx's Concept of Man* by Erich Fromm (New York: Frederick Ungar Publishing Co., 1963), p. 135.

exceeds any abstract form. For Lacan, as for poststructuralists, what is real is unavailable to human beings because social experience is limited to the relations of language.[37] This suggests that the closest representation can come to reality is in so-called realistic representations which reproduce not reality but our alienation from reality. It is because of such assumptions that the novelists I am concerned with can be said to depart from realism. "Realistic" experience comes to be recognized as a constraint on experience as these writers insist on the reality of human relations that exceed the divisions of alienation. And they represent such excesses implicitly with language that often itself remains embroiled rather than clear, implying the excesses of social relations in its own indeterminacy.

In the relations of human beings in these novels, the alien qualities of self and other are apparent, to the extent that Pamela and B, for example, are clearly different and have little in common. But these differences do not result in the separation or division of the characters. Rather, the expression of their differences elaborates the characters' very dependence on each other, implicating such differences in each other. Disparities of self and other and disparities within self, such as the love and enmity both Pamela and B feel, seem to be inseparably bound to each other *for* their difference. Different elements of experience, that is, are experienced fully *as* differences only because they differ in relation to other elements. This means that Pamela and B, for example, are bound to differ, but always in relation to each other and always in a relation that renders differences indeterminate rather than distinct. Differences are not settled, and so differences cannot be resolved or disposed of. Rather than a binding together of

[37] The work of Jacques Lacan emphasizes that the mediation of a symbolic order causes a split "between the self, the innermost part of the psyche, and the subject of conscious discourse, behaviour and culture." Thus "mediated by language, the subject is irremediably divided, because he is at once excluded from the signifying chain and 'represented' in it." See Anika Lemaire, *Jacques Lacan*, trans. David Macey (London: Routledge and Kegan Paul, 1977), pp. 67, 68.

differences that limits their difference, this is a binding relation that intensifies and mobilizes differences, continually discharging and recharging differences. It is an ongoing process of differing rather than a structure that contains or limits differences.

The effect of such a process on the relation of the narrative is, as I suggested earlier, various kinds of redundancy: the same things seem to happen repeatedly, as differences are discharged without making a determinant difference. Its effect on the relations of characters is also redundant, as characters differ from each other but in no way that either distinguishes them from or equates them with each other. Rather than working to distinguish or resolve such differences, the exchanges among characters both express and leave room for differences. Alien differences, which would be divided in a determinate exchange, become the very fabric of commitment in these novels, as alienation itself becomes impossible to distinguish from union.

Thus "alienation" is apparent only in embroiled relations of committed alienation. Alienation becomes a relation of, rather than a division of, differences. The very freedom from negating alienation, the type of alienation familiar in an economical rendition of self or society, is dependent on relations of self and other in which self-possession is given up and meaning is found instead *in* relations. This freedom, then, depends on a commitment *to* difference rather than on an attempt to control disparity. The latter results in double binds: the self that finds security in self-possession achieves such security only by assuming others' values in place of the "unacceptable" parts of the self and thus comes into possession of itself only by giving up part of itself.[38] The binding relation

---

[38] I am using the term "double bind" to denote situations in which a person does or wants to do two things, at least one of which negates the other. Gregory Bateson has identified schizophrenia with the experience of the double bind, as "a situation in which no matter what a person does, he 'can't win.' " Among the "necessary ingredients for a double bind situation," he says, are "a primary negative injunction" and "a secondary injunction conflicting with the first at a more abstract level, and like the first enforced by

of self and other that I am identifying, however, displaces that double bind into the doubly binding relation of two different beings who are therefore bound to be double—or multiple— rather than doubly or multiply bound. Unlike the binding that can be identified as part of a plot, this process does not repress or stabilize but seems actually to generate differences. For differences are not securely bound *by* other differences; they are bound to differ, in constant relation to other differences.

What is given up here is self-possession and self-control, and in a sense these are the cost of freedom for the writers I am considering. Yet the redundancy of the exchanges that occur in such relations suggests that in fact nothing is given up; in their indeterminacy, these exchanges, occurring as processes rather than as determinations, always insist on the excesses of meaning on both "sides" of any exchange. Moreover, the distinction and security of differences are identified in these works with loss rather than with any gain of meaning; they are themselves losses of meaning, and therefore to give them up is to lose nothing. If distinction is lost, then, substantial differences, because they are not negated or repressed, are gained or regained. This involves, too, the refusal to equate or "match" differences. The recognition that no difference can make up for another difference, or the inherent incom-

---

punishments or signals which threaten survival." See *Steps to an Ecology of Mind* (New York: Ballantine Books, 1972), pp. 201, 206-207. I am identifying the alienated ego as doubly bound by the desire on the one hand to be self-possessed, to separate the self from others, and the necessity of repressing parts of the self and assuming others' values in order to do so. I also identify deconstruction's exposure of conflicting meaning with the creation of double binds. An example of this is Cynthia Chase's "The Decomposition of the Elephants: Double-Reading *Daniel Deronda*," *PMLA*, 93, no. 2 (1978), 215-27, in which Chase identifies conflicts of meaning in Eliot's novel in terms according to which Eliot works against things she is working for: "The narration of Deronda's relationship with Mordecai both stresses the authority of recognition or knowledge and undermines the basis of this authority. The contradiction here resembles the one involved in the disclosure of Deronda's birth, which both stresses the causative power of origin and draws attention to the questionable status of cause." (221). The double bind depends on conceiving conflicts in terms of contradiction or opposition in which one of two things done negates the other.

parability of different elements of experience, is crucial to the processes of exchange in these narratives. Because adequate compensation cannot occur in exchanges, these exchanges occur in terms that leave room for differences to remain different. The resistance to "even exchange" is perhaps the most consistent common characteristic of these novels, which thereby avoid the loss of meaning that such exchanges entail.

To say that characters in these novels are committed to difference, committed even to the extent that the experience of alienation is qualified into an experience of commitment, is to mark the crucial difference between these narratives and masterful realistic representations of experience. But it is also to signal again their difference from deconstructive representations of experience. These works preclude deconstruction just as they preclude mastery; in a sense, they preclude deconstruction *because* they preclude mastery. For what deconstruction undermines is the mastery of meaning. It occurs, as Barbara Johnson says, as a "careful teasing out of warring forces of signification *within the text itself.* If anything is destroyed in a deconstructive reading, it is not meaning but the claim to unequivocal domination of one mode of signifying over another."[39] Thus the concept of meaning that emerges in novels of Richardson, Eliot, and James differs from a deconstructive sense of meaning not only because deconstruction limits the struggle of meaning to the experience of language but because it limits that struggle to a struggle for and against mastery.

Language itself is a structure which deconstruction identifies in conflict with itself for mastery:

> The very fact that a word is divided into a phonic *signifier* and a mental *signified*, and that, as Saussure pointed out, language is a system of differences rather than a collection of independently meaningful units, indicates that language as such is already constituted by the very distances and differences it seeks to overcome.[40]

[39] Johnson, "Translator's Introduction," p. xiv.
[40] Ibid., p. ix.

This is to say that deconstruction, though it assumes that meaning consists of dependent differences and therefore cannot be mastered, identifies the preclusion of independence and mastery as a loss: overcoming differences is always desirable if unattainable. Similarly, Leo Bersani's "deconstructed selves" are constantly differing from themselves, but they are essentially working against themselves. "I think," Bersani writes,

> that an imagination of the deconstructed, perhaps even demolished, self is the necessary point of departure for an authentically civilizing skepticism about the nature of our desires and the nature of our being. . . . For what we call character is also a partial self. Its appearance of completeness, of wholeness, may be nothing more than the illusion created by the *centralizing* of a partial self. . . . An exuberant indefiniteness about our own identity can both preserve the heterogeneity of our desires and rescue us from the totalitarian insistence natural to all desire.[41]

A deconstructed self, then, like a deconstructed text, is a self which both seeks totalitarian mastery and undermines any such possibility, for it seeks to overcome what constitutes its very nature. If we cannot say exactly that the deconstruction of a self or a text is self-centered, since the process of deconstruction constantly displaces or de-centers meaning, we can nevertheless recognize that deconstruction always assumes the limits of a structure which claims or seeks self-sufficiency or mastery. The process of deconstruction, then, is limited to undoing constructions, or to defeating mastery; and the work of deconstruction is thereby limited *by* the work of construction and mastery. If attempts to master meaning leave us doubly bound, then, deconstruction, working to expose that double bind, is limited *to* the work of the double bind.

Deconstruction works as such, I am suggesting, precisely because it works within the confines of selfhood: when we deconstruct, we recognize any given structure of meaning as

---

41 Bersani, *A Future for Astyanax*, pp. 313-14.

claiming the same independence and sufficiency that the divided ego claims for itself. Thus the limitation of meaning to the structure of language becomes the limitation of meaning to a divisively alienating conflict. Fiction deconstructs itself, Paul de Man has suggested, precisely because it knows itself to be a fiction; that is, a construct unrelated to anything outside itself. Unlike writing that claims to represent empirical reality, fiction cannot be said to be alienated from reality, according to de Man, as the object it seeks but cannot grasp. It is alienated from itself, or self-negating. Fiction does not present us with an absence of something but with "the presence of a nothingness."[42] At the "imaginary source of fiction," de Man states, "the human self has experienced the void within itself and the invented fiction, far from filling the void, asserts itself as pure nothingness, *our* nothingness stated and restated by a subject that is the agent of its own instability."[43] Within its own terms, then, the fiction comes apart, precisely, in fact, because limited to its own terms.

Deconstruction, then, as I suggested at the beginning of this chapter, because it is intent on relations internal to a specific structure, denies the differences that other relations make to meaning in the novels I am considering. A process of deconstruction is in fact recognizable in these novels. But it differs from most deconstruction in that it exceeds the confines of a structure that claims sufficiency and so exceeds the capacity of most deconstructions to do no more than defeat mastery or claim nothingness. Deconstruction occurs in *Pamela*, for example, not within a self but as a social process. Pamela does not, except at the very beginning of her narrative, claim self-sufficiency or self-control, and the deconstructive tactics that are recognizable in her relation with B therefore effectively bind the two together rather than take apart any self. The individual self in such a relation is demonstrated to be partial and incomplete, as is the deconstructed self in Bersani's work.

[42] Paul de Man, *Blindness and Insight: Essays in the Rhetoric of Contemporary Criticism* (New York: Oxford University Press, 1971), p. 18.
[43] Ibid., p. 19.

But the displacement of deconstruction into the relation between two selves means that the very partiality and incompletion of the self are discovered to be relative to another self.
Selves are partial, then, but they also take part in other selves.
This does not occur as the completion of self or other, but it
does bind the self to what lies outside the self and thereby, in
a sense, supports the self in its very partiality and difference.
Though incomplete, the meaning of such a self is not limited
to a "void within itself," for it is part of a binding relation
to what lies outside it. Such a relation of self and other effectively precludes the self-mastery of an independent self, as
it precludes the deconstruction of self that depends on the
assumption of mastery to deconstruct. The identification of
the self in a relation to another therefore also precludes the
negating alienation of self. For the partiality of the self is
precisely what commits the self to what lies beyond the self
for its meaning.

I am using the term "partiality" in a double sense here:
both in the sense that the self constitutes, in itself, only part
of its meaning and in the sense that the self is biased and
therefore arbitrarily favors certain meanings more than others.
Whereas for Bersani the deconstruction of the self into a partial self enables skepticism, my sense of the partial nature of
the self is what enables belief to take part in meaning. To
identify the self as partial in both senses is to identify the
double commitment of the self to what lies beyond the self
and to suggest how, in these novels, to partialize the self is
not to demonstrate its incompleteness or insufficiency but precisely to realize its power. For the self is empowered in the
extension of itself into another, and the self is empowered by
the recognition that its own arbitrary partiality is what makes
meaning meaningful. It is because the partial self believes in
certain meanings, that those meanings are realized; and this
is the power of partiality to make meaning.

If deconstruction claims that to recognize the meaning of
language as a fiction is to recognize the nothingness of meaning, the experience of the heroines and heroes of these novels
asserts that to recognize the meaning of language as a fiction

is to recognize the power of the self to create meaning. It is the self that makes the difference between the fiction of meaning and the realization of meaning. Or, it is the self, in its arbitrary partiality, that realizes meaning. The narratives that I am considering suggest that the very indeterminacy of meaning functions as a kind of guarantee that experience is never subject to determining and that, therefore, it leaves room for the self's own partial and indeterminate meanings. The indeterminacy of the meaning of language, then, allows the self to find itself in the spaces left open by language, as an indeterminate, partial, and relative being.

Though meaning in these texts by Richardson, Eliot, and James is bound to language, then, that commitment is experienced as a liberation of meaning rather than as a double bind. For meaning is not bound *by* language; it is something that language cannot contain and therefore lets go. Meaning is in fact free to differ in time and space by its very commitment to language because language is itself unable to contain or limit meaning. Such a concept finds in the very differences of language and meaning the dependent but indeterminate relation that constitutes freedom in commitment. And that freedom is also available to the self who identifies herself or himself as indeterminate and partial. It is the commitment of the partial self to indeterminate meaning—meaning of the self and of experience in general—that frees the self to realize meaning through its own partiality. Thus the partial self in fact demands or requires the indeterminacy of the meaning of language, just as the indeterminacy of the meaning of language demands or requires the partiality of the self in order to be meaningful: both insofar as partial meaning is all it provides for the self and insofar as such meaning depends on interpretation by human selves.

Realization is therefore not limited to language but is limited only insofar as the commitment of the self to meaning is limited. Realization is thus a matter of making believe or of belief making meaning. And making believe is thus discovered to be not a counter to or a negation of reality but an extension of reality, as all realizations are recognized and accepted as equally fictitious, or equally real. The pressure exerted by these narratives is the pressure to include within our realizations of experience what conventional realizations exclude: the indeterminate excess of the human capacity to make believe. Because all representation is recognized as indeterminate, that is, belief itself cannot be excluded from realization. Fiction is always part of human reality, these works insist, not separable from or exclusive of it.

What I am suggesting, then, is that the indeterminacy of meaning—the meaning of selves and the meaning of experience—is an enabling condition: one that empowers the self to exercise its partiality and arbitrariness in ways that bind the self to what lies beyond it rather than separating the self either from parts of itself or from what lies outside it. The concept of power in these narratives, then, as I have already noted, is a concept radically different from concepts of control or mastery. The power to exercise control is exercised as a divisive alienation of parts of experience; and similarly the power of deconstruction, which defeats control, is exercised to take meaning apart. But such divisions and breaks do not occur in the novels I am considering insofar as the power of human belief, or the power of fiction itself, is discovered to be a binding power, with the capacity to hold meaning, indeterminate though it remains. The binding relation that constitutes power is therefore crucial to these writers' concepts of authority and to their vision of fiction itself as a power.

The idea of power that has no clear source or objective but works as a relation which exceeds control has been considered by Michel Foucault, whose work "undoes" the distinction of masterful and repressed behavior on which the Freudian economy of self-control, among other similar economies, rests. For Foucault, power is more productive than repressive:

> What makes power hold good, what makes it accepted, is simply the fact that it doesn't only weigh on us as a force that says no, but that it traverses and produces things, it induces pleasure, forms knowledge, produces discourse. It needs to be considered as a productive net-

work which runs through the whole social body, much more than as a negative instance whose function is repression.[44]

If for Freud the indeterminate experience that exceeds individual control is repressed, in Foucault's uneconomical descriptions of society what seems to be repressed by social powers are in fact phenomena that serve the interests of power. Thus sexuality, for example, is identified by Foucault not so much as a repressed phenomenon but as a creation of the power network.[45] Power in fact creates its own opposition, and this is a mark of its power. For it thereby controls not only positions of power but positions of powerlessness. This means that no one in any position is outside the system that constitutes power.

The excesses of power that Foucault identifies mean that power itself is not determinate but indeterminate, and that power lies in indeterminacy. "For Foucault power is relational, not substantial," as Frank Lentricchia emphasizes; it is not a property or a possession but a process in which every-

[44] Michel Foucault, *Power/Knowledge: Selected Interviews and Other Writings 1972-1977*, ed. Colin Gordon, trans. Colin Gordon et al. (New York: Pantheon Books, 1980), p. 119.

[45] In *The History of Sexuality, Volume 1: An Introduction*, trans. Robert Hurley (New York: Pantheon Books, 1978), Foucault says that sexuality has not been repressed but "deployed" by the powers that be. Our society's very investment in sex, then, serves the purposes of established power: "By creating the imaginary element that is 'sex,' the deployment of sexuality established one of its most essential internal operating principles: the desire for sex—the desire to have it, to have access to it, to discover it, to liberate it, to articulate it in discourse, to reformulate it in truth. It constituted 'sex' itself as something desirable. And . . . it is this desirability that makes us think we are affirming the rights of our sex against all power, when in fact we are fastened to the deployment of sexuality that has lifted up from deep within us a sort of mirage in which we think we see ourselves reflected—the dark shimmer of sex" (156-57). For sex to be talked about, then, is not a sign of freedom from repression but a sign that sexual experience has been assumed as a discourse of power. It is neither repressed nor free but part of the deployment of power in society. Moreover, "the idea of 'sex' makes it possible to evade what gives 'power' its power; it enables one to conceive power solely as law and taboo" (p. 155). For Foucault, power is never so simple a matter.

one takes part. Thus Foucault's theory of power suggests the possibility of real structural changes; for the dominated "seem more realistically placed to break their chains and to emerge."[46] It is precisely because power is a process that always exceeds possession and determination that it seems to leave room or make room for more power than can be controlled and thus may work against itself. As Leo Bersani says, "the ambiguous energetics of the *pouvoir-savoir* network works to defeat the orders of power and knowledge" as "it defeats its own objective by always producing in excess of the calculable requirements of a strategy of domination."[47] Even as Foucault's power network seems to take over everything, then, it opens up the possibility of changing the relations of power.

The most revolutionary aspects of the considerations of power in the novels on which I am focusing here may be seen, in the context of Foucault's writings, as the location of power in experience that exceeds the terms of mastery and repression. The powerful subject finds power in relations with others in which neither subject nor object is ruled or ruled out by the other. The most important excess involved here is meaning in excess of the terms of any opposition. Most explicitly in *Pamela*, what initially is identified by both Pamela and B as an effort on the part of the other to control the self comes to be recognized as behavior that in fact leaves the self free to differ—free to exceed any position that can be defined as exclusively controlling or controlled.

But the most crucial effect of this excess of power is one that cannot, perhaps, be termed revolutionary. For the recognition of power as an empowering relation that exceeds control by anyone does not mean that power changes hands; it is not something that can be possessed or defined anyway. The powerful self, moreover, in the revised terms of Richardson, Eliot, and James, is a character who assumes power *as*

[46] Frank Lentricchia, "Reading Foucault (1) (Punishment, Labor, Resistance)," *Raritan*, I, no. 4 (1982), 14.
[47] Bersani, "The Subject of Power," p. 5.

relational and indeterminate. Such power is exercised "non-repressively," but this is not a strategy for domination. The desire to dominate does not function in these characters. Unlike the powers that Foucault considers, their desires are not doubly bound by the conflict of a desire to dominate and the fact that power exceeds the terms of domination. Though there are characters in these novels of whom this can be said—Richardson's Lovelace and Eliot's Gwendolen Harleth, for example—such characters differ most from the authorized heroine or hero of their novels precisely in their desire for mastery.

Yet if the heroic characters are never doubly bound, neither are they exactly free, since their power is the power of commitment. If concepts of power are revised by these narratives, so are concepts of freedom. To be empowered in relation to others is never to be free, if we assume freedom entails independence of others.[48] But to be free of others constitutes a loss of meaning in these novels, and a loss of the freedom to perceive the self as an indefinite and relative being. Freedom and commitment are in fact conflated in this concept of human relations, just as alienation and union are conflated, in relations that realize these experiences inseparably.

It is, moreover, only in terms of such an "embroiled" relation of freedom and commitment, I think, that Richardson's, Eliot's and James's concepts of narrative authority can be represented. In Richardson's works, the power of the binding

---

[48] This concept of freedom, then, as freedom to exceed independence through relations, differs emphatically from that held by theorists such as Nietzsche and Foucault, for whom freedom would be without relations or commitment. They suggest that even to conceive of freedom is a contradiction in terms, since thought itself would constrain freedom by forms and conventions, among them language. Thus Leo Bersani, too, identifies freedom in James's fiction as the freedom of being "unrelated"; for "the only absolute escape from power is to escape from relations themselves." See ibid., p. 12. The freedom I am concerned with is never separable from the constraints of chosen commitment. I am arguing for the freedom to be committed to relations rather than to be independent, which is to be involuntarily constrained in one's meaning; and I am arguing that such freedom liberates human beings to experience excessive power.

relations of self and other is clearly reflected in the binding relations of language that characterize Pamela's and Clarissa's writing. They themselves share the power of their representations: a power both to exceed control or determination and to bind differing elements of experience together so that the losses necessitated by control do not occur. In Eliot's *Middlemarch* and *Daniel Deronda*, the characterizations of Dorothea Brooke and Deronda also identify them with narrative authority. These characters find power in the very arbitrariness and partiality of their beliefs and thereby authorize the very qualities that may be thought to frustrate realistic novelists. For Eliot's as for Richardson's heroic characters, meaning lies in a reflexive relation of self and world, and it is because the self actively participates in meaning that both self and meaning are bound to be meaningful.

In George Eliot's novels, the will to power can thereby be said to be displaced by the will to believe. On the one hand, the power of both Richardson's and Eliot's heroic characters lies not in their mastery of meaning but in their capacity to make a difference to meaning through their representations. On the other hand, this capacity to make a difference to meaning becomes indistinguishable from the capacity to invest with meaning differences that already exist, both in self and world and in relations of self and world. For the power of these characters' relations—of their relations to others and of the ways they tell about experience—is the power of their commitment to the world. The most crucial difference these characters make, then, in their interpretations of experience, is not the creation of new experience but the acceptance of elements of experience that more conventional interpretations rule out or repress. What is novel here is in part something that already exists rather than something newly created. It is such acceptance that results in the excesses of meaning in characters' and narrators' perceptions of experience. And this acceptance is itself the result of human belief in meaning that can neither be controlled nor determined.

It is George Eliot, perhaps, who, at least explicitly, comes closer to William James's justification of faith than does his brother. William James insists in "The Will to Believe" on the power of faith to effect what is believed in. In questions of personal relations, he says,

> The desire for a certain kind of truth . . . brings about that special truth's existence; and so it is in innumerable cases of other sorts. Who gains promotions, boons, appointments, but the man in whose life they are seen to play the part of live hypotheses, who discounts them, sacrifices other things for their sake before they have come, and takes risks for them in advance? His faith acts on the powers above him as a claim, and creates its own verification.
>
> . . . There are, then, cases where a fact cannot come at all unless a preliminary faith exists in its coming. And where faith in a fact can help create the fact, that would be an insane logic which should say that faith running ahead of scientific evidence is the "lowest kind of immorality" into which a thinking being can fall.[49]

It is the power of such commitment—what she calls "that passionate belief which determines the consequences it believes in"—that George Eliot wishes her characters to achieve.[50] This sort of power is in itself coercive, not only in its demands on others but in the commitment of the self it entails. But if the commitment of belief excludes certain possibilities of meaning and denies the freedom of meaning to mean anything at all, it is, for Eliot, crucial to the liberation of meaning that the self accept its own partiality as part of meaning. Partiality is one of the indeterminate excesses of experience that she renders acceptable. Her characters' commitment to the partiality of their beliefs is an act of acceptance of part of the self that logic, for example, rules out of significance. But, though indeterminate and partial in its effects,

---

[49] William James, *The Will to Believe and Other Essays in Popular Philosophy* (New York: Longmans, Green, 1937), pp. 24-25.
[50] Eliot, *Daniel Deronda*, p. 572.

belief constitutes the uniquely human capacity to make experience meaningful.

Partiality is binding for George Eliot, as it is for William James. Moreover, for Eliot as for James, each human being is always engaged by her or his feelings, even in the recognition of "truth." As William James says,

> practically one's conviction that the evidence one goes by is of the real objective brand, is only one more subjective opinion added to the lot. . . . There is this,—there is that; there is indeed nothing which some one has not thought absolutely true, while his neighbor deemed it absolutely false; and not an absolutist among them seems ever to have considered . . . that the intellect, even with truth directly within its grasp, may have no infallible signal for knowing whether it be truth or no.[51]

For Eliot, a similar recognition of the reliance of meaning on subjectivity demands the inclusion within meaning of human feelings. If partiality is assumed to be excluded from meaning, as it is in rational thought on rational grounds, the self is separated from meaning and doubly bound by the conflict of partiality and meaning. To commit the partiality of the self to the meaning of the world is an act that empowers both self and world with an increase of meaning.[52]

[51] James, *The Will to Believe*, p. 16.

[52] Walter Benn Michaels has argued that meaning is always a matter of belief, whether critics believe in separating the two or not. He considers various critical attempts to make this separation, including New Criticism and deconstruction, but asserts that "the text which simply is, meaningful or meaningless, denies ideology without escaping it. Ideology (like common sense) is what we believe." Moreover, "we have no choice about whether or not to invoke these beliefs: to read is already to have invoked them." Belief or ideology, then, as Michaels considers it, is not a choice, whereas the novelists I am considering here, particularly Eliot and James, insist that it is commitment of the self to beliefs that makes meaning meaningful. As Michaels points out, one can be committed by one's beliefs to being noncommittal, or insignificant. But in novels of Eliot and James, this sort of belief constitutes a refusal of commitment because it denies that the self makes a difference to meaning. This is not to deny ideology, but it is to say that the act of taking responsibility for the difference one makes to meaning and the willingness

A recognition of the indeterminate nature of knowledge and of truth itself underwrites all of the narratives I am considering here. Truth cannot be contained in any representation and always exceeds the grasp of representation or verification. In Richardson's novels, for example, truth is something that language comes closest to approximating when language is explicitly ambiguous and indeterminate in meaning. Both groundless and relative, truth occurs in indeterminate relations that hold true precisely because of human belief or human commitment to the world outside the self. In the reliance of truth on belief in these novels, truth is both recognized to exceed the grasp of logical proof or determination and recognized to be a binding but changeable relation of human belief in the world. Truth is, therefore, indeterminate and partial, both in that all the truth is never identified and in that it depends on belief. But what is believed holds true because of the commitment of human partiality.

As for Nietzsche, then, the recognition of truth depends on what a person believes true in the first place. It is not discovered as an independent or objective phenomenon; it is created. "The world seems logical to us," therefore, "because we have made it logical."[53] For Nietzsche, truth is thus essentially redundant and circular: "What distinguishes the true from the false belief? What is knowledge? He 'knows' it, that is heav-

---

to be fully implicated in meaning by one's partiality are what make meaning meaningful. See "Saving the Text: Reference and Belief," *MLN*, 93 (1978), 771-93. The above quotations are on pages 791 and 782.

[53] Friedrich Nietzsche, *The Will to Power*, ed. Walter Kaufmann, trans. Walter Kaufmann and R. J. Hollingdale (New York: Random House, 1967), p. 283. For Nietzsche not only is truth a fiction, it is a masterful fiction: "'Truth' is the will to be master over the multiplicity of sensations:—to classify phenomena into definite categories" (p. 280). Foucault, following Nietzsche, insists that truth "is a thing of this world: it is produced only by virtue of multiple forms of constraint. And it induces regular effects of power." Like other powerful phenomena, truth is both productive and constraining: not something that simply is but something that works as part of the relations of power. See *Power/Knowledge*, p. 131. The complicity of truth and human relations is implicit in all the novels I am considering, though in these novels the binding power of partial truth is identified as a liberation of human power.

enly!"[54] Persistently redundant themselves, the novels I am considering similarly insist on the groundlessness of truth. Such means of truth as logic are exceeded, then, because logic denies its own excesses, among them its dependence on belief; and such means of truth are considered less than meaningful because they negate the subjective power that enforces their truth. Rather than pretending that truth is objective or static, these novels insist that truth is a fiction with a capacity to change the way things are. Exceeding conventions of truth, they suggest that truth itself is meaningful only when it exceeds both impartiality and determination.

For Richardson, Eliot, and James, then, the concept of meaning must be extended beyond logic and other forms of knowledge in order to include irrational elements. For Eliot, the acceptance of the meaning of our own partiality—itself incomparable and inexplicable in its differences—makes possible the acceptance of other elements of experience that exceed knowledge and rationality. The acceptance of partiality makes room for other differences—even the difference of brute reality that exceeds any attempts at human realization—to be accepted in their incomparability rather than repressed or assimilated. Once the involuntary and coercive nature of feelings is accepted into meaning, Eliot's work implies, the recognition of other elements of the world that exceed determination is made possible. The emphasis of *Middlemarch* and *Daniel Deronda* finally seems, then, to be an emphasis on making room for the irreducible nature of differences that exceed control rather than an emphasis on changing the nature of things. Or we might say it is an emphasis on changing the relations of things rather than on changing things themselves.

The coercive power of belief that enforces acceptance of rather than escape from the irreducible and indeterminate nature of experience is most relentlessly represented by Henry James in *The Golden Bowl*. Like Eliot, James does not claim to be realistic. But whereas Eliot insists that reality always exceeds the terms of thought, James insists that his fiction

---

[54] Nietzsche, *The Will to Power*, p. 287.

deals with the reality that real life wastes. What we cannot deal with in real life, he suggests—what is never conventionalized or economized by realistic economies—constitutes the excess of meaning with which the "sublime economy" of fiction is concerned.[55] For James, too, then, fiction entails the acceptance of otherwise unacceptable excesses of experience rather than new experience. This "economy," practiced by the Ververs in the novel as well as by James, remains "sublime" and coercive in its denial of the limits of meaning imposed by orders of determination or knowledge. For this denial operates as a pressure to resist the ease of determination and a pressure to believe in what exceeds any means of determination. Yet for James, as for Eliot, the refusal to determine meaning constitutes freedom as it constitutes the believing self as a power: a power to make indeterminate excesses of experience meaningful.

The power of belief itself in *The Golden Bowl* is a power that depends on human relations. For Eliot, the human being is committed by belief to her or his particular perception of meaning, and that belief seems to come both from within the self and as a reflection of others' belief. For James, characters are coerced into believing *in* themselves by the belief of others. Faith is "catching" in the novel, and in this his narrative shares with "The Will to Believe" his brother's conviction that "Our faith is faith in some one else's faith, and in the greatest matters this is most the case."[56] Thus belief itself becomes part of the relations of human beings rather than an independently held conviction. Like Richardson and Eliot, James thereby insists that the relation of self and other can provide binding support for the groundless propositions of arbitrary and partial meaning. In *The Golden Bowl*, James and the Ververs *make* belief, and the novel's insistence on the fundamental indistinction of fiction and reality rests on the real human power to do so.

Richardson, Eliot, and James claim the power to transform

---

[55] Henry James, *The Art of the Novel: Critical Prefaces*, intro. R. P. Blackmur (New York: Scribner's, 1934), p. 120.
[56] James, *The Will to Believe*, p. 9.

experience in indeterminate terms: not only to transform experience but thereby to redeem experience from the constraints of determination. For to claim the power of indeterminacy is to empower the human being to be true to his or
her own indeterminate being and to be true to the indeterminate relations of self and others. The discovery of such
fidelity is not the discovery of truth, if we think of truth as
an objective and unchanging phenomenon, external to human
subjectivity. It is the discovery of what Webster's dictionary
calls an "archaic" sense of truth—"the quality or state of being
faithful." And it is the discovery of faith in what Freudian
theorists have called an archaic sense of self and in such "embroiled" human relations as Marcel Mauss describes in archaic societies. The discovery of such commitment—a commitment of self to other powerful enough to commit the self
to the very differences of self and other—is the subject of the
following chapters.

I consider these novels in the order in which they were
written, despite the fact that the priority, or the privileged
importance, of the past in relation to the present and future
is a hierarchy of meaning I am challenging and one challenged
in the novels themselves. The essential redundancy of these
narratives is an excess characterized in part by repetitions that
radically qualify any sense of historical progress. But at the
same time, past events are not excluded from meaning. Thus,
though historical precedence is subject to question here, this
is not to say that it makes no difference when events occur;
it is to say that such differences are also indeterminate. It
made a difference to James's work, for example, that he read
George Eliot's fiction. And it made a difference to *Clarissa*
that Richardson had already written *Pamela*. Though I do not
consider these differences here, I leave the works in chrono-
logical order partly because in the cases of all three novelists,
their later works constitute more complex and intensified considerations of the issues in which I am interested. This is
apparent in *Pamela* and *Clarissa*; it is apparent in *Middlemarch* and *Daniel Deronda*; and it is apparent in *The Portrait
of a Lady* and *The Golden Bowl*, though I consider only the

latter of James's novels because it seems to me to represent
sufficiently James's differences from Richardson and Eliot.

To have introduced the following chapters in a theoretical
context of human and narrative relations, however, is in a
sense to have put the cart before the horse, or to have broken
with the sense of sequence in which I consider the novels. For
the theoretical significance of the issues of experience in these
five novels became apparent to me only through reading the
novels themselves. But, as I hope the following readings will
show, the concerns introduced here, though seldom abstracted
by Richardson, Eliot, or James from the events of their narratives, are crucial concerns of their fiction. They are most
clearly crucial, in fact, just because they cannot be abstracted
or separated from those events or from the relations of characters in the novels. If, then, my introduction of theoretical
issues in a sense seems alien to the novels, these are nevertheless issues to which the five works of Richardson, Eliot,
and James are deeply and forcefully committed.

CHAPTER TWO

CORRESPONDING FREEDOMS:
LANGUAGE AND THE SELF IN
PAMELA

Ian Watt, considering the eighteenth-century novel in a historical context, emphasizes "the transition from the objective,
social and public orientation of the classical world to the
subjective, individualist and private orientation of the life and
literature of the last two hundred years."[1] Finding in Defoe's
"total subordination of the plot to the pattern of the auto-
biographical memoir . . . as defiant an assertion of the primacy
of individual experience in the novel as Descartes' *cogito ergo
sum* was in philosophy," Watt identifies "the rise of the novel"
with the increasing social, political, and philosophical sovereignty of the individual in the eighteenth century.[2] At the
same time, the epistolary novel's focus on private experience
makes possible a deeper identification between its readers and
its characters: "there had never before been such opportunities
for unreserved participation in the inner lives of fictional characters as were offered by Richardson's presentation of the
flow of consciousness of Pamela and Clarissa in their letters."[3]

But if in the historical perspective it is the detailed privacy
of experience that is most striking in the novel form, in another
sense the form of a correspondence actually undermines any
perception of the subject—either the subject as self or the
subject of the narrative—as a separate and private individual
phenomenon. The sense of "unreserved participation" in the
life of another that Richardson's novels encourage implies that

[1] Ian Watt, *The Rise of the Novel: Studies in Defoe, Richardson and Fielding* (Harmondsworth, Mx.: Penguin, 1970), p. 182.
[2] Ibid., p. 15.
[3] Ibid., p. 208.

individual meaning exceeds the individual. As Roy Roussel suggests, it is because Richardson "conceives of human identity as an intersubjective relationship" that "he is led naturally to the letter as the most appropriate medium to express it."[4] Roussel's reading removes *Pamela* from the tradition of individualism by insisting on the "act of correspondence" as "a rejection of the isolation of the self in society": "insofar as it is the form of love, it involves the choice of another as the ground of a new identity."[5]

Yet the implications of an intersubjective identity involve not so much an extension or displacement of the grounds of meaning as a loss of any firm grounds whatever for meaning. The experience of individual identity in the novel can be described as a recognition of a self with multiple and equivocal meanings that exceed the bounds assigned by individualism. The self is given meaning in relation to others and thus becomes a social and relative rather than an individual and independent phenomenon: subject to change, and a changing subject. It is neither self-possessed nor determined by others but is always part of a relation, in a narrative that precludes individual sovereignty or distinction just as it precludes the social distinctions of class and sex. Richardson's first novel suggests that to shift emphasis from public to private concerns does not represent a shift of priorities or a changed order such as Watt describes, but represents a shift from the experience of order to experience that exceeds order.[6]

---

[4] Roy Roussel, "Reflections and the Letter: The Reconciliation of Distance and Presence in *Pamela*," *ELH*, 41, no. 3 (1974), 398.

[5] Ibid., p. 394.

[6] Terry Eagleton suggests that what begin as personal, social, or sexual distinctions in the novel not only come to correspond; they come to collaborate, he suggests, in the re-enforcement of the hierarchical orders they seem to challenge. Eagleton puts pressure on the deconstructive standoffs he identifies in the narrative, both by considering their political and historical implications and by bringing to bear analogous conditions in Richardson's life, given as necessarily of political and historical significance. In reality, Eagleton says, such tensions are either resolved or, in their irresolution, make no difference to the prevailing structure of power. Eagleton's reading is compelling in its capacity both to acknowledge and resolve the irresolutions of

If the heroine of *Pamela* begins in correspondence with her parents, who insist on her sovereignty and sufficiency, she continues writing only "in correspondence" with B, a relationship characterized by indecisive and inconclusive exchanges. Moreover, the indeterminate exchanges in which Pamela and B take part are not resolved by but repeated by her representation of them. And it is just this indeterminacy that enables Pamela and B to come together, after B reads Pamela's expression of sympathy for him even among her expressions of enmity. Roussel, in considering the characters' dependence on writing, emphasizes the ability of letters to "reveal as they conceal"; thus writing maintains the tension of distance and presence necessary to Pamela and B in their fears of exposing their feelings.[7] This is, however, only one advantage offered the characters by the fact that their correspondence depends on language. Their correspondence entails both spoken and written language, and in fact their conversations insist that the meaning of spoken words is as indeterminate as the meaning of written words. Thus they argue about the meaning of the terms they use. Pamela's and B's insistence that they use the same words differently, moreover, is a crucial discovery, for it means that they are already engaged in a relation that leaves room for both of them as radically different beings.

To identify the excess of meaning in language with gain rather than with loss is to contradict prevalent eighteenth-century as well as more modern concepts of order and excess. Martin Price, in *To the Palace of Wisdom*, writes of the Augustan enterprise as an attempt "to define an ideal order of mind" that would unite disparate human interests that threaten to defy order. Price insists on the Augustans' need to come to terms with excess, in order both to construct an inclusive order and to avoid the division of different individ-

---

the novel. Yet his method, it seems to me, insists on more resolution than the novel provides. See *The Rape of Clarissa: Writing, Sexuality and Class Struggle in Samuel Richardson* (Minneapolis: University of Minnesota Press, 1982), pp. 1-39.

[7] Roussel, "Reflections and the Letter," p. 389.

uals, "locked in self-enclosed and self-subsistent orders, seeming to use the same words but in fact unable to comprehend
each other's meaning."[8] In an essay that considers Pope coming to terms with the breakdown of order, Murray Krieger
has suggested that Pope represents the distinction between
order and discord as the distinction between classical unity,
in *The Rape of the Lock*, and modern historical reality, in
The Dunciad. Pope displays a nostalgia for the inconsequential, sufficient, and unified form of art as well as a recognition
of the real and consequential discord and partiality of human
beings. Krieger thus suggests that Pope wishes for the unified
world of art even as he recognizes the world as what Price
calls a "self-subsistent" order, cut off from reality.[9]

Pamela, however, by embracing the disorderly excess of
experience, may be seen to constitute a reconciliation, both
of the real differences of human beings and of reality and art.
B and Pamela are partial and they are different; but they are
increasingly incapable of self-subsistence and increasingly subject to change in relation to each other. The characters begin
as "self-enclosed" orders, exactly in Price's terms: "seeming
to use the same words but in fact unable to comprehend each
other's meaning." Yet, I want to suggest, it is the capacity of
language to include their different meanings that makes their
union possible. Thus partiality and difference are "realized"
in a relation that makes them inconsequential; for they do
not lead to division. Pamela's art is thus precisely the means
of representing both the differences between individuals as
indecisive differences and representation itself as an inclusive
phenomenon. In *Pamela*, life and art come to correspond in
their mutual acceptance of excesses, and this is the means by
which human beings are united in their differences.

The novel's excesses are multiple, for the narrative itself is
difficult to "order" and therefore difficult to place in a de-

[8] Martin Price, *To the Palace of Wisdom: Studies in Order and Energy
from Dryden to Blake* (New York: Doubleday, 1964), pp. 290, vii.

[9] Murray Krieger, "The 'Frail China Jar' and the Rude Hand of Chaos,"
in *The Play and Place of Criticism* (Baltimore: The Johns Hopkins Press,
1967), pp. 53-68.

velopment or history of the novel. Verging on tedium, it exceeds the bounds of plot with a representation of experience that is both repetitive and redundant. Although it is usually assumed, by critics who read in the context of a history of the novel, that this is a mistake of an early and inexperienced novelist,[10] it may in fact be one of the various refusals of *Pamela* to treat experience or representation as a means to an end. For the experience of reading the novel is one of episodes that do not contribute to a clear objective.[11] We cannot even reread the narrative and see that early episodes lead to an end; they remain ambiguous, as likely to lead to rape as to marriage. Any episode could go either way, since Pamela does not determine their significance. Although the content of episodes varies, the form is a replay, in which she goes back to him and he tries it again. Even after the marriage, the confrontation and the evasion of resolution are re-enacted by Pamela with B's sister, Lady Davers, whose threat similarly forces Pamela to escape out of a window.

[10] Mark Kinkead-Weekes, in *Samuel Richardson: Dramatic Novelist* (Ithaca: Cornell University Press, 1973), insists convincingly that the "faults" of the novel are technical: "The first plank in the 'hypocrisy' platform, for example, is supplied by inadequacies of plotting. Richardson often overlooked the need for invention, as his habit of repeating himself shows, but he seems never to have noticed how failures to contrive could have unwanted psychological effects" (p. 89). I do not claim that Richardson intended my reading, but neither do I think that Richardson, any more than Pamela, carries through his intentions with determination.

[11] Many readers identify an objective, of course, but my argument is that, on the basis of what Pamela writes, this is difficult to do. If marriage is the objective of the narrative, for example, it would not need to exceed that point by more than a hundred pages. Robert Alan Donovan, acknowledging this excess, suggests that "Pamela's central concern is with the clear and unambiguous definition of her social identity" and that the novel must extend beyond the wedding in order for her to accomplish this. See *The Shaping Vision: Imagination in the English Novel from Defoe to Dickens* (Ithaca: Cornell University Press, 1966), p. 58. Mark Kinkead-Weekes provides an objective more sympathetic to my reading of the novel: "Human relationship and happiness can only be established when faith and trust, however dangerous and difficult, replace war and sexual intrigue." See *Samuel Richardson*, p. 56. It seems to me that "war" and "trust" are not so distinct in *Pamela*, however, but that the one makes the other possible.

This is to say that events are not plotted, or that they are present in excess of the requirements of a plot. And the order imposed by a plot is always suspect in this narrative. The suspicion on the part of Pamela and B that the other is plotting is exactly a suspicion that the self is being imposed upon. If we read the novel as a struggle for mastery and possession, B wants to possess Pamela and she wants to marry him; or, he wants to get her and she will not give herself unless she gets him in return. And the fact that Pamela and B remain engaged in their struggle can be assumed to mean that each has an end in view; critics like Henry Fielding assume this, and the characters assume it of each other. But if we take their words for it, we cannot plot their desires. Instead, we must accept their meaning as ambiguous or inconsistent, as difficult to get hold of as Pamela is for B and B is for Pamela. The narrative is unwilling to allow impositions, either those of one character on another or those of one event on another, to be final or determinant. Thus the novel proceeds as a repetition of exchanges that evade rather than effect possession. The evasion of mastery and possession seems to me to be a goal of the narrative, even as it is a goal that precludes finality and certainty. The cumulative experience of the novel seems to be to allow meaning to exceed plots: to accept redundancy rather than impose consequential or decisive development on experience.

I will consider the fact that both the narrative and its characters are redundant, therefore, not as a sign of a lack of development or a mark of the novel's immaturity but as a mark of *Pamela*'s engagement with the issue of development itself. The novel suggests that in such "undeveloped" forms as the unplotted narrative and the dependent self, in both of which distinction remains dubious, lies a realm of freedom and power unavailable to forms of development, which define differences and reduce excesses. This unsettling consideration is generated by the recognition that language itself refuses to settle differences and instead encourages ambiguity and redundancy. It is through its engagement with the power of language to unsettle determination that *Pamela* is able to exceed the bounds that usually limit our conceptions of meaningful experience and meaningful selves.

Pamela begins her narrative with determination: "I will die a thousand deaths, rather than be dishonest any way," she writes to her parents (47), and she proclaims to B that, " 'if you were a prince, I would not be otherwise than honest' " (55).[12] She represents a clear sense of choice and a clear sense of her own independence and consistency. The two most crucial values in the novel, truth and individual meaning, are invariable and definite here. No matter what else is offered, both statements imply, Pamela will hold on to what she is. Her self-possession entails definitions of truth and self that clearly distinguish both values, making them independent of what differs from them.

But it is this conception of meaning that is threatened in Pamela's dealings with B:

> "Well may I forget that I am your servant, when you forget what belongs to a master."
> ... "Have I done you any harm?" "Yes, sir," said I, "the greatest harm in the world: You have ... lessened the distance that fortune has made between us, by demeaning yourself, to be so free to a poor servant." (55)

It is self-possession that is lost here with the failure of memory to keep hold of things. Having vowed never to "forfeit my good name" (47), Pamela here describes her relationship with B as one of mutual forfeiture in mutual forgetfulness. Both the losses and the mutuality involved endanger her ability to claim her own meaning as a secure possession. For not only does she let go her grasp of what she is and what belongs to her; she does so because he forgets what belongs to him. Her meaning is now doubly insecure, both subject to being lost

---

[12] Samuel Richardson, *Pamela* (Harmondsworth, Mx.: Penguin, 1980). All quotations are taken from this edition and page numbers are cited in the text.

by her and subject to what lies outside her bounds in its
dependence on his behavior. That she is not distinct from him
is suggested by her recognition that he has " 'lessened the
distance' " between them. But it is even more forcefully suggested by her failure to differentiate his behavior from her
own. Hers is no longer her own; it is owing to him. The turn
from claims to disclaimers, by which she moves from owning
up to her actions to disowning responsibility for them, marks
a further loosening of her determination. Not only has she let
go of her meaning as determined, but she has lost the sense
that that meaning is exclusively hers.

But this loss is mutual. B also finds that he cannot maintain
his determination because of Pamela's behavior, and who is
responsible for or benefits from the "freedom" of their exchanges is not itself determined. Shortly after the above exchange, Pamela dresses in her peasant clothes, in which she
plans to return home. And B, seemingly mistaking her for
someone else, again makes advances, for which he blames her:
" 'I was resolved never again to honour you with my notice;
and so you must disguise yourself, to attract me.' " She then
speaks "disrespectfully" to him, but she blames that on his
provocation (90-92). The freedom of their behavior with each
other lies in the impossibility of confining what either character means to that character. Neither "means" to do what
she or he does. Their meaning is thereby opened up to include
more than they can determine and made fluid rather than
fixed as it changes, relative to each other. Meaning is free here
because it is neither confined nor stable. But Pamela and B
speak suspiciously of the freedom of the other's behavior,
identifying it with their own loss.

On one level, their freedoms are a matter of stepping out
of the bounds of their proper social positions. He has moved
lower than his position, having "degraded himself to offer
freedoms to his poor servant" (54). She has moved higher,
having exhibited pride and having "taken" freedoms with his
name (63). When free, then, they are out of place. But that
such freedom is threatening seems due not simply to the insecurity of place or possession but to the assumption that they

can therefore be placed or possessed by the other. For the economic language that is used or suggested in their accusations implies a conception of exchange that identifies all values as subject to possession and determination; so that if someone loses something, someone else gets it. That B "offers" freedoms or Pamela "takes" freedoms makes freedom itself an object that can be exchanged and possessed. That both characters see the freedom of their behavior as something due to the other identifies such freedom as a loss of self that is the other's gain.

In fact, neither claims anything or feels the gain of anything in these exchanges. But because both experience freedom as a loss of what they have had, and because they represent this economically, they are threatened by the perception that if one is out of control, the other must be in control, or that one's losses must be the other's gains. Giving up something for nothing is exactly what Pamela's parents have warned her against: "we *fear*—you should be *too* grateful, and reward him with that jewel, your virtue, which no riches, nor favour, nor any thing in this life, can make up to you" (46). This conception of exchange insists that Pamela must get equivalent compensation in return for whatever she gives up; to exceed a fair exchange, to be *too* grateful, is frightening. The difficulty, then, is not just that Pamela and B no longer have secure possession of what they are. It is that they call this sheer loss, one for which they can identify no compensation. It is the conception of their exchanges as matters of definitive and exclusive gain and loss that endangers their freedom, for what they are potentially freed from *is* definitive gain and loss. What they actually do in the novel is to give up possession of themselves and get nothing definite in return but freedom from possession, freedom to be indeterminate. To recognize this as liberation, as the freedom to mean more than definition permits, is the project for which the experience of language is crucial.

The meaning of words is a matter of constant debate early in the novel as Pamela and B question the meaning of each other. And Pamela expresses disapproval of the "free" talk of the ladies who visit B because she insists that ambiguous words are neither true nor trustworthy. The ladies "toss their jests about, and their *double meanings*, as they own them, as freely as the gentlemen. But whatever reputation these freedoms may give to their *wit*, I think they do but little credit to their *hearts*" (84). The freedom of double meanings from definition is equated here with duplicity. Pamela herself, when confronted with B's freedoms, and with the sudden multiplication of meanings that his freedoms make possible, wants to single out one version as the truth:

> O this angel of a master! this fine gentleman! . . . (yes, I *must* call him gentleman, though he has fallen from the merit of that title) has degraded himself to offer freedoms to his poor servant: he has now shewed himself in his true colours. . . . (53-54)

Calling him both a gentleman and not a gentleman, Pamela gives B two conflicting meanings. She reads him as duplicitous and identifies that duplicity as part of a design against her. The truth, then, is not that he is genuinely variable or ambiguous but that he is tricking her. Similarly, B identifies Pamela as a " 'hypocrite' " when she dresses in those other clothes (90), someone who pretends to be what she is not in order to attract him. Arguing with his housekeeper about Pamela's character and the freedom of her behavior, B recognizes that there is more than one meaning for her; but he insists that the truth is that she is artful:

> "She is," replied she, "an innocent young creature. . . ."
> "*Innocent*! again; and *virtuous*, I suppose! . . ."
> ". . . she keeps herself so much to herself, and yet behaves so prudently, that they all esteem her. . . ."
> "Ay," says he, "that's her art. . . ." (60)

For both Pamela and B, the fact that the other can be given more than one meaning is suspicious and means that the other is both untrue and artful. Artful representation here is misrepresentation, or misinterpretation, of true meaning. It involves turning one thing into another thing that it is not and thus is identified with artifice. This art is practiced not only in the misrepresentation of the other by the other, but in the misrepresentation of the self by the other. And thus each feels that the other makes her or him into something she or he is not.

> As light as he makes of the words *virtue* and *innocence* in me, he would have made a less angry construction, had I *less deserved* that he should do so; for then may be, my *crime* would have been my *virtue* with him, wicked gentleman as he is! (61)

> "Precise fool!" said he, . . . "I was bewitched I had not gone through my purpose last Sunday night; and then your licentious tongue had not given the worst interpretation to little puny freedoms, that shew my love and my folly at the same time." (248)

Pamela insists in the first passage above that B's constructions of meaning would make a virtue of crime, and that she would only deserve his kindness if she were in truth an undeserving person. B, in the second passage, sees that she misrepresents him to a similar extent, though. For he interprets his failure to go through with the rape as a sign of both love and folly; and she interprets it at its worst, an intended rape. He, then, she thinks, would see her crime as a virtue; and she, he thinks, would see his virtue as a crime. Both feel the other is artful, making the self into something the self is really not.

Art, then, is the realm of freedom in which things are what they are not: crime can be virtue and virtue can be crime, and artful meaning is multiple meaning. Pamela and B open up meaning for each other. They exceed its confinement and stability as they recognize room for interpretation. And although they do not trust meaning that shifts its grounds in such ways, their experience of each other is an experience of meaning that is not clear or stable. "Is it not strange," Pamela writes of B's inconsistent behavior, "that love borders so much upon hatred? But this wicked love is not like the true virtuous love, to be sure" (86). In order to be sure, truth and virtue must be unambiguous. Like the lessening of distance between Pamela and B that she identifies with his freedom, love and hatred are too close here to remain distinct. And the confusion of the properly distinct and exclusive opposition threatens the security of truth just as it threatens the security of self.

Yet Pamela uses language in her exchanges with B in ways that increase such confusions and preclude the security of truth. Her ability to shift the bounds of meanings, and her ability to shift the grounds of meanings, make truth itself a shifty proposition. This is the art of her representation; and it is in the practice of this art that she frees truth from the confinement of secure borders. Truth itself becomes something that cannot be told except as an excess of meaning that defies definition, as Pamela's way with words allies the forces of art and truth. And it is in the increasing inability of the narrative to tell the difference between the artful and the truthful that its characters find their freedom.

Pamela's refusal either to keep her words within bounds or to admit that she is doing anything dishonest—her refusal to discriminate between her excessive writing and the truth—is what angers B:

> "And so I am to be exposed, am I," said he, "*in* my own house, and *out* of my house, to the whole world, by such a saucebox?" "No, good sir," said I, "and I pray your honour not to be angry with me; it is not *I* that expose you, if I say nothing but the truth." (62)

Here what seems to be at issue for B is his exposure; and his description of how that occurs emphasizes that it is Pamela's refusal to make proper distinctions that is most threatening to him. He sees her as breaking through the bounds of propriety, property, and privacy by sending her stories "out of a family" (44). She thus refuses to distinguish properly what is his own and what she can give away to the rest of the world, or what lies inside and what lies outside his house. She does not seem to accept his limits as determinant or decisive; she acts as if they make no difference.

Refusing, by writing letters home, to keep what she says

about B within bounds, Pamela initiates the most fundamental confusion in the novel. By making dubious the difference between inside and outside, her narrative will unbind the limits imposed by that distinction and so replace fixed bounds with shifting possibilities of meaning. The difference between inside and outside stands simply in their opposition, but the opposition is what Pamela's writing ignores. And because that distinction is arbitrary, her refusal to accept it makes it disappear. Rather than accept the distinction as fixed, she makes its meaning subject to interpretation. Since she is part of two "families" at once, her own and his, Pamela can interpret her behavior as well within the prescribed bounds of propriety even as it exceeds them.

Doubling meaning, Pamela both remains within and exceeds bounds; and this opens up a multitude of improper possibilities. That B cannot enter her body and that she cannot enter his social class, both of which are definite and exclusive assumptions at the beginning of the novel, are rendered uncertain by the undoing of the elementary difference between in and out. That these concepts can be confused leads to the eventual recognition that she has already incorporated him, and his class her, even as he and she remained on the outside. They can both be in two places at once. Thus once the difference between inside and outside is made dubious, numerous boundaries are subject to dispute and not subject to clear settlement.

But this is not the only confusion Pamela is responsible for in this passage. She does not answer the question B poses and changes the subject by disagreeing not with the substance of what he says—that he is being exposed all over the place— but with his assignment of responsibility to her. The issue thus shifts from whether the exposure occurs to who is doing the exposing. Pamela's ability to elude B is suggested here by her ability to open up holes in his argument. Through these, she gets out of answering the question he poses and gets out of the position in which his words put her.

"Interpretation is like a football game," Geoffrey Hartman has written. "You spot a hole and you go through. But first

you may have to induce that opening."[13] Pamela responds to
that part of B's question with which she can take issue and
in which she can make room for another interpretation. She
opens up the meaning of his question by undermining any
definite sense of causality. What she says implies that maybe
the truth will come out on its own or maybe B himself is at
fault. Moreover, in a sense she does not have to reinterpret
the exposure itself: that already leaves him wide open. Her
interpretations and representations work to put more meanings into things, insisting on meaning in excess of definition
and thereby also dependent on other meanings, or dependent
on interpretation, *for* meaning.

Able in this passage to combine what B perceives as clearly
distinct (inside and outside) and able to separate what he
perceives as obviously connected (her behavior and his exposure), Pamela unsettles meaning because she keeps differences in play, refusing to let them settle. She opens up the
boundaries that keep differences distinct and takes apart the
connections between such differences as cause and effect. She
demonstrates, then, both her power to change meaning and
the inability of language to fix meaning so that it is not subject
to change, even as she seems to claim, for both herself and
language, the capacity to speak the truth. But she does not,
of course, exactly make that claim. Instead, truth itself is left
in the realm of possibility rather than certainty as it is located
only conditionally. Truth becomes "iffy"; it depends. Pamela's
true role in this depends on whether she speaks the truth; or,
her true role in this depends on how you interpret it.

And so although she keeps changing the subject, Pamela
does not privilege or certify any version or any subject. She
makes the limits of meaning indefinite, perceives oppositions
as inclusive rather than exclusive of each other, allows meanings to overlap, and insists that meanings are dependent on
rather than independent of other meanings. Related to each

[13] Geoffrey H. Hartman, "The Voice of the Shuttle: Language from the
Point of View of Literature," in *Beyond Formalism: Literary Essays 1958-
1970* (New Haven: Yale University Press, 1970), p. 351.

other but in constant flux, differences vary; differentiation is mobilized and shifts around. Like the agent of exposure in the above exchange that is never positively identified, truth is not something Pamela can claim to know. Nor does she allow any claim to be made on her; the self is also a changing subject here. The possibility of truth really functions as part of Pamela's disclaimer of her own role in B's exposure: if she in fact is writing exposition, she is only the means which elucidates, rather than the cause of, exposure. Like B's passive construction, which frees *him* from responsibility, Pamela's own representation of self gets her out of rather than owns responsibility for what is going on. She also, that is to say, represents herself as dependent (" 'I pray your honour not to be angry with me' "), making no claims for self whatever. The implicit disclaimers of both characters' speeches, as if to say "*I* am not doing anything," insist that the self remain as shifty as the other subjects of this exchange: subject to the other and subject to differing interpretations.[14]

Pamela's and B's relationship thus works as the "undoing" of both self and other. The tactics of deconstruction are socialized in Richardson's novel, as each character uses language to undermine the claims of the other and to disclaim responsibility for doing so. But this results in no loss of meaning. Critics have identified, in other eighteenth-century writers, the "absence" or "fiction" of selfhood. Homer O. Brown, for example, has suggested that "Defoe's project seems to have involved the creation of more or less autonomous voices, themselves without a center. . . . Or, rather, voices whose center is a felt lack of center."[15] And Juliet Flower Mac-

---

[14] In a discussion of psychoanalytic narratives, Roy Schafer identifies the use of disclaimers in the reconstruction of experience by language as elements of fantasizing in which the self is "split up or split off" rather than a coherent unit. The worlds constructed by disclaimer tend to be animistic, full of surprises, and unmanageable: worlds such as the one Pamela inhabits. See "Action and Narration in Psychoanalysis," *New Literary History*, XII, no. 1 (1980), 61-85.

[15] Homer O. Brown, "The Displaced Self in the Novels of Daniel Defoe," *ELH*, 38, no. 4 (1971), 583.

Cannell, focusing on Rousseau's "deconstruction of the concept of self-love," has concluded that for Rousseau "The self is a hypothesis, a fiction, that exists, as do all fictions, in the manner of its presentation. Its mode, that of the *as if*, suspends from the outset questions of definite knowledge."[16] In *Pamela*, the self is also suspended in its meaning as it is suspended between one person and another. But this does not render the self absent.[17] The suspension seems instead to extend the self and enlarge its powers, even as it renders the self groundless and dependent for its meaning on what lies beyond it, in exchanges that disable any sense of self-possession. Precisely because it is no longer clear to whom it belongs or how it can be located, given representations that keep it indeterminate, the self is freed from the limits of individuality and self-possession. To come undone, *Pamela* suggests, is to gain a self of potentially limitless meaning.

The struggle in which Pamela and B engage even while they try to disengage themselves is the central focus of the pressure the narrative exerts in order to keep meaning at issue. Their opposition never clearly *is* an opposition. That is why the novel is subject to interpretations such as Fielding's *Shamela*, in which roles seem to be reversed as the scheming whore plots to marry the simple minded squire. In fact, Pamela and B are, at various points in the novel, liable to turn into each other or switch positions. The beginning of their relationship is clear enough as a kind of property dispute, in which he

[16] Juliet Flower MacCannell, "Nature and Self-Love: A Reinterpretation of Rousseau's 'Passion primitive,' " *PMLA*, 92, no. 5 (1977), 900.

[17] Patricia Meyer Spacks, in *The Adolescent Idea: Myths of Youth and the Adult Imagination* (New York: Basic Books, 1981), pp. 19-30, identifies Pamela's power as "Nobody's Power" because Pamela conquers B by means of her adolescent helplessness and inability to assert herself. Spacks sees Pamela's lack of coherent identity as something we all grow out of and suggests that Pamela loses power once she takes on adult status and marries B. I am suggesting, however, that Pamela's dependence and power are not a matter of her youth and are realized because of B.

wants to possess her and she claims a self-possession that makes her independent of him. But this is almost immediately confused by his sense that she, with her letters and talk, is giving him away. The issue of B's mastery and possession of Pamela keeps slipping into the issue of B's humiliation and dispossession by Pamela, with each supposedly distinct objective verging on its opposite. As in the exchange about his exposure, it is also often difficult to tell the exact difference between the two characters themselves, for that difference is not clear. Pamela is not absolutely denying B here and is even praying for his favor; but she is not in agreement with him either. Because she is dependent on him and differs from him, it is impossible to say exactly where she stands in relation to B. She is both subordinate and insubordinate, as he is both master and victim. The characters' meaning is thus suspended between the poles of oppositions which provide distinct and decisive meaning.

The loss of the clear subordination of one character to another is implied in all the lost distinctions of the narrative, and it is because subordination shifts from one side to another of any proposed distinction that those constructions fail *as* distinctions. This is why Pamela and B are not simply reversing the sexual and social hierarchy of their society: they are disabling hierarchy altogether by identifying positions as always reversible and always in flux. Other oppositions are represented as convertible and insecure in similarly indefinite exchanges. This is true not only of exchanges between the characters but of exchanges set up between one word and another. If, especially at the beginning of her narrative, Pamela can insist that some values are subject neither to change nor exchange (as with " 'if you were a prince, I would not be otherwise than honest' "), it is more characteristic of her, once she sets up an exchange, neither to define nor redefine by means of it. Instead, she identifies flexible equivalences.

When, for example, Pamela seems to want to clarify differences between herself and B by insisting that each values the same thing in opposite ways, the results are not definitive:

"My *crime* would have been my *virtue* with him. . . ."
(61)

"What does *he* call honour, think you?" "Ruin! shame!
disgrace!" said I, "I fear." (160)

These differentiations do not provide clear distinctions. For
if they insist that things are different for B than they are for
Pamela, they also insist on the equivalence of opposite values.
That crime equals virtue and honor equals disgrace suggests
not that distinction prevails between Pamela and B but that
he, or she, can undo distinctions by equating them and then
converting one into the other. What seems a means of distinction in fact makes distinction uncertain, putting meaning
in flux rather than settling it.

When Pamela constructs maxims, something similar happens. "Your *poverty* is my *pride*," she writes to her parents.
And she preaches to Mrs. Jewkes that " 'an *hour* of innocence
. . . is worth an *age* of guilt' " (175). Such statements seem to
mean to confirm the value of Pamela's poverty and innocence.
But they also mean that these qualities are dependent for their
meaning on their opposites, and the expression of the opposition as an equivalence means that such qualities as poverty
and innocence are interchangeable with their opposites.
Meaning becomes convertible. If Pamela's parents' poverty is
the equivalent of Pamela's pride, then they cannot really *be*
poor, and she cannot really be proud, even as they are these
things. Or, if the grounds for poverty and pride are the same
grounds, they can all be both at once. The second exchange
also denies the determination of its own differential. The equation of an hour of innocence and an age of guilt distinguishes
the qualities by the quantities. But if an hour is worth an age,
this can increase or decrease its value: increase it in that sixty
minutes is as great as sixty years, or decrease it in that it is
an hour that seems to last an age. And if an age of guilt is
the same as only an hour of anything, it does not seem to
amount to much. Thus the implication is that there is not in
fact much to choose between them, or the choice does not
make much difference. To conflate such contradictory mean-

ings in these ways, then, is to challenge the certainty of difference and to free language from security. But it is also to risk undifferentiation and meaninglessness.

"Art does not add itself to the world of meanings: it makes room in meaning itself." Geoffrey Hartman's essay "The Voice of the Shuttle" considers how, in the language of literature, "words are released from their bondage to meaning."[18] Such language, he says, both underspecifies and overspecifies, both crowds meaning with an excess of possible interpretations and compels silence. Pamela uses this kind of language. The power of her representation lies in its ability to increase the variable potential of meaning: both because she conflates meanings, by interpreting apparent differences as similar, and because she breaks meanings apart, by interpreting apparent similarities as different. In a sense, the pressure she exerts is the pressure of the pun that Hartman calls "the redundancy principle": "You can define a pun as two meanings competing for the same phonemic space or as one sound bringing forth semantic twins, but, however you look at it, it's a crowded situation."[19] Pamela crowds. She crowds B even as she eludes him so that he feels as threatened as she; and she crowds her narrative with a constant sense of excess meaning. There often seems to be more meaning in words when Pamela uses them than any use can account for. She threatens with a kind of oppressiveness, then—a uselessness or meaninglessness—even as she delivers freedom. For her language is both overdetermined and indeterminate.

If to crowd meaning with an excess of possibilities is to risk exceeding meaning itself, Pamela threatens her narrative with the death of meaning. And she literalizes this version of the struggle of meaning to be free when she considers suicide in order "to free myself from all their persecutions" (211). But her conception of the effects of her death is not one of freedom. What Pamela foresees is that because of her suicide B will know that she " 'really was the innocent creature she pre-

---

[18] Hartman, "The Voice of the Shuttle," p. 352.
[19] Ibid., p. 347.

tended to be'" (212). Her end would thus secure and limit her meaning; it would be known. Pamela is driven to consider suicide, compelled to silence, by the very impossibility of otherwise knowing or proving anything; but it is also this very impossibility that compels her to live.

Physically weak from her fall from a wall as she tried to escape, Pamela cannot decide if that weakness is "meant" to make it easier to give up her life or if it is a weakness she would only take advantage of in order to take the easy way out. She does not know, that is, if suicide would be a strong or a weak act; she cannot tell the difference.

> "Who authorized thee to put an end to [thy life] ? Is it
> not the weakness of thy mind that suggests to thee that
> there is no way to preserve it with honour? . . . Art *thou*
> to put a bound to the Divine Will . . . ? " (213)

In a series of questions that extends more than a page, Pamela finds that though her own authority may only authorize questions and guarantee no answers, or even *because* her authority cannot thereby put a bound to anything, it authorizes only life. Moreover, she recognizes that the choice of death, if it would fix bounds, would fix them only arbitrarily. For it would be the choice of " 'one rash moment,' " as insignificant and temporary as any other moment. Death, then, and finality, in the kind of reversal that Pamela's art authorizes, become the arbitrary choice, and life becomes the compulsion. It is because she cannot tell the difference, because she is unable to know or finalize meaning, that Pamela is bound to live. Thus, her crowding of meaning so that it exceeds bounds may threaten meaninglessness; but that threat can never be carried through while she lives. Alive, Pamela is bound to be free of finality.

The pressure Pamela puts on meaning, therefore, is not the pressure of a plot. The intensity of meaning in her narrative is not generated by the question of how things will turn out; and things do not become meaningful as part of a larger context or as contributions to an end. Her meanings turn in as well as out, as in "your *poverty* is my *pride*." One element is not subordinate to another, nor does one lead to another. That these values can turn into each other as well as open each other up to include more meaning, and that it is difficult to distinguish any inherent from any externally determined meaning, are the factors that intensify and increase meaning here. And the pressure increases precisely because such meaning cannot turn out to mean with any finality but turns, or reverses, to unsettle meaning further. Elements or events under such pressure are crucial in themselves. They cannot, then, be plotted.

Even when she means to plot, Pamela does not effect a plot. The episode in which she contrives to escape from the house in the country clarifies why she cannot construct a plot and clarifies this inability, again, as a confusion of the difference between "inside" and "outside":

> As I continue writing here, when I ought to act, that will shew you my strange irresolution, and how I am distressed between my hopes and my fears! But I will go down again . . . What a contriver is your Pamela become!
> . . .
> Well, here I am, come back again! frighted, like a fool, out of all my purposes! The gardener was in another part of the garden . . . when I looked, and saw the horrid bull, as I thought, making to get between me and the door, and another bull coming towards me the other way. Well, thought I, here seems to be the spirit of my master in one bull, and Mrs. Jewkes's in the other; and now I am gone for certain! "O help!" cried I, like a fool, nobody near me! and ran back to the door as swift as if I flew. When I had got the door in my hand, I ventured to look back, to see if these supposed bulls were coming; and I saw they were only two poor cows, grazing in distant places, that my fears had made so terrible to me.
> But as every thing is so frightful to me, as things have not so black an appearance as they had at first, I will not think of escaping: and, indeed, if I were to attempt it, and were to have got at distance from this house, I should

too probably be as much terrified at the first strange man that I met with. I have heard it said, *That there can be no prudence without apprehension*: but I am persuaded, that fear brings one into more dangers than the caution, that goes along with it, delivers one from. (192)

Acknowledging contrivance, Pamela nevertheless constructs experience as something other than a plot here. Rather than identifying different things and actions so that they come together to contribute to her ends, she represents a world in which she cannot tell differences with any consistency at all and therefore loses her determination. Her most striking confusions are those in the field, where she is unable to tell the very differences on which her own distinction and integrity depend. In her interpretation of grazing cows as charging bulls who are both Mr. B and Mrs. Jewkes, Pamela conflates rather than differentiates male and female, master and servant, passivity and activity, safety and danger. All these oppositions shift positions. And this is true also of inside and outside. There seems to be no difference between them, she realizes: things are equally bad out there and in the house. Thus, at the moment she could get out, Pamela interprets experience so that she might as well stay in. But the more significant result—the really meaningful "end" of this—is that she interprets experience to mean that interpretation itself cannot get her anywhere. Her representations do not contribute to ends. She disables plot as she "concludes" that looking forward will only cause her to retreat backward.

Pamela's interpretation of the meaning of things disables decisive action as it disables plot. At the beginning of the passage, she sees her writing as a sign of irresolution, an indication that she is somewhere "between" hopes and fears. But her action brings her no closer to resolution. She remains in the midst of activity, unable to take an action and follow it through to an end, suspended in the middle of the plot she has contrived, by her own suspension of the difference between such things as passive cows and charging bulls. In fact, Pamela's activity brings her less resolution than she has at first; for although she comes to a conclusion, it is to do nothing conclusive. Plot, action, and conclusion are not just disabled here but are turned against themselves, as is determination. Unable to get out of the indeterminate middle of activity, Pamela decides that this is so because fear opens up more possibilities of meaning than caution resolves. In the maxim she cites, apprehension is a necessary and subordinate part of prudence. The two are plotted: one contributes to the other. Her experience, though, is that fear is greater than caution; the part exceeds the whole. The plot of the proverb thereby comes apart.

If what is inside and what is outside the house become indistinguishable here, the indistinction of what is inside and what is outside Pamela's self seems the most important confusion. In the field she cannot tell the difference between what her fear makes things mean and what things are in themselves. She has no sense of her own difference or of the difference she makes. Sitting in her room, Pamela recognizes that her fear causes danger, but she cannot count on keeping hold of that difference. Although she owns up to responsibility for her false interpretations, then, she owns up not to falseness but to a loss of self-possession and determination. The meaning of things is both excessive and open in this passage, as elements of experience are either jammed too full of meaning to be clearly differentiated or break apart as they lose integrity. Both also seem to be happening to Pamela. As she decides in the episode of the possible suicide, she will see what happens next rather than act. The means to an end are discarded; and the end of the plot comes apart as Pamela's resolution disintegrates. When experience is left to her to determine, we learn here, meaning breaks loose of determination.

Now this passage may be read as a plot if it is read as the expression of a repressed wish to remain in the house. This would concur with Fielding's reading of hypocrisy in its insistence that the apparent confusion is only a cover for an underlying determination. But to insist on an underlying truth is to insist on a kind of meaning unauthorized by this narrative, in which the possibility of determining truth or any

other meaning is itself at issue. We cannot say that the truth
comes out here, nor can we say that Pamela admits the truth.
What is both coming out and being admitted is that truth can
go in two directions or exist in two places; and so true meaning—the true meaning of the object of desire or of the objective
of her action—cannot be fixed. Nor can the repression be
fixed; for what is clearest about repression in this novel is that
it is both externally imposed by objects and internally imposed
by fears. The narrative's inability to define repression is analogous to its inability to fix subordination. The determination
of such orders is unresolved.

   The failure of resolution, in both character and narrative
structure, renders problematic not only the existence of a plot
but the whole concept of causality. Pamela's decision to see
what comes next rather than determine her future is one factor
contributing to the loss of causal connection. This is also a
decision given in the structure of the narrative, with its daily
rather than single perspective. Pamela can narrate events only
sequentially and not as matters of consequence, which remains
unknown even if it is expected; and increasingly in the narrative consequences are not predicted. Consequence assumes
that events are connected causally: that past events lead to,
or precedents determine, the present and future. And consequential relations are exclusive, ignoring or discounting what
does not contribute to an accumulation of meaning or value.
Sequence, however, assumes that things just happen, and sequence is inclusive: anything that happens is equally valid.

   Early in the novel, Pamela conceives of her experience as a
matter of consequence:

   "I know this, that he is vexed at what he has done; he
   was vexed the *first* time, more vexed the *second* time,"
   [said Mrs. Jervis].
   "Yes," said I, "and so he will be vexed, I suppose, the
   third and *fourth* time too, till he has quite ruined your
   poor maiden; and who will have cause to be vexed then?"
   (73)

"The fruits of being of consequence to him, might be to make me of none to myself, or any body else." (78)

In the first passage, Pamela seems to recognize a consequential plot: incidents will accumulate and culminate in her ruin. But she also implies the recognition of the consequential as a purely arbitrary relation. Whereas Mrs. Jervis identifies one sort of accumulation—B's increasing vexation—Pamela will identify another result—her ruin. Moreover, she denies the significance of B's increasing vexation, by insisting that it will not be the consequence of his acts; the consequence will be her vexation. Thus the constituents of the consequential relation are themselves inconsequential here. This suggests what the second quotation makes explicit: what has consequence for one person has no necessary consequence for another. Here Pamela identifies consequence with another form of exclusiveness: if I matter to him, I will not matter to anyone else; or, his gain is my loss. But the exclusiveness is not determinate; it is arbitrary, and it renders the concept of consequence itself relative and dubious. As Pamela is increasingly concerned to escape B's plots, she denies consequence as her value:

"Pray, Mrs. Jewkes," said I, "don't *madam* me so: I am but a silly poor girl, set up by the gambol of fortune, for a may-game; and now I am to be something, and now nothing, just as that thinks fit to sport with me." (147)

Consequence, here a matter both of being called madam and being determined, is denied, to be replaced not by self-determination but by the subjection of self to indeterminacy.

Causality is further undermined by the inability of the narrator to determine what will happen next. Plot demands planning. But often, as in the passage about the cows and the bulls, the forms of expectation with which Pamela looks forward are fear and doubt, which decide nothing. " 'Your doubts will only beget *cause* of doubts,' " B tells her (257), suggesting the repetitive and circular movement of her narrative. When, on the other hand, Pamela and B are determined and decisive about the future, they are simply wrong. Having decided she hates him in Letter xxxi, Pamela is still intending to six weeks later: "Now will I hate him most heartily" (260). And B, too, repeatedly believes that *now* he has had enough. What gets repeated are both doubts and certainties, because neither doubt nor certainty has consequence. Each present is inconsequential, discrete rather than a result determined by the past or a cause determining the future.

Experience is repetitive here, and its representation is repetitive. The failure to develop suggests stasis; and the repetition suggests the regressive form of ritual, which we may consider boring, rather than the progressive form of history, which we consider more interesting. Yet this choice of forms is inadequate to contain the experience of the novel. For the choice itself does not leave room for Pamela's defiance of formulation. The forms of both ritual and history secure experience. Ritual guarantees stability by repeating events. History guarantees security by denying loose ends, by tying events together so that they are parts of other events. *Pamela*, however, suggests that any moment is crucial in itself, neither bound to repeat nor bound to any other moment.

Some events repeat others in this novel; and some events seem plotted. But neither the repetitive nor the plotted event seems *determined* as such. Repetition is not acknowledged as old; nor are plots acknowledged as predictable. Even after experiencing and evading multiple plots that threaten her, Pamela remains doubtful about predicting a plot—"if this should turn out to be a plot, nothing I fear but a miracle can save me" (187)—and surprised when one appears—"what a plot, what an unexpected plot was this!" (241). Both repeatedly unexpected and repeatedly ineffectual, plot becomes as redundant and inconsequential as the repetitious events in this narrative. Rather than fitting into the form of either ritual or history, which give definite meaning to temporal sameness or difference, *Pamela* makes both repetitious and plotted events seem indeterminant and unformed.

In the economy of the narrative, this means that the inconsequential repetition of a single event replaces reserve, the accumulation of interest, and a pay-off. As each character holds on to the other only to withhold from the other the offer of his hand and the offer of her body, the standoff threatens to neutralize rather than generate interest. To consider how the novel maintains the standoff as a tension rather than stasis is to consider again the issue of difference. If indistinction of meaning and events prevails, so that there is nothing to choose between for characters incapable of making choices, what can happen? " 'I can neither *bear*, nor *forbear* her,' " B says (90). But, though unable to be with her and unable to be without her, he is nevertheless not disabled, as he finds in the very indistinctions or choices not a cancellation but an increase of value. Pamela's and B's choice *of* indistinction is also the choice of the narrative as it repeats its events. And it is in the freedom of their exchanges that the radical potential of that choice is clearest. Pamela's and B's relationship is one in which they lose themselves as distinct beings; they come together. That they come together only by taking each other apart and giving up any sense of individual integrity constitutes the most radical exchange of Pamela's narrative.

The loss of both the individuation and the independence of the self implies that the meaning of the self in *Pamela* comes apart in the same ways as do other meanings in the narrative. The bounds of the self come undone as confusion increases about what is self and what is other, about what lies inside and what lies outside the self. And this disintegration is both temporal and spatial. Such a self, like the narrative that represents it, cannot be plotted in time or space.

That the disintegration of narrative plot is linked to the disintegration of conventional concepts of the self in *Pamela* is suggested by several critics' identifications of plots with selfhood. Like Ian Watt, who suggests that much of the novelty of early narrative plot lies in its resemblance to personal memoirs, Peter Brooks identifies narrative plot with the work of individual memory. And he identifies memory as a means

of self-possession or mastery. Reading Freudian theory as providing a model of the self that stresses consistency and stability, Brooks posits that the individual gains control of what
he or she has been and is by remembering his or her past as
a history. Repetition, in memory and in behavior and in their
representation, works "economically," "as a process of *binding* toward the creation of an energetic constant-state situation
which will permit the emergence of mastery, and the possibility of postponement." This is also the process of written
narrative:

> Serviceable form must in this case mean perceptible form:
> repetition, repeat, recall, symmetry, all these journeys
> back in the text, returns to and returns of, that allow us
> to bind one textual moment to another in terms of sim-
> ilarity or substitution rather than mere contiguity. Tex-
> tual energy, all that is aroused into expectancy and pos-
> sibility in a text . . . can become usable by plot only when
> it has been bound or formalized.[20]

This is economical and useful. Exchanging the felt experience
for language that is coherently organized, with bounds and
definition, the process makes experience itself something that
can be exchanged.

The ability to remember and tell with coherence is thus the
ability to come into possession of experience, as Sharon Cameron emphasizes:

> Our minds produce images for which there are no verbal
> equivalents; more impenetrable than the images are vague
> intimations; words are absent or lost. Unable to say what
> we mean, we also fail to know it. We haven't names for
> our experiences, and after a while we haven't even the
> experiences.[21]

Moreover, to *have* the experience, in language that makes it

[20] Peter Brooks, "Freud's Masterplot: Questions of Narrative," *Yale French
Studies*, no. 55/56 (1977), 289-90.
[21] Sharon Cameron, *Lyric Time: Dickinson and the Limits of Genre* (The
Johns Hopkins University Press, 1979), p. 54.

distinct, means, Cameron explains, that the individual can separate it from the self: "telling changes, externalizes, puts one outside of and beyond."[22] Such representation is not a matter of truth, then, but a matter of realization. Realized by representation, the plotted experience can be both possessed and, because it can be possessed as something distinct, gotten rid of. This concept of the representation of memory as a coherent unit is thus linked to the concept of a securely bound self, securely separate from the rest of the world. It is allied to the Freudian model of the development and differentiation of ego, a development that coincides with the discovery of objects as external to and distinct from self. Such a self uses exchange as a means of corroborating its independence; whether one gains or loses by exchange, the process of exchange, because it occurs as a process of realization and distinction, cannot threaten but in fact reaffirms the distinction of the self and self-possession.

Pamela's refusal to represent a coherent memory corresponds to the novel's refusal to represent selves in these terms. That the consistency of a self, like the coherence of a story, can be imposed by "binding," which excludes differences that cannot be tied together, and that both are dependent on repetition in memory, are facts that Pamela recognizes. Yet her narrative, in its inconsequentiality, has no single memory. It has no power to render coherence, because the point of view is not totalized but broken up in time and space, a series of points of view related only contiguously. This disjunction is formalized by the use of letters. Each letter or journal entry is written, or recalled, at a different time. Without a single point from which to remember the past, and without a single point to which the past can lead, events are not held together. They are free to lead in various directions, and each moment is free to be a crisis. This narrative proceeds as a dispersal rather than a binding or integration of separate moments. And the integrity of character is similarly precluded by the

[22] Ibid., p. 53.

absence of any point of view that differentiates definitively what was from what is.

That Pamela's self is coming unbound is clear in that episode in which she dresses up again in her "own" kind of clothes in preparation to return home. Attempting to remember her place, to construct an identity and maintain self-possession by repetition of the past, she finds herself only displaced again into another "false" position of the kind she is trying to avoid. B makes another pass at her, then claims he thought she was someone else. Reclaiming herself in repetition, Pamela only increases the threat of B claiming her; she even, from his point of view, asks for it. This sort of return cannot, of course, be considered therapeutic or integrating, because Pamela does not differentiate past and present and returns to the past at the cost of her present difference from it. But this is the only recovery of past that she seems capable of. She cannot realize the difference between moments but only realizes one at a time. Thus she cannot determine on a past to repeat that will not also increase her present indeterminacy. "Meaning" to get away from B, she pulls him closer; and she cannot tell these effects apart or separate herself from either. Thus Pamela's present insecurity makes her memory and her use of memory dubious and incoherent. Remembering, that is to say, as in the episode in which she remembers that the cows are not bulls but doubts if she can remember such differences for long, is no more constructive than the forgetting that threatens her with the loss of self.

The internal binding of events, then, is replaced in this text by a process of internal unbinding. The self, for both Pamela and B, is experienced as coming undone and going out of control. Neither bound nor determined by internal consistency or mastery, these selves seem the archaic self of Freudian theory in which ego and non-ego are undifferentiated. What is inside overlaps with what is outside, or what is felt as part of the self is also felt to be part of someone else, so that there is no clear boundary between self and other. This involves a number of other indistinctions, too. The primitive ego is thought to be unable to distinguish between love and destructiveness, for example, because incorporation, which means both love and destruction, remains the most satisfying means of relating to objects. And external stimulation and internal reaction to it—being acted on and acting—are not distinguishable. Moreover, such confusions of self and other coexist with the apparent interchangeability of self and other. For by means of the processes of projection and introjection, which constitute reversals of the separation between ego and non-ego, the narcissistic self can project what is internal onto outside phenomena and internalize the external world, by introjection, for a sense of omnipotence.[23]

Such a self has no sense of independence whatever. The development of an independent self requires that narcissistic needs become internally satisfied by the interaction of ego and super-ego. But without this internal exchange, the self remains dependent on what is external to it and has no means of achieving self-regard or self-determination. Such a self is conceived, then, and perceived in terms of what is outside it; and it identifies its experience as interaction or reaction rather than action. The difference between inside and outside and between active and receptive positions is not recognized.

Pamela and B seem to perceive and represent experience in terms of such indistinctions. Differences seem convertible and insecure, and distinct identities become borderline cases. As meaning shifts, that is, from one side to another of the boundary that separates a thing from what is different, that shift is not perceived as unrealistic even though it disables the realization of secure meaning. This is what happens when Pamela sees B as both a gentleman and not a gentleman. It is also what happens when B sees Pamela as another person, and then as herself, when she is dressed in different clothes; she is both Pamela and not Pamela. The issue is complicated, and the indistinctions pile up, when each character insists that it is the other character who is making the self lose sight of

---

[23] See Otto Fenichel, *The Psychoanalytic Theory of Neurosis* (New York: W. W. Norton, 1945), pp. 34-41, for a discussion of the Freudian archaic ego.

differences and differ from her or his own customary behavior. That neither feels responsible for her or his own confusion makes them feel unable to prevent it.

The inability to realize or represent secure differences implies the inability to realize the self *as* different. If it is by means of representation that an individual is able to distinguish the self and control experience, Pamela and B have no means of distinction or mastery. The exchanges in which they take part do not serve these ends. Language represents their correspondence rather than their distinction and confirms their sense of themselves as interdependent and interchangeable. They in fact experience extraordinary power in these exchanges; but they do not possess power. Theirs is not power over the self or over the other; nor is it a power distinct from the other. For power is not exclusive here. To be in power is to be in relation to each other; for to be in relation to each other is to be potentially anything, both self and other.

Unable to exclude either self from power, Pamela and B make it impossible to identify their relationship as one of mastery because neither assumes any position that the other does not also assume. Roles of master and subordinate, and of aggressor and victim, shift back and forth between them. Because the grounds of dispute shift, and the boundaries of both possessions and positions become indistinct, it is hard to tell which side anyone is on, and it is not clear who is in possession of what is in dispute. It is also true that each character seems to be on both sides of any dispute: to be both master and subordinate, both in possession and dispossessed. The reversibility and indistinction of all such positions mobilizes the relation of the characters, insisting that their meaning is relative rather than independent. Their corresponding shifts of meaning both preclude the possession of individual identities, since neither secures any meaning for the self, and increases the meanings of both self and other, since both can have multiple meanings.

The two passages on which I will focus in considering how the exchanges of Pamela and B always defy rather than effect distinction and possession do not function as decisive passages in the novel. Each seems merely to repeat other indecisive exchanges, and each seems of minor importance both in that larger context and in the context of the passages themselves. These are picky and petty fights. But if to argue about one word, as happens in the first passage, seems childish, as if Pamela and B will use the smallest excuse for their mutual retaliations, the issues at stake are large. They are large because they are psychologically primitive issues. These characters pick on each other's words in order to take apart the linguistic constructions with which they defend themselves against incursions by the other. For it is in the reinterpretation of the other's representations that each finds room for the self. Here the defenses of each self are also used as the offenses of the other. But the persistence with which Pamela and B repeat the maneuvers that insist that neither can have anything the other cannot also have suggests that it is not really possession they are fighting for. Pamela and B seem to push these exchanges so far not in order to establish possession but in order to establish that possession cannot be determined: that they, therefore, have nothing to lose. Their exchanges work to get them out of exchange as a means of determination and possession.

The first of these representative exchanges is a larger section of the conversation about B's exposure:

> "And is it thus, insolent as you are! you taunt and retort upon me! But still I will be answered directly to my question." "Why then, sir," said I, "I will not tell a lye for the world: I *did* tell Mrs. Jervis; for my heart was almost broken; but I opened not my mouth to any other." "Very well, bold-face," said he, "and equivocator again! You did not open your *mouth* to any other; but did you not *write* to some other?" "Why . . . you could not have asked me this question, if you had not taken from me my letter to my father and mother, in which (I own it) I had broke my heart freely. . . ."
>
> "And so I am to be exposed, am I," said he, "*in* my own house, and *out* of my house, to the whole world, by

such a saucebox?" "No, good sir," said I, "and I pray
your honour not to be angry with me; it is not *I* that
expose you, if I say nothing but the truth." (62)

In this passage, each character represents the self as both
helpless before and threatened by the aggressive behavior of
the other. Neither Pamela nor B claims self-possession or self-
determination here. Both "own" only what is not or is no
longer their own: she claims the privacy of her letter, and he
claims the privacy of his house, but these are exactly the
properties whose bounds the other has transgressed. Their
claims are claims of dispossession. And both only own up to
behavior that can be blamed on the other. The identification
of the self as passive and dependent contributes to each character's denial that she or he has any responsibility for what
is happening.

Thus neither perceives his or her self as initiating or causing
anything. Each demand on his part and each acknowledgment
on her part is qualified by a passive construction of self: B
demands answers in the passive voice, and Pamela admits
telling things only because, in the first instance, her heart was
broken and, in the second, he has stolen her letter. Each presents the self as the victim of the other's duplicity. And each
practices duplicity here. For if neither actually lies, each shifts
the grounds of the argument repeatedly so that the other is
at fault or is the cause of what is going on.[24] The characters
not only pull the ground out from under each other but refuse
to take a stand.

[24] The fact that Pamela and B do not qualify as liars also suggests that they
cannot realize their selves as individual or separate entities. For lying is a
practice that assumes the clear distinction of self and other as it insists on
the difference between what the self knows and what others know. Thus
lying can be considered a sign of improvement by psychotherapists: "The
therapist working with the psychotic can be grateful when the patient can
genuinely 'lie' again. He has at least restored secrecy, privacy, a separate
identity." For the successful lie puts an end to the infantile stage of "omnis-
cience of thought" and helps to establish ego boundaries. See John M. Schlien,
"A Client-Centered Approach to Schizophrenia: First Approximation," in
*Psychotherapy of the Psychoses: Perspectives on Current Techniques of
Treatment*, ed. Arthur Burton (New York: Basic Books, 1961), p. 299.

Exchange is somehow dodged, then, as the agreement necessary to exchange—an agreement between or adequation of things given and taken—is deferred, and as each character defers to the other. And so is any distinct sense of self dodged. For if each time one is deferred to, that one responds with some version of "I'm not doing anything," there are no grounds for constructing a self there. Both mastery of the other and self-mastery are evaded by such disclaimers. Neither self can be located in this exchange at all. Although each puts the other in place of the self and so gets out of the other's representation of the self, such evasions are the limits of the characters' attempts at self-representation. There is no self-assertion, and evasions provide no limits to meaning.

Neither self draws the line that distinguishes what the self is independently of the other. In order to realize a difference between the characters, who is doing what to whom, and why, need to be distinguished. If Pamela said that she exposed B in order to protect her virtue, and if B said that he opened her letters in order to protect his name, these claims and defenses would distinguish them and their interests. But instead Pamela implies that she does not expose him or does not mean to expose him; she writes because her heart is broken, and if he is exposed that is only the effect of the truth. And B implies that he opens her letters because those letters hurt him. Both represent their actions as if they were involuntary reactions and emphasize their dependence rather than independence: if the outside world were different, they would be different. They do not, then, determine themselves; what determines what they are and do is a confusion or interaction of internal and external causes and interests. Selves do not stand their ground here and claim no ground to stand on; they shift around, like the changing subjects of the conversation. Neither self nor other is ever put in possession, as each resigns mastery to the other but then evades any determination.

There is thus no security of meaning and no give and take that provide security about the meaning of things; for what is given by one character and what is taken by the other never

agree. More problematic, though, is the fact that Pamela and
B do not even discriminate between the acts of giving and
taking. They thus have no means of determining whether they
stand to win or to lose. Each offer either character makes is
discounted by the other as not enough, and each demand as
too much; and this seems to happen because the characters
do not distinguish an offer from a demand. Each offer made
is perceived by the other *as* a demand, and neither character
admits making any demands that are not offers. B's "offer"
of "freedoms" and "kindness" in the summer-house is interpreted by Pamela as exactly his sexual demand. Her offers to
leave and get out of his way are interpreted by B as really
demands for more money: " 'If the terms I have offered are
not sufficient, I will augment them to two thirds of my estate' "
(232). This follows Pamela's rejections of B's written pro-
posals of money, land, jewels, and clothes: offers she cannot
accept because they demand her body in return. Pamela and
B cannot enter into exchanges because they cannot give without feeling that they are giving up or take without feeling that
they are being taken. The desire on the part of each self to be
admitted by the other is indistinguishable from the fear of
being "taken in" by the other.

    This is to say that there is really no exchange at all between
the characters, or at least none that will settle the differences
between them or enable them to get anywhere. They seem
always to be at a standoff. For the same thing occurs on both
sides of any exchange, rendering any exchange redundant.
That no differences can be determined threatens to mean that
there are no differences; most frighteningly, that the self, because indeterminate, can disappear into the other. That the
other can take over is what B and Pamela recognize in each
other's behavior. There is for each character the sense that
the whole exchange has been initiated or caused by the other
and that the self cannot help it. B claims to have been only a
" 'little kind' " in the summer-house, where he tried to kiss
Pamela; Pamela claims to have told " 'hardly' " anyone about
it. Each implies: I did nothing, but you make something of it.
And so the other is seen to determine meaning. This indicates

the sense of helplessness and dependence with which Pamela repeatedly begs B, as she does in the above passage, not to be angry with her even as she insists that he is the cause of that anger. B, similarly, repeatedly begs Pamela's sexual compliance but always accuses her of enticing him to do it. So it is his fault that he finds fault with her, her fault that she finds fault with him. Such exchanges are short-circuited, for each character implies that both the demand and the response lie with the other. The other has taken over and overdetermines meaning.

But if this ought to mean that there is nothing more to say, it also means that everything is left to say. For if exchange is frustrated or by-passed, it is also generated by the evasion of any common ground. Each character always finds something that the language of the other has implied, or left room for, but left unsaid. " 'You did not open your *mouth* . . . ; but did you not *write?*' "; " 'you could not have asked me this question, if you had not taken from me my letter.' " In these responses, B and Pamela seem to fill in meaning; but they always also make room for more. Meaning is pushed wide open, as each punches holes in or, in Hartman's terms, induces openings in the other's representations. For even while claiming to be helpless, each character makes clear that he or she is able to open up such spaces and so able to get the self out of any position assigned by or any accusation made by the other. The misrepresented self insists on such openings *as* the representation of his or her own misrepresentation. In this sense, then, the realization that the other leaves things out or leaves things open is the realization that the self can be in the other, or represented in the other's language, but not confined or held there. Each identifies the self in the other as an opening, indeterminate and able to be free.

The exchange of evasions, as the evasion of exchange, recurs as a continual reversal of meaning in scene after scene. Although B cannot get hold of Pamela and Pamela cannot hold B to his word, it is by their evasions that they in fact hold each other. For their willingness to take part in such exchanges represents their willingness to let each other go even as they remain committed to each other. Yet because it is only in their misrepresentations of each other that they find room for themselves, their relationship proceeds as an exchange of inadequacies that implies the inadequacy of each self. If we can say of the experience of language in the narrative that to be able to secure no determined meaning is to free meaning of confinement and bondage, the recognition of this freedom in the character's experience of self is more difficult. For the individual experience of indeterminacy seems a much more loaded issue. If we assume that we can live with language that threatens to be meaningless, we do not assume as easily that we can live with the threat that our selves are worthless.

Pamela's early recognition that B is "demeaning" himself when he is free with her persists in the narrative, and she is demeaned as well as he. That their relationship works as a demeaning process, a process of devaluation of both self and other that verges on debasement, is the novel's greatest risk. If we call the novel risqué, we associate its risk with indecency and impropriety and especially emphasize the sexual nature of that impropriety. But if we recognize that the real indecency of this relationship is that it continues at the risk of individual worth, we come closer to the threat it represents.

In a much later passage, after the attempted rape in the bedroom, Pamela goes back to B in the garden to ask his permission to return to her parents. What follows is another inconclusive exchange, but an exchange more threatening, in its confusions, to the value of the self.

> He made me sit on his knee; and still on my struggling against such a freedom, he bid me rely on his honour, solemnly assuring me that I might. But then kissing me very often, though I resisted every time, I told him . . . that I would not stay with him in this place. I would not be so freely used. And I wondered he could so demean himself. (247)
>
> "Who then am I?" "Why," said I, (struggling from him, and in a great passion) "to be sure, you are Lucifer himself in the *shape* of my master, or you could not use

me thus." "These are too great liberties," said he, in
anger. . . .
   I was running from him; and had got at a little distance,
when he in a haughty tone, called out, "Come back!
Pamela, come back when I bid you!" . . .
   What could I do? With unwilling feet, and slow, I went
back . . . and wept, and said, "Pray, sir, forgive me."
"No," said he, "rather say, pray, Lucifer, forgive me.
You have given me a character, Pamela, and blame me
not if I act up to it." (248)
   . . . "But begone," said he, taking my hand, and tossing
it from him, "and learn more wit. I will lay aside my
foolish regard for you, and assert myself." . . .
   . . . "I cannot quit your presence till you pardon me.
On my knees I beg you will"; and I kneeled to him. "I
am truly sorry for my boldness. But I see how you go
on: now you soothe, and now threaten me: and have you
not as good as avowed my ruin? What then is left me
but words? . . . judge for me, and pardon me."
   "Pardon you," said he, "what! when you have the
boldness to justify yourself in your fault?" (248-49)

Here the shifts of feeling in each character and the shifts in
power from one character to the other make any determination of feelings or power impossible. Reacting to each
other's reactions, neither B nor Pamela seems in control of
the self or the other. Again, in this passage, neither seems to
determine what he or she is, but each demands to be determined by the other: " 'Who then am I?' " B asks her; and
" 'What could I do?' " Pamela demands, recognizing no choice
but to do as he tells her. But this giving in to the other does
not last long. For although each insists on his or her own
subordination, each also rejects any meaning given by the
other. Thus, neither character maintains subordination or
mastery. Once one character seems to be subordinated, either
the subordinate or the master switches positions. B grabs Pamela, and she runs away, refusing him control. But she comes
back, and he then rejects *her*, refusing to allow her subordi-

nation. She both denies his mastery and does what he tells her to do; he both insists on her subordination and insists that she makes him do what he does. It is again impossible to distinguish a victim or an aggressor here. The concurrent subjection of the self and rejection of the other dislocate both selves from determination, as if the self were lost in the space between, belonging to and determined by no one and rendered ineffectual.

Yet this passage insists on the indeterminacy of the self as a devaluation of self. Dependent on each other for meaning, Pamela and B effect no exchange in which anything is taken as given; and so the self is rendered unacceptable rather than simply indeterminate. Both Pamela and B are able to make offers to the other. But neither is able to go through with an exchange. Neither will accept what the other gives, for one thing, as if any meaning given by the other is demeaning. When B gives her a kiss, or Pamela gives him a name, these acts seem to take away more than they give. But if neither can accept the other, nor is either character able to be accepted by the other. For if the other's behavior is an act of acceptance of the proffered self, it still seems that the other takes too much: he takes too many freedoms when she sits on his knee, and she takes too great liberties when he asks her to name him.

Whether anyone's behavior here is an act of giving or taking is difficult to tell. For each character interprets any response given by the other as a response that takes something away from the self. Their exchanges of words are as demeaning as the physical rejections by which Pamela runs away from him and B throws her hand away. Instead of giving and taking, they give and take back or, as B does with her hand, take in order to give back. Unlike the incomplete exchanges in the earlier passage, these failed exchanges do not suggest a freedom of meaning from determination. For each character seems to determine that there is no room for the self in the representations of the other. The failure to find any adequate representation threatens to mean that they are inadequate to each other.

This is not because the characters do not ask anything from each other. But the very demands of the other character that something be given by the self seem to demean the self further. When Pamela, at the end of the passage, begs B to pardon her, his response points out that she is really giving him no say. For she is asking for something she has already gotten on her own: " 'what! when you have the boldness to justify yourself in your fault!' " Earlier, when she begs forgiveness, he also insists that she has already identified him as a figure who cannot be forgiving, so she again is just getting what she has already determined on. Pamela, too, perceiving that B has avowed her ruin, implies that he only asks her for what he is determined to get on his own if she does not give it.

Thus each feels excluded and diminished by the other's representation, which seems to leave no room, either because it excludes the self altogether or because it confines the self to a prescribed position. It is as if each recognizes a plot on the part of the other: the other has determined meaning, independently of the self, and the other has taken over the part of the self in any exchange. B puts words in Pamela's mouth: " 'rather say, pray, Lucifer, forgive me.' " Pamela puts words in his: " 'have you not as good as avowed my ruin?' " Assigning parts to the other, each character insists that there is a plot afoot. Both Pamela and B turn the other's words against the other, as in previous exchanges. But each thereby uses the other's words not to make room but to diminish open spaces and take away any choice about meaning. Feeling either thrown aside altogether or totally absorbed, the self feels completely discounted either way.

The other is thus seen as self-sufficient in his or her capacity to fill in meaning independently of the self, even though dependence is expressed by both characters. Pamela's request that B " 'judge for me, and pardon me' " is not a request that leaves him any room to differ from her. If you take my part, she says, you will pardon me; she is not asking him to make a difference but to fit the part as she determines it. So, similarly, when B later that day says to her, " 'Now, Pamela, judge for me' " whether he can marry her or not, she refuses to tell

him what she thinks he should do: for " 'what I can truly say
to your question, may pave the way to my ruin' " (253). Thus
each character refuses to give the words that might fit the self
into the plot of the other. Even to be asked to judge for the
other is perceived as a trap and an imposition rather than an
expression of dependence by the other. To be offered any part
by the other, even to be put in the place of the other (as in
" 'judge for me' "), is suspect here, and suspect because it
seems determined.

Again here, giving the self and taking the other are indistinguishable; any offer may take away from the self, just as
any gift may allow the self to be taken. The standoff here
suggests that Pamela and B perceive their separateness. But
although each resists being taken in by the other's determination, each also insists that she or he is dependent. If the
indistinction of " 'judge for me' " threatens to make the difference between them disappear, then, it is not the indistinction that is resisted. What is resisted is the loss of the freedom
to differ. Determination is resisted, even as the characters insist
that their selves are inseparable.

But their responses to each other are thereby limited to
demeaning responses. To give what the other asks is to fit into
a prescribed space; and so their responses take away rather
than give and thereby risk taking away meaning. Whereas in
the earlier passage each takes away the words of the other,
here each takes away the value of the self. In the former case,
representations are shown to leave room for the self; here,
the self is so reduced and devalued that no representation can
positively hold it. Not only do they see themselves left out,
but their own actions take themselves further away. And they
take away the value of each other, demeaning even what they
themselves want. It is B's good name that Pamela demeans.
Although that name is desirable to her, it is that name that
he refuses to give her; so she takes it away, replacing it with
"Lucifer." It is Pamela's body that B wants, but it is what she
will not give; so he takes hold of it and throws it away. B
does the same in his insistence that Pamela is not in fact
virtuous, demeaning her virtue because it is not offered to

him: " 'I shall not touch her: . . . she is for any fool's turn, that will be caught by her' " (222).

These responses replace exchange with a kind of theft, although no one gets anything by it. Value is taken away from the other but not acquired for the self, which is also, in fact, correspondingly diminished. Pamela takes away B's good name but still kneels to him and begs of him, asserting his inadequacy but also representing herself in postures of submission that proclaim her own inadequecy; as if the real fault is hers because she is not worth marrying. And when B represents Pamela as a cheap slut, he also represents himself as someone who wants but is unwanted by a cheap slut.

No one gains in these exchanges. All value is taken away— except the value of the correspondence. For if nothing is exchanged, because nothing is gained by either character and everything is taken away, all valuation nevertheless remains a matter of correspondence between Pamela and B. The devaluation of the one means also the devaluation of the other. And their devaluations and demeanings function as another form of the indeterminacy that marks their freedom. Selves without value, devalued out of exchange, they remain free of determination. For if one form of freedom is to go beyond the bounds of meaning, another is to fall short of these bounds, to become small enough to slip out of bounds. Both kinds of unfitness exceed the limits of definition and preclude the possession of exchanged meaning. Both insist that the loss of "fit" meaning is a loss without compensation, but therefore also a loss beyond the scope of determination: a loss free to be gain.

The exchange that *is* effected in this passage is the exchange of freedoms. This is not a fitting exchange, and there is no representation given that fits or fixes the meaning of what is represented. Indecent and improper, and always demeaning insofar as they defy any determination of meaning, those freedoms are what Pamela and B get from each other throughout the narrative. It is the exchange of freedoms that moves their relationship out of the realm of definitive exchange and renders it indeterminate. Give and take, gain and loss, self and other all become indistinct and reversible, impossible to secure

or determine, as all meanings, even of the self, become subject
to the conflict of interpretations that is the guarantee of freedom. Once made free with, those things that are invaluable
are also without value. His name and her body are the possessions that the other takes liberties with. But once liberated,
that name and that body cannot be had. They cannot be taken
away, and they cannot be held onto in any way that excludes
the other from taking part in them. Once the freedoms are
admitted, the self is free to admit the other.

That the loss of secure value is indistinguishable from the
gain that exceeds valuation is given in Pamela's admission of
love:

> I must own to you, that I shall never be able to think of
> any body in the world but him! Presumption! you will
> say; and so it is: but love, I imagine, is not a voluntary
> thing—*Love*, did I say! But, come, I hope not: at least it
> is not, I hope, gone so far, as to make me *very* uneasy:
> for I know not *how* it came, nor *when* it began; but it
> has crept, crept, like a thief, upon me; and before I knew
> what was the matter, it looked *like* love. (283)

Here is what we may read as Pamela's acknowledgment that
she belongs to B. But that is not the way she puts it. The gift
of herself is given here as a presumption: she has taken upon
herself what she has no warrant to take. But if she presumes
herself, she does so because love has presumed with her. Love
has "crept like a thief" upon her, to take over, without warrant, her own volition. Thus Pamela does not represent herself
as losing by the theft; she in fact repeats it with her own
presumption. Unauthorized and improper, her feelings come
to her without determination or choice and commit her to
take what she has no justification for taking, even as she herself
has been taken, by illegitimate means. This is not an exchange
so much as a reflexive reaction, one such as characterizes the
exchanges between Pamela and B throughout the novel.

Volunteering her love, Pamela volunteers here only an involuntary admission. Love has entered her mind; she did not
let it in, but she nevertheless admits it. She admits love, then,

because it has taken liberties with her. But she also admits love because her love has let her go: she is on her way home to her parents. Having been freed from the threat that B will take away "that jewel, your virtue, which no riches, nor favour, nor any thing in this life, can make up to you" (46), Pamela is free to see in herself the theft she had thought would come from the outside. She takes his part here and, taking him in, admits him without loss but with presumption. If love has taken liberties, then, it has also freed her to take liberties. The "liberty" of love seems to mean that Pamela cannot tell the difference between herself and B and that she cannot tell the difference between her losses and her gains.

The theft here entails the loss of volition and the loss of security. Involuntary, inexplicable, without cause and unpredictable, love is recognized by Pamela in terms that preclude definition and determination. Identified with loss of determination, loss of consequence, and loss of possessions—only "owned," that is, as a loss of self-possession—love is the resolution of Pamela's experience precisely because it is represented in terms of irresolution. She did not mean this, and she is not sure what this means: it only "looked *like* love." Both claiming and disclaiming love, Pamela represents love itself as something that cannot be adequately represented. This is not "true love," unless truth itself is always uncertain and only approximately subject to definition and possession by representation. She is not "*very* uneasy" then, because meaning itself is so uneasy that it cannot be determined. Free to exceed determination, love stands for her own freedom to be more than can ever be owned. Love corresponds to Pamela as Pamela corresponds to B.

The "history" of love given us in this novel, like the story given us in the above passage, is unplotted in its course and uneasy in its effects. It settles nothing as it leaves meaning indeterminate. The recognition of love does not clearly make much difference to Pamela; it only makes it impossible to tell the differences that would separate her from B. Pamela remains suspicious, perhaps more suspicious than before, even as she goes back to him again. Yet she goes back precisely because she cannot tell the difference, finally, even between her imprisonment and her freedom: "I have made an escape from my prison, only to be more a prisoner" (284). Thus the narrative, in the "form" of the correspondence, redundancy, and indecisiveness of differences, has given us the relation that will bind Pamela and B to each other. It is Pamela's representation, and the art of her representation, that insists that differences cannot be told with any finality and that the very impossibility of telling them opens up the possibility of being both committed and free.

CHAPTER THREE

RICHARDSON'S *CLARISSA*:
AUTHORITY IN EXCESS

Like *Pamela*, Richardson's *Clarissa* exceeds the bounds of economical narrative. Its very length is a sign of this excess, as is the multiplicity of narrators whose letters make up the text. Authorizing excess, Richardson and his heroines never reduce meaning to terms according to which differences can be either clearly opposed or clearly equated. Such a vision of meaning is represented and realized in *Pamela*, in the interdependence of characters whose differences neither distinguish them from each other nor enable them to rule each other out of significance. In *Pamela* we find two characters doing essentially the same thing to one another in a reflective relationship that renders their opposition itself a redundant relationship. *Clarissa*, however, is more complex in its representations of the relations of different characters.

The conflict of the central characters in the later novel seems easier to resolve, in a sense. The fact that Clarissa and Lovelace never "get together" signals some more fundamental difference between them than is possible to identify between Pamela and B. But if Clarissa and Lovelace cannot come together, neither can they easily be separated in terms of the oppositions usually employed to represent their differences: the opposition of male and female, for example, or the opposition of aristocracy and bourgeoisie. This narrative, too, resists the reduction of meaning to the terms of any exclusive opposition, even as Lovelace repeatedly imposes those terms in his insistence that opposition is functioning. The most crucial difference between Lovelace and Clarissa is that only he finds any meaning in such terms. For whereas Lovelace perceives experience as a struggle to master meaning and disable his opposition, Clarissa's vision of meaning disables opposition itself. This means that, although Lovelace and Clarissa are like B and Pamela in that they never really come to terms with each other, only Clarissa is willing to recognize such an indeterminate relationship as meaningful. The difficulty of coming to terms with the novel itself is thus the difficulty of considering characters who, though related to each other, are not commensurable in any way.

If we read the novel, as most critics do, as a struggle for power between two opponents intent on mastering each other, we are able to see the differences of the characters in common terms. They are opposed, but they are opposed because they are fighting for the same end. Thus Leo Braudy identifies the opposition of "Penetration and Impenetrability" as the crucial opposition of the novel because these "poles" represent the terms in which Clarissa and Lovelace define themselves, as they attempt "to penetrate, control, and even destroy others, while they remain impenetrable themselves."[1] William Beatty Warner depicts the opposition in different terms: as a "play of rival significations," a series of confrontations in which "power . . . consists in being the active encoder of significations, the controller of language, and the director of the unfolding scene."[2] Terry Eagleton describes the novel as a "great warring of discourses."[3]

Thus warfare is given as the structure of the relationship of Clarissa and Lovelace; each character thereby means to control or defeat the other. But their opposition is confirmed by critics in other terms too, terms which clarify why the one can win only at the cost of the other. For critics insist that Clarissa and Lovelace find meaning in such radically different

---

[1] Leo Braudy, "Penetration and Impenetrability in *Clarissa*," in *New Approaches to Eighteenth-Century Literature: Selected Papers from the English Institute*, ed. Philip Harth (New York: Columbia University Press, 1974), p. 186.

[2] William Beatty Warner, *Reading "Clarissa": Struggles of Interpretation* (New Haven: Yale University Press, 1979), p. 60.

[3] Terry Eagleton, *The Rape of Clarissa: Writing, Sexuality and Class Struggle in Samuel Richardson* (Minneapolis: University of Minnesota Press, 1982), p. 79.

terms that the meaning of one rules out the meaning of the other. Braudy opposes Clarissa's "essential" concept of self, for example, to Lovelace's seventeenth-century character of surfaces, "character constructed by rhetoric and viewed from without."[4] Warner contrasts "the stability and identity of the 'self' Clarissa creates," which "is grounded on her inner nature," with Lovelace as "a function of the manifold of struggle and the interplay between self and other."[5] And Cynthia Griffin Wolff identifies Clarissa with "an order which Richardson would identify with moral righteousness" and Lovelace with "the violent rejection of any form of order."[6] According to the terms of these distinctions, Clarissa's concept of meaning is stable, orderly, and grounded in nature, while Lovelace's is unstable and groundless. Her meaning is true, and his duplicitous. Thus Clarissa can be said to be a "naive exegete" who is "made to confront the interruption of that 'natural' relation she assumes between text and meaning, the sign and reality. A gap is opened up in her vision of the world: sign and 'Nature' split apart."[7] And Lovelace, on the other hand, can be considered a powerful and sophisticated exegete who, in his constant displacements of meaning, "helps to undo the matrix of truth and value through which Clarissa would have us see, know, and judge."[8]

It is such distinctions between the two characters that my reading will attempt to "undo," though I do not mean to emphasize similarities in Clarissa and Lovelace. Richardson's narrative, insistent itself on the indeterminate nature of meaning, never equates the two characters. Yet it does insist that Clarissa and Lovelace "correspond" to a great extent: the extent to which they commit themselves to the indeterminacy of meaning. What they thereby have in common is just their

[4] Braudy, "Penetration and Impenetrability," p. 179.

[5] Warner, Reading "Clarissa," pp. 21, 39.

[6] Cynthia Griffin Wolff, Samuel Richardson and the Eighteenth-Century Puritan Character (Hamden, Conn.: Archon Books, 1972), pp. 117, 102.

[7] Terry Castle, Clarissa's Cyphers: Meaning and Disruption in Richardson's "Clarissa" (Ithaca: Cornell University Press, 1982), pp. 58-59.

[8] Warner, Reading "Clarissa," p. 30.

resistance to the reduction or definition of meaning, and thus what they have in common does not provide any grounds or common terms for their relationship. But that both Clarissa and Lovelace share the capacity to recognize meaning as indeterminate is crucial to the engagement of each with the other, just as Clarissa's capacity to be "true" to such indeterminacy constitutes the crucial difference between her and Lovelace. It is my contention that Clarissa finds meaning precisely in the gaps of representation as she insists that truth is neither knowable nor representable in just terms. It is Lovelace who is interested in such determinations. Though he opens up meaning, as in his displacements and misrepresentations, he is also driven to fill in any open space, even the space in Clarissa's body. It is crucial to Clarissa's heroism that she, like Pamela, is committed to indeterminacy.[9] And it is crucial

[9] It may seem here that I find continuity in the two novels exactly in the context in which most critics find the greatest difference. Clarissa always seems less morally dubious than Pamela because she stands by her principles whereas Pamela marries the man who threatens hers. *Clarissa* is considered a superior work in both moral and formal terms by critics who emphasize the more realistic complexity of its multiple points of view, as Ian Watt does, and of its "probing" characterizations, as does Mark Kinkead-Weekes. (See Watt's *The Rise of the Novel: Studies in Defoe, Richardson and Fielding* [Harmondsworth, Mx.: Penguin, 1970], pp. 216-20; and Kinkead-Weekes's *Samuel Richardson: Dramatic Novelist* [Ithaca: Cornell University Press, 1973], pp. 123-276.) The greater power of the later novel is thus identified in the greater difficulty it presents. As Watt says, "Even the most apparently implausible, didactic, or period aspects of the plot and the characters . . . are brought into a larger dramatic pattern of infinite formal and psychological complexity. It is this capacity for a continuous enrichment and complication of a simple situation which makes Richardson the great novelist he is; and it shows, too, that the novel had at last attained literary maturity, with formal resources capable not only of supporting the tremendous imaginative expansion which Richardson gave his theme, but also leading him away from the flat didacticism of his critical preconceptions into so profound a penetration of his characters that their experience partakes of the terrifying ambiguity of human life itself" (248). Thus though Watt emphasizes the unity of form and substance in *Clarissa*, they are united in their ambiguity. It is Richardson's effort to be true to the ambiguity of experience that I believe characterizes both *Pamela* and *Clarissa*, and in this context my emphasis on heroic indeterminacy is not so far removed from recognitions of other critics.

to Lovelace's betrayal of meaning that he is committed to his own ends, though he can only achieve those ends by first undoing values that he identifies as contributing to others' ends.

If we read the novel as a struggle for power, it is necessary to make some such distinctions as the above critics make, for opponents must be opposed. But the fact that Lovelace and Clarissa cannot be so clearly distinguished is linked to the fact that power itself is not at issue in the novel in the sense that most critics find it at issue. Lovelace and Clarissa are not in opposition to each other, that is, because they are not struggling for the same end. There are two concepts of power in *Clarissa*. If Richardson, on the one hand, is aware of the power of language to assert control, he is also aware of the power of language to exceed control; and it is the latter power that the narrative authorizes. For the power of the narrative itself is a power that makes distinctions difficult. The multiple vision of the text, in which it is impossible to identify a single controlling voice, insists on the power of differing representations to extend meaning beyond the control of authority. Thus power is at issue in the novel not because Lovelace and Clarissa are both struggling to gain it, but because only one character regards it as a possession from which others must be excluded. Lovelace's sense of power depends on order and control in order to impose limits on meaning. But Clarissa neither submits to nor exercises control and instead empowers meaning to move out of control in order to extend meaningful

---

On the other hand, I may be considered far removed indeed in my insistence that Clarissa does not stand her ground and that, in fact, she claims no grounds to stand on. William Beatty Warner gives a brief discussion of Richardson's " 'loyal' " and " 'subversive' " critics in *Reading "Clarissa"* (pp. 270-71), distinguishing those who read the novels in terms of Richardson's stated intentions and those who insist that the power of his work lies in his unintentional representation of "cultural myths and psychological drives which he was unwilling and unable to apprehend." My own reading of Richardson may thus be considered "subversive," since my emphasis is not on his intended achievements. Yet because intentionality is not sufficient to determine meaning for the characters he creates, it seems to me reasonable to consider it insufficient grounds for Richardson's own meaning.

experience to include more than can be controlled or determined. Whereas Lovelace is intent on opposition and distinction in order to gain control, Clarissa is intent on exceeding
those terms altogether.

One indication of this is that, whereas Lovelace is always
plotting experience and so always has an end in view, Clarissa
neither plots experience nor recognizes ends in life. The narrative itself undermines all plots and acknowledges only one
end, and that is death. Once she loses, by rape, the indeterminacy of her own meaning, Clarissa loses her commitment
to life. But she remains always committed to meaning that
cannot be settled by oppositions or plots. Whereas Lovelace
is committed to the division of experience into means and
ends, insignificance and significance, Clarissa is committed to
the indeterminacy of such distinctions: she recognizes all elements of experience as meaningful or, after the rape, she recognizes no elements of experience as meaningful. Meaning,
for Clarissa, is either absolutely in suspense or absolutely over.

Like *Pamela*, then, *Clarissa* is a narrative in which Richardson struggles for a representation of meaning that refuses
to effect "realistic" reductions. Realistically, recent critics
have insisted that Clarissa is defeated because she cannot escape the controlling powers of her society. Terry Castle maintains that Clarissa loses because she does not have the advantages of a man: "The battles of interpretation, in the text,
in the world, are seldom fair fights."[10] And Terry Eagleton
insists that any behavior on Clarissa's part that attempts to
escape victimization is ultimately complicitous with her
victimization:

> What Clarissa will discover in particular is the most de-
> moralizing double bind of all: the truth that it is not so
> easy to distinguish resistance to power from collusion
> with it. . . . Power reproduces itself by engendering in its
> victims a collusion which is the very condition of their
> survival.[11]

[10] Castle, *Clarissa's Cyphers*, p. 193.
[11] Eagleton, *The Rape of Clarissa*, p. 82.

Yet, like Pamela, Clarissa never really comes to terms with the reality of hierarchy and control, just as she never comes to terms with the capacity of plots to control meaning. She does not want a fight, even a fair fight. Moreover, Clarissa wishes to be complicitous with others. She does not want to collaborate in others' control of her, but she wants to collaborate with others in mutual correspondences of meaning that preclude control altogether.

If this is unrealistic, it is nevertheless crucial to Richardson's relentless refusal to conform his narrative to the forms of power and control that Lovelace imposes on experience. Lovelace represents both the most powerful threat to Richardson's concept of meaning and the self-negation that Richardson associates with any effort to impose conventional forms of distinction and determination on meaning. It is Lovelace who represents experience in terms of determination, plots, and double binds; and Lovelace's experience insists that attempts to control reality are condemned themselves to be doubly bound. Lovelace's commitment to determination and possession coexists with his recognition that reality always exceeds determination and possession. He is bound to keep trying, therefore, and bound to be frustrated. In Clarissa, however, we are offered an alternative to Lovelace. She is not an alternative that defeats him, because her difference lies precisely in her refusal to find meaning in exclusive or determinant terms. Clarissa represents an alternative because she represents Richardson's recognition that to oppose determination by counterdetermination or to oppose plot with counterplot is to work for a victory as empty of meaning as Lovelace's victory. Clarissa never reduces herself to those terms.

I will be focusing, during this chapter, on the first half of the narrative of Clarissa, in order to consider the indeterminate "midst" of experience in which Clarissa finds meaning and in order to consider how her representations maintain the suspension of meaning that others would determine and settle. Those characters who attempt to control Clarissa, restricting her movements and restricting her speech by "shutting her up" in two senses, are confronted with a power in her which does not function as an exercise of power over others. She is initially besieged by two antagonists, both of whom attempt to control her. Her father demands absolute obedience: "No *buts*, girl! No qualifyings! I will be obeyed" (I.37).[12] And Lovelace demands unqualified possession; he "will secure her mine in spite of them all; in spite of her own inflexible heart: mine, without condition" (I.148). Both men require unconditional surrender and exclusive possession, at the cost of Clarissa, who is ruled out by their attempts to rule her. She is to have nothing to say or, in the language of conflict, no room to maneuver. Yet Clarissa always has something to say, and the difficulty with considering the novel as a struggle for power is that what she has to say is precisely *not* inflexible in its opposition to others. She never clearly assumes the role of opposition, for, in her disagreements with others, she refuses to take a firm stand. She qualifies and conditions with those whom she ought, if she were engaged in opposition, to refute.

The attempts to restrict Clarissa's movements on the part of those who want to control her suggest that it is her rhetorical and physical mobility that is most threatening to their power. She seems, indeed, to be able to get out of anything; evasion is her most effective "tactic" against control. Yet her evasive mobility has more than defensive or negative effects. For not only does Clarissa evade the opposition; she threatens to move the opposition, too. Her mother commands her to "restrain . . . your powers of moving!" (I.70); and Lovelace himself is repeatedly "diverted from all my favourite purposes" (II.182) by Clarissa's ability to move people out of the positions they take in order to control experience. Her power of movement is a power of both motion and emotion, and this suggests that if meaning resists control, it nevertheless is bound to other meanings. Clarissa moves in response to others, and she moves others to change in response to her.

[12] Samuel Richardson, *Clarissa*, intro. John Butt (London: Dent, 1972). All references are to this edition; volume and page numbers are cited in the text.

Thus, if she is able to qualify any opposition to include more meaning than opposition can rule or rule out, she also extends relations with others to include the indeterminate realm of feelings. She demands that all differences be relative rather than distinct, and she demands relations with others that preclude definition and distinction. Meaning becomes sympathetic, and as it becomes sympathetic it exceeds any grounding, it exceeds any terms of representation, and it exceeds the distinction of differences.

If we read *Clarissa* in terms of opposition, then, we read it in Lovelace's and the Harlowes' terms, terms which the narrative and its heroine both evade and exceed, in exchanges which render meaning much more difficult to locate. The exchanges of letters by corresponding individuals, for example, diffuse rather than define meaning and include more differences than they either settle or distinguish. The evasion of conventional exchange is crucial to *Clarissa*, and the later novel entails a more searching criticism of conventional assumptions about exchange than does *Pamela*. *Clarissa* focuses this consideration on the marital exchange and the experience of a heroine who is unable to enter into such an exchange. There is no "match" for Clarissa; nor does the narrative suggest that one is possible. The assumption of the Harlowes and Lovelace that exchanges occur *as* matches, or that equivalent values are given and taken in any exchange, is an assumption that Clarissa defies and disables. The Harlowes identify Solmes as a fit match for Clarissa, and Lovelace identifies her as his own match:

> Tell me not of politeness; tell me not of generosity; tell me not of compassion—is she not a match for me? *More than a match?* Does she not outdo me at every fair weapon? (II.34)

The difficulty is that Clarissa is always "more" than his match, as she is more than a match for Solmes. But this is not because she meets or outdoes Lovelace on his own terms. It is because, for Clarissa, differences are not reducible to the common terms necessary to any even exchange.

Thus Clarissa's exchanges with others tend to proceed as evasions of exchange; and such evasions are far more complex in their implications about human relations than are Lovelace's evasions of others' power. In order to clarify the capacity of Clarissa's language both to undermine and preclude conventional exchange, and how that capacity both resembles and exceeds Lovelace's own, I want to focus for a moment on the very beginning of the narrative. We are immediately presented with two evasions: one is Lovelace's evasion of Arabella, and one is Clarissa's evasion of Anna Howe. Both "escapes" are effected by interpretation, or misinterpretation, of another's words. The narrative thus immediately focuses on the indeterminacy of language and the difficulty of completing exchanges by means of language. Not only is meaning difficult to determine because what is meant by one character differs from the meaning taken by another, but more goes on in any exchange than the words indicate, as the meaning of words gets turned around.

Arabella has said no to Lovelace's proposal of marriage, but she did not mean it. And Clarissa assumes that Lovelace knows that she did not mean it and so assumes that he, because he has taken Arabella at her word, did not really mean to propose. Arabella's response, Clarissa writes, was

> A good encouraging denial, I must own—as was the rest of her plea, to wit: "A disinclination to change her state. Exceedingly happy as she was; she never could be happier!" And such-like *consenting negatives*, as I may call them. . . . And thus, as Mr. Lovelace thought fit to *take it*, had he his answer from my sister. (I.8)

Arabella's words do not in fact seem ambiguous; but the convention is that her no's mean maybe. Therefore, it is Lovelace whose sincerity is at issue here because he did not respond to the insincerity of the "consenting negative."

By placing his characers in this context—the context of conventions that assume that people do not mean what they say—Richardson not only makes it difficult to distinguish sincerity from insincerity but also insists that language will not necessarily provide that distinction. But if we look to Clarissa to rectify this by establishing firmer grounds for meaning or by behaving differently from Arabella and Lovelace, we do not find a clear difference between them. For if Lovelace can be faulted for taking advantage of Arabella by turning her words against her, Clarissa opens her narrative with an even shiftier evasion of Anna Howe. Like Lovelace, she frees herself from a threatened oppression by misinterpreting:

> How you oppress me, my dearest friend, with your po-
> liteness! I cannot doubt your sincerity; but you should
> take care that you give me not reason from your kind
> partiality to call in question your judgment. You do not
> distinguish that I take many admirable hints from you,
> and have the art to pass them upon you for my own. . . .
> So pray, my dear, be more sparing of your praise for the
> future, lest after this confession we should suspect that
> you secretly intend to praise yourself, while you would
> be thought only to commend another. (I.3)

If this is on the one hand a contorted effort to prevent Anna from praising her, it is also a sweet expression of Clarissa's own love for Anna. And it is certainly innocent and harmless, even as Lovelace's own initial manipulation of meaning is one with which we can sympathize. Yet Clarissa *is* oppressed by praise, and the means by which she here avoids taking something she does not want are characteristic of her behavior. She turns the implications of Anna's praise inside out, reading into Anna's words a meaning so at odds with their literal meaning as to turn subject into object and the act of giving praise into the act of taking credit. Not only does Clarissa interpret Anna's words to mean something quite different from what they were intended to mean, she also re-enforces the uncertainty of meaning by insisting that it is impossible to choose between the two interpretations. Like Lovelace's interpretation of Arabella's no, moreover, Clarissa's interpretation of Anna's praise prevents the exchange intended by the other.

To see these episodes as analogous is not to suggest that

there is no difference between them or that there is no difference between Lovelace and Clarissa. But it does suggest that not only Lovelace, but Clarissa and Richardson, too, render meaning indistinct rather than distinct in exchanges that are indecisive and inconclusive. As Clarissa's first letter suggests, she is always aware that words, no matter how decisive they may seem, leave room for differing meanings. The words exchanged, therefore, do not literally represent or determine the exchange. Rather, words represent, in their ambiguity, the very impossibility of locating what is being given and taken in exchanges that do not define or control meaning.

And the fact that exchanges are indefinite and words are indefinite is not frustrating so much as necessary to Clarissa. For Clarissa, meaning depends on what lies beyond any given exchange; it is qualified and amplified by surrounding conditions and contexts as it is by others' interpretations. This suggests that Clarissa remains in the midst of meaning, which is suspended between the poles of opposition that distinguish, for example, yes and no. "Consenting negatives" do not commit the speaker to decision. Their meaning depends on how they are taken, and if they are taken with sympathy, they are read ambiguously. Clarissa herself, when Lovelace proposes to *her*, is unable to say yes or no but is dependent on him to understand that her inability to declare herself is also a sign of favor:

> The man saw I was not angry at his motion. . . . Would he have had me catch at his first, at his *very* first word? I was *silent* too—and do not the bold sex take silence for a mark of favour? (II.28)

Silence is another kind of open space that Clarissa is willing to employ in order to leave room for interpretation. Her silence here is intended to suspend her relation to Lovelace; it represents her genuine confusion and uncertainty, and she expects Lovelace to understand this. Such evasions of distinct meaning characterize both her speech and her writing as she tries to leave room for meaning to exceed definitive representation.

Lovelace does something quite different when he interprets
or creates meaning. Although he, like Clarissa, recognizes and
takes advantage of the variability and insecurity of meaning,
Lovelace interprets indeterminate meaning as always subject
to final and exclusive determination. To him, Arabella's "consenting negatives" mean that he has a choice of yes or no;
they do not mean maybe. And to him Clarissa's silence in the
above passage means not indeterminacy but one of two things:

> Charming creature! thought I . . . , is it so *soon* come to
> this? Am I *already* lord of the destiny of a Clarissa Har-
> lowe? Am I already the reformed man thou resolvedst I
> *should* be, before I had the *least* encouragment given me?
> . . . (II.33)
>   Then what a triumph would it be to the *Harlowe pride*
> were I now to marry this lady! (II.34)

What Clarissa regards as the spacious capacity of indeterminate meaning to exceed determination and control, Lovelace regards as a duality or opposition of conflicting meanings,
one of which will negate and exclude the other in the end.
Thus Clarissa's silence signifies either that he has already won
or that he has already been triumphed over. What keeps Lovelace in suspense here is that he cannot tell the difference between winning and losing; but that distinction is the only
difference he values.

This indicates another crucial difference between them.
Lovelace's interpretations of indeterminate meaning are also
a means of separating himself from others. He separates himself from Arabella by denying her ambiguity, and he separates
himself from Clarissa by denying her silence any genuine indeterminacy. But Clarissa's interpretations preclude such separations. If Clarissa also rejects Anna in the passage quoted
earlier, her evasions are clearly not evasions of Anna herself.
In fact, Clarissa's evasions of praise bind her more closely to
Anna than an acceptance of praise could. For Clarissa identifies herself with Anna, making the two indistinct, whereas
Anna's praise would make a distinction between them. What
Clarissa seems to evade here is her own distinction. It is be-

cause Clarissa's representations bind her to others by means
of indistinctions and indefinite sympathies that she, like Pamela, may threaten others' self-sufficiency.

Clarissa's attempts to exceed the limits of independent and
self-sufficient meaning are also attempts to exceed the limits
that independence and self-sufficiency impose on the self. Repeatedly, Clarissa refuses to distinguish herself from others
and works instead to reconcile self and other by representations that do not settle but leave room for differences. She
thus represents herself as neither distinct nor determined, indecisive in ways we identify with immaturity, confused about
the limits of selfhood in ways we identify with narcissism. Yet
this is her heroism, in a narrative that also insists on the
capacity of human beings to be corresponding rather than
distinct in their meaning.

   With her family, Clarissa attempts to prevent the separation
which their behavior demands and which Anna Howe also
advises. "Your merit is your crime," Anna writes, insisting
that Clarissa acknowledge the irreconcilable difference between her own and her family's values. "You can no more
change *your* nature than your persecutors can *theirs*. Your
distress is owing to the vast disparity between you and them"
(I.282). The relation of Clarissa to her family becomes explicitly a rhetorical concern after Clarissa has left the house.
Anna sees the separation as final because there is no way to
represent Clarissa's behavior in terms acceptable to the
Harlowes:

   And how, my dear, can one report it with any toler-
   able advantage to you? To say you *did not intend it* when
   you met him, who will believe it? To say that a person of your known steadiness and punctilio was *over-per-
   suaded* when you gave him the meeting, how will that
   sound? . . .

I want to see how you put it in your letter for your
clothes. (II.7)

Anna is sure that there can be no advantageous representation
of Clarissa going off with Lovelace and that the family will
reject any grounds on which Clarissa can justify her behavior.
Yet for Clarissa the reconciliation of herself with her family
is both possible and necessary; it is their separation that is
unacceptable to her.

Clarissa's letter for her clothes suggests how she tries to get
around the difficulty: not exactly by representing her behavior
advantageously or acceptably or justifiably but instead by insisting on the very difficulty of representing it at all.

> My dear sister,—I have, I confess, been guilty of an action
> which carried with it a rash and undutiful appearance.
> And I should have thought it an inexcusable one had I
> been used with less severity than I have been of late; and
> had I not had too great reason to apprehend that I was
> to be made a sacrifice to a man I could not bear to think
> of. But what is done is done—perhaps I could wish it had
> not; and that I had trusted to the relenting of my dear
> and honoured parents. Yet this from no other motives
> but those of duty to them. To whom I am ready to return
> (if I may not be permitted to retire to The Grove) on
> conditions which I before offered to comply with. (II.12)

Here Clarissa invokes the indeterminacy of meaning and the
difficulty of interpretation. It is not what is true but what
might be true that she represents: the appearance and reality
of her actions may differ and, most emphatically, all her actions are conditional. Thus her letter evades the issue of cred-
ibility or acceptability, not insisting that Arabella believe her
version but instead refusing to have a version that is unconditional. Each claim she makes is qualified so that in fact she
makes no claims; there seem to be no grounds at all for her
representation. Rather than assert that because one thing is
true the next is true, Clarissa insists that each possibility is

subject to qualification. Her use of conditional and qualifying terms multiplies rather than limits her meaning.

Clarissa's evasions are thus also reconciliations as she represents differences in ways that leave room for differences. She offers here to leave room for others' interpretations as well as demands that others leave room for her to differ: to differ from them and even to differ, over time, from herself. Clarissa represents reality, then, with words that identify reality as multiple and irreducible rather than claiming truth or reducing reality to a single version. She does not come to terms with such differences by identifying what they have in common; she instead leaves room for them all.

This is to say that, in Clarissa's relations with others, exchange does not occur as we usually understand it. For Clarissa does not give anything up in order to get something else. She is willing to give things up: to give up marriage altogether, to give up her property, to give up her life, to give up her self: "How willingly would I run away from myself, and what most concerns myself, if I could!" (I.282). But such offers are not part of any exchange; they are offers that are not linked to any return and offers that would evade exchanges demanded by others. She refuses to take anything from others, similarly, if such taking requires giving something up on her part. The multiple offers of marriage that she refuses, for example, and her family's offers of clothing and jewels if she will agree to marry Solmes require that she lose something in order to win something. Anna's offers of money and servants and Lovelace's offers of money require that she place herself in debt. Rather than enter into such exchanges, Clarissa usually prefers to have things both ways, in the sense that she neither lays claim to anything herself nor gives up anything. Rather than get one thing by giving up another, she prefers to ignore the categories of possession altogether and leave possession undetermined. Thus she refuses to choose between her family and Lovelace and refuses to accept that one excludes the other. She chooses to remain in between them. No longer theirs and not yet his, and making no claims herself,

Clarissa puts relations into a context different from exclusive possession.

Words and letters seem to be the only satisfactory objects to exchange for Clarissa precisely because they cannot be possessed by any individual exclusively. Words can always be taken as something else, and their exchange therefore does not entail definitive gain and loss. No bargain can be concluded if no common value can be decided; nothing can be gained or lost conclusively. Language, subject to differing interpretations, provides a means of exchange that does not allow exclusive possession of values. This is why Clarissa's family refuses to see her or read her letters to them. They want something definite and they want to have their own way; and Clarissa's way with words threatens to disable both definition and possession.[13]

Even in her "opposition" to marrying Solmes, Clarissa wants nothing definite. Her substitutions, as she tries to qualify the exchange her family has arranged, are all offers to give up something. She posits nothing and takes no position:

I then offered to live single; never to marry at all; or never but with their full approbation.

If you mean to show your duty and your obedience, Clary, you must show it in *our* way; not in *your own*. (I.78)

What the family can think of only in terms of exclusive distinctions—our way or your way—Clarissa tries not to distin-

[13] John Allen Stevenson has suggested that Clarissa and her family attempt to evade conventional structures of exchange, in that both attempt to have things two ways at once. He identifies the family's insistence on Solmes as an attempt to escape the social imperative of reciprocal exchange and to satisfy instead incestuous desires. By fostering a marriage that would keep Clarissa and her property, in addition to incorporating Solmes and his, they would give up nothing. Stevenson identifies both the Harlowes and Clarissa at impasses. See "The Courtship of the Family: Clarissa and the Harlowes Once More," *ELH*, 48, no. 4 (1981), 757-77. But whereas the Harlowes' actions are essentially conservative, as Stevenson argues, Clarissa's evasions of exchange are not. She refuses to choose not in order to hold on to what she has and get more but in order to avoid exclusive possession altogether.

guish at all. Where the family identifies an opposition, Clarissa identifies ways of circumventing opposition and diverting each side from a way of its own. She offers multiple alternatives as "her" way and thus has no single way. And she thereby suspends the sense of differences, rendering indeterminate the opposition identified by others.

The kinds of exchanges in which Clarissa takes part are usually identifiable, therefore, as evasions or denials of exchange: inconclusive and incomplete, with no clear end in view. Her evasion of marriage occurs in these terms. Because Clarissa is never finally committed to any man, her relations to men seem always in suspense. As she writes about Solmes,

> How much easier to bear the *temporary* persecutions I labour under, *because* temporary, than to resolve to be *such* a man's for *life*? Were I to comply, must I not leave my relations, and go to him? A *month* will decide the one, perhaps; but what a *duration of woe* will the other be! (I.287)

Here she represents her refusal of Solmes as a preference for the temporary over the decisive situation. For Clarissa, anything temporary is preferable to anything determinant, for the temporary is always inclusive of different possibilities. She attempts repeatedly to render any situation in which she finds herself a temporary situation, never conclusive or exclusive or lasting in its meaning.

Such suspension of meaning is also achieved by her refusal to determine her own ends. With no definite object or objective, Clarissa refuses to differentiate means from ends and refuses to limit the meaning of things to terms that make such a distinction possible. She wants to obey her parents, for example. But she cannot assign to that act a greater significance than she assigns to marrying Solmes; nor can she equate them in order to identify a fair exchange. Because Clarissa perceives differences in different rather than comparable terms, she is unable to do one thing for the sake of another. Objects tend to carry much more meaning for her than for others and tend to be seen therefore as incomparable. As in her perception of what it would mean to agree to marry Solmes, what others see as an act of obedience assumes incomparable dimensions for Clarissa. This is another exchange she cannot make, for she cannot give priority to one act over another or equate them. Instead, she extends the meaning of any single act beyond the limits that are accepted by others and that are necessary to a fair exchange, which must define some arbitrary limits in order to make values comparable.

But because she does not limit the meaning of any act, the meanings of actions also overlap, and therefore it is difficult to identify Clarissa as doing anything for its own sake either. Because meaning is always dependent, pending in time and space, no meaning is sufficient in itself or limited to its own terms. Clarissa begins her correspondence with Lovelace, for example, not in order to write to Lovelace but in order to prevent trouble between him and her brother. She chooses Lovelace over Solmes not so much because of any positive value she attaches to Lovelace as because she cannot bear Solmes. Thus, any act has multiple causes and multiple effects, and each separate act is entangled in others without being distinguished in terms of cause and effect or means and ends. One act does not take priority over another, and one act does not cancel out another or render it insignificant. And this makes it difficult to identify any plot in Clarissa's experience, on her part or on our part. For we cannot identify any choice on her part; she evades choice by evading the definition of objects or actions, refusing to distinguish them from their implications and extensions and thus diverting action *from* objects or objectives.

Such extensions and suspensions of meaning also characterize Clarissa's sense of self. Anna's advice is to "make yourself independent" (I.255); this would mean taking possession of her own property, living alone in her own house, and locking out those who mistreat her (I.125). But Clarissa does not separate herself from others. As her first paragraph suggests about herself and Anna, the distinction of self and other and what belongs to each is one she precludes: "You do not distinguish that I take many admirable hints from you, and have the art to pass them upon you for my own" (I.3). What she wants distinguished here is the inseparability of herself and Anna.

This confusion of self and other leaves her in situations in which "your merit is your crime": the difference between her self and her family should be distinct but instead is indistinct. Subject to confusion rather than distinctions, the boundaries of self remain undecided. Part of what Clarissa is, such as the characteristics praised by Anna, may belong to others as much as to her. Part of what others have, such as her father's control over her estate, may belong to her as much as to others. In herself, therefore, she is incomplete and indefinite. And left to herself, Clarissa is not determined: she makes no claims that she holds to and initiates no action. She suspends decisive action, waiting for others to do something: for Cousin Morden to arrive from Italy, for Anna's advice to arrive, for her parents' responses to her letters to arrive. Definitive assertions and decisive actions on her part are identified as responses to others' demands, so that she admits to her family that she has a preference for Lovelace only because "they will have it" that way (I.136), and she runs off with Lovelace only because she is tricked "out of *myself*" (I.487). Thus her statements are responses to others, and her actions are reactions to others, and her meaning is suspended between self and others even when it appears determined.

"Only one thing must be allowed for me," Clarissa writes to Anna; "that whatever course I shall be *permitted* or be *forced* to steer, I must be considered as a person out of her own direction" (I.345). This is Clarissa's continual demand. Although she seems to wish to determine herself here, she only demands in the passive voice and only claims by disclaimer: whatever I am or do is due to others. What she does, that is to say, is to remain in the rhetorical position of having no position, just as she remains free of confinement to any phys-ical space. She locates herself not in terms of places she holds but by her mobility: her ability to get out of any place or position in which she considers herself put. But if she cannot be committed by her self or others to any permanent or limited commitment, she is always committed *to* others, whom she regards, like herself, as changeable and qualified beings. The commitments she refuses are commitments that leave her no room for movement or changes; but she will be committed to others as long as such commitments leave room for her indeterminacy. Thus her initial admission that she may come to care for Lovelace is an admission that others direct her actions: "I will acknowledge that I believe it possible that one might be driven, by violent measures, step by step as it were, into something that might be called—I don't know what to call it—a *conditional kind of liking*, or so" (I.135). Tentative, dubious, qualified, and conditional, even as she is driven by what lies outside her, Clarissa represents herself in a process of change and dependence that precludes any determination of her meaning, by her self or anyone else, but includes both self and others in her indeterminate meaning.

Clarissa thus represents herself in a correspondent relation to others, by exchanges that resemble the exchange of letters in the narrative. This is a correspondence in which meaning always depends, for the reader, on something else: on others' responses, on later information, on different points of view. Like Clarissa herself, the narrative acknowledges no single authority. Representing itself as an unauthorized narrative, it insists on multiplying the possibilities of meaning yet resists choosing between possibilities. In its "form" it resembles Clarissa's formlessness, and, in complicity with her own behavior, the narrative both exceeds and evades the orders of distinction and possession and the concept of fair exchange on which those orders depend.

The differing interpretations and representations may attempt to restrict meaning but in fact always amplify and qualify meaning as they are suspended in the midst of the exchange that provides meaning. Every point of view is qualified by another, and we can perceive each letter, and each self, only as a partial, tentative, and suspended element of the whole. Thus the narrative insists that meaning is a process rather than an exchange: a process in which what is given and what is taken differ from and qualify each other. The qualifying responses, moreover, always increase the meaning of what is given and what is taken, even as they solicit more meaning in response to them. Meaning thus grows into more than any construction can hold, more than anyone can claim as her or his own. The process exceeds exchange and construction as it includes disparities—different points of view, different points in time, different interests, different conditions—rather than choosing one difference at the cost of others.

Not only is truth rendered indistinct by this process; so is the purpose or direction of the text. The objects and objectives of writing are difficult to define, as are the objects and objectives in Clarissa's behavior. The correspondence of characters occurs as a circulation rather than an exchange of meaning, not only because meaning is qualified and increased by different points of view but because the letters themselves never arrive at any final destination. They are given to other readers, copied for other readers, and thus circulate among the characters, exceeding the bounds of the exchange intended by the writer. Circulating both at first- and secondhand, the letters of the narrative can be said to belong to no one and to have no clear origin or end. The narrative shifts its grounds, then, not only because the narrators vary but because the letters themselves change hands. The mobility of the narrative is extraordinary: moving back as well as forward in time, covering "original" as well as secondhand material, changing places and points of view. In constant circulation without control, its parts go in multiple directions. Yet, on the other hand, different points of view may overlap, so that there is both coverage and recoverage of events. Both diffusive and redundant, the letters behave in accordance with Clarissa's perception of differences and defy the logic of any structure or order.

The fact that this circulation and fluidity of meaning dissolve distinctions is nowhere clearer than in the representation of the principal characters' principal correspondents, Anna and Belford. In their correspondence with Clarissa and Lovelace, these two characters serve to extend and qualify the central characters' individuality. They serve both as extensions and repetitions of them. And they cover the same ground in at least two senses: not only do they serve as outlets for Clarissa and Lovelace and respond to them, but they re-present at secondhand and from another point of view what those characters have discussed in their letters. Thus the two pairs of correspondents diversify the meaning of any individual self.

But if they correspond to their correspondents, Anna and Belford also correspond to their correspondents' "opposition" and thus preclude the opposition itself. Both Clarissa and Lovelace regard the other's correspondent as a part of the other, identifying the two. But in fact Anna begins by writing in support of Lovelace, and Belford of Clarissa. Anna begins by telling Clarissa not to be so modest, and Belford advises Lovelace not to carry through his plot. And both Anna and Belford eventually change from speaking for their friends' opponent to being identifiable with that opponent, as his or her "match." Thus the correspondences multiply. It is Belford who, as he becomes acquainted with Clarissa, actually reforms because of her. And it is Anna who responds to Lovelace in his terms, striking back at him, even hitting him in the face at one point, and plotting so strategically that Lovelace comes to plot against her in order to plot against Clarissa. Anna and Belford, corresponding with both central characters at once, preclude their opposition as the determination of their differences. Their presence complicates the correspondence of selves, even crossing the lines of sexual distinction, and thus insists on evading the opposition of both self and other, man and woman.

In the context of Clarissa's behavior and the sympathetic "behavior" of the text, the promise of Clarissa lies in the potential excess of meaning, in the allowance of meaning that is insecure and uncertain. The promise of Clarissa's representation to remain unreduced and uncontrolled by definitive exchanges offers the possibility of individuals being allowed to be both indistinct and incommensurable: corresponding even in their

differences, with room to change themselves and room to
differ from others without losing connection with others. It
is because of his own uncertainty and variability that Lovelace
seems to exceed the distinctions which the narrative exceeds.
He is thus not quite ruled out by and not quite opposed to
the uncertainty of differences that prevails in the novel. For
Lovelace, too, fluctuates in his meaning, unclear about the
distinction between what he is and what others are.

"A perfect Proteus," according to Clarissa, Lovelace seems
to himself to be not a hypocrite but simply inconsistent: "I
have as good motions, and perhaps have them as frequently
as anybody; all the business is, they don't hold; or, to speak
more in character, *I don't take the care some do to conceal
my lapses*" (II.69). Conscious of himself as a character, so
that he is always aware of his own difference from himself,
Lovelace seems to himself less hypocritical than others, for he
is truly dubious or genuinely inconsistent. His real meaning
cannot be determined, but this is not because he withholds it
or covers it up. He is open about its deceptiveness, which he
does not control:

> Thou knowest my heart, if any man living does. As far
> as I know it myself, thou knowest it. But 'tis a cursed
> deceiver; for it has many and many a time imposed upon
> its master—*master*, did I say? That am I not now. (I.145)

Like Clarissa, then, Lovelace experiences his self as out of
his own control, and although he is famous within the novel
and among its readers as a plotter, he is usually unable to
hold to any purpose because his objectives and motivations
are constantly changing. "I have three passions that sway me
by turns; all imperial ones. Love, revenge, ambition, or a desire
of conquest" (II.494-95). Because he experiences himself by
"turns," as subject to turns, Lovelace turns against himself
repeatedly. Unable to stick to a single objective—for instance,
to want Clarissa for love or for revenge—he is unable to carry
through his plots. Although control over others and circumstances is his goal, then, his own variability interferes with its
accomplishment: "Never was man in greater danger of being

caught in his own snares," he writes to Belford after having, "quite destitute of reserve," begged Clarissa to marry him (II.140-41). Lovelace repeatedly switches motives and sides; he "lapses" from his own purposes just as he lapses from the consistency society demands of good character. His genuine and involuntary inconsistency threatens his own ends and disables both his mastery of others and self-mastery.

Moreover, for Lovelace, as for Clarissa, what he is depends on what others are. He repeatedly refuses to own up to his actions, seeing them instead as reactions to others. His treatment of women he blames on the woman who first rejected him (I.145-46); and his treatment of Clarissa always seems to him to be demanded by her treatment of him. He insists that even his false pretenses are her fault: "To make an honest fellow look like a hypocrite; what a vile thing is that!" (I.514). Furthermore, as William Beatty Warner demonstrates, Lovelace's various roles are always assumed in relation to others, so that his sense of self is dependent on others' interaction with him:

> Because Lovelace has consciously committed himself to the interplay of struggle, he looks outside to his opponent instead of inside to his own "heart" . . . He does not try to decide what "the nature of things and actions" is in itself, but considers how things and actions exist in relation to the "characters of the actors."[14]

The paradox of Lovelace's identification of himself and others as "functions" of relationships, then, is that his mode of power over others is inseparable from his dependence on others for meaning. Having no "grounds" for his meaning, he, like Clarissa, needs others in order to have any meaning at all. And, like Clarissa, he recognizes that no meaning is exclusively his. The fact that others make him do things, and the fact that he chooses what position to take depending on others, mean that no position belongs solely to him.

But Lovelace, unlike Clarissa, sees all differences as parts

[14] Warner, *Reading "Clarissa,"* p. 33.

of potentially exclusive oppositions, in which one difference will rule out the other. He does not acknowledge the inclusive "middle ground" of meaning in which Clarissa lives, for he is always either one thing or its opposite. Even his own indeterminacy is experienced by "turns" that turn him against himself or switch him from one side of an opposition to another. And although he is dependent on others for meaning, that meaning opposes him to others, as each position he assumes is part of an opposition. These oppositions insist on a final and exclusive determination of meaning. If his plots, for example, do not snare his enemy they will snare him. If a turn occurs—as when Clarissa turns him from victor to victim— it is a turn against something else that is thereby canceled out: his control, or his purposes. He is never in between such oppositions but always one thing at the cost of another. Lovelace imposes the structure of conventional exchange on experience that Clarissa attempts to free from that confinement and the losses it entails.

Lovelace is therefore always in a double bind. He is dependent on those he would master, for example, and mastery remains his goal even as he recognizes that mastery, even of himself, is impossible. For Lovelace knows reality to be indeterminate, even as he insists on trying to determine his own superiority. Moreover, the structure of exchange Lovelace imposes on relations with others is itself a double bind. Because any determinant exchange requires the reduction of meaning to the terms of a match, the means of his own distinction or mastery are also the means by which others can master him. Once he limits his meaning to the terms of opposition, he is both aware that that meaning is uncertain because it is unrepresentative of him and aware that he is comparable to others and so can be mastered by them. He is always subject to the double bind, and he knows it. It is what he most fears as the means of his own undoing, even as it is what he most wishes to effect against his enemies:

It would be a confounded thing to be blown up by a train

of my own laying. And who knows what opportunities
a man in love may give against himself? (II.21)

Had I been a military hero, I should have made gun-
powder useless; for I should have blown up all my ad-
versaries by dint of strategem, turning their own devices
upon them. (II.55)

Because he reduces all meaning to the equivalent terms of
opposition, Lovelace can as easily be on one side as another;
yet one side can defeat the other. The terms of opposition
condemn him to be divided from his own meaning and to be
divided from the meaning of anything else, because such terms
can as easily work against him as for him.

Although Lovelace evades definition, then, he never identifies meaning as indeterminate; suspense, for him, is only
temporary. His constant plotting is evidence of this; for plotting enables him to determine both significance and insignificance: ends matter, and means do not matter except as means
to ends. Making the distinctions Clarissa cannot make, Lovelace assigns priority or privilege to certain elements of experience and discounts other elements. His plots to possess Clarissa, therefore, are plots to determine meaning at the cost of
part of experience. Her anger and her tears, for example, when
confronted with his determination, are treated by him as insignificant, as is his sympathy for her. They do not contribute
to his ends and are therefore devalued. His lies and disguises,
on the other hand, are valid because they do contribute to his
ends. Lovelace's end thus validates some meaning and invalidates other meaning, ruling out some according to the rule
of the other.

Moreover, Lovelace plots others' behavior as well as his
own; and as long as he can believe that all meaning is plotted
by someone, he need not be confused by others' differences
from him. When, like Clarissa's family, Lovelace can read her
behavior as part of a counterplot, he is secure. She, then, is
calling him dishonest and cruel only in order to have her way
with him: to reform him or negate him. To identify her behavior as part of an opposition, moreover, is to justify her

defeat, since an opposition can be settled only if someone wins and someone loses. Thus it is possible for Lovelace to interpret even what exceeds his code of values in terms of that code: what is not his way is another's way. Therefore, he is en-
.couraged to plot for more control rather than be diverted by Clarissa's behavior:

> can art and design enter into a breast so celestial; to banish me from thee . . . in order to bring me closer to thee . . . ? Well do *thy* arts justify *mine*, and encourage me to let loose my plotting genius upon thee. (II.33)

Lovelace here reduces all meaning to equitable terms. Insisting that Clarissa is doing what he wants to do, he identifies her as his match and thus justifies defeating her. Because his own desire for her seems to him to give her power over him, Lovelace identifies it as plotted by Clarissa. And by thus defining his loss of control as her assertion of control, he both masters the loss of control, by determining its meaning, and justifies his own attempt to master Clarissa. Determined to ignore the reality of differences, he can determine meaning and assume the possibility of controlling meaning.

The fact that his plots "unravel" threatens Lovelace's mastery, of course, and this happens repeatedly, as he is "totally diverted from all my favourite purposes" by the behavior of Clarissa (II.182). She often does not act in ways that he can identify as a counterplot or that enable him to know where he stands. Repeatedly he will begin in letters to write about his plans to master her and then become confused about positions of mastery and subjection and about where he stands, as he recalls her power to move him.

> What signifies her keeping me thus at distance? She must be mine, let me do or offer what I will. Courage whenever I assume, all is over: for should she think of escaping from hence, whither can she fly to avoid me? . . . And what then is the matter with me, that I should be thus unaccountably overawed and tyrannized over by a dear creature . . . ! (II.275)

I more than half regretted that I could not permit her to enjoy a triumph which she so well deserved to glory in. ... But her *indifference*, Belford! That she could resolve to sacrifice me to the malice of my enemies; and carry on the design in so clandestine a manner—yet love her, as I do, to frenzy!—revere her, as I do, to adoration! These were the recollections with which I fortified my recreant heart against her! Yet, after all, if she persevere, she must conquer! Coward, as she has made me, that never was a coward before!

... The women below say she hates me; she despises me! And 'tis true: she does; she must. And why cannot I take their advice? (II.316)

In this passage, extraordinary in its shifts—of syntax, as when he shifts referents, as well as of feeling, as he moves from regret to frenzy to anger to puzzlement—Lovelace is completely disarmed. But this is not because he is fairly beaten by Clarissa; she does not outmaneuver or outplot him. Her real power is a power that disables plots and one that cannot be plotted, and Lovelace seems to recognize that here. If Clarissa's indifference could be interpreted as a strategy, as it is in the earlier passage when she has locked herself in her room, Lovelace could be sure of her. But she now seems genuinely undifferentiating to him: to be unable to choose, unable to know whether she wants him or not. She is suspended between choices and seems to suspend choice even when, in such cases as Lovelace presents in the first passage, she has no choices. And so he is also in suspense, even about his own meaning. In the face of her suspension of meaning, he turns from mastery to submission, from fortification to cowardice. He cannot determine his meaning, cannot determine her meaning, and cannot determine on an act that would decide them.

Yet for Lovelace, even as plots come apart, meaning remains plotted. For the above uncertainty is immediately recognized as only temporary: "I will not long, my fair one, be despised by *thee*, and laughed at by *them*" (II.316). And throughout the passage, even though he is uncertain and indecisive, he represents his uncertainty in decisive and exclusive terms: he is either friend or enemy, either in possession of her or triumphed over by her, either fortified against her or conquered by her. Thus the order imposed by his plots remains the order of significance, reducing the two characters to the terms of exclusive opposition, even when plots fail. And mastery remains the priority, even as mastery is disabled. Thus Lovelace is always "caught in his own snares" as he is caught by his need to determine the meaning he sees as indeterminate.

Engaged in opposition, Lovelace recognizes no real diversity or incomparability of differences. Nor does Lovelace recognize diversion except as an interruption of determination. Any diversion, like any suspense, is seen as the mere middle of a plot. For Clarissa, the diversity, diversion, and suspension of meaning constitute the reality of experience; and this assumption is necessary to her freedom from the losses that ends determine. Her diversion seems absolute. When she feels diverted from her purposes, therefore, the result is not a trap or a double bind.

I had begun a letter to my cousin; but laid it by, because of the uncertainty of my situation . . . I know not how it comes about, but I am, in my own opinion, a poor lost creature: and yet cannot charge myself with one criminal or faulty inclination. . . .

Yet I can tell you *how*, I believe—one devious step at setting out!—that must be it—which pursued, has led me so far out of my path, that I am in a wilderness of doubt and error; . . . and the poor estray has not one kind friend, nor has met with one directing passenger, to help her to recover it.

But I, presumptuous creature! must rely so much upon my own knowledge of the right path!—little apprehending that an *ignis fatuus* with its false fires . . . would arise to mislead me! And now, in the midst of fens and quagmires, it plays around me, and around me, throwing me back again, whenever I think myself on the right track. . . .

But how I stray again, stray from my intention! I would
only have said, that I had begun a letter to my Cousin
Morden some time ago: but that now I can never end it.
(II.263)

Unable to relate her intentions and her actions, Clarissa remains here "out of her own direction." For her, deviation has
been indistinguishable from the right path. Whereas Lovelace
is immediately aware of deviations from his purposes, Clarissa
is not and continues to proceed by way of diversion.

This seems due to several causes here. One is the fact that
Clarissa depends on others, and others are not there to help
her; for she would recover her direction through others' direction. Another is that, on her own, Clarissa identifies goals
that are as "devious" as her steps. Misled by an *ignis fatuus*,
she is unable to determine a goal. Or, what seems a goal turns
out to be indeterminant, and she travels toward something
that "plays around" her, precluding any "right" track. Left
on her own, then, Clarissa finds that her objectives evaporate
or that they shift ground, as her movements do. It is self-
reliance that seems to be at fault, for she cannot trust her
"own knowledge." Confused and lost because she is on her
own and independent of others, Clarissa identifies her loss of
meaning in terms radically different from Lovelace's terms.
He is confused and loses meaning when subject to others'
behavior; and it is others who are perceived as the causes of
his deviations from purposes. Moreover, for Lovelace such
losses are losses *to* others, whereas for Clarissa the loss of her
way is simply an experience of being lost. She does not perceive
her loss in terms of others or as another's gain but precisely
as a loss of relation to others.

Clarissa's loss of direction, then, is due to the loss of others'
direction, a shiftiness of purpose, and initial deviation. Recognizing the diversity of action and intention, and recognizing
thereby her own diversity, Clarissa also recognizes diverse
causes for her loss. The fact that she cannot track down the
reason for her loss of direction seems to account to some
extent for the fact that she is not on the right track. For her

sense of a "track" or direction of meaning is clearly always devious, just as her sense of a beginning is always also a sense of deviation. Because the discussion of her lost way is itself a deviation in this letter—she meant to write about something else—it is clear that Clarissa does not stick to intentions. She "strays" in this letter because she is led off the subject by corresponding concerns that are not relevant to any single purpose, proceeding by indirection rather than direction. The prose is not evasive of purpose, but it slips off its "track" as it includes more meaning than could be contained by a coherent organization of points leading in a single direction.

Whereas Lovelace, aware of a purpose, is aware of the need to consider only meaning relevant to that purpose or, when he considers irrelevant meaning, to identify it clearly as an aside or digression, Clarissa often does not discriminate the point from asides or does so only after the fact, after she has strayed. Thus, once she arrives at any point in time or space, she can look back and recognize it as a deviation from intention. But she holds to neither intention nor objective in the process of experience. One reason for this in the above passage may be that the "starting point" of the discussion in which she strays is itself a letter to Morden that she has laid aside. If the point at which Clarissa begins is already a displacement of objects due to uncertainty about ends, this indicates that Clarissa never is at a proper starting point or end. If she corresponds with Lovelace because of her family's interests, likes Lovelace because she dislikes Solmes, and goes off with Lovelace in order to escape attackers, she is never clearly at a beginning that can be clarified as an intentional beginning of a particular action or direction that will lead to a particular end. Objects and objectives are correspondingly difficult to identify as such, as beginnings always look like "asides."

"So poor a plotter," as Lovelace says of her (III.388), Clarissa does not exercise the power of a plot. It is precisely her attempt to rely on self-determination that she identifies as part of her loss. Lost because self-reliant, she exists in a "wilderness" that might be identified with individualistic freedom, since she is absolutely on her own, independent of others. But it is meaningless to Clarissa. What she misses, and what she identifies as the means of finding meaning, are others. The recovery of what she has lost, therefore, is not to be accomplished by knowledge or determination. Knowledge gets her nowhere, and both knowledge and determination are undermined or precluded in this passage. She would not limit the diversity of differences in order to win back meaning but would include more differences by referring her direction to others. This is to say that being "out of her own direction" is not the difficulty here. For the solution would also put her "out of her own direction." This is not a double bind but a recognition that she is bound to others for meaning. She has come undone here because she has come apart from others. She is bound to others for meaning, therefore, though she will put no other bounds on meaning.

When Clarissa has her way, then, it is not a way that excludes others or excludes diversity. Her "will" has been identified by critics as a commanding, assertive, independent will. But her will, insofar as it is resolute, is also subject to change. What Leo Braudy calls "her assertion of will and freedom, the step outside the garden gate that ends in her death,"[15] is not presented as an "assertion of will and freedom." Clarissa's escape from home is presented, on the one hand, as a contradiction of her will. For what she asserts to Lovelace in the garden is " 'I will not go with you! . . . And, once more, I will *not* go' " (I.477). Her will is contradicted, then, though it is already, in its expression, a contradictory will, as it attempts to deny the decisive break with her family that going with Lovelace entails. Clarissa is able to be definite about what she will not do, though she is seldom definite about what she will do; for negation still leaves what *is* indefinite. As with her insistence that she "will not" marry Solmes, she contradicts Lovelace's will to control her but, in place of asserting control herself, seeks to suspend decisive action: "to suspend, for the present, my intention of leaving my father's house" (I.461).

On the other hand, insofar as Clarissa does represent the

¹⁵ Braudy, "Penetration and Impenetrability," p. 197.

event as the result of her independent will, she identifies the assumption of independence as a mistake. In a passage typical of her indeterminacy, she writes to Anna in terms that both assert her independence and qualify it.

> You know, my dear, that your Clarissa's mind was ever above justifying her own failings by those of others. God forgive those of my friends who have acted cruelly by me! But their faults *are* their own, and not excuses for mine. . . .
>
> O the vile encroacher! how my indignation, at times, rises at him! Thus to lead a young creature (too much indeed relying upon her own strength) from evil to evil!
> . . .
>
> How much more properly had I acted, with regard to that correspondence, had I, once for all, . . . pleaded the authority by which I ought to have been bound, and denied to write to him! But I thought I could *proceed* or *stop* as I pleased. I supposed it concerned *me, more than any other, to be the arbitress of the quarrels of unruly spirits*—and now I find my presumption punished—punished, as other sins frequently are, by *itself*! (I.486)

"Above justifying her own failings by those of others," Clarissa goes right on to blame Lovelace for what she has done. And this self-contradiction is compounded by the following contradiction of will, by which will itself, *because* a matter of self-assertion and independence, constitutes its own negation. It is precisely, as in the passage in which she is diverted from her way, the extent to which she has assumed self-control and privilege that constitutes her loss. Will is self-contradictory, finally, because it assumes the isolation of self from others whereas the self in fact remains dependent on circumstances and others. Clarissa perceives herself in a double bind, then, not because she cannot have her own way but because she wanted her own way: because she assumed that will can limit meaning to the bounds of self.

Even the will Clarissa writes before her death—the will which, Braudy says, "makes clear that it is not will alone which controls one's identity and relation to others, but will as embodied in writing"[16]—leaves room for others to differ from it.

> I have always earnestly requested that my body might be deposited in the family vault with those of my ancestors. . . . But as I have, by one very unhappy step, been thought to disgrace my whole lineage, and therefore this last honour may be refused to my corpse; in this case, my desire is that it may be interred in the churchyard belonging to the parish in which I shall die. . . . (IV.416)

> And I could wish, if it might be avoided without making ill-will between Mr. Lovelace and my executor, that the former might not be permitted to see my corpse. But if, as he is a man very uncontrollable, and as I am nobody's, he insist upon viewing *her dead* whom he ONCE before saw in a manner dead, let his gay curiosity be gratified. (IV.416)

And of the money from her grandfather's estate, Clarissa's will is to

> hope I may be allowed to dispose of [it] absolutely, as my love and my gratitude . . . may warrant: and which therefore I shall dispose of in the manner hereafter mentioned. But it is my will and express direction that my father's account of the above-mentioned produce may be taken and established absolutely. . . . (IV.418)

Even after the rape, then, when she has accepted that she is isolated, or "nobody's," Clarissa's will expresses itself as subject to qualification by others, and her intentions take into consideration the differences of others on whom her "will" depends.

Clarissa's will, then, is both divergent and diverse in its expression. Moreover, she wishes to allow for similarly diverse behavior in others. In the same letter in which she strays from her intention and loses her way, she hopes that Lovelace's

[16] Ibid., p. 202.

behavior may also be unintentional: "If it be necessary, in support of the parental authority, that I should be punished by *him*, [I pray] that it may not be by his *premeditated* or *wilful* baseness; but that I may be able to acquit his *intention*, if not his *action!*" (II.263). Here Clarissa insists on the possibility of Lovelace diverging from his will as she does from hers. Thus she, like Lovelace, sees the other as a version of self. But whereas Lovelace needs to be able to plot his own and others' meaning, Clarissa wishes to perceive him as well as herself in terms that preclude control. Whereas Lovelace chooses between differences, she hopes to increase differences: to diversify his meaning in order to make room for significance in which mixed values coexist. Thus she will be able to acquit him if she must condemn him, qualifying and thereby exceeding judgment and knowledge themselves. Doing this, she would "let him off," and it is characteristic of her to do so. It is because she does so, moreover, that Lovelace is not caught in his own snares. For, at moments when he turns against his own purposes, Clarissa does not take advantage of it:

> Well, but what was the result of this involuntary impulse on my part? Wouldst thou not think I was taken at my offer?—an offer so solemnly made, and on one knee too?
> No such thing! The pretty trifler let me off as easily as I could have wished. (II.142)

Clarissa lets him off from being caught in his double bind as she would let him off from justice and determination, allowing him to deviate from his own purposes without paying for it and allowing him to escape the limits of a just determination.

Thus Clarissa identifies meaning *as* so diverse that it cannot be plotted. But Lovelace never identifies meaning as anything but part of a plot, his own or another's. Although William Beatty Warner identifies Lovelace with creative "play," Lovelace never plays for the sake of play, or diversion, or freedom. He plays for an end. He knows that ends are empty of meaning: "*Preparation* and *expectation* are in a manner everything: . . . but the *fruition*, what is there in that?," he writes to Belford (I.172-73). But he nevertheless directs all his actions toward an end, thus working against his own understanding as well as against others. Lovelace's representations repeatedly reduce the indeterminacy of meaning to determinant terms, as Warner makes clear in his discussion of Lovelace's "portraiture":

> In isolating Clarissa as a self-complete object, and naming the splendid elements she holds in tension, Lovelace feels her overabundance, her excess of energy. . . . As Clarissa's image appropriates all power to itself, Lovelace feels himself to be abject and worthless. . . .
> . . . In framing Clarissa and making her a portrait, Lovelace abstracts aspects of her into one reduced but intensified image. But he is so generous in his adornment of the surface, he gives it such complex tones and enigmatic shadings, that it threatens to overcome him. . . . Now it can master (i.e. seduce) its creator.[17]

Perceived as sublime excess of meaning, Clarissa is not allowed to remain indefinite. For Lovelace gives form and direction to the meaning she confuses, turning her reconciliation of differences into a form of control. He really does frame her by such interpretations, confining her excesses and forcing her into the position of opposition. Clarissa's excesses are not the mark of Lovelace's gift as an artist or of his generosity. She is always excessive: inconsistent and confused. The difference that Lovelace's representation makes is the identification of those excesses as her means of mastering him. Because he can conceive of meaning only in terms of appropriation, and because he cannot quite appropriate her, she must therefore be appropriating him. Lovelace is not generous in his "treatment" of Clarissa: he is always, finally, reductive, and reduction is the end to which he is committed, even as he recognizes such an end as a loss.

Lovelace's sense of the difference between one thing and another is therefore never a sense of play but of war. In one of the most extraordinary confusions he exhibits, Lovelace

---

[17] Warner, *Reading "Clarissa,"* p. 48.

acknowledges that he is not sure there is much difference between himself and women. But the effect of the comparison is not playful:

> I was *originally* a bashful mortal. Indeed I am bashful still with regard to this lady—bashful, yet know the sex so well! But that indeed is the *reason* that I know it so well. For, Jack, I have had abundant cause, when I have looked into *myself*, by way of comparison with the *other* sex, to conclude that a bashful man has a good deal of the soul of a woman; and so, like Tiresias, can tell what they think, and what they drive at, as well as themselves. The modest ones and I, particularly, are pretty much upon a par. The difference between us is only, what they *think*, I *act*. . . .
>
> One argument let me plead in proof of my assertion: that even we rakes love modesty in a woman; while the modest women, as they are accounted (that is to say, the *slyest*), love, and generally prefer, an impudent man. Whence can this be but from a likeness in nature? And this made the poet say that every woman is a rake in her heart. It concerns them by their *actions* to prove the contrary, if they can. (II.55)

Here Lovelace begins by identifying himself with women and proceeds to undermine any grounds for their distinction. The bashful man is like a modest woman: the only difference is the difference between thought and action: what they think, he acts. Thus modesty is denied as a distinction: for if women have modest actions, they have impudent thoughts, just as he has modest thoughts and impudent actions. Moreover, modest women are attracted to impudent men, just as rakes are attracted to modesty in women; modest women are not, therefore, really modest; they are really sly, which is to say again that they are no different from Lovelace himself.

Thus Lovelace proceeds, by putting differences into what looks like a deconstructive play. But Lovelace is not interested in destroying "the claim to unequivocal domination of one mode of signifying over another" that Barbara Johnson identifies as the method of deconstruction.[18] He is interested in destroying women's claims to domination and establishing his own claims to domination. And he does so by denying any difference in women that he cannot also claim and then insisting that women must try "to prove the contrary, if they can." Having undermined all sense of contraries here, Lovelace reimposes a sense of contraries, as he does in Warner's description of his creative procedure, where he recognizes excesses of meaning in terms of domination. Unwilling to leave the differences indistinct or unsettled, Lovelace demands that women attempt to prove their difference "by their *actions*." Yet he has already claimed that actions are unreliable: for his own impudent actions belie his bashful thoughts. Thus he demands that women prove a difference that cannot be proven, for actions and thoughts may differ.

By the end of the passage, differences are no longer in play: they are at an end. There is no such thing as modesty, which is equated with slyness. And there is no such thing as woman. There are only active and inactive rakes; and the inactive rake, itself a contradiction in terms, is the meaningless condition of women. Thus Clarissa will, as Lovelace's equally sly counterpart, deserve what she gets. But what she gets, of course, is exactly representative of one real difference between men and women: for men can accomplish at least one action, literal rape, that women cannot accomplish. Lovelace denies differences when they dispute his superiority and exploits them when they enable him to assert mastery.[19]

---

[18] Barbara Johnson, "Translator's Introduction" to *Dissemination* by Jacques Derrida, trans. Barbara Johnson (Chicago: University of Chicago Press, 1981), p. xiv.

[19] Judith Wilt considers the passage I have just discussed as evidence of Lovelace's profound identification with Clarissa. But Wilt clarifies that this does not signal an indistinction of men and women on Richardson's part. For if Lovelace is part woman, it is the part that is feminine that destroys him and Clarissa too: "So far as the novel is Lovelace's story it is the record of a man-woman—woman as his culture defines woman, that is, split into harlot and Harlowe—trying to become whole, trying to fit the masculine half with a workable feminine half. And neither harlot nor Harlowe is workable inside him. Lovelace's masculine aspect seems in Richardson's eyes worthy;

This is what Lovelace does repeatedly with Clarissa. Not only does he find a way to represent what exceeds his control in terms that justify control—as he does by insisting that women are no better than he is; he also deconstructs meaning only to the extent that she has nothing more than he has. And then he insists that she prove that she is better than he is. By doing so, Lovelace confines her to determinant grounds and limits her to the terms of opposition to him, and always to terms of an opposition he can win. It is Lovelace, then, who puts Clarissa in the position of proving her virtue. She never claims to be able to do that. Whereas she is always willing to let him off when there is any possibility of qualifying judgment, as when she separates his intentions from his actions, he insists that she be proven in her meaning by a "just" trial, even as he knows that no such proof is possible. Her meaning cannot be determined, even as she is confined by him to terms according to which not to be determined is to have no meaning at all.

The trial that Lovelace requires in order to keep Clarissa confined to terms of winning and losing is justified by rendering the grounds of her virtue uncertain. But again, Lovelace's deconstructive tactics are partial, as the following selections from his extended justification suggest:

---

he is shown as courageous, resourceful, intelligent. . . . But there is another side to him, an aspect that "drives at" unceasing sexual relationship, that suffers ungovernable rages and will not be reasoned out of obsession, that delights both in cruelty and in bending to the cruel fair. It is difficult to escape the impression that for Richardson this other side that ruins Lovelace is the woman-internal, powerfully dramatized internally in the crazed servitude to obsession by which Lovelace finally achieves his own rape-death at the hands of the manly Morden, and externally in the figures of Sinclair and the harlots." It is Sinclair, a woman, Wilt argues, who is in fact the rapist in the novel. And thus if woman is the victim in *Clarissa*, she is also the criminal. Wilt's reading of the novel, in "He Could Go No Farther: A Modest Proposal about Lovelace and Clarissa," *PMLA*, 92, no. 1 (1977), 19-32, is compelling in its insistence on Richardson's ambivalence and in its insistence that therefore it is impossible to regard Clarissa as in any sense pure. The above quotation is on page 22.

Is not, may not, her virtue be founded rather in *pride* than in *principle*? Whose daughter is she? And is she not a *daughter*? . . .
Then who says Miss Clarissa Harlowe is the paragon of virtue?—Is Virtue itself? (II.35-36)

. . . Has her virtue ever been *proved*? Who has dared to try her virtue? (II.36)

To the test, then, as I said, since now I have the question brought home to me whether I am to have a wife? And whether she is to be a wife at the *first* or at the *second* hand?
I will proceed fairly. I will do the dear creature not only strict, but generous justice; for I will try her by her own judgment, as well as by our principles.
She blames herself for having corresponded with me, a man of free character. (II.36-37)

Whoever was the *tempter*, that is not the thing; nor what the *temptation*. The *fact*, the *error*, is now before us. (II.37)

Let LOVE, then, be the motive—love of whom?
A *Lovelace*, is the answer. (II.38)

But has she had the candour, the openness, to *acknowledge* that love?
She has not. (II.38)

And what results? "Is then the divine Clarissa capable of *loving* a man whom she ought *not* to love? And is she capable of *affectation*? And is her virtue founded in *pride*?" (II.38)

"Nor is *one* effort, *one* trial, to be sufficient. Why? Because a woman's heart may be at one time *adamant*, at another *wax*"—as I have often experienced. (II.41)

But what, methinks, thou askest, is to become of the lady if she fail?

What?—Why will she not, "*if once subdued*, be *always subdued*?" (II.41)

In the long passage from which these lines are taken, Lovelace again both renders meaning indeterminate and insists on its determination. He does so by reducing meaning to the terms of exclusive oppositions and demanding a trial that will decide between the two sides, choosing "just" one. Among the decisions to be made are these: whether virtue is grounded in pride or in principle; whether Clarissa will be a firsthand or a secondhand wife; whether Clarissa is adamant or wax. His trial will decide which. Clarissa's love, moreover, is made to oppose virtue. For if she loves a Lovelace, and if she will not admit it, she is in conflict with virtue on two counts. This clarifies that virtue may be an affectation and thereby also demands a trial. Yet the trial will occur as often as Lovelace pleases, since a woman may change from adamant to wax. Thus the justification for trial—the fact that Clarissa is variable—is also the justification for the fact that he must keep trying: because Clarissa is variable, a trial is necessary, but because she is variable no trial is necessarily adequate or proof against her. Unless, of course, she fails, in which case Lovelace will consider the trial final.

Here, too, Lovelace is working against himself. He insists, on the one hand, that firsthand and secondhand make a difference in a wife; but whether the trial is the first or second makes no difference. He insists at one point that the facts stand on their own, without extenuation: the tempter and the temptation make no difference. But the circumstances surrounding her love—its object and the fact that it is unacknowledged—make a difference to it. He insists that Clarissa cannot be two things at once, but he clarifies that she always is two things at once. And he insists that virtue must be proven but no trial will prove it. The only proof possible is proof that she is not virtuous; given Lovelace's capacity to undermine the meaning of anything here, it is clear that only what he wants to prove can be proven. For Lovelace, the rigor of any form of thought—constructive or deconstructive—gives way to the need to win. Whether meaning is groundless or grounded is irrelevant; what is relevant is what gives him meaning and takes meaning away from others.

The passage about the trial, which extends over several pages, is both illogical and inconsistent. And it seems playful, too, in the sense that there is seldom any attempt on Lovelace's part to be serious about what he is doing. But he is playing in order to win, and the passage is characteristic of him in its insistence on using any means at all to get what he wants. He shifts grounds, shifts standards, and misrepresents meaning; but he does so in order to gain control of it. Thus his inconsistency is not "genuine" inconsistency: it is inconsistency demanded by the end he has in view. If the meaning he represents is inconsistent in some ways, moreover, it is consistently reductive. One of the "ends" of the passage, for example, seems to be to reduce Clarissa to Lovelace's own terms, to represent her as no different than he is: proud, dishonest, disobedient, undependable. Yet this identification is accomplished only at the cost of Clarissa's multiple nature. As in his other plots, Lovelace interprets experience in order to reduce it to common terms which enable him to "get" it. What he cannot get, either by the grasp of his hands or the grasp of his understanding, is reduced to "graspable" terms in order to enable him to get what he can and deny the meaning of what he cannot get. This, too, further "ensnares" him, though. For in order to see Clarissa as something he can possess, he must rule out her excesses; just as, in order to plot, he must rule out the significance of those elements of experience that do not serve his ends. Yet any sense of possession, therefore, is also a sense of loss, for he is always aware that something is missing.

Once he completes his "trial," this is what he experiences. He is able to possess Clarissa only because she is drugged, and thus understands in his act of possession that he cannot completely possess her: "Why say I *completed*? when the *will*, the *consent*, is wanting—and I have still views before me of obtaining that?" (III.203). As always, Clarissa exceeds Lovelace's terms of possession and defeats his ends, but, as always,

Lovelace does not think in different terms because of his failure. He thinks of her excess as his own lack, insistent that he
can still get it.

If the above passage suggests that justice is not taken seriously by Lovelace, it is nevertheless characteristic of him to
claim justice, just as it is characteristic of him to claim knowledge. Such structures of meaning need never be taken seriously
by him, because they are subject to multiple interpretations
of their terms which conflict with their claims that those terms
define and settle meaning. Such structures suit Lovelace's purposes because he can deconstruct them and so has the power
to undermine their claims. He can get the better of them, or
turn them against themselves. Clarissa, however, though
equally subject to multiple interpretations, can never be turned
against herself or bettered, for she cannot be structured.

Clarissa cannot, therefore, be confined to the terms of justice
or knowledge. She cannot, for example, be reduced to "just"
terms, which is what Lovelace attempts in the above passage.
We as readers are unable to define her as guilty or not guilty
throughout the narrative; she simply is not only one of these.
Nor is it possible for Lovelace to do justice to her in any
representation: "*Imagination* cannot form; much less can the
pencil paint; nor can the soul of painting, *poetry*, describe an
angel so exquisitely, so elegantly lovely!" (II.499). Clarissa
always leaves room for differing interpretations, and she herself resists laying down the law in order to allow behavior
and meaning to exceed the limits of any terms. What she
demands is neither justice nor a fair deal:

> Let me tell you what *generosity* is, in my sense of the
> word: TRUE GENEROSITY is not confined to pecuniary
> instances: it is *more* than politeness: it is *more* than good
> faith: it is *more* than honour: it is *more* than *justice*: since
> all these are but duties, and what a worthy mind cannot
> dispense with. But TRUE GENEROSITY is greatness of soul.
> It incites us to do more by a fellow-creature than can be
> strictly required of us. . . . Generosity, sir, will not surely
> permit a worthy mind to doubt of its honourable and

beneficent intentions: much less will it allow itself to
shock, to offend any one. . . .

What an opportunity had he to clear his intentions,
had he been so disposed, from the *latter part* of this home
observation! But he ran away with the *first*, and kept to
that.

Admirably defined! he said. But who, at this rate,
madam, can be said to be *generous to you*? Your *generosity* I implore; while *justice*, as it must be my sole
merit, shall be my aim. (II.304)

Finding value in *more* than can be determined by any exchange
or confined to any terms, Clarissa values indeterminacy itself.
She does not disclaim indeterminate values, as do structures
of justice or politeness; she insists that meaning is to be found
in indeterminacy.

As always in his relations with Clarissa, Lovelace ignores
here any more meaning than he can control. His evasions of
the excess of generosity are accomplished by dividing experience into parts and ignoring the part that he cannot lay claim
to. He can claim justice. But true generosity cannot, according
to Clarissa's "terms," be claimed, because it cannot be defined
or limited *to* terms. Generosity is part of no exchange, for it
exceeds the equivalence that exchange depends on. Generosity
proceeds without either demand or return, as giving without
regard to what is given by others; it is never, therefore, part
of any match. The fact that Clarissa here does attempt to
represent it—the fact that she must reduce it to terms of exchange by talking about it and by, implicitly at least, making
it a demand—is a fact that she recognizes as a mark of the
unsatisfactory nature of her relationship with Lovelace. "Under the sad necessity of telling a man . . . what true generosity
is" (II.305), she is under the necessity of reducing her values
to the terms of exchange. Yet her attempt to represent those
values still leaves room for their meaning to exceed exchange.

Because Clarissa exceeds the bounds of determination and
Lovelace repeatedly imposes those boundaries, the disparity

between the two can be termed a match or an opposition only from Lovelace's point of view. From Richardson's and Clarissa's points of view, which include rather than exclude disparities, the relation of their differences remains unsettled because those differences are not reduced to common terms. This means that in place of a rhetorical opposition or a "warring of discourses," we are presented with a relation that resembles the relation of differing statements that Paul de Man identifies in writing that both asserts and qualifies knowledge:

> It is necessary, in each case, to read beyond some of the more categorical assertions and balance them against other much more tentative utterances that seem to come close, at times, to being contradictory to these assertions. The contradictions, however, never cancel each other out, nor do they enter into the synthesizing dynamics of a dialectic. No contradiction or dialectical movement could develop because a fundamental difference in the level of explicitness prevented both statements from meeting on a common level of discourse; the one always lay hidden within the other as the sun lies hidden within a shadow, or truth within error.[20]

Like the assertive and tentative utterances that de Man identifies in unresolved tension in a literary text, Lovelace's and Clarissa's statements, in their differences, never quite meet on common grounds or in common terms. It is characteristic of their relation, for example, that when one is categorical, the other is tentative. Their utterances never quite come together, but neither do they come apart distinctly enough to oppose or exclude each other. As in the above exchange about generosity, Clarissa does not demand anything that cancels out Lovelace's sense of justice; she demands something more, something different but in addition to justice rather than disputing justice. Nor does Lovelace's behavior ever manage to

[20] Paul de Man, *Blindness and Insight: Essays in the Rhetoric of Contemporary Criticism* (New York: Oxford University Press, 1971), pp. 102-103.

deny Clarissa's excesses; he is in fact unable to stop trying to possess her because she always exceeds his grasp.

Because of this relationship, however, the characters are often included or implicated in each other's attempts: she in his attempt to possess her, and he in her attempt to remain free of possession. The complicity of differences that de Man identifies in language that includes indistinct differences suggests the complicity of Lovelace and Clarissa in behavior that differs from their willed behavior. It is complicity that readers have recognized when they claim that Clarissa really wants to be raped or that Lovelace is really self-destructive. But their complicity is never a complicity in these ends. For Clarissa does not recognize ends at all; and Lovelace, when complicitous with her, is complicitous with her suspension of ends.

The complicity of categorical assertions and tentative utterances that do not exclude each other and that, for de Man, represent the complicity of truth and error, is the complicity that characterizes Clarissa's understanding. She recognizes truth as something difficult to distinguish or arrive at and perceives truth as including multiple differences rather than as an end of difference. When she "confesses" to Anna that she may love Lovelace, for example, the confession is not a direct statement but a circuitous and evasive recognition, mostly in the form of questions: "Am I not guilty of a punishable fault, were I to love this man of errors? And has not my own heart deceived me, when I thought I did not?" (II.438). Recognizing the conflation of pure and impure values—love and error, heart and deception—Clarissa represents dubiously the dubious nature of her experience. Tentative in her "confession," she does not acknowledge the truth or claim to know it but represents instead the ambivalent nature of truth, knowledge, and representation itself:

> What can we do more than govern ourselves by the temporary lights lent us?
> You will not wonder that I am grave on this detection—*detection*, must I call it? What can I call it?
> ... I never was in such an odd frame of mind. I know

not how to describe it. Was *you* ever *so*? Afraid of the
censure of her you love—yet not conscious that you deserve it?

Of this, however, I am convinced, that I should *indeed*
deserve censure, if I kept any secret of my heart from
you. (II.439)

Here truth is complicitous with error, and representation is
complicitous with misrepresentation as Clarissa disallows the
separation of truth and error or knowledge and ignorance and
allows for the inadequacy of language to represent experience.
Even as she clearly does not know the true meaning of her
thoughts, since she cannot define them categorically, she is
sure that she must tell them to Anna. Yet she is not sure that
she can call her discovery a detection, for she has not previously hidden anything. The sense of a secret here is as uncertain as the sense of truth, because neither term represents her
experience. The secret is not something she has been conscious
of knowing herself; and the truth is indefinite. Thus it is the
very complicity of knowledge and ignorance that Clarissa feels
compelled to represent, in order to be true to the uncertainty
of meaning.

As in de Man's consideration of language, truth is represented here as both dubious and temporary. Clarissa's representation is a representation of constant change: what *is*
changes, and the ability to perceive what is also changes. It
is her insistence on the ambivalent character of any representation of truth that differentiates her from Lovelace. She is
committed to the complicity of truth and error as she is committed to the complicity of self and others. But because she
is committed to these complicities, she is committed to no end
or resolution; she is, in fact, committed to precluding ends.
Given her perception of complicitous meaning, meaning itself
cannot be resolved: it includes differences that cannot be settled. Because she represents meaning in these inclusive terms,
moreover, her representation is not subject to contradiction.
Positing nothing as certain, she cannot be negated.

Clarissa's clarity, then, lies in her clear expression of the very impossibility of determining or representing the truth. She is dubious in her representations because she is representing the dubious nature of experience that exceeds the terms of distinction and determination. Lovelace, however, as his name suggests, recognizes meaning only in terms that can also be negated. He posits singular meanings, and the positing determines the meaning as also subject to negation. Giving only what he can also take away, Lovelace never lets go of determination, never allowing meaning to exceed definitive terms. Although he both represents and misrepresents, he does not recognize the complicity of the two but keeps them distinct. Unlike Clarissa's "secret," which is only a secret from others as long as it is a secret from herself, Lovelace's secrets and lies and disguises insist that he can have something more than others have. He thus profits by the indeterminacy of meaning, dividing it into possessions and lacks and keeping more than others have.

In Lovelace's representation, therefore, the complicity of differences is subject to the same treatment as other kinds of indeterminacy. Only if complicity contributes to an end does it have significance for him. It is a means to an end, insignificant in itself, and it serves someone's purposes. His own complicity with Clarissa's interests is thereby always interpreted by him as a loss of meaning: either because insignificant or because part of a double bind. Always clear about the distinction between one thing and another, especially between what he has and what others have, Lovelace conceives of meaning in terms of possession and loss. Insistent on ruling out of significance whatever exceeds those terms, he is committed to lack itself. Always condemned to attempt to make up for lacks, he is also condemned, by his conception of meaning, to discover new lacks. His inventions always make up things that cancel out other things, and his expression is thereby always tied to repression. Lovelace himself generates lack and is condemned to try to make up for the lacks he himself imposes on experience. Thus he dies saying "Let this expiate!" (IV.530), insistent to the end on the possibility of compensating for the losses he has himself created.

Lovelace, then, is a character who, for all his capacity to render meaning indeterminate, is committed to the repression of meaning. His recognition of the groundless and arbitrary character of meaning is not a recognition of the necessary instability of meaning. He insists that determination occurs, that "*once subdued . . . always subdued.*" For Clarissa, once subdued is not always subdued. But to be subdued by Lovelace at all is the end of meaning for her, because, with the rape, Lovelace imposes on Clarissa the same divisions he lives by: the division of one part of herself from others; the opposition of self and other; the recognition that to leave room for others in the self is to subject yourself to loss.

Terry Castle argues that "Lovelace's ultimate gesture of 'force' (as he calls it) exposes a truth about meaning itself. The power to determine the significance of events, to articulate one's reading of experience and impose it on others, is a function of political advantage alone, and identified finally with physical force."[21] But Lovelace's rape of Clarissa may also be considered a rape of meaning itself, which is not exposed in its truth but mastered by determination and possession, robbed of part of itself by the repression of its indeterminacy. The rape can be considered, as Castle represents it, as a violation by fragmentation that breaks Clarissa apart;[22] or it can be considered a violent totalization that fills up her body. It is both. Its effect on the one hand is to divide her; and its effect on the other hand is to insist that such divisions are masterful divisions, in which one part takes over, repressing and ruling out the other. In both ways, the binding relations of differences that have constituted meaning for Clarissa are broken.

To call the rape a robbery of meaning is not to identify it as a theft of property. A theft of property is in fact implicitly what occurs when meaning is meaningful for Clarissa, in the sense that meaning always exceeds the bounds of exclusive possession. Pamela's experience of love as a thief—an expe-

[21] Castle, *Clarissa's Cyphers*, p. 116.
[22] Ibid., p. 111.

rience of loss of self-possession and self-control, as love breaks down the bounds of property—would also be a meaningful experience for Clarissa. But that theft occurs from the inside and marks the indistinction of self and other, inside and outside, that is meaningful in both novels. The rape of Clarissa occurs as a violation of meaning as well as a violation of Clarissa in that Clarissa takes no part in Lovelace's forced entry. As the figure of speech suggests, the rape turns her into a piece of property as it forces her to know the difference between self and other, inside and outside. The rape does not take away Clarissa's distinction, then; it makes that distinction.[23]

Not only does the rape occur by force of mastery, then. It enforces mastery as the means of meaning, as it forces Clarissa

[23] Patricia Klindienst Joplin has written of rape as theft in "The Voice of the Shuttle Is Ours," *Stanford Literature Review*, I, no. 1 (1984), 25-53. She considers the story of Philomena not like Geoffrey Hartman, in "The Voice of the Shuttle: Language from the Point of View of Literature," in *Beyond Formalism: Literary Essays 1958-1970* (New Haven: Yale University Press, 1970), for what it says about figurative language, but for what it says about the voice of women silenced by men. Joplin identifies rape with property theft as she identifies women as objects of exchange in male-dominated society. The woman's body, she suggests, is used by men to represent their control of the body politic. "The exchange of women articulates the culture's boundaries, the woman's hymen serving as the physical or sexual sign for the limen or wall defining the city's limits" (p. 37). Given and taken in marriage, the woman represents the capacity of male sovereignty to maintain control over possible invasion of its property. Raped, the woman represents "the very violence the exchange of her body was meant to hold in check" (p. 38). Joplin suggests, however, that if we look at the situation from the woman's point of view instead of from a "universal" point of view, from which she remains a mere sign, the raped woman "stands radically outside all boundaries. . . . There, she may see just how arbitrary cultural boundaries truly are; she may see what fictions prepared the way for her suffering" (p. 42). Whereas Hartman identifies an excess of meaning in figurative language, for Joplin it is the woman who experiences herself in excess of the boundaries of properly controlled social values.

When Clarissa is raped she does not learn "how arbitrary cultural boundaries truly are"; I have argued that she at some level has known that throughout her narrative. But she learns, as Joplin's raped heroines learn, that those boundaries are created by mastery and enforced by repression.

to master herself unless she would be mastered by another. For hereafter Clarissa must live with the recognition that parts of herself—the part that loved Lovelace, the body that could not resist rape—are the enemies of other parts of herself. Acknowledging that enmity, she must repress, or subdue, parts of herself. The rape thereby robs her of her involuntary differences, of her very freedom from determination and will, and forces her to conform her meaning to the meaning of a determinant will. His will or hers: one at the cost of the other, just as part of herself excludes other parts of herself. Once mastery takes control, she is divided from others and from self.

But for Clarissa, this is the loss of meaning itself. If for Lovelace, as Castle says, the rape is "trivial,"[24] an event that he wishes to repress or discount, for Clarissa the rape is also insignificant in that it represents meaninglessness. And rather than having to live with what is for her the meaningless repression of meaning, she chooses to die and give up meaning altogether.[25] In doing so, she moves from the midst of meaning, in which all values have significance, right beyond the ends of meaning to the recognition that nothing whatever matters. Unable to choose between alternatives earlier because she values all differences, Clarissa moves toward such absolute indifference in the later part of the novel that she does not care for anything. Terry Eagleton describes this choice as a choice to be "utterly autonomous" and utterly transparent:

Such transparency—the baffling enigma of that which is merely itself—is bound to appear socially opaque, a worthless tautology or resounding silence. There is noth-

[24] Castle, *Clarissa's Cyphers*, p. 116.
[25] Warner insists that Clarissa finally subjects the world to her sovereign self, trying to "assume a Godlike authority and dominion" over others and thus exposing "a more insidious will to power" than Lovelace's (*Reading "Clarissa,"* p. 75). Although Clarissa does eradicate "otherness" at the end of her narrative (p. 114), she does so in indifference, it seems to me, rather than in an exercise of mastery. Indifference, of course, can be interpreted as a power play, and Lovelace, like many critics, does see her behavior as an exercise of power. But Clarissa, I think, does not much care.

ing to be done with it, as the patriarchs can finally do nothing with Clarissa, the stubborn little minx who perversely insists upon dying and leaving them with blood on their hands.[26]

With no meaning at all, defiant of understanding and as defiant of realistic likelihood as she ever has been, Clarissa refuses to go to law, refuses justice, and refuses compensation. She leaves Lovelace with his guilt as an irreducible phenomenon: one that cannot be exchanged for anything else, one for which there is no compensation.

It is Lovelace, however, whose conception of meaning prevails in the history of the realistic novel as it prevails in the history of reality. This is suggested clearly by the fact that critical readers of *Clarissa* tend to see the novel in Lovelace's terms—terms of mastery, determination, possession. We tend to think of fiction, too, as compensatory and to insist on the division of fiction from reality. Yet Richardson offers an alternative in the indeterminate and indecisive representations of both Pamela and Clarissa: representations in which differing values are free to differ without cost yet are so bound to one another that they cannot be separated. Embracing the groundless excess of meaning that threatens Lovelace with the loss of determination, Richardson's narratives identify the potential freedom from loss to be found in the indeterminacy of meaning.

[26] Eagleton, *The Rape of Clarissa*, p. 75.

CHAPTER FOUR

POWER AS PARTIALITY IN
MIDDLEMARCH

Dorothea Brooke, the heroine of *Middlemarch*, has as uneasy an effect on the world around her as do Richardson's Pamela and Clarissa. She, too, is hard to take and difficult to place, and, as in Clarissa's case, the difficulty is initially posed as a problem of "marriageability."

> And how should Dorothea not marry?—a girl so handsome and with such prospects? Nothing could hinder it but her love of extremes, and her insistence on regulating life according to notions which might cause a wary man to hesitate before he made her an offer, or even might lead her at last to refuse all offers. A young lady of some birth and fortune, who knelt suddenly down on a brick floor by the side of a sick labourer and prayed fervidly as if she thought herself living in the time of the Apostles—who had strange whims of fasting like a Papist, and of sitting up at night to read old theological books! (6-7)[1]

Loving extremes, Dorothea seems unlikely to be accepted as, or accepting of, a match. The problem is not only that her excesses threaten to make her unacceptable. The difficulty also lies in the fact that she does not want a "match." Sir James Chettam is unthinkable as a husband for Dorothea precisely because he is so agreeable: "an amiable handsome baronet, who said 'Exactly' to her remarks even when she expressed uncertainty—how could he affect her as a lover?" (7-8).

[1] George Eliot, *Middlemarch*, ed. Gordon S. Haight (Boston: Houghton Mifflin, 1956). All references are to this edition, and page numbers are cited in the text.

Dorothea's desire is not a desire to be met but a desire to be exceeded by something larger than herself.

Her mind was theoretic, and yearned by its nature after some lofty conception of the world which might frankly include the parish of Tipton and her own rule of conduct there; she was enamoured of intensity and greatness, and rash in embracing whatever seemed to her to have those aspects; likely to seek martyrdom, to make retractations, and then to incur martyrdom after all in a quarter where she had not sought it. (6)

Theoretic rather than realistic, Dorothea desires an idea rather than an object and marries, in Casaubon, an ideal rather than a man. This is a mistake, a mistake due to her idealistic yearnings; but the narrative does not resolve the mistake in realistic terms. For Dorothea turns around and marries, in Will Ladislaw, a second husband who is also more an idea than a man. This is not so much the fault of Dorothea, perhaps, as of George Eliot, who simply never, as critics point out, presents Ladislaw as a convincingly realistic character.[2] But if Ladislaw is considered a failure on George Eliot's part, he is a "failure" congruent with Dorothea's own need to idealize characters.

Middlemarch insists, however, that we reconsider our sense of both failure and success. Dorothea's theoretic mind may

[2] U. C. Knoepflmacher suggests that "If Ladislaw's unsatisfactoriness persists, this is so, not because of his unsuitability as Dorothea's husband, but because, as a character, he serves too many different roles in the novel's ideological scheme." See *Religious Humanism and the Victorian Novel: George Eliot, Walter Pater, and Samuel Butler* (Princeton: Princeton University Press, 1965), p. 96. This is to suggest that Eliot is more concerned with relations of characters to larger structures of experience in the novel than with individual or independent selves. Mark Schorer also suggests that characters in *Middlemarch* suffer a lack of substance because Eliot's "view of character in general" insists that character changes in relation to others and in relation to circumstances. Because they are subject to such changes, then, characters are necessarily less complete or substantial than realistic demands allow. See "The Structure of the Novel: Method, Metaphor and Mind," in *"Middlemarch": Critical Approaches to the Novel*, ed. Barbara Hardy (New York: Oxford University Press, 1967), pp. 18-20.

imply her alienation, since ideas are not men; and in this the
novel may seem realistic. Georg Lukács, for example, identifies
the form of the realistic novel with the form of human desire
that seeks satisfaction in a world inadequate to satisfy it.[3] As
in the Freudian reality principle, human desire and the real
world are discovered to be incommensurable. *Middlemarch*,
however, though it discovers such incommensurability, affirms it rather than identifying it with frustration. If Dorothea
is typical of heroes and heroines in that she does not settle
for things as they are and, like Saint Theresa, to whom she is
compared, sees the world in unrealistic terms, she also, like
Theresa, has an "unrealistic" power to change things into
something different. This is clear, for example, in the effect
she has on Will Ladislaw:

> He felt, when he parted from her, that the brief words
> by which he had tried to convey to her his feeling . . .
> would only profit by their brevity when Dorothea had to
> interpret them: he felt that in her mind he had found his
> highest estimate. (565-66)

Those who respond to Dorothea's power thus become something different, and something more, than they are in themselves. Her power is not, then, a matter of assuming control
over others but a process of becoming part of others and so
changing and extending the meaning of both herself and
others. Thus her power is generative rather than controlling
of meaning; and it in fact depends on her own and others'
willingness to "let go" of meaning. As the above passage
suggests, Will does not control or even know the part of his
meaning that lies in her mind. But his increase of value depends
on allowing his meaning to go out of bounds and out of his
possession. What he is in himself and what he is in Dorothea

---

[3] Lukács insists that in the novel, unlike the epic, the central experience of
seeking takes place only in incommensurable terms. The disintegrated civi-
lization offers no fulfillment of the individual's desire to find his or her place
in the world, and there is no correspondence between the individual's goals
and the surrounding world. See *The Theory of the Novel*, trans. Anna Bostock
(Cambridge: M.I.T. Press, 1971), especially pp. 56-58.

are in these ways incommensurable. But the incommensurability constitutes an increase, not a loss.

This is the relation with the world for which Dorothea yearns. But it is an unsettling relation, unsettling because it demands that meaning be allowed to exceed knowledge and possession. If in the above passage, for example, Dorothea interprets Ladislaw's words to have a meaning he does not even know, it is difficult to say whether the meaning belongs to him or her. Thus we, confronted with such meaning, cannot say who means it. Dorothea's authority to create meaning—like the authority of Pamela and Clarissa—is an authority that is not exactly her own: it is dependent on others and inseparable from such dependence, a matter of corresponding differences rather than of control. More explicitly in *Middlemarch* than in Richardson's novels, however, the interdependence and indeterminacy of meaning which result demand that knowledge and determination be given up. Rather than learning to acknowledge reality, Dorothea learns to deny the limits that knowledge imposes on experience. She proceeds according to the belief that things can be different because she believes them to be different. And the narrator works with her in this. For the narrative consistently evades and undermines knowledge, insisting that we cannot know all that is meaningful but that we can make room for it if we do not limit ourselves to knowledge.

The narrative itself thus becomes hard to take at its word. The narrator is always conscious of the misrepresentation of any representation and insists on the incommensurability of representation and reality and the incommensurability of different representations. Her prose often exceeds the bounds of logical representation and thus precludes any understanding that would determine meaning. On the other hand, the narrator often is difficult to understand not because she gives us indeterminate prose but because, in another sense, she represents as meaningful something that we are accustomed to view as a loss of meaning. Perhaps the most familiar example of the difficulty readers have accepting her words at face value is the resistance they tend to feel to the conclusion of the novel. The narrator insists that Dorothea gets what she wants:

> No life would have been possible to Dorothea which was not filled with emotion, and she had now a life filled also with a beneficent activity which she had not the doubtful pains of discovering and marking out for herself. . . . Dorothea could have liked nothing better, since wrongs existed, than that her husband should be in the thick of a struggle against them, and that she should give him wifely help. Many who knew her, thought it a pity that so substantive and rare a creature should have been absorbed into the life of another, and be only known in a certain circle as a wife and mother. But no one stated exactly what else that was in her power she ought rather to have done. . . . (610-11)

"Absorbed into the life of another," Dorothea has achieved what she wished for at the beginning of the novel: to be part of something larger than her own life. That this incommensurable relation of self and world is difficult to accept as fulfillment is recognized by the narrator's reference to those characters who cannot accept it as such. In order to accept what the narrator is saying about Dorothea, we must recognize that those characters "who knew her" are incapable of accepting what she is. It is knowledge that fails here as Dorothea succeeds, for knowledge fails to make room for the incommensurable differences she values.

The problem here, then, is not that others do not get to know Dorothea. The problem is that we do not recognize the value of the unknowable. Dorothea's effect on the world is "incalculably diffusive" and thus cannot be known because knowledge is a matter of calculation and determination. Yet knowledge is also, therefore, an interpretation of reality; it is one limited representation among other possible interpretations, such as the narrator's own. One of the means Eliot uses to insist on the indeterminacy of meaning in *Middlemarch* is her recognition that meaning is always a matter of interpretation. It is a major concern of the narrative to represent not only what happens to characters but how other characters interpret what happens. And the multiple interpretations undermine the possibility of knowledge, even though knowledge, as in the above passage, is claimed by some. Those who know Dorothea always identify her, however, in terms that place her out of bounds. She is known as someone who cannot be understood, for example. Thus the only way to know or determine her meaning is to determine it as excessive. The terms of knowledge, therefore, exclude her from knowledge, but in doing so they also claim to define her and to limit her meaning by ruling it out of bounds. It is because of the exclusive terms of knowledgeable interpretation that Eliot insists that it is a particularly inadequate interpretation.

The only way to represent Dorothea's meaning as significant is to represent her in indeterminate terms. This is what the narrative does. I will be considering in this chapter how the narrator's commitment to indeterminate meaning that exceeds the bounds of knowledge revises our conceptions of truth, of power, and of authority. Insisting that none of these phenomena is itself knowable, because they really exceed the orderly limits of knowledge, Eliot also insists that none of them be considered a matter of control. Like Dorothea's power, the narrator's power does not impose limits on meaning but attempts to open up the possibilities of meaning. Doing this, she insists on the increased potential of meaning, for such meaning is always subject to change. In order to indicate the mutual concerns of Dorothea and her narrator, I will consider the excesses they have in common. From the very beginning of the narrative, Dorothea is represented by the narrator in terms that allow for her excesses; and thus Eliot suggests an alternative to other characters' interpretations of Dorothea's behavior that rule out those excesses.

Consistently interpreted as outside the bounds of proper behavior, Dorothea is unacceptable at times because she gets carried away and goes too far, and at other times because she falls short of the standards of propriety. As the Prelude puts it, her behavior is seen alternately as "extravagance" and "lapse" by those around her. Kneeling on laborers' floors and fasting might be interpreted with equal ease either way. But whichever way Dorothea is interpreted, she is too much to take. Her excesses and others' responses to them suggest again Geoffrey Hartman's "redundancy principle," cited in the chapter on *Pamela*. Hartman's thesis that poetic language is indeterminate emphasizes that its excesses can be read in two ways: "Poetry either says too much—approaches the inexpressible—or too little—approaches the inexpressive." On whichever side one sees it, there is always an excess, and this is what "allows, if it does not actually compel, interpretation."[4] Such meaning demands interpretation, but it precludes knowledge. Dorothea's behavior is similarly excessive, indeterminate, and demanding. But others do not respond to that demand, for it demands too much: that her meaning depends on them and thus that they take part in uncertain meaning.

We are not accustomed to seeing people as poems, of course, nor is the world of *Middlemarch*, which tends to interpret Dorothea as without worth because she exceeds determinate worth. With no more practical use than a poem, Dorothea is responded to by other characters with some version of Mrs. Cadwallader's " 'I throw her over' " (45). Impractical and unrealistic, she is identified with waste because there is nothing to be done with her. But Will Ladislaw's insistence to her that " 'You *are* a poem' " (166) suggests that the difficulty of saying what she is is a difficulty crucial to her extraordinary value. Clearly, for Ladislaw, Dorothea's excesses do not exceed but extend the bounds of meaning to include "incalculably diffusive" effects. Dorothea's excesses, like the excesses of poetic language, are what make her meaningful, precisely because her meaning is incalculable: indeterminate and changeable.

"Likely to seek martyrdom, to make retractations, and then to incur martyrdom after all in a quarter where she had not sought it" (6), Dorothea is repeatedly "martyred" not because she is "true" to certain beliefs but because she is inconsistent,

---

[4] Geoffrey H. Hartman, "The Voice of the Shuttle: Language from the Point of View of Literature," in *Beyond Formalism: Literary Essays 1958-1970* (New Haven: Yale University Press, 1970), pp. 347, 339.

not true at all if truth is unchanging. She will seek martyrdom
by sacrificing her youth and intensity to Casaubon, regret it,
then sacrifice her estate to marry Will Ladislaw. She will "be
spoken of to a younger generation as a fine girl who married
a sickly clergyman, old enough to be her father, and in little
more than a year after his death gave up her estate to marry
his cousin—young enough to have been his son, with no property, and not well-born" (612). From this point of view, Dorothea does not "get" anywhere; rather, she proceeds by veer-
ing from one extreme to the other, neither of which is
satisfactory in others' eyes. According to the gossip of Middlemarch, "she could not have been 'a nice woman,' else she
would not have married either the one or the other" (612).
Inconsistent but also repetitive from this point of view, Dorothea's marriages go too far in opposite directions to be acceptable. She is outside the bounds of propriety either way,
having missed the happy mean of proper behavior.

   If in this case she goes too far, in other cases she does not
go far enough to be acceptable. In the first scene of the novel,
Celia asks Dorothea to divide with her the jewels left them
by their mother. Indifferent to the jewelry on religious principles, Dorothea at first seeks a sort of martyrdom by giving
up all claim to them. But she retracts when she sees the emeralds, which are the best pieces in the collection. She puts
them on, "all the while . . . trying to justify her delight in the
colours by merging them in her mystic religious joy" (10).
The merger, however, is not successful in Celia's eyes: "she
repeated to herself that Dorothea was inconsistent: either she
should have taken her full share of the jewels, or, after what
she had said, she should have renounced them altogether"
(11). Dorothea, who does neither, thus incurs an unlooked-
for martyrdom, subject to Celia's interpretation that she has
things both ways in her effort to combine her mixed feelings
rather than choose between them. Here again, she gets nowhere. She is wrong both at the beginning and the end, and,
in addition, her behavior lacks resolution because she cannot
carry through either alternative but tries to combine them. In
order to satisfy Celia, Dorothea would have to do one thing

or the other. Yet she remains in between the two alternatives that Celia sees as mutually exclusive. She takes part of the jewels, so beautiful that her pleasure in them may be merged with religious feeling, and thus allows herself part of both the jewels and the religious joy.

In the case of the marriages, Dorothea's alternations go too far; she lacks any middle ground. In the case of the jewels, her sense of alternatives seems itself to be lacking, so that she falls short of proper distinctions, in the midst of undistinguished differences. In both instances, whether going too far or falling short of the boundaries of proper meaning, her behavior seems redundant. Others cannot make sense of her because she does things that do not fit together, either logically or chronologically. She is inconsistent, and she does not get anywhere with others, because one action neither agrees with nor leads to the next.

But to Dorothea's disparities are added the disparities of others, for in both cases it is others' interpretations that make her behavior unsatisfactory. Differences in her own behavior are compounded by differences between her self and her beholders as the narrative shifts among differing points of view. Others' interpretations make distinctions where Dorothea does not; their distinctions are exclusive, and her sense of difference is inclusive. Yet the representation of her husbands as one "old enough to be her father" and the other "young enough to have been his son" suggests that exclusive distinctions are more a matter of representation than reality. For one might say that Casaubon is old enough to be her father and Ladislaw is her own age. But then Dorothea would not be represented as consistently out of bounds; she would be even more difficult to place. Exclusive distinctions enable representation to avoid such confusions. But the representation of distinctions avoids the reality that the narrator is attempting to represent: a reality in which differences and inconsistencies abound without being contained by the limits of clear distinction and agreement. The clarification of differences depends on representations that the narrator is unwilling to make with any consistency.

The Prelude to the novel prepares us for this when comparing modern women to the martyr Saint Theresa. The description insists on their similarities but also insists that the difference between them is the difference between agreement and difference themselves. Modern women are different because of the irreconcilable disparities in their lives:

> Many Theresas have been born who found for themselves no epic life wherein there was a constant unfolding of far-resonant action; perhaps only a life of mistakes, the offspring of a certain spiritual grandeur ill-matched with the meanness of opportunity; perhaps a tragic failure which found no sacred poet and sank unwept into oblivion. With dim lights and tangled circumstance they tried to shape their thought and deed in noble agreement; but after all, to common eyes their struggles seemed mere inconsistency and formlessness; for these later-born Theresas were helped by no coherent social faith and order which could perform the function of knowledge for the ardently willing soul. Their ardour alternated between a vague ideal and the common yearning of womanhood; so that the one was disapproved as extravagance, and the other condemned as a lapse. (3)

Such lives are unfitting and "ill-matched": formless, without coherence, without agreement between spirit and opportunity or thought and deed. The inability to find any object or objective that meets the subjects' spiritual grandeur is due to multiple causes: to circumstances, to others' interpretations, and to the lack of anything that functions as knowledge. Because they do not *know*, such women not only lack the means of integrating thought and action but also lack the means of knowing whether such integrity is possible. With no fitting object for their ardor, they shift between two incommensurable relations to the world. In one, ardor goes too far to be suitable to others, as in Dorothea's rejection of all the jewels according to a "vague ideal." In the other, ardor falls short of suitability to others, as when she takes only the best emeralds in "common yearning" for their beauty.

The alternating behavior of such women and the alternative interpretations of their behavior by others, both of which contribute to the confusion of their experience, are reflected in the prose of the passage. The narrator, like the women she describes, is involved in "irreconcilable disparities" which are represented as shifting alternatives rather than resolved differences. Nothing provides coherence: not the individual, nor her society, nor those who observe her, nor the narrator. For, like Dorothea in her marriages or in the scene with the jewels, the narrator alternates among rather than choosing between alternatives. We are told, for example, that for any of the possible kinds of failure, there are different explanations: others do not understand such women, and they themselves do not know what they are doing. If we want to choose between these alternative explanations, we are not allowed to do so. For the sentence actually says that others do not understand these women *because* they themselves do not know what they are doing, making the alternative explanations dependent on each other.

> With dim lights and tangled circumstance they tried to shape their thought and deed in noble agreement; but after all, to common eyes their struggles seemed mere inconsistency and formlessness; for these later-born Theresas were helped by no coherent social faith and order which could perform the function of knowledge for the ardently willing soul. (3)

This is not logical; the three statements do not fit together to give us a clear sense of causality. They seem to be out of order, and we thereby alternate among explanations rather than distinguishing specific causes and effects. The prose itself is redundant: it either says too little or says too much to be knowledgeable.

We can read the Prelude, therefore, as about the narrator as well as about her heroine. For the narrator, too, finds in her narrative "no epic life wherein there was a constant unfolding of far-resonant action"; and her efforts, too, often seem "mere inconsistency and formlessness," as in this passage. She represents meaning by a process that shifts meaning: from one point of view to another, from one point in time to another, and among all points so that they cannot be seen as points of a logical progression. The narrator's authority will not be used in *Middlemarch* to impose order. It will instead authorize the recognition of incommensurable differences whose representation exceeds the bounds of orderly prose. The project of the narrator, as her prose suggests, is not to create an alternative form of secure meaning that can take the place of knowledge. It is to insist on the greater significance of meaning that includes insecure and "undistinguished" differences; and so, including multiple alternatives, it precludes an alternative order.

Though *Middlemarch* is supposed to be a "masterpiece" of Victorian fiction, the project I have been describing is a project that disables any mastery of meaning and precludes any formal ordering of meaning. By considering the differences between the meaning that *Middlemarch* offers and the meaning we traditionally expect to find in a realistic novel, I wish to suggest here the potential of *Middlemarch* to change our assumptions about realistic meaning. The mastery we associate with "masterworks of Victorian fiction" lies in their ability to integrate multiple characters, places, events, and actions into a consistent whole. In *Middlemarch*, J. Hillis Miller says,

> a fragment is examined as a "sample" of the larger whole of which it is a part, though the whole impinges on the part as the "medium" within which it lives. . . . Eliot's strategy of totalization is to present individual character or event in the context of that wider medium and to affirm universal laws of human behavior in terms of characters. . . .[5]

5 J. Hillis Miller, "Optic and Semiotic in *Middlemarch*," in *The Worlds of Victorian Fiction*, ed. Jerome H. Buckley (Cambridge: Harvard University Press, 1975), pp. 126-27.

This suggests that the novel both presents each separate character and event as part of a whole and presents the whole truths about experience that are recognizable in each of the characters and events; in this way it would attempt a "totalization" of meaning. In realistic novels, then, the correspondence between parts and whole provides consistency and stability. Their integration settles meaning by allowing us to know the differences as parts of a larger assimilating structure that is implicit in each different part.

Such a narrative would provide what Leo Bersani calls a "commanding structure of significance": "Realistic fiction serves nineteenth-century society by providing it with strategies for containing (and repressing) its disorder within significantly structured stories about itself."[6] Bersani perceives the realistic novel as an even greater exercise of power than does Miller, for he sees it tolerating disorderly differences in order to demonstrate its capacity to contain even disorder. But Eliot exceeds this power, too, as she insists on the partial and indefinite nature of both experience and authority in her narrative.

Eliot does not see her world as an orderly structure. She sees it as a "web," one which she is "unravelling": "I at least have so much to do in unravelling certain human lots, and seeing how they were woven and interwoven, that all the light I can command must be concentrated on this particular web, and not dispersed over that tempting range of relevancies called the universe" (105). Such an image implies much more openness and diversity than an orderly structure of integrated parts. For the web implies a suspension rather than a determination of meaning. Various elements of experience in the novel are bound together as related differences, but, as in a web, the "lines" of the narrative are both bound together at points and go in different directions, converging with and diverging from other lines. There are multiple intersections, but the lines do not go in a single direction and are not clearly

[6] Leo Bersani, *A Future for Astyanax: Character and Desire in Literature* (Boston: Little, Brown, 1976), pp. 53, 63.

traceable to a single beginning. The meaning is thus suspended in midair, without grounds or with multiple grounds, and held in suspension by the interdependent binding of its parts that makes distinction impossible, and logical and causal connections unclear. This is not the sort of binding that a traditional or containing plot entails, because binding differences within a masterful plot creates a tension that is finally, and only finally, discharged.[7] Eliot's prose, on the other hand, creates tensions that are confusing and unresolved, with differences mixing together and changing each other as they proceed to change independently as well. Differences intensify differences rather than being discharged of difference eventually or with any finality. Moreover, a web has holes in it— open spaces in which the lines can fluctuate. To choose to represent meaning as a web is to insist that some meaning is left open.[8]

The characteristics of a web of meaning are suggested by the narrator's description of the mobile society she is concerned with. In a passage which functions as a historical and social overview, and which thus might be expected to provide "background" for the particular events of the novel, Eliot

[7] Here again I am indebted to Peter Brooks's discussion of narrative plots as forms of Freudian mastery in "Freud's Masterplot: Questions of Narrative," *Yale French Studies*, no. 55/56 (1977), 280-300.

[8] Critics tend to regard Eliot's "web" of meaning as an attempt to unify and complete meaning. Thus Mark Schorer, though recognizing that the various stories in the novel are connected by "a thin and wavering line of relationships," emphasizes the "wholeness" we recognize in the conception of the novel ("The Structure of the Novel," pp. 12, 24). Knoepflmacher gives an interesting description of the "organic" and "three-dimensional web" but emphasizes finally the "balance" of the novel as a whole (*Religious Humanism*, pp. 72, 114). J. Hillis Miller considers the "metaphor of the web" as one of numerous metaphors whose multiple presence undermines the meaning of any single metaphor. But his argument, too, rests on the assumption that Eliot attempts to "totalize" meaning. See "Optic and Semiotic in *Middlemarch*," pp. 129-37. Barbara Hardy, however, though she perceives Eliot as moving from particulars to moral generalizations, considers the novel as more open-ended than most critics do. She emphasizes the "diffused structure" of a pattern that is "rotating" in the novel. See *The Novels of George Eliot: A Study in Form* (London: Athlone Press, 1959), pp. 96-108.

chooses to use historical and cultural perspectives to insist on
the reality of fluctuating meaning rather than to provide secure
grounds for meaning.

> Old provincial society had its share of this subtle move-
> ment: had not only its striking downfalls, its brilliant
> young professional dandies who ended by living up an
> entry with a drab and six children for their establishment,
> but also those less marked vicissitudes which are con-
> stantly shifting the boundaries of social intercourse, and
> begetting new consciousness of interdependence. Some
> slipped a little downward, some got higher footing . . . ;
> some were caught in political currents, some in ecclesi-
> astical, and perhaps found themselves surprisingly
> grouped in consequence; while a few personages or fam-
> ilies that stood with rocky firmness amid all this fluctua-
> tion, were slowly presenting new aspects in spite of so-
> lidity, and altering with the double change of self and
> beholder. (70-71)

It is not possible to determine meaning in this passage. As in
the passage quoted from the Prelude, in which one disparity
is considered in relation only to other disparities, here changes
are identified only in relation to other changes. There are no
stable grounds in opposition to which difference and change
can be defined as different. Changes are differentiated from
more or less marked changes but not from any stable element.
Differences, then, are not distinctly different from anything.
No single element of society is absolutely distinguished from
another. Not only are all elements of society shifting, but they
are shifting interdependently. So that not only can none be
distinguished as unchanging, but none can be distinguished
as independent of other changing elements. Because the parts
of the process are not separated, there is no way to distinguish
cause and effect; therefore, causality cannot be determined
either. No difference causes another difference; things change
together, responding to each other. Moreover, individuals do
not determine their positions in this situation. They do not

even have positions that hold but are placed involuntarily and surprisingly, caught and carried by currents into places that keep moving. Those who stand firm change even as they stand firm. And if distinctions are precluded by the interdependence of differences, such confusions are compounded by the indistinction of changes in "self and beholder." The "double change of self and beholder" itself entails changes, presumably in addition to those already described, even as it makes it impossible to locate the source in one or the other. Thus all elements of the society and its meaning are bound to others, but not in any way that limits differences.

And the prose, like the situation it represents, remains in flux. This writing refuses to impose determination. On the one hand, virtually all the statements are intransitive or passive constructions that implicitly disclaim mastery. Things change, or they are changed. On the other hand, in the single statement that is structured clearly as a determination, with a subject, transitive verbs, and objects affected by them, the subject itself is "vicissitudes," the verbs are "shifting" and "begetting," and the objects are matters of "intercourse" and "interdependence." What is affected is in any case a relative condition; and what causes changes are changes that are still occurring. So that even when the construction seems to determine a difference, the difference is rendered indistinct. Grammatical subjects and objects, like self and beholder, are clearly different on one level and inseparable on another, like the "rocky firmness" and the "alteration." Logically, these exclude each other; but they are nevertheless present at the same time in the same things. Meaning, then, gets confused here. The elements of meaning in the prose, like the elements of the society, double up rather than gain distinction as shifting spatial and temporal differences also merge together.

Thus the narrative shifts the boundaries that contain meanings and keep differences separate by making all differences continuously respond to other differences. It generates more meaning than it limits, for all limits are themselves subject to change. Such a passage cannot order or "command" significance, then. This narrative *demands* significance, and this is partly why it is unsettling.

The most essential structure that is given up in *Middlemarch* is the concept of exchange by which we lose one thing and get another in return: especially the exchange of reality for language. Eliot's narrative assumes that language cannot quite *get* reality; the exchange does not occur definitively because there is always something left over, some unrepresented reality or some aspect of the representation that does not fit the reality. What Eliot's narrative attempts is a representation that acknowledges such excesses with prose that leaves itself open to dispute and differences. To say that the narrative demands significance rather than commands significance is to emphasize that it does not complete or attempt to complete the representative exchange. Its demand for meaning, therefore, is not a demand for which there is a definite return possible. Neither demand nor return can be defined: what is demanded is more meaning than can be represented, and the demand can be "met," therefore, only by giving up determination. The relation of representation and meaning is not an exact relation but a relation of excess. Each side of the exchange exceeds the other, so that the meaning is uneasy and unsettling. But, without definitive structures, the narrative gets what it demands: more meaning than we can define. The demand keeps differences differing, even as they are bound together.

The force of *Middlemarch*, therefore, does not lie in mastery. The novel is not a determining order, nor can it be determined as an opposition to order. It does not defeat orders, that is, or work against them, so much as it finds meaning in experience and expression that preclude or ignore order. The novel is not, therefore, a negative enterprise. The meaning of the narrative is difficult to identify except in terms of what it is not, just as Dorothea is difficult to identify except in terms of what she exceeds. That is because we are accustomed to and have words for the orderly structures of novels and fewer words for what works without order. The fact that we can say distinctly only what the narrative and Dorothea are not

is due to the fact that their meaning is not a matter of
distinctions.

The release of meaning from grounds and distinction in this
novel entails the release of all phenomena from definition.
Once this happens, meanings become confused even to the
point of verging on their traditional or conventional opposites.
Knowledge, for example, is not always a matter of form in
Middlemarch; it is also a matter of feeling. This is confusing.
It is confusing in theory, because to call feelings knowledge
is not logical; and it is confusing in practice because feelings
themselves are confused and partial. And the consideration
of knowledge is confusing because the word has different
meanings in different places in the text. Language, as can be
seen in that passage about the mobile society, shifts meaning
rather than structuring or limiting meaning. This is always
confusing. And like the grammatical confusions of subject and
object in that passage, the narrative's representation of the
psychological subject and the objects it perceives is always in
flux. There is no clear distinction between subject and object.
The powerful subject, therefore, represented by Dorothea, is
not a masterful subject; her power is always partial. Thus
even to identify Dorothea as powerful is problematic because,
although she clearly has a powerful effect on others, she never
seems to have power over anyone. Hers is not a power that
determines or masters anything.

Interpretations of the novel, however, tend to resemble the
interpretations of Dorothea in the novel in their refusals to
accept the narrator's inconsistencies. Critics suggest that the
narrator's refusal to make clear distinctions—a tendency, like
Dorothea's, to have things "both ways" at once—results in
kinds of lapse and extravagance. Those who emphasize the
novel's commitment to "the petty medium of Middlemarch"
recognize the novel as a compromise in which Dorothea's
experience falls short of her heroic aspirations. Eliot's attempt
to merge differences can then be seen as part of a "process of
swallowing and assimilating would-be individualists," as potentially distinguished characters lapse into the mediocrity of

a middling society.[9] Other critics see the inconsistencies of the narrative as leading meaning in opposite directions, even to the extent that different meanings are opposed and so cancel out each other's validity. The narrative's differences are so extravagantly different, that is, that we must choose some and not others in order to find meaning. Thus Leo Bersani finds *Middlemarch* working against itself; for, although Eliot recognizes that " 'embroiled' and strained relations . . . are the only connections she can realistically conceive of," she nevertheless "won't abandon the dream of structured significance."[10] Such criticism leads logically to Miller's insistence that the text deconstructs itself, and that this can be seen in "certain all-encompassing metaphors which are proposed as models for Middlemarch society" but do not work as such. For "each group of metaphors is related to the others, fulfilling them, but at the same time contradicting them, canceling them out, or undermining their validity." Thus the narrator's web of meaning is implicitly undermined by the metaphor of vision according to which all views are partial, subjective, and distorted.[11]

Such interpretations use against the text the very means by which it resists both the grounding of meaning and the negation of meaning. To perceive that differences are undistin-

---

[9] John F. Hulcoop, " 'This Petty Medium': In the Middle of *Middlemarch*," in *George Eliot: A Centenary Tribute*, ed. Gordon S. Haight and Rosamary T. VanArsdel (Totowa, N.J.: Barnes and Noble, 1982), p. 164. Hulcoop, who identifies the medium of prose in the novel with the "petty medium of Middlemarch," insists that the narrative's "epic aspirations are persistently undermined by the petty medium in which it has its existence, and by the prosaic conditions of an imperfect social state against which it struggles" (p. 164).

[10] Bersani, *A Future for Astyanax*, p. 64.

[11] Miller, "Optic and Semiotic in *Middlemarch*," p. 128. The text, Miller says, "suggests that one gets a different kind of totality depending on what metaphorical model is used. The presence of several incompatible models brings into the open the arbitrary and partial character of each and so ruins the claim of the narrator to have a total, unified, and impartial vision" (144). In an earlier article, "Narrative and History," *ELH*, 41, no. 3 (1974), 455-73, Miller considers the "self-defeating turning back of the novel to undermine its own ground" in the context of Eliot's treatment of history (p. 462).

guished and so the heroine must be middling is to suggest a loss of meaning; to perceive a deconstructive standoff is to suggest that meanings are neutralized. It is true that the narrative refuses to separate meaning from its medium; and thus all meanings are parts of other meanings rather than distinct or free. But the novel does not want distinction or freedom. It demands commitment: the commitment of meanings to each other rather than to an end beyond the means. It is also true that the narrative is arbitrary and partial. But this refusal to ground meaning enables meaning to occur as a process that commits meanings to each other rather than to an origin or end. Demanding significance without grounds, *Middlemarch* demands that all differences become parts of meaning that never stops or determines meaning but constantly generates more meaning. *Middlemarch* undermines grounds because the security of grounds is itself recognized as a loss of meaning. Partiality, moreover, entails a gain of meaning. The narrator's web is admittedly partial; but that is what commits her to its meaning. This precludes any objective representation or history because those forms preclude the kinds of commitment Eliot values.

The narrative's insistence on including multiple differences insists that representation exceed the bounds of history. Recognizing the variables that contribute to meaning, Eliot recognizes the difficulty of telling the story of any person or event. Lydgate, for example, is introduced "at a starting-point which makes a man's career a fine subject for betting." And "the risk would remain, even with close knowledge of Lydgate's character; for character too is a process and an unfolding" (111). Knowledge of character, then, would provide no security, for character changes. Extending the meaning of Lydgate's character beyond his or anyone's determination, the narrator insists that its discovery can be neither straightforward nor steady. For his meaning will shift, because it is subject to shifting external elements, "the thwartings and furtherings of circumstance," as well as to different internal elements that can go different ways: "both virtues and faults capable of shrinking or expanding" (111). Because of both external and internal differences that differ constantly and can go in different directions, character is impossible to predict or historicize.

Moreover, not only the self but the beholder changes. The interdependence of characters and circumstances is complicated, as the narrator warns us, by the dependence of what is seen on who is seeing it and from what point of view. And the narrator's point of view shifts around. That anything may be seen in multiple ways and interpreted differently, even by the same person, is re-emphasized repeatedly as the narrator takes different points of view herself and allows those of her characters to change. At times, the narrator insists that one point of view is as valid as another. But such inclusiveness does not provide consistency. As in the passage quoted about the mobile society, the recognition of multiple and mobile meaning increases the fluctuations of meaning.

The narrator's most abrupt shift of point of view, for example, insists that there is another way of looking at Dorothea's marriage to Casaubon:

> One morning, some weeks after her arrival at Lowick, Dorothea—but why always Dorothea? Was her point of view the only possible one with regard to this marriage? ... In spite of the blinking eyes and white moles objectionable to Celia, and the want of muscular curve which was morally painful to Sir James, Mr. Casaubon had an intense consciousness within him, and was spiritually a-hungered like the rest of us. (205)

Here the inclusion of a different perspective disperses rather than unifies meaning. The narrator not only shifts her ground from Dorothea to Casaubon, but she shifts from one shaky sense of grounds to another. She makes Dorothea's point of view dubious and partial by switching to Casaubon's. But Casaubon's is also made insecure by the allusions to Celia and Sir James. The narrator includes those differences but goes on nevertheless to identify Casaubon as "like the rest of us." So that in the cases of Dorothea and Casaubon, differ-

ences remain partial and inconsistent; and the sense of character is differing but inclusive.

In other shifts of point of view, one perspective may in fact
act as a corrective or completion of another, as in the discussion of Mrs. Cadwallader as a bossy busybody:

> Even with a microscope directed on a water-drop we find
> ourselves making interpretations which turn out to be
> rather coarse; for whereas under a weak lens you may
> seem to see a creature exhibiting an active voracity into
> which other smaller creatures actively play as if they were
> so many animated tax-pennies, a stronger lens reveals to
> you certain tiniest hairlets which make vortices for these
> victims while the swallower waits passively at his receipt
> of custom. In this way, metaphorically speaking, a strong
> lens applied to Mrs. Cadwallader's match-making will
> show a play of minute causes producing what may be
> called thought and speech vortices to bring her the sort
> of food she needed. (44)

In this case, the second perspective is more revealing and
clarifies what was misperceived with the "weak lens." But
what is clarified is not a clear situation. Instead, the closer
look clarifies an interdependence of action that makes it impossible to say who is doing what. Mrs. Cadwallader becomes
passive rather than active in a process that is seen as something
like a whirlpool of thought and speech. This is a process that
cannot be attributed to any one person's behavior and that
proceeds without an object, though it does have an effect. The
"play" of causes and the vortices of thought and speech mean
that causality cannot be identified in determinate terms. Thus,
the weaker lens may distort the reality; but the clearer focus
presents a picture so complex that it cannot be clarified by
means of causal or otherwise discriminate explanation.

The alternations among differing points of view, then, extend and diffuse meaning but do not separate meaning into
distinct parts. Meaning is both taken apart and connected, as
strands of the web both diverge and converge. Thus Eliot
disables the sense of history that the other historian in the

novel, Casaubon, imposes upon the past. He interprets history
as a predictable and unified progression and reduces all differences to variations of a single and knowable truth:

> he had undertaken to show . . . that all the mythical sys-
> tems or erratic mythical fragments in the world were
> corruptions of a tradition originally revealed. Having
> once mastered the true position and taken a firm footing
> there, the vast field of mythical constructions became
> intelligible, nay, luminous with the reflected light of cor-
> respondences. (17-18)

This is what Bersani calls a "commanding structure of significance." Once the fragments are interpreted as corruptions,
even their differences mark the power of the tradition. And
Casaubon limits the significance of differences to what they
have in common with the tradition, thereby managing both
to define their meaning and claim that their differences are
insignificant. For Eliot's narrator, however, the web of meaning is difficult to unravel because no clear origin or truth is
identifiable. Thus no single position is taken exclusively and
no clear pattern can be identified. There are interweavings of
weavings, and there are gaps that separate as well as threads
that tie together the various elements of experience that she
perceives.

The narrator's procedure, unlike Casaubon's, identifies parallels that remain parallel only temporarily and then converge
or diverge. In the following passage, which identifies intellectual passion with sexual passion, a conflation renders differences indistinct:

> Is it due to excess of poetry or stupidity that we are never
> weary of describing what King James called a woman's
> "makdom and her fairnesse," never weary of listening to
> the twanging of the old Troubadour strings, and are com-
> paratively uninterested in that other kind of "makdom
> and fairnesse" which must be wooed with industrious
> thought and patient renunciation of small desires? In the
> story of this passion, too, the development varies: some-

times it is the glorious marriage, sometimes frustration and final parting. And not seldom the catastrophe is bound up with the other passion, sung by the Troubadours. (107)

Presented in terms usually reserved for stories of love between people—"makdom and fairnesse," passion, wooing, marriage, parting—the experience of intellectual desire is rendered familiar by being identified with more common experience. But then, just as the "reflected light of correspondences" that Casaubon works for in his project seems to make the second story clearly and newly intelligible as a version of the first, all clarity is lost by tying the two parallel strands together. No longer parallel, the one is "bound up with the other," compounding the relation between them so that they are no longer distinguishable though not the same either.

As the story of Lydgate proceeds, the confusion is acted out: we are not able to tell which catastrophe—his marriage or his career—causes which, nor whether he or Rosamond is at fault. Disallowing such exclusive alternatives, the narrative suggests something like the vortex that replaces Mrs. Cadwallader as the "active agent" in her experience: mixing things up so that we cannot tell what is causing what or otherwise distinguish them. In the narrator's initial use of historical parallel, the identification of the Spanish martyr and "later-born Theresas," the parallel strands, on the other hand, diverge rather than converge, as more and more disparities are identified in the modern lives. But in divergence the distinction between the two strands becomes as difficult to find as does the distinction of converging passions in the above passage. For diverging differences do not provide exclusive alternatives either. Modern women and Saint Theresa cannot be considered different for any determinate reason.

Whether they converge or diverge, then, such strands of meaning can result in confusions or vortices, in which distinctions whirl around inseparably. Differences seem to collapse together in such cases, although they still remain in tension. Just as often, however, as different narrative lines are conflated, they are thrown out in dispersions and not brought back together. The two paragraphs that contain the above historical "parallels" conclude by letting different possibilities go in different directions. The paragraph that considers love and intellectual passion continues with a discussion of how men's intentions differ from their outcomes and concludes:

> Nothing in the world more subtle than the process of their gradual change! . . . you and I may have sent some of our breath towards infecting them . . . ; or perhaps it came with the vibrations from a woman's glance. (107)

The Prelude concludes: "Here and there is born a Saint Theresa, foundress of nothing, whose loving heart-beats . . . tremble off and are dispersed among hindrances, instead of centering in some long-recognisable deed" (4). Each of these conclusions disperses meaning beyond the focus or recollection of the narrator, insisting that what is meaningful goes beyond her grasp.

The web of meaning in the novel, then, does not allow us to keep track of meaning or keep meaning straight; often it does not allow us to keep meaning at all. Alternately pushing together and pulling apart the kinds of meaning that Casaubon would develop as linear and parallel progressions, the narrator violates the form of traditional history and of meaning itself. Just as Dorothea's behavior is subject to alternating interpretations as lapse and extravagance, the narrative alternately risks collapsing differences and dispersing them so extravagantly that, uncentered, they verge on meaninglessness.

The vortices and dispersions of meaning in the novel insist on the arbitrariness and partiality of the web that the narrator weaves. She picks up some strands of meaning and lets others go; any that are let go might be picked up by someone else if looked for or recollected. But although to "ground" the narrative in the arbitrary is to partialize its meaning and to replace any sense of grounds with partiality, it is this choice that constitutes the generative power of the narrative. For in *Middlemarch* partiality itself is the means by which meaning occurs; and it is a means of generation rather than loss.

Partiality is not a structure. It relates elements of meaning temporarily, unsystematically, and arbitrarily. Insisting on her own arbitrariness and partiality, the narrator in fact evades any formulation or deconstruction; for neither can be applied to the partial or the arbitrary or to unsystematic alternations among differences that cannot be distinguished as opposites. Allying herself with the arbitrary as a partial arbiter of meaning, the narrator indeed makes choices, as an arbiter: choices of a partial and inconsistent will. But such arbitrariness makes possible a concept of meaning that cannot be undermined. For meaning is held together by the very power of partiality, a power that cannot be limited or grounded. For Eliot, arbitrariness and partiality are necessary to meaning rather than faulty grounds of meaning, for it is the commitment of the arbitrary and partial self that is binding here and that binds meaning together. The commitment of the narrator generates meaning: committed, she is bound to the meaning of the narrative and part of its meaning. Though arbitrary and partial, the commitment is irrefutable; it is irrefutable, in fact, because it is arbitrary and partial. It rests on faith and belief which, groundless themselves, cannot be undermined either.

Commitment of this sort defies impartiality and objectivity. The narrator's is not a commitment to truth or knowledge but a commitment of the self to the world as part of the meaning of the world. Partiality does not decide the difference between one thing and another or know such distinctions. But partiality is a difference that makes more differences, since it reinterprets everything in the unique terms of its own partial perspective. And partiality holds meaning together because all the meaning it perceives is relative to the self and part of the self. Thus all differences are bound together. Yet partiality, because recognized as partial—both in the sense that it is prejudiced and in the sense that it is incomplete—commits meaning to differences. Meaning is bound to differ if it is bound by partiality. The arbitrary will that behaves in accordance with its own partiality, rather than being determined by codes of behavior to be consistent and integrated, behaves as Dorothea behaves in the scene with the jewels. Such a will alternates among different possibilities, depending in part on what happens in the world around it. Responding to the sudden appearance of the emeralds, Dorothea changes her mind; she differs in response to other differences. Her will is inconsistent, and the world is inconsistent. But they are bound together as will responds to the world. Thus the partial and arbitrary will is only a part of meaning, but a part always bound to other elements of the world. Meaning is never limited to the self but is never exclusive of the world. Partiality commits to each other the differences that objectivity attempts to separate and thus makes room for the subject that objectivity rules out.

The binding of partiality is uneven, like a web. Interdependent and relative, all meanings are bound to other meanings even as they change. Thus all meanings are also always committed; for they are committed to other meanings *for* their meaning at any given moment. But if differences are bound to other differences, they are not bound by boundaries; they are not limited. Differences converge and diverge and can be unraveled as well as woven together or lost track of, fluctuating in response to the differences made by partiality. If differences are bound in the novel by partiality, then, this means that differences are bound to keep differing. This is a disorderly process of meaning, generating more meaning than distinction can provide in its continuous discovery of differences.

Dorothea's story re-presents a similar discovery of meaning, for her experience is an experience of the power of partiality to create a more meaningful world than others perceive. This is a discovery that depends on the partial nature of the self, on the recognition that any self is only part of its meaning. The concept of binding meaning in the narrative entails, then, a radical revision of the concept of self to which we are accustomed. Heroic desire in this novel is a desire for bondage rather than freedom. In traditional terms, the process that

gives meaning to the self goes in the wrong direction. Dorothea's commitment to others, for example, verges on narcissistic confusions about what she is and what others are.[12] For,
as in Richardson's novels, the meaning of the individual is
suspended rather than determined by the narrative. Any one
character's meaning depends on others and on circumstances
that lie beyond her or his control. Bound to change in relation
to what lies outside the self, the meaning of any character is
beyond determination. The self is given as an inconsistent and

[12] Neil Hertz, in "Recognizing Casaubon," *Glyph* 6 (1979), 24-41, considers narcissism as an issue for both characters and narrator in *Middlemarch*.
Hertz identifies the arbitrary and partial nature of meaning that Miller finds
in the novel in the novel's concept of self. Although Eliot affirms "the consistency of the self as a moral agent," he writes, the novel is in fact unable
to choose between such an "ethically stable notion of the self" and the self
as a "cluster of signs" that is variable in its meaning. Instead, "those two
notions of the self are held in suspension in the novel" (p. 26). Hertz identifies
Dorothea as alternating between a stable and an unstable sense of self, between a sense of self as different and a sense of self identified with the world
around her. And this instability, he suggests, also characterizes the narrator's
alternating presentation of *her* self and her relation to the world of the novel.
    "Writing," says Hertz, "like the self-doubling of narcissism, is disturbing
not simply because it may seem 'self-centered' but because it is both that and
self-dispersing at once" (p. 28). Writing resembles narcissism because of two
kinds of confusion about the identity of the self, then: it may seem an act of
including the world within the self—a kind of introjection—or an act of
dispersing the self into the world—a kind of projection. Hertz recognizes
how the narrator alternately identifies with and separates herself from her
characters and suggests that she withdraws from Dorothea at points because
she recognizes the danger of excesses of sympathy in terms analogous to other
literary experiences of the sublime (pp. 38-40).
    It is true, I think, that Eliot rejects the sort of experience associated with
the sublime: both because such experience is self-centered and because it is
absolutely indeterminate. This becomes more explicit an issue in *Daniel Deronda*. But it seems less clear that Eliot rejects the unstable alternations of
difference and identification that can be identified with narcissism. For the
confusions of identity with others and of differentiation of self and others
are confusions that characterize the narrator and her heroine, not Casaubon.
If both the narrator and Dorothea have consciousnesses "capable of shrinking
and expanding," Casaubon consistently shrinks himself into smaller and
smaller confines. He is "banished," I think, precisely because he lacks the
mobile sense of meaning that characterizes authority in Dorothea and the
narrator.

dependent being whose meaning alters over time and alternates among degrees of identity with and difference from
others.

A character may determine to do something, of course. But
no such determination holds, insofar as no determination prevents change in meaning. Characters do not proceed to do
what they "mean" to do at any given moment. This is to risk
a loss of meaning for some, just as critics may identify the
discrepancy between the narrator's own intentions and ac-
complishments as a discrepancy that undermines meaning.
But, as early as the Prelude, the narrator does not recognize
the disparity of intention and action as a negation of either.
Intention does not ground meaning in this narrative; it is a
part of meaning, but a part in flux rather than a part that
determines meaning. Similarly, knowledge does not determine
character, as the narrator insists when introducing Lydgate.
Characters themselves do not know what they are doing or
what they are going to do. Nor is any character except Casaubon, who is repeatedly identified with death, represented
as separable from other characters. The grounds for determining individual meaning—consistency over time, distinction, and independence—are not grounds in *Middlemarch.*

Like the shifting differences that make Middlemarch what
it is but make it indeterminate, changes alter individual lives
continuously: both changes in the self and changes in circumstances and in those around her or him. We are never given
singular meanings for individuals, and we are not allowed to
identify any character as self-determined. Any difference between what someone means to do and in fact does, moreover,
cannot itself be determined as her or his fault or on any other
grounds. For

in the multitude of middle-aged men who go about their
vocations in a daily course determined for them much in
the same way as the tie of their cravats, there is always
a good number who once meant to shape their own deeds
and alter the world a little. The story of their coming to
be shapen after the average and fit to be packed by the

gross, is hardly ever told even in their consciousness. . . .
Nothing in the world more subtle than the process of
their gradual change! In the beginning they inhaled it
unknowingly: you and I may have sent some of our breath
towards infecting them. . . . (107)

In this discussion of the failure of men who mean to make a
difference in the world, the individual act of determination is
recognized only as a temporary and indeterminant effort. Intention itself changes, for one thing; and it can change un-
intentionally, "unknowingly." The unintentional, moreover,
is more meaningful here than what a man means to do, and
the untold more "telling" than what such a man tells himself.
What is really significant, then, remains unknown and untold.
Occurring "much in the same way as the tie of their cravats,"
the determination of these lives is so indefinite as to include
us as possible determinants, though our involvement is presumably unintentional.

Intention, then, is only a partial and temporary element of
one's meaning, which involves interdependently what one
means to do, what one does or says, and how others respond
to oneself. These elements always differ. Though Will comes
to welcome the disparity between his and Dorothea's minds,
earlier in the novel he is less aware of the difference between
what words mean to him and what they mean to her:

"I suspect that you have some false belief in the virtues
of misery. . . ." Will had gone further than he had intended, and checked himself. But Dorothea's thought was
not taking just the same direction as his own, and she
answered without any special emotion. . . . (163)

Will again feared that he had gone too far; but the
meaning we attach to words depends on our feeling, and
his tone of angry regret had so much kindness in it for
Dorothea's heart . . . that she felt a new sense of gratitude
and answered with a gentle smile. (164)

Here the difference between what Will thinks he is saying and
what Dorothea hears is due to the different contexts of their

thoughts and to the fact that she responds to his tone and intensity rather than to his words. Such differences are neither predictable nor determinable. The variability of the meanings of his speech is compounded by the difference between how far Will "means" to go and how far he in fact goes. He intends something different when he begins to speak than he intends in the middle of the speeches. No one here, then, seems to be in control of meaning or able to determine it; meaning is carried away from intention, and carried in different directions, by Will's emotional involvement in what he is saying and by Dorothea's involvement in her own thoughts. The dispersion of meaning that occurs is also a partialization, for Dorothea does not pay attention to Will's words but only to their passion; and of the passion she does not hear the anger but only the regret, which she can translate as kindness. To identify their verbal exchange as in fact an exchange of tone or feeling rather than words, moreover, is to suggest again that what is not verbalized functions even more meaningfully than words. This is true even though it also seems that the interpretation of feeling is even more partial and arbitrary than the interpretation of words. To open up the realm of meaning to include the unspoken, as in the passage quoted earlier about middle-aged men, and to include what is not expressed by language, is greatly to increase the possibilities of interpretation.

To replace knowledge with interpretation is itself a partialization of meaning. And this is augmented by the partiality of feelings that generate particular interpretations:

> in girls of sweet, ardent nature, every sign is apt to conjure up wonder, hope, belief, vast as a sky, and coloured by a diffused thimbleful of matter in the shape of knowledge. They are not always too grossly deceived; for Sinbad himself may have fallen by good-luck on a true description, and wrong reasoning sometimes lands poor mortals in right conclusions: starting a long way off the true point, and proceeding by loops and zigzags, we now and then arrive just where we ought to be. Because Miss Brooke

was hasty in her trust, it is not therefore clear that Mr.
Casaubon was unworthy of it. (18)

Interpretation functions here by a process incompatible with
any definitive knowledge. This is a process that can be described only vaguely: it is "apt" to deal in conjury, which is
groundless, and in the conjury of attitudes that are also ungrounded. The ardent nature interprets signs in terms of wonder, hope, and belief "coloured" by something "in the shape
of knowledge," something both miniscule and diffused and
not knowledge itself. Unknowing, such a process is also unknowable, and the passage proceeds by a method analogous
to the "interpretation of one metaphor by another metaphor"
that Miller recognizes as "characteristic of Eliot's use of figure."[13] Interpretation is not contrasted to more dependable
means of discovering meaning. Instead, luck, wrong reasoning, and loops and zigzags are brought in, and their possible
efficacy corroborates the undependable, unpredictable, and
haphazard possibilities of wonder, hope, and belief. Moreover, if Dorothea's trust in Casaubon is a mistake, it is not
necessarily because that trust is groundless. In fact, the burden
of value is finally shifted here from the process of interpretation to the object of interpretation, as if the invalidity of
the one might lie in the inadequacy of the other. Her interpretation is hasty and groundless, but he is not necessarily
unworthy of it.

To state the situation in this way is to suggest that the
meaning given by means of wonder, hope, and belief is more,
and worth more, than what can be known. Dorothea certainly
cannot know Casaubon by such means. For knowledge limits
the meaning of things to what things are, whereas wonder,
hope, and belief make more of things than they are. Knowledge also limits meaning to characteristics that can be demonstrated. To say that what things are is demonstrable is to
say that meaning lies in what we all can "see," either physically
or logically. Knowledge, then, is established in impartial terms
and is always a form of agreement. But Dorothea's vision does

13 Miller, "Optic and Semiotic in *Middlemarch*," pp. 133-34.

not see things that are demonstrable; she uses "wrong reasoning" rather than clear logic. And she does not agree with
others about what can be seen: " 'You always see what nobody else sees,' " Celia tells her, " 'yet you never see what is
quite plain' " (27).

Hers is a vision that refuses to know meaning, one that is,
in fact, dependent on blindness:

> She was blind, you see, to many things obvious to
> others—likely to tread in the wrong places, as Celia had
> warned her; yet her blindness to whatever did not lie in
> her own pure purpose carried her safely by the side of
> precipices where vision would have been perilous with
> fear. (273)

Here Eliot risks presenting Dorothea in terms that suggest a
likeness to Casaubon: a heroine with a "pure" purpose who
refuses to see what lies outside that purpose. But Dorothea's
purity is not a matter of singularity or determination. Her
vision is pure in its partiality. Hers is not, that is to say, a
blindness that could enable her to master meaning, for mastery
depends on repressing our dependence on an undependable
world. We master the fear that we will not be satisfied by
such a world by discovering our independence from it. But
Dorothea's is a blindness that precedes repression in the Freudian development of self. She retains the more primitive blindness that is associated by Freud with a narcissistic confusion
of self and world and remains blind to the boundaries that
conventionally separate the self from others. She perceives her
meaning as part of something greater than her self; and the
inconsistency of that meaning is not a source of anxiety because it is bound to others even as it changes. As long as
Dorothea can identify herself with others, she has no fear, for
fear comes only with the recognition of separation.

Dorothea's partiality, then, does not know anything at all;
it precludes the recognition of distinctions on which knowledge depends and it recognizes meanings in feelings rather
than judgment. The novel can be said to "regress" on two
counts here: the powerful self is identified as dependent rather

than independent, and knowledge is replaced by feelings. Thus Dorothea cannot tell Celia the story of herself and Will: " 'you would have to feel with me, else you would never know' " (602). The telling relation depends on partiality, both in the narrator and the listener. Dorothea thus insists that partiality constitutes meaning and demands that our conception of knowledge be extended beyond any means of determination.

There is thus no objectivity to Dorothea's vision; nor does her vision know or see things as objects. In knowledge, as in seeing, we assume the distinction of subject and object: the object is there to be seen as it is. Interpretation, however, changes the object, making it something different than it is on its own. Its meaning depends on the subject; and so the meaning of the object cannot be separated from the subject. Meaning is carried away from the object into the subject, too; and so distinction and determination are both given up. In order for Casaubon to be worthy of Dorothea's interpretation, then, he would have to be able to be more than he is and allow his meaning to depend on her.

This suggests how interpretation opens up the process of meaning, the meaning of individuals as well as of other phenomena, as it carries meaning away from determination and grounds. Knowledge must have grounds. Interpretation requires no grounds at all and is always partial. But whereas possibilities of knowledge are limited, "interpretations are illimitable" (18). Dependent on partiality, interpretations, like feelings, get carried away from any referent, as happens in the conversation between Dorothea and Will quoted earlier. Dorothea's interpretation of Casaubon is similarly far removed from any objective aspects of Casaubon. But the interpretation is not mistaken until Casaubon fails to respond to it except by rejecting Dorothea. For in Eliot's interdependent process of meaning, interpretation is itself a means of meaning.

Will Ladislaw becomes more than he is because of Dorothea's interpretive capacity: "he felt that in her mind he had found his highest estimate" (566). And Dorothea finds her own meaning increased by him, because "Ladislaw always seemed to see more in what she said than she herself saw"

(265). These are not knowledgeable relations; the characters do not know but "estimate" each other. In order to have one's meaning expanded by others, one must give up being known and give up self-possession, open the boundaries of the self to include others and so become dependent on others for meaning. Dorothea's belief in others is binding, therefore, though it is groundless. Such people "bind us over to rectitude and purity by their pure belief about us" (565). The power of her belief in others is "one of the great powers of her womanhood" (565), but it is both generative and demanding. It demands that meanings be "responsible," but responsible to pure belief. Generating a demand as well as a gift, the purity of her belief replaces exchange with a pure relation. The grounds and the referents of meaning she gives cannot be distinguished; it is not possible to say whose meaning it is, for each person is part of it. She does not give something that Will gets; she believes something that enables him to believe something. These beliefs have no grounds but are committed to, or dependent on, each other. Her belief is sheer credit; his increase or profit lies in her. It is not possible to secure such meaning by identifying grounds for it or by separating subject from object. And the relation is pure, or purely relative, by reason of such indivisibility. The meaning of interpretation depends on both subject and object but belongs to and originates in neither exclusively. Meaning is freed from determination; but it binds others to the purity of dispossessed meaning, without distinction or determination.

Dorothea herself is subject to others, and her behavior is determined partly by external circumstances, as is every individual's according to the narrator: "for there is no creature whose inward being is so strong that it is not greatly determined by what lies outside it" (612). Yet Dorothea desires this condition, and her demands to be useful, even to be used by others, make it impossible to identify her power with any sort of mastery. In fact, her power is identified in terms usually associated with powerlessness. Freedom, for example, is something she doesn't want:

"What shall I do?" "Whatever you please, my dear:" that
had been her brief history since she had left off learning
morning lessons. . . . Marriage, which was to bring guid-
ance into worthy and imperative occupation, had not yet
freed her from the gentlewoman's oppressive liberty. . . .
(202)

Such a passage emphasizes the dubious nature of Dorothea's
self and of her power. But it does so with language that is
itself dubious, language that tells us two conflicting things at
once: liberty is oppressive, and freedom lies in freedom from
liberty.

Perhaps the most dubious aspect of Dorothea's power is
that she has no sense of independence. She wants someone to
tell her what to do; and if no one tells her what to do she
feels worthless, because she is unable to do anything "on her
own." On the other hand, when Casaubon does decide "to
demand much interest and labour from her" (349), Dorothea
is not satisfied either: "she had thought the work was to be
something greater" (351). In this particular inconsistency, we
can see the confusion of submission and demand that characterizes her, a confusion that makes her difficult to deal with
for characters like Celia and Casaubon. Dorothea wants to
be part of Casaubon's work, but she demands that the work
be great enough to make room for all she has to give.

Excessive in her demands, Dorothea demands to identify
herself as part of everything. Yearning "for a binding theory
which could bring her own life and doctrine into a strict
connection with that amazing past, and give the remotest
sources of knowledge some bearing on her actions" (63), she
wants to be implied in or included in everything. This is asking
"too much" because it is an uneconomical demand. It cannot
be identified in terms of exchange. In fact there is no structure
that can hold such meaning, no structure for such a desire or
such a relationship to the world. Her demand is to be demanded by something outside herself, as she conceives of
meaning originating outside and beyond her. It is thus excessive or pure demand: demand is identified on both sides of

the exchange as subject demands a demanding object. Practically, the excess threatens to mean only frustration and dissatisfaction, for practical experience structures experience by exchange. The fact that the demand on Dorothea's part is not definite or distinct means that she does not know what she wants and others cannot know what she wants. She thus seems insatiable, and others seem inadequate, for they cannot meet a demand that has no object. And in order to take part in Dorothea's demand, others would have to give up more than their sense of adequacy. Because her demand is grounded in neither subject nor object and is impossible to define by a beginning and end, the demand insists that there is no distinction between such differences.

Thus, as I have suggested earlier, Dorothea's dependence demands that what is external to her lose independence and determination. Her demand to be used by others is a demand to be able to make a difference to others and a difference to the world through others. In order to use her, then, Casaubon would have to want to be more than he is and identify himself and his work in relation to others. It is therefore unacceptable to Casaubon and others that Dorothea does not demand anything specific. Not to define the exchange between self and others is to give no one anything to hold on to. As long as the relation of subject and object is conceptualized as an exchange, Dorothea's demand must be seen as unacceptable, frustrating, and alienating. But her demand is not part of an exchange exactly, for it demands an infinite process of interdependently changing meanings rather than a definitive exchange which limits meaning by defining differences. All elements of meaning have infinite potential for more meaning in her perception of the world.

It is because this is what she wants that, when Will Ladislaw accepts her, Dorothea finds satisfaction in her dependence on him for meaning. Her life becomes filled with "a beneficient activity which she had not the doubtful pain of discovering and marking out for herself," for she is "absorbed into the life of another" whose work is to serve others (610-11). Secure because she is bound to others, Dorothea "ends up," then,

with no distinction: both absorbed by another who is committed to others and with only an "incalculably diffusive"
effect on the world around her (613). But if this means that
she has no distinction and that what she is cannot be accounted for, it also means that her meaning is limitless. The
narrator herself refuses to make the exchange of representation for reality that would define what Dorothea is. But Dorothea's demand has been met by the end of the novel, with
an end that refuses to limit her meaning to herself or to definite
ends.

Dorothea's "selflessness" prevails. But that it prevails as a
power is not possible unless we accept a concept of power
that entails neither domination nor possession. Power occurs
here for the wrong reason, we might say, as the narrative
proceeds with interpretations that resemble Dorothea's own
"wrong reasoning." For Dorothea is powerful only as part of
someone else, as a partial self. To identify power with partiality is to identify power in differences that are always committed to each other and always differing. Different elements
are powerful insofar as they are related to other elements,
because power depends on relations themselves rather than
the determination of relations. The committed and partial
individual, then, is in power because she or he is selfless,
without the independence or distinction we associate with
mastery. Power is shared willingly by characters who recognize that power lies in their dependence on others and is
generated in relation to others.

Leo Bersani, considering the realistic novel in the context
of Michel Foucault's ideas about power, insists that the heroine or hero of such novels strives for freedom from commitment and in this is alienated from the form of the novel
itself. Such a character, attempting to exceed the limits of
convention, attempts "escapes from the very constraints and
agreements into which [the novelist] has entered in order to
produce realistic fiction." One such escape is the escape from
literal imprisonment "by an extravagant conversion to spirit."
Commitment, according to Bersani, is alienating; it is imposed
on characters by a prison or other confining structure, and it

is evaded only by death, spirituality, or some other version of "a dream of wholly unrelated being," since "the only absolute escape from power is to escape from relations themselves."[14] But for Eliot freedom lies in commitment *to* relations because only in relations can a character escape the confines of the individual and unrelated self. Her heroine is so committed to relations that she seems to exist *as* a relation between self and others rather than as an individual. The escape from confinement occurs in the loss of the self in relations, for the separate self is Eliot's idea of imprisonment. And the relations in which she sees generative power are not confining structures but relations of shifting and indistinct differences that therefore cannot be structured.

The relations of Dorothea and the world around her are characterized by such indefinition; and her demand for significance is for meaning that cannot be limited or distinguished. To authorize such a character's authority, as *Middlemarch* does, is to insist that authority has little to do with either the totalization of meaning that Miller identifies as the intention of authority, or the "commanding structure of significance" that Bersani identifies with realism. Dorothea's authority is clearly differentiated from the "authorities" in the town of Middlemarch, and it is this difference that I want to consider here.[15]

---

[14] Leo Bersani, "The Subject of Power," *Diacritics*, 7, no. 3 (1977), 10, 9-10, 12.

[15] Two critics who have considered authoritative characters in the novel have identified the narrator with characters less committed to others than Dorothea is. George Levine insists that the "progress" in the novel "is progress toward the centrality of the disengaged figure, the writer himself. . . . In *Middlemarch* the world of 'common sense' becomes monstrous, one to which the best must refuse unreflecting commitment. Ladislaw is right to stand at its edges and is horrified at the disaster caused by Dorothea's premature faith." See *The Realistic Imagination: English Fiction from Frankenstein to Lady Chatterley* (Chicago: University of Chicago Press, 1981), p. 316. U. C. Knoepflmacher suggests that George Eliot "is closest perhaps to Mary Garth, the homely observer without illusions. Of all the characters, Mary alone is

Dorothea authorizes an excess of meaning. She wishes nothing to be meaningless, hoping when she marries Casaubon that " 'there would be nothing trivial about our lives. Everyday things with us would mean the greatest things' " (21). This means that she cannot secure meaning, for Dorothea, like the narrator, envisions and enacts meaningfulness by a process that intensifies rather than contains differences. She authorizes more meaning than she controls. And the fact that she sees herself as part of all meaning both increases and further unsettles meaning. Because she allows for so many differences, her meaning is always in the midst of a process which would determine significance only if grounded or concluded. But Dorothea never makes those distinctions and insists instead that any difference, including her own partiality, is one difference among many, making a difference and differing itself in response to other things. She is thus neither omniscient nor omnipotent as an authority; for her demand is never to be the center or determinant of meaning. Her resemblance to the narcissistic self is not a matter of self-centeredness but lies in her refusal to make a clear distinction between self and world, so that the difference between them is never settled.

Because Dorothea refuses to distinguish herself from others, she insists on her ability to enter into others' problems. When she does so, her behavior provides an alternative to conventional forms of behavior in the novel and an alternative to conventional forms of fiction, too. The situation in Middlemarch following Raffles' death is subject to multiple interpretations, for no one knows the truth about the affair. Raffles has died. Bulstrode profits by his death. Lydgate gave medical advice that was not followed by Bulstrode. Lydgate has borrowed money from Bulstrode. Those are facts, but the connections between them, such as which occurred because of which, are not available. "Who could say that the death of

---

able to laugh at the human scene." See *Religious Humanism*, p. 114. The disengagement of both Will and Mary seems to me to differentiate them from George Eliot's authority.

Raffles had been hastened? Who knew what could save him?"
(521). Or, as Lydgate thinks, "There seemed to be no use in
implying that somebody's ignorance or imprudence had killed
him. And after all, he himself might be wrong" (522).

When Dorothea demands that the powerful men in the
community—Farebrother, Sir James, and Mr. Brooke—support Lydgate in the face of suspicion and scandal, she is answered with logic:

> "It is a delicate matter to touch," [Farebrother] said.
> "How can we begin to inquire into it? It must be either
> publicly by setting the magistrate and coroner to work,
> or privately by questioning Lydgate. As to the first pro-
> ceeding there is no solid ground to go upon, else Hawley
> would have adopted it; and as to opening the subject
> with Lydgate, I confess I should shrink from it. He would
> probably take it as a deadly insult. I have more than once
> experienced the difficulty of speaking to him on personal
> matters. And—one should know the truth about his con-
> duct beforehand, to feel very confident of a good result."
> (537)

Regarding the affair as a sort of vortex of meaning, because
the facts cannot be causally or logically distinguished and
related, Farebrother responds with reasoned impartiality.
There are two ways to find out the truth, he says. But for one,
the public inquiry, there is " 'no solid ground to go upon.' "
And the other, asking Lydgate, would not be certain unless
they knew the truth beforehand. Thus, something must be
predetermined in order to determine the truth; or you have
to know something in order to know something. Farebrother
thus recognizes the need to construct a plot in order to determine the meaning of reality. It is because he cannot identify
a structure of meaning with a beginning, a middle, and an
end that he cannot deal with this situation. Here he cannot
tell even where to begin an inquiry; not enough is known
about the affair even to know what questions to start with.
In order to know where to begin, he implies, he needs to know
the end. He needs at least some sense of what he wants to

know, some object to inquire after or move toward. As in a structured plot, therefore, the end is needed to determine the beginning and middle.

Because they cannot plot the events of the scandal, Farebrother and Sir James insist on staying out of it. As in Freud's story of the developing ego, they have learned to separate themselves from uncertain reality in which anything can happen. " 'Whatever you do in the end, Dorothea, you should really keep back at present, and not volunteer any meddling. . . . We don't know yet what may turn up' " (539). They assume a plot will become apparent eventually, or that the truth about this situation will come out; and they want to wait for the end in order not to be involved in the insecure middle of meaning that will be determined according to a beginning that has already begun. Since they cannot predict the end, any meddling in the middle would threaten their own meaning. Thus Dorothea risks a dubious reputation if she interferes without knowing the truth.

Without grounds and without an object, these men can do nothing and remain neutral. In economic terms, it is a risky business, for because nothing is known, there is no security. Thus for Farebrother and Sir James to credit Lydgate would be to take part in an exchange that guarantees no return. For other characters, the noncommittal stance takes a different form. Because neither knowledge nor returns is guaranteed, the gossips of Middlemarch are free to make up all sorts of stories and believe anything at all. The uncertainty of events produces endless possibilities of meaning:

> this vague conviction of indeterminable guilt . . . had for the general mind all the superior power of mystery over fact. Everybody liked better to conjecture how the thing was, than simply to know it; for conjecture soon became more confident than knowledge, and had a more liberal allowance for the incompatible. Even the more definite scandal concerning Bulstrode's earlier life was, for some minds, melted into the mass of mystery, as so much lively

metal to be poured out in dialogue, and to take such
fantastic shapes as heaven pleased. (529)

For the gossips, forms of conjecture are preferable to forms
of knowledge because of their freedom from determination.
There are no bounds to the fantasies. But such freedom of
interpretation is as indifferent and neutral in meaning as Farebrother's demands for a plot. Its neutrality also lies in its
separation from uncertain reality. For whereas Farebrother
and Sir James insist that the meaning of the event will be
determined independently of them, the gossips insist that the
meaning of the event will remain indeterminate. They do not
discover but cover up reality by imagination that works independently of reality. In each case, something is excluded
from consideration, as characters separate themselves from
other elements of the world. Rather than perceiving the situation as a vortex of meaning, so confused that one cannot
afford to become involved in it, the gossips perceive an endless
dispersion of meaning, so boundless and groundless as to
enable them to give it any form they please. The economy of
these interpretations is one of endless productivity but no use,
for it applies to nothing at all. Gossip requires no credit; it
commits no one to anything. The gossips too, then, provide
only unrelated meanings. Although meaning for them gets
"carried away," it carries nothing with it. It involves neither
investment nor return; it is "just gossip."

The fact that no one can know the truth of the situation
thus makes possible two modes of mastering uncertainty. The
responses of Farebrother and Sir James enable them to separate themselves from uncertainty because they see all meaning as plotted. They master the uncertainty by assuming it
will eventually be resolved. The gossips, on the other hand,
master the uncertainty by producing more if it, thus confining
meaning to uncertainty. Nothing can come of gossip, which
is insignificant and dubious in itself; and it thereby guarantees
that Lydgate also is insignificant and dubious. The gossips
cannot depend on him, so they want no part of him either.
Each of these forms of fiction insists that all that is significant

is knowable and thereby denies the significance of uncertain or unknown things. In both cases, people can relax when confronted with uncertainty. In the first case, they wait and see; in the second, they indulge in "idle talk" because they have already written Lydgate off.[16] The neutrality of these reactions is the impartiality of the realistic plot and the fantasy, both of which authorize impartiality as they authorize the separation of fiction and reality. Whether committed to truth or committed to make-believe, such authorities are equally uncommitted to the reality that confronts them.

But for Dorothea, ease is impossible: " 'I cannot bear to rest in this as unchangeable' " (560). She does not separate herself from the uncertainty because of ignorance, as Farebrother does. Nor does she separate herself because of suspicion, as the gossips do. She takes part in it, committing herself to uncertainty, risking her reputation and money on Lydgate. With no grounds for knowing that Lydgate is not

---

[16] My consideration of interpretation in *Middlemarch* depends in part on the Heideggerian concept of "idle talk." Paul Bové describes the relation of "idle talk" and language in *Destructive Poetics: Heidegger and Modern American Poetry* (New York: Columbia University Press, 1980), p. 60: " 'Idle talk' not only covers-up something disclosed, but it also reifies language itself. In the process of transforming the insight or discovery made by language into the mime of hearsay, of what is overheard without understanding, the 'they' world reduces language itself to an instrument which is present-at-hand. Language becomes a 'thing' to be studied objectively, shaped, and abstracted. 'Truth' in the world of the 'they' becomes the degree to which the solidified 'statement' 'about' some solidified 'object' corresponds to the observable 'facts of the case.' The reification of the discovered by the idle talk of the 'they' parallels the traditional metaphysical insistence that truth is a matter of judging the degree of correspondence between proposition and object." This is to suggest that the conception of truth which Farebrother acknowledges is itself a form of "idle talk" insofar as truth for him is a matter of the correspondence of "proposition and object." Both those in Middlemarch who want to know the truth and those who enjoy making believe rather than discovering anything are, in their disengagement, responsible for kinds of reification that separate them from their observations. It is partiality that Eliot demands in order to find meaning, and in this her concept of meaning resembles Heideggerian thought. I will be considering partiality and its contribution to meaning again in the following chapter.

in fact guilty, Dorothea simply " 'will not believe it' " (536). Arbitrarily and illogically, she knows:

"I know the unhappy mistakes about you. I knew them from the first moment to be mistakes. You have never done anything vile. You would not do anything dishonourable." (558)

Now this is not true, so far as anyone in the novel, including Lydgate, knows. But Dorothea's partiality invalidates truth. She does not depend on grounds; her belief ignores origins and ends. She meddles with both and insists that she knows what Lydgate has been and will be. This precludes any plotting of meaning, for the consistency of her vision is purely arbitrary and partial, with no logical grounds. Yet her partiality also invalidates fantasy, for she commits herself absolutely to her belief in Lydgate.

Dorothea increases the realm of significance by making room for uncertain values. She makes room for all of Lydgate:

The presence of a noble nature, generous in its wishes, ardent in its charity, changes the lights for us; we begin to see things again in their larger, quieter masses, and to believe that we too can be seen and judged in the wholeness of our character. . . . [Lydgate] felt that he was recovering his old self in the consciousness that he was with one who believed in it. (558)

This is not to say that Dorothea knows Lydgate. His "wholeness" is accepted as indeterminate; it includes "his doubts" and "his uneasy consciousness" of dubious interpretations of his behavior (559). But Dorothea's trust enables him to tell her what cannot be determined in him; she makes room for unresolved differences. She accepts all differences because nothing can make a difference to her belief.

Dorothea's authority thus authorizes the telling of anything. But she also believes that anything is potentially something else. She thus intensifies rather then settles the tension of difference. She demands to be able to make a difference. If Lydgate accepts her trust, he can become more than he is. But there are no grounds for such change. And Lydgate himself cannot meet the demand for change because he cannot be certain of the result:

> "I prefer that there should be no interval left for wavering. I am no longer sure enough of myself. . . . It would be dishonourable to let others engage themselves to anything serious in dependence on me." (562)

Unable to trust himself, Lydgate takes the position of Farebrother when confronted with an unknowable future. In order to avoid the wavering uncertainty, he disengages himself from others, insisting on his own independence from others.

Those characters who insist on the determination of meaning can rest in security. They are able to know where they stand and hold their ground because they separate themselves from uncertainty. They can confine meaning within limits by plotting it; as Sir James says of Lydgate, he " 'must know—at least he will soon come to know how he stands. . . . He must act for himself' " (558). This confines people to stable positions. Or, the gossips can confine Lydgate by saying that he could be anything. He thus becomes subject to what Dorothea feels as oppressive liberty in her married life, in which no one cares what she does and she makes no difference to others. Lydgate is seen by those who would determine meaning as either too little or too much to be acceptable; either they make nothing of him or too much of him to determine his significance. Both "lapse" and "extravagance" in these interpretations, Lydgate, because he and others do not know where he stands, is subject to the same readings as those unfitting women in the Preface to the novel. Fitting no place, they are nevertheless placed by their society into categories of excess. Lydgate, who is indeterminate, is determined as too little or too much to be acceptable. His real excess of meaning is determined as meaningless, for he is placed outside the bounds of meaning, like Dorothea, by the determination of others.

Lydgate's lack of meaning for others, or their refusal to recognize his value, depends, that is, on a strict definition of the boundaries of meaning itself. Such boundaries define the differences between significance and insignificance; what is unaccountable or indeterminate does not count at all. Lydgate's failure in the novel lies in the fact that he agrees to become, in the eyes of others, a "successful man" (610). He writes about gout rather than the "common tissue" that once interested him, giving to others what is acceptable to them and what they pay for. For Dorothea, however, as for her narrator, the unaccountable is always worth more than the accountable, precisely because it cannot be counted as anything definite.

The power of Dorothea's interpretations lies in her refusal to distinguish the boundaries between herself and others. That is the essential indistinction necessary to her arbitrary and partial interpretations, for it commits those interpretations to others. On such "grounds," anything can be meaningful if the self is invested in or takes part in its meaning. But with the difference between her own meaning and the meaning of the world always indeterminate, no determinant exchange can occur between Dorothea and others. To say that she sees her self in others is to suggest something similar to the recognition that what she demands is a demand: in her relations with others, the same thing tends to be identifiable on both sides of any exchange. Unlike Lydgate, who finally meets others' demands, Dorothea always exceeds them. She never seems to meet others in common terms or in a fair exchange. Her relations thus seem redundant rather than economical.

This makes her subject, again, to accusations of lapse and extravagance; she is accused of trying to get everything to herself and of giving everything up to others. And it is difficult to tell the difference. " 'You can't undertake to manage a man's life for him in that way,' " Sir James says to her about Lydgate (538). She is seen here as someone who wants to take over. But she is also seen as an extravagant spendthrift who wants to throw herself away by marrying Casaubon and Will or throw her money away on schemes "which would interfere with political economy" (7). From this point of view, she is wasted or used, given nothing in return for her gifts. The difficulty is that both interpretations are valid; and sometimes both are valid when applied to the same act. One can say that she tries to manage Lydgate, and one can say that she wastes her money on him. She both takes over and gives up.

Dorothea always interferes with economy, even with the economy of language that would give words adequate to hold her meaning. Here again, she has things two ways at once. But if her behavior can be interpreted as both lapse and extravagance, it is not clear whether she is the problem or whether it is the economy that cannot determine her meaning that is problematic. Through the representations that attempt to deny her significance, we learn that Dorothea is unaccountable. But we also recognize that the economical determination is itself unaccountable, as arbitrary and indefinite as she is. For in order to define her behavior as either lapse or extravagance, characters must themselves practice some lapse or extravagance. If she is both, to call her one or the other is either to leave something out or represent something more than is there. If determination can determine her only as invalid, then, she also invalidates determination. Confronted with Dorothea's behavior, we cannot tell the difference between lapses and extravagances. By this I do not mean to suggest that one sense of meaning is as flimsy as another. For although the determination of meaning is a structure of meaning that subjects itself to deconstruction, Dorothea's interpretations lie outside that structure, evading both its grounds and the undermining of those grounds. She cannot be "gotten" either way, for she depends on no grounds. She cannot be determined, even as lapse or extravagance.

Using economic terms, her behavior can be identified only as uneconomical, because her relations to others occur as something other than fair exchanges. When Dorothea goes to Rosamond, for example, to plead for sympathy for Lydgate, something extraordinary occurs between them, but no definite or definitive give-and-take occurs. Both characters are carried away by their emotions from any prior determination on their parts and from any determinant exchange. Dorothea's intention is to keep her own interests to herself and act in the interests of Rosamond and Lydgate. Rosamond intends "cold reserve" (580). But both fail to keep themselves in reserve. When Dorothea includes her own experience, speaking of her own marriage as well as Rosamond's, Rosamond is moved to tell her that Will loves her. "Taken hold of by an emotion stronger than her own," Rosamond is compelled to give Will's love back to Dorothea (584). Yet it is not a voluntary act, and what is given is not exactly a gift: "With her usual tendency to over-estimate the good in others, [Dorothea] felt a great outgoing of her heart towards Rosamond for the generous effort which had redeemed her from suffering, not counting that the effort was a reflex of her own energy" (585). Here the boundless but binding power of Dorothea seems to constitute the whole relationship. Just as Will is bound to purity by her pure belief in him, and Lydgate sees himself differently because she sees him differently, here Rosamond is given a different identity from her own by Dorothea's identification with her. It is not that anyone gives up or takes away anything; they move together into a different relationship in which such distinctions are not clear. Both are moved by Dorothea's emotions out of the bounds of determination, "in a new movement which gave all things some new, awful, undefined aspect" (584), and the object becomes reflexive of the subject rather than remaining separate. Each loses self-possession and determination in this relationship, with Rosamond giving them up in response to Dorothea giving them up, to be carried away into an indefinite relation, dispossessed of grounds and of definitive distinctions of subject and object, origin and objective.

Dorothea takes over, then, only by losing control. Her power lies paradoxically in her ability to let herself go, for it is her letting go that compels Rosamond to let herself go. Dorothea's partiality—both her intense feelings and her insistence on taking the other's part—compels meaning to change yet suspends the determination of meaning. It makes a difference that is unaccountable, both in that we cannot explain it logically and in that we cannot define its effects. Her power demands indeterminacy. Rosamond, for example, does not "really" change. She momentarily, in response to Dorothea, behaves selflessly; but she is not "really" generous, for this is the only time we see her behave generously. As the above passage suggests, what Rosamond is during this conversation cannot be "counted" as Rosamond; it does not hold true of her. She is taken hold of, temporarily, by something other than truth: the power of Dorothea's partiality, which enables her to be more than she is. Similarly, what Dorothea gets through Rosamond is not valued as the truth about Will but as the ability to believe in him again. Entering into Rosamond's suffering, Dorothea compels Rosamond to "open up," and this opens up Dorothea's perspective, giving her another point of view that changes the meaning of what she saw in Will's behavior the day before. But this does not determine his meaning for her. It enables her to suspend it again, to believe in him rather than to know him or to doubt him. She does not return to Will; she returns to her belief in him.

Because Dorothea takes over by losing control, there is no way to represent her behavior "economically." We cannot define Dorothea's relations using Farebrother's requirements: logical grounds and clear beginnings and ends. She seems to do two logically exclusive things at once, and cause and effect become similarly confused. She is given, on the one hand, as the origin of meaning; so that what happens throughout the novel between her and others is due to Dorothea. Thus she is repeatedly represented as generating meaning, with "an enthusiasm which was lit chiefly by its own fire" (20). And others in relation to her tend to function as reflexes of her own energy, like Rosamond above, or as reflections of her own ideas, like Casaubon, into whose mind she "looked deep ..., seeing reflected there in vague labyrinthine extension every quality she herself brought" (17). Dorothea, therefore, generates the meaning she finds, arbitrarily. Yet on the other hand, she does not perceive this. She insists on her dependence on others for meaning: her partiality always includes others, and it is always part of a relation. The partiality of her feelings is thus neither self-contained nor stable. It moves her to identify with others, and others are moved by it to relate them-

selves to her. Her partiality is not experienced by Dorothea
as wholly hers, then, and such partiality does not function as
a limitation of meaning. It is not purely subjective, and her
arbitrariness is not purely subjective either. She does not perceive her choice as free choice but as involuntary and com-
pulsory. Her freedom of interpretation, therefore, unlike gossip or fantasy, is not exercised as pure freedom: "the objects
of her rescue were not to be sought out by her fancy: they
were chosen for her" (577). The arbitrary choice is demanded
of her. Neither the partiality nor the arbitrariness of Dorothea's interpretations, then, is represented as limiting meaning
to her own terms or as freeing meaning from constraint.

Dorothea makes up meaning, therefore, but without attempting to control that meaning or perceive it as free. She thereby
seems unauthoritative and indeed demands that she herself be
authorized. She wants an external imperative, and "if she had
written a book she must have done it as Saint Theresa did,
under the command of an authority that constrained her conscience" (64). In this, she resembles the narrator, who never
regards herself as free either. Rejecting the "copious remarks
and digressions" of Fielding's novels, the narrator claims that
"I at least have so much to do . . . that all the light I can
command must be concentrated on this particular web, and
not dispersed over that tempting range of relevancies called
the universe" (105). Thus both these authorities resemble Edward Said's characterization of the novelist, whose condition
is always one of authority and "molestation": "Every novelist
has taken the genre as both an enabling condition and a re-
straint upon his inventiveness." For Said,

> in the written statement, beginning or inauguration, aug-
> mentation by extension or possession and continuity
> stand for the word *authority.*
>   . . . [But] no novelist has ever been unaware that his
> authority, regardless of how complete, or the authority

of a narrator, is a sham. Molestation, then, is a consciousness of one's duplicity, one's confinement to a fictive, scriptive realm, whether one is a character or a novelist. And molestation occurs when novelists and critics traditionally remind themselves of how the novel is always subject to a comparison with reality and thereby found to be illusion.

Said's thesis is that "authority" and "molestation" "ultimately have *conserved* the novel because novelists have construed them together as *beginning* conditions, not as conditions for limitlessly expansive fictional invention."[17]

But Dorothea and her narrator willingly embrace what is regarded by Said as molestation, and they embrace that condition as the enabling condition of their power. Dorothea's authority to make things up is always constrained by a sense of something external to herself; and that constraint does mean that she cannot possess or continue what she generates. But it is desirable to her that she not determine the meaning she generates; it is desirable to her that that meaning becomes part of what is beyond her and beyond her control. For this is what enables her to believe in her power as a generation of meaning that cannot be limited and that can make a limitless difference. Wanting neither to possess nor continue her "own" meaning, Dorothea authorizes the "letting go" of meaning. She authorizes meaning to proceed regardless of possession and continuity. The sense of authority in the novel is thus itself released from the bounds of possession or the bounds of beginning, continuity, and end. Such distinctions are not authorized and cannot be identified in Dorothea's authority.

The realistic novel is realistic, according to the descriptions I cite earlier in this chapter, because it includes multiple differences: the recognition and representation of different points of view, for example, is realistic. Knowing the difference between them, however, is also realistic, and it is this distinction that Dorothea refuses to realize. Moreover, a novel is realistic,

[17] Edward W. Said, *Beginnings: Intention and Method* (Baltimore: The Johns Hopkins University Press, 1975), pp. 83-84, 83.

as Said insists, because it knows the difference between fiction and reality. Any realistic novelist, or any realistic character, is always aware that her or his vision is different from reality. But Dorothea Brooke does not know this difference either; she does not see any necessary distinction between her interpretation and reality but experiences each as always subject to differing, in response to the other. Dorothea can be said to be, as she is said to be throughout the narrative by other characters, unrealistic. But that is because we use the term "realistic" to represent the knowledge that self and other, subject and object, fiction and reality are distinct. Dorothea does not *know* the difference between these things; she confuses them, just as she thereby confuses the concept of authority.

In *Middlemarch*, reality consists of different characters living different fictions. As Miller says, characters are as if so many texts or fictions themselves.[18] For the most part, these fictions are fictions that separate characters from others. They are "realistic" fictions, in part, because they isolate individuals: "Poor Lydgate! or shall I say, Poor Rosamond! Each lived in a world of which the other knew nothing" (123). Knowledge, however, is part of such fictions; knowledge demands separate worlds. For when people recognize only what they can know, they separate themselves from what cannot be known, as Farebrother and Sir James separate themselves from Lydgate. Knowledge, like other limiting and limited fictions, is subject to the experience of molestation, for something is always known to be missing whose existence threatens the authority or completeness of the fiction. Dorothea's fiction, however, is that she is not an authority, and she believes there is no authority for limiting or knowing meaning. Real authority in the novel, the authority to generate meaning, depends on such indeterminacy: on the willingness not to own meaning and not to limit meaning to what can be determined

[18] Miller, in "Narrative and History," writes that "Casaubon is a text, a collection of signs which Dorothea misreads, according to that universal propensity for misinterpretation which infects all the characters in *Middlemarch*" (p. 466).

or known. Creative authority authorizes all differences and determines none. It authorizes meaning to change: it does not experience change or difference or otherness as molestations, but as increases of meaning. Unlike other fictions in the novel, then, the generative fiction is neither masterful nor possessive but carries meaning away from determination. Giving up the distinction of self and other, subject and object, Dorothea generates a fiction that defies even the distinction of fiction and reality.

Using Said's distinction of authority and molestastion as conditions of realistic novels, we can see Dorothea, again, both as lapsing and as extravagant. It can be said that she collapses the distinction, since authoritative and molesting characteristics seem to overlap in her behavior. Or it can be said that she goes so far in either direction that she exceeds distinction. Taking over the determination of meaning or giving up determination to others, she takes all or loses all; either way, the exclusive distinction of differences—between self and others, or between authority and molestation—is lost. But since Dorothea can be said to do all these things, she in fact cannot be determined by the distinction at all.

Yet Said's distinction is useful not merely as another economy that clarifies Dorothea's unfitness to economical categories. Said's thesis is particularly relevant here because he recognizes that the tension between authority and molestation is a tension generative of meaning: to know that one's own fiction is different from reality is to know that one has the power to create novel meaning. Because the representation will never "get" the reality, however, the difference between novel and reality traditionally consigns the novel to "secondariness": not quite what it pretends to be. Yet Said insists that it is only because novelists "have construed [authority and molestation] as *beginning* conditions" that the tension has made the form conservative. It is, then, because the tension undermines any sense of grounds that it is restrictive. But what *Middlemarch* attempts, as it evades all grounding of tension and differences, is to maintain differences without perceiving some as grounds for others, some as prior and some as sec-

ondary. Dorothea's fictions are as likely to make reality uncertain as reality is to make her fictions dubious. The novel
does not miss the grounds that it lacks. The difference between
fiction and reality is always there, but it remains a shifting
and indeterminate difference. Neither Dorothea's authority to
generate meaning nor other elements that differ from her in
different interpretations masters the uncertainty; and the difference between them is never determined either. No difference can be determined as prior or secondary, or even as
independent; fiction and reality interact indistinctly. Dorothea's fictions thus open up the potential of meaning rather
than restrict it, insisting on differences as generative of
meaning.

This is both to increase the potential power of authority
and to lose the power of mastery. For the genuinely creative
will is limitless in its effects but not in control of them, and
Dorothea's creative interpretations of reality never serve herself but give more meaning to others. That she is selfless is
necessary to her power to generate unmastered meaning. But
the concept of a distinct and separate self, as I have suggested
throughout this discussion, is a concept that Eliot wants to
give up: not in an act of martyrdom and loss, though that is
the interpretation usually given, but in an act of dispossession
that makes possible an extension of meaning of the self and
of reality.

Thus Dorothea, demanding to be demanded, wills that she
be willed by a Will external to her self. The riskiest, because
the most unrealistic, move that Eliot makes in *Middlemarch*
is to move Dorothea's will outside her and give its name to
another character. This effectively precludes any determination of either character and insists that the human will need
not serve as a means of mastery and determination. Binding
her self to her Will rather than obeying Casaubon's will, Dorothea chooses a will that is committed to taking part in the
world without mastering the differences between self and
world.

Casaubon's written will is a conventionally authoritative
text, a form of mastery that is aware also of its molestation.

It is an attempt to secure meaning by separating Casaubon and what belongs to him from uncertainty. The will states that Dorothea will inherit Casaubon's money except under one condition: if she marries Will Ladislaw, she will have none of it. Identifying the world in terms of an exclusive opposition of self and other and in terms of exclusive possession, Casaubon attempts to defeat another Will which would take away what is his. He determines his own security by identifying the difference between what is his and what is not his as an exclusive opposition and thus protects himself from loss.

Casaubon's will is thus a masterful plot: it imagines what Casaubon most fears and defeats it by predicting that he can remain separate from it and retain what is his in opposition to it. Casaubon, unlike Dorothea, never recognizes what lies beyond him as part of himself. He commits himself to nothing, because commitment would bind him to what might exceed his mastery. "Marriage, like religion and erudition, nay, like authorship itself, was fated to become an outward requirement" (207). Uncertain of mastery in these areas of life, Casaubon separates himself from them, shrinking himself within smaller and smaller confines. To separate the self in this way, which excludes uncertainty from the self, is to live in what Dorothea experiences as a "nightmare of a life in which every energy was arrested by dread" (275). This is the condition of Casaubon's will. For the will expressed is a will arrested by, and limited to, fear; and its authority is arrested by its sense of what would molest it. Because Casaubon needs to determine meaning in order to separate himself from uncertainty, the result is that his will is itself determined by the fear of uncertainty. Here Eliot suggests what she will consider more explicitly in *Daniel Deronda*: "the desire to conquer is itself a sort of subjection."[19] The individual who cannot experience the self as bound to others arrests his or her own energy with fear of what lies beyond his or her control. Casaubon's will,

[19] George Eliot, *Daniel Deronda*, ed. Barbara Hardy (Harmondsworth, Mx.: Penguin, 1967), p. 139.

both in his life and after his death, accomplishes nothing but negation in its separation of himself from what lies beyond him. Will Ladislaw, on the other hand, cannot be defined or determined by any means. Unknowable, he cannot be identified by a family, a past, or a profession that would designate his future. A product of two generations of runaway women, a grandmother who " 'lost herself' " at marriage and was disowned by the Casaubons and a mother who disowned her own family and fortune, Will's inheritance is one of dispossession. He does not belong clearly anywhere, and he cannot be accounted for—except as a " 'frightful mixture' " (599). Even at the end of the novel " 'it is difficult to say what Mr. Ladislaw is' " (599). Even physically he materializes mobility and indefinition with "the uncertainty of his changing expression. Surely, his very features changed their form " (155). Nor does Will believe in certainty, as he debunks Casaubon's whole intellectual undertaking with a preference to imagine rather than know things, exceeding knowledge with a belief in what lies beyond it.

As a character, Will Ladislaw has seldom, as I suggested at the beginning of this chapter, been considered satisfactory by critics. "He is not substantially (everyone agrees) 'there,' " as F. R. Leavis puts it.[20] As a "match" for Dorothea, he seems inadequate to critics and Middlemarchers alike. As her will, however, Will's unfitness as a character is his qualification. For his indefinition and mobility are linked to his capacity to commit himself with intensity to multiple concerns. "Without any neutral region of indifference in his nature, ready to turn everything that befell him into the collisions of a passionate drama" (587), he invests all that he experiences with excessive

[20] F. R. Leavis, *The Great Tradition: George Eliot, Henry James, Joseph Conrad* (New York: George W. Stewart, 1950), p. 75. Gordon S. Haight, in "George Eliot's 'eminent failure,' Will Ladislaw," in *This Particular Web: Essays on "Middlemarch,"* ed. Ian Adam (Toronto: University of Toronto Press, 1975), pp. 22-42, considers critics' objections to Ladislaw and defends him against them. Haight even claims that Ladislaw provides "the only coherent focus" in the novel's plot (p. 39).

meaning. Everything matters to him; he excludes nothing from significance. He is incapable of indifference and instead perceives that anything may make a difference to him.

Will's excesses are what qualify him for marriage with Dorothea, though to identify him as her will is to emphasize that their union is essentially redundant. Redundancy is crucial to this narrative, crucial as a denial of the distinction and independence of different meanings. "Absorbed" into his life, Dorothea cannot be distinguished from Will; they seem to merge together. But her meaning may also be lost sight of because her effect on the world is "incalculably diffusive." Both lapse and extravagance, Dorothea's meaning may not count because it can be neither distinguished nor known. But to limit significance to these means of determination, the narrator insists, is to lose much of the meaning of experience.

The narrator's own final statement is not an apology for insignificance but a demand for the significance of what we cannot know: "the growing good of the world is partly dependent on unhistoric acts; and that things are not so ill with you and me as they might have been, is half owing to the number who live faithfully a hidden life, and rest in unvisited tombs" (613). Thus George Eliot concludes her narrative, insistent on extending the bounds of significance beyond calculation and knowledge. " 'Every limit is a beginning as well as an ending,' " she writes as she begins her Finale (607), conflating beginnings and endings as she rejects any total or determinate representation and proclaims the partiality and arbitrariness of her own choice. Refusing herself ever to master the meaning of her novel, Eliot persists in her commitment to the freedom of meaning to proceed beyond knowledge into unlimited possibilities of meaning. That partiality itself is the power which can convert endings into beginnings is the recognition that is diffused throughout the narrative. Partiality is the claim and pride of her authority. For it precludes the ends of meaning as it precludes the limits of any individual and moves meaning instead into a limitless capacity for meaning that Eliot insists is real.

CHAPTER FIVE

GEORGE ELIOT'S REDEMPTION OF MEANING: *DANIEL DERONDA*

To consider the redemptive vision of *Daniel Deronda* is to consider again a concept of meaning that challenges, even reverses, our assumptions about what is meaningful. If we consider the central characters, for example, we have a hero who, like Will Ladislaw, is subject to readers' accusations that he is not there at all. "We see through him," Barbara Hardy says, because of an "absence of personality" as well as an absence of ironic critical perspective on the part of the narrator.[1] Yet Deronda, like Ladislaw, seems to satisfy the terms of his own description of human character, perceived as part of a relation: " 'generally in all deep affections the objects are a mixture—half persons and half ideas' " (470-71).[2] This suggests several crucial elements of Eliot's belief about human character: one's meaning is not necessarily one's own; it changes according to who is perceiving the self; and it consists partially of what is inside the self and partially of what is in the mind of others who are related to the self. Here the relation that suspends the meaning of a self between self and other is not an ironic but a committed relation: one which binds self and other together rather than imposing a distance between them. Given this sense of human meaning, we cannot expect Deronda to be "fully realized" as a distinguished character. Gwendolen Harleth, however, may be thought of as a char-

[1] Barbara Hardy, "Introduction" to *Daniel Deronda*, ed. Barbara Hardy (Harmondsworth, Mx.: Penguin, 1967), pp. 19-20.
[2] George Eliot, *Daniel Deronda*, ed. Barbara Hardy (Harmondsworth, Mx.: Penguin, 1967). All references are to this edition, and page numbers are cited in the text.

acter who is "there," since she and her experience are given in terms that distinguish her from others as well as from the narrator. Ironic about her relation to the world, Gwendolen is also represented with irony by the narrator. Yet it is in this "fully realized" character that George Eliot represents her conception of an empty and meaningless life.

This is to suggest that one way in which *Daniel Deronda* exceeds the conventions of realism is that it tends to identify as meaningful what we more easily identify as a lack of meaning. Yet the excesses of the novel get in the way of any such definitive distinction. The relation of *Daniel Deronda* to realism is itself, as Cynthia Chase has suggested, a suspended relation; for its modes of realization are inconclusive and indeterminant. Though realism is a matter of changing conventions about what reality is and how it can be represented, as George Levine says, it nevertheless "always implies an attempt to use language to get beyond language, to discover some nonverbal truth out there."[3] Chase clarifies how, although *Daniel Deronda* is realistically referential, its "specific referent" is an extralinguistic fact that is excluded from the text:

> Insistence on the hero's specifically Jewish identity not only puts in question the authority of the discourse but effectively disrupts its coherence. . . . The plot can function only if *la chose*, Deronda's circumcised penis, is disregarded; yet the novel's realism and referentiality function precisely to draw attention to it.

The historical fact is that Deronda must have been circumcized; but the literary fact is that he has not noticed that he is Jewish, "an idea that exceeds, as much as does magical metamorphosis, the generous limits of realism."[4]

If realism refers beyond language but the novel excludes the fact to which it refers, this suggests that meaning is incomplete

---

[3] George Levine, *The Realistic Imagination: English Fiction from Frankenstein to Lady Chatterley* (Chicago: University of Chicago Press, 1981), p. 6.

[4] Cynthia Chase, "The Decomposition of the Elephants: Double-Reading *Daniel Deronda*," *PMLA*, 93, no. 2 (1978), 222.

in the novel. Chase represents this incompleteness as the novel's suspension of "the principle of identity between two
modes: the performative mode, which would define it as a
form of activity, and the constative mode, which would define
it as a matter of knowledge."[5] Repeatedly, the narrative identifies meaning in terms of both modes, as when Mordecai
Cohen preconceives Deronda's Jewish identity—so that identity is given by the subject—and recognizes that identity—so
that identity is provided by recognition of objective evidence.
Both kinds of realization are thus present; but neither is given
"full affirmation," because each is thereby exceeded in the
text and neither is sufficient in itself. Thus "the narrative
structure" becomes "a strictly groundless construct."[6]

    With meaning suspended between internal and external ref-
erents or grounds, as it is acknowledged to be in Deronda's
description of the meaning of an object in an affectionate
relation, the narrative does insist on the "constitutionally fictional status" of both "knowledge and action."[7] For language
and thinking are always fictions in this narrative. These processes always differ from reality, and what is realized is thereby
always an effect of realization rather than reality itself. Insistent on the "inevitable makeshift of our human thinking,"
George Eliot recognizes that "No formulas for thinking will
save us mortals from mistake in our imperfect apprehension
of the matter to be thought about" (572). As Chase clarifies,
Eliot's narrative itself exceeds formulation. But the imperfect
apprehension of reality is not the condition from which its
redemption of meaning can save us. Rather than use language
either "to discover some non-verbal truth out there" or to
confirm our capacity to create what is out there in terms of
our thinking, Eliot uses language to suspend the very difference between what is inside and what is outside language, or
between what is inside and what is outside the human mind.
The exclusion of the fact of circumcision can be understood

5 Ibid., p. 223.
6 Ibid.
7 Ibid.

in these terms. The language of the narrative does exclude the fact and substitutes for its recognition other means of recognizing Deronda's Jewishness. If reality is thereby excluded from representation, it is not the lack of reality that concerns Eliot but the capacity of representation, in its very indeterminacy and incompleteness, to realize a gain of meaning that conventions of realistic referentiality preclude. The meaning of the excluded referent is redeemed *by* the suspension of modes of realization that characterizes her representation.

Circumcision is read by Chase as a sign that would cut off the narrative, because if it were read, the narrative would not need to be written. Thus the "narrative must cut out or cut around the cutting short of the cutting off of narrative."[8] But circumcision would also signal that Deronda is cut off from significance in the society in which he lives. Suspicious "that there was something about his birth which threw him out from the class of gentlemen to which the baronet [Sir Hugo, his guardian] belonged," Deronda never asks about his birth; "in his imagination he preferred ignorance" (209). He cannot read the sign of circumcision, presumably, because he is unwilling to recognize the parts of himself that are insignificant and unacceptable to others. Such a repression of self in order to be acceptable to others is recognized as "realistic" by the Freudian development of self: certain elements of the self are repressed, and the self thereby becomes constituted in terms of exchangeable, or acceptable, elements—the elements of language, particularly, according to Jacques Lacan. If Deronda represses knowledge of his birth in order to belong to others, he is thereby engaged in a theoretically "realistic" alienation of self and others. For, given language as the means of relating self and world, he will never fully belong.

But the narrated discovery of Deronda's birth that takes the place of discovering the circumcision, though it is in a sense superfluous, makes a great difference. For it enables Deronda to accept his Jewishness: not as a sign that cuts him off from others but as a sign that suspends his meaning between self

[8] Ibid., p. 224.

and others. The narrative substitutes a binding relation for the excluded fact. Deronda's Jewish identity is rendered acceptable by its representation as part self and part other: partly Deronda's own identity and partly Mordecai's idea of Deronda's identity. The represented recognition of his Jewish identity, however, does not resolve the difference between himself and others, just as it does not resolve the difference between language and reality. Deronda identifies himself, even after he acknowledges his birth, as a mixture of incommensurable differences:

> "The Christian sympathies in which my mind was reared can never die out of me. . . . But I consider it my duty— it is the impulse of my feeling—to identify myself, as far as possible, with my hereditary people. . . ." (724)

If Deronda is to satisfy Mordecai's prophetic vision of Judaism, moreover, he will not establish a homeland that will give the Jews a distinct and separate identity either. For the " 'new Judaism,' " like Deronda himself, will be " 'poised between East and West' " (597), suspended in its differences rather than a distinct difference in itself.

The redemption of meaning in the novel thereby insists on suspending meaning between differences that remain meaningful though they remain incommensurable. It is thus difficult to say who or what Deronda is, and this difficulty may be represented as an absence of meaning, since it is an absence of determinate meaning. But Deronda is not lacking meaning; Eliot's suspension of meaning leaves him with too much, rather than too little, to be defined or distinguished. Deronda remains a man of differing elements, none of which cancels out or represses another. He does not lack differences but is full of them, even though this precludes the kind of identity we call integrity, as his binding relations to others preclude the kind of identity we call distinction.

Eliot's redeeming suspension of meaning thus depends on the fact that realization is limited to the indeterminate terms of realization rather than being able to determine reality. The excluded fact of circumcision is not recovered by representation. Instead, a relation is discovered—the kind of dependent relation that characterizes meaning in language; and the relation provides meaning that does not separate Deronda from others or from differing parts of himself. The very indeterminacy and incompleteness of representation thus allow for the redemption of meaning from loss. For the indeterminacy and incompleteness preclude differences being cut off from significance as they leave meaning open to difference.

Eliot's meaning thus exceeds the realistic literary convention that language can reach beyond language even as it exceeds the realistic psychological convention that identifies the inability to reach beyond language as a loss. For Lacan, the fact that language and reality are incommensurable commits the self to experience desire as a metonymic "displacement of the 'real' object of the subject's desire onto something apparently insignificant." Metonymy thus "represents the *manque d'être* (lack of being) which is constituent of desire itself."[9] The assumption here is that real needs are never satisfied, or that what we can ask for will never coincide with what we really need. This is a convention which Eliot acknowledges, though she acknowledges it only *as* a belief or convention: "Wishes are held to be ominous; according to which belief the order of the world is so arranged that if you have an impious objection to a squint, your offspring is the more likely to be born with one; also, that if you happen to desire a squint, you would not get it" (432). If we assume that real people, and therefore realistic characters, lack satisfaction and that the experience of lack is the experience of reality, we are, according to Eliot, imposing a lack of meaning on experience by believing in lack. But "This desponding view of probability the hopeful entirely reject, taking their wishes as good and sufficient security for all kinds of fulfillment" (432). The gaps in meaning that occur in any representation are not, therefore, constituent of desire itself unless we desire it to be so; for the

9 Anthony Wilden, "Lacan and the Discourse of the Other," in *The Language of the Self* by Jacques Lacan, trans. Anthony Wilden (New York: Dell, 1968), p. 242.

gaps in any form of realization can be filled with belief, trust, or hope, powers that bind the self to meaning and bind meaning itself. Meaning depends, for Eliot, on what we believe in. For "Who is absolutely neutral?" (432).

Rather than imposing a lack on meaning by insisting that we are neutral and so have nothing to do with and are excluded from the meaning of the world, Eliot insists that each perceiving self takes part in meaning. The partiality of any realization, therefore, is reflective of the partiality of any self. Eliot thus acknowledges the ironic or neutral disjunction of self and world only as a choice. It is her insistence that those whose lives are experiences of lack choose to have it so. So we are given a choice in the novel, and we can consider this choice as a choice between two plots. One of these is "realistic," in that it concerns a heroine who confronts the incommensurability of self and world; and one exceeds the conventions of realism with a hero who finds that self and world coincide to a great extent.

The realism of Gwendolen's story lies in its irony. She cannot satisfy her desire to distinguish herself, a desire " 'not to go on muddling away my life as other people do, being and doing nothing remarkable' " (58). For the opportunities the world offers her do not correspond to her desires; circumstances dispute her will. At the very beginning of the novel we see her gambling away money, for example, that becomes desirable almost as soon as she loses it, when she receives the letter telling her that her family is bankrupt. The bankruptcy, moreover, comes just at the time when Grandcourt is ready to renew his proposal of marriage, so that marriage to him is the only alternative to being a governess and thus the only available means of achieving social superiority. If this incommensurability of desire and reality seems realistic in its irony, however, the narrative insists that it is in fact a condition predetermined by Gwendolen's noncommittal attitude to the world. Gwendolen would not have lost her money in the first place if she were not gambling, and, in fact, she is always taking chances. Though she is determined not to marry Grandcourt, for example, her resolve is "a form out of which the blood had been sucked—no more a part of quivering life than the 'God's will be done' of one who is eagerly watching chances" (341).

Because Gwendolen's only resolve is to distinguish herself, her very determination makes her variable. Whatever offers distinction in others' eyes becomes desirable. For example, when she has less money than others, money becomes desirable. Yet when distinction depends on something else, money does not matter; thus she gambles all her money away in the Casino at Leubronn in order to make a striking impression on Deronda. Even Gwendolen's "uneasy longing to be judged by Deronda with unmixed admiration" is "a longing which had had its seed in her first resentment at his critical glance" (376-77). What generates desire in Gwendolen is anything that would provide superiority. But since her desire is always to have more than she has or more than others have, circumstances are necessarily incommensurable with desire. For it is only lack that generates desire in her, and thus she only values what she misses. The ironic incommensurability of self and world is thus given as a reflection of Gwendolen's desire to be different from the rest of the world. It is in fact, Eliot insists, the response she demands.

In Deronda's plot, on the other hand, coincidences seem always to serve his needs, and thus experience seems to realize his desires. His mother, for example, exposes her identity just when he would in fact like to find out that he is a Jew. And Mordecai, rather than the vulgar pawnbroker, turns out to be the real Ezra Cohen, Mirah's brother. But these coincidences occur in a life in which desire itself is very different from Gwendolen's desires. Deronda desires to find himself in agreement with others: the object of his desire is to participate in others' lives and make a difference to them rather than to distinguish himself from others. The discovery that he is the Jew he is willing to be is not, therefore, just good luck; for Deronda wishes to acknowledge ties to circumstances and to others. In his discovery of Mirah's brother, too, Deronda has more than luck. The discovery of a noble Mordecai is determined not by fate but by Mirah's faith in her memory of him as a noble man. Moreover, the discovery comes only after Deronda has been "forced to admit some moral refinement" even in the pawnbroker Ezra Cohen (579). Thus Deronda's experience is a recognition that there is increasingly less distance between himself and what the world offers him; and his desire to decrease this difference enables his ideas to coincide to a great extent with what he discovers in the world.

Thus, in *Daniel Deronda*, any realization of experience is dependent on the assumptions in the mind which realizes as well as on the objects which are to be realized. This is to emphasize not the separation of representation and reality but the inseparability of representation and realization. There is no separating the perceiving mind and the perceived object, and there is no separating desire and realization. Gwendolen's ironic experience is inseparable from her ironic attitude to the world, and Deronda's satisfying experience cannot be separated from his desire to accept the world even as it differs from him. Like the difference between himself and the pawnbroker that Deronda gradually recognizes as a partial rather than a distinct difference, differences in his experience remain different without being either assimilated to or distinguished from other differences. It is this willingness to accept a world of incommensurable differences that accounts for the excesses of the novel. Like the two plots that coexist in the novel yet coincide only in places, and like the hero and heroine who are emotionally bound to each other yet never are united, the different elements of *Daniel Deronda* remain suspended in relations that acknowledge their incommensurability.

Recognizing the unsettled relation of different parts of the novel, critics tend to take it apart or insist that it can be divided into separate parts. Thus U. C. Knoepflmacher suggests that

> *Daniel Deronda* is a novel about belief and disbelief. That only the latter has been extended to the book itself is unfortunate, but logical. Unlike the Shakespeare whom she so consciously imitated, George Eliot was unable to mingle actuality and phantasy or to combine the prosaic with the heroic. She finally demanded a heightened belief

which would rise above the quasi-idealistic "realism" dis-
played in her earlier work, but she also remained a skeptic
at heart.[10]

Here Knoepflmacher presents the novel as divided against
itself because in it reality is divided from fantasy, and he
attributes this to George Eliot's own self-division. The only
consistency he identifies is in readers' reactions, and in this I
think he is wrong. For readers, too, tend to be divided in their
response to the novel: liking the part about Gwendolen and
conventional English society and disliking the part about Deronda and Judaism. The difficulty Knoepflmacher identifies
as the inability on the part of the novelist to "mingle actuality
and phantasy" is a difficulty recognized by most critics, in a
number of different contexts. *Daniel Deronda* is undoubtedly
strained by the inclusion of material that does not belong in
a realistic novel. The narrative just does not fit together, and
its excesses can be identified in its form, themes, characters,
ideas, and language.

"It is a novel which shows the effort in effects not totally
achieved, ideas not perfectly embodied in character, language
not having quite the intended impact," Barbara Hardy says.[11]
Again, as in Chase's discussion of the novel, the narrative is
seen in terms of incompletion and lack. Hardy's assumption
that Eliot cannot quite do what she means to do is one way
of explaining why parts of the novel do not fit together. Presumably the goal was unity, but she did not achieve it. Another
way to explain the novel's excesses is to say that it goes in
different directions; the narrative is confusing because it does
conflicting things simultaneously. Thus F. R. Leavis writes
that "the nobility, generosity, and moral idealism are at the
same time modes of self-indulgence," and that "the 'duty' that
Deronda embraces . . . combines moral enthusiasm and the
feeling of emotional intensity with essential relaxation in such

---

[10] U. C. Knoepflmacher, *Religious Humanism and the Victorian Novel:
George Eliot, Walter Pater, and Samuel Butler* (Princeton: Princeton University Press, 1965), p. 119.
[11] Hardy, "Introduction," p. 9.

a way that, for any 'higher life' promoted, we may fairly find an analogy in the exalting effects of alcohol."[12] Hardy demands unity and Leavis demands more careful distinctions from a novel that is seen, in the terms Eliot uses in *Middlemarch*, both as extravagance and lapse.

We tend to make sense of such excesses by making distinctions. Hardy separates intent from achievement, and Leavis separates duty from relaxation, just as Knoepflmacher distinguishes reality and fantasy. And most readers separate the novel into two parts: the English part and the Jewish part, or, as Leavis judges, the good half and the bad half. Yet to do this is to do what George Eliot does not do: such differences are inseparable for her. We cannot dismiss the novel because of its excesses, since excess is emphatically what the novel is *about*. It is not a mistake, for example, that ideas are "not fully embodied in character." To demand that characters embody ideas is to demand that the ideas they represent be clearly secondary to personal characteristics; characters are people, we might say, though ideas can be derived from character. But both the distinction and the priority assumed here are not shared by George Eliot, if we take her to agree with Deronda that " 'generally in all deep affections the objects are a mixture—half persons and half ideas' " (471). Eliot does not intend to provide us with characters in whom the person takes priority over the idea or the personal embodies the abstract. In this as in other contexts, she both refuses to integrate what we are accustomed to having unified and refuses to separate what we are accustomed to having distinguished.

Thus her narrative insists on its own incommensurable differences. With characters who are " 'half persons and half ideas,' " for example, the novel insists on *not* "mingling" fantasy and actuality, though it also insists that both exist together. This incommensurability is itself, however, the fullness of meaning that constitutes Eliot's redemption of meaning, precisely because differing elements are allowed to co-

[12] F. R. Leavis, *The Great Tradition: George Eliot, Henry James, Joseph Conrad* (New York: George W. Stewart, 1950), pp. 82, 84.

exist, or are put in contact with each other, even as they are not reduced to common terms that would make them commensurable. Thus it is not skepticism that accounts for the excesses of the novel. It is Eliot's recognition of real disparity—of idea and object, for example—and her refusal to give up either difference.

Such disparities remain incommensurable, therefore. But the disparity adds to rather than detracts from meaning as Eliot conceives of meaning. She insists, for example, that enthusiasm must acknowledge

> the pressure of that hard unaccommodating Actual, which has never consulted our taste and is entirely unselect. Enthusiasm, we know, dwells at ease among ideas, tolerates garlic breathed in the middle ages, and sees no shabbiness in the official trappings of classical processions; it gets squeamish when ideals press upon it as something warmly incarnate, and can hardly face them without fainting. . . . But the fervour of sympathy with which we contemplate a grandiose martyrdom is feeble compared with the enthusiasm that keeps unslacked where there is no danger, no challenge—nothing but impartial mid-day falling on commonplace, perhaps half-repulsive, objects which are really the beloved ideas made flesh. (430-31)

Here Eliot identifies the burden of meaningful experience in a representation that may make us uneasy in more than one respect. Insistent that the Actual presses upon enthusiasm as something "which has never consulted our taste" and that ideals press upon enthusiasm as "incarnate" things, she both implies the difference between thoughts and things and implies that there is no difference. Pressing the actual and the belief together even in their differences, the passage insists that belief must not slacken under the pressure of the Actual but must bear it. This is not presented as a compromise, for enthusiasm and belief must not give way, even as the Actual remains "hard" and "unaccommodating" itself. It is in sympathy rather than idealism that Eliot finds the redemptive relation of subject and object here, and, in sympathy, the subject stands as firm as the object. The two do not "mingle," for their sympathy is due to what seems an arbitrary commitment on the part of the subject to what lies beyond his or her ideas as a version of those ideas, just as it is due to what seems an arbitrary commitment on the part of the narrator here of subjective and objective differences to each other. What is required is a projection of partiality onto what lies beyond the self and appears impartial. Thus belief reconstitutes itself as belief as it reconstitutes what lies outside the self as both partial and objective.

In such a relation, each element carries a burden of excess meaning. Not only does the subject carry the burden of the "unaccommodating Actual," but, as in Deronda's affectionate relations, the object carries the weight of the subject's ideas about the object even as it remains different. It is in the acceptance of such mutual pressures that Deronda sees Gwendolen's redemption: " 'You are conscious of more beyond the round of your own inclinations—you know more of the way in which your life presses on others, and their life on yours' " (508). In this process, meaning becomes burdensome, but it is only by assuming such burdens that Eliot can commit different meanings to each other without reducing them to common terms. The real burden of Eliot's meaning is the burden of its commitment to incommensurable differences. This is a burden that she perceives as a positive burden, unlike the burden of lack that characterizes the alienation of self and world in more "realistic" representations.

The burden of meaning in the novel thus entails a number of excesses. If on the one hand the novel seems to fall apart because Eliot puts together elements so various that they do not fit together, on the other hand her writing puts such pressure on differences that they seem to overlap. Either way, there is an excess of meaning: too many differences and too much sameness, both interfering with clarity and unity. But the means by which we might reduce such excesses are identified by the narrative with a loss of meaning. Meaning is threatened by two conditions in this narrative. One is distinction, by which something is identified as separate and independent of other things; the other is indifference, by which something does not count for anything or makes no difference to anything else. Gwendolen, in her ironic and noncommittal attitude to the world, characterizes the loss of meaning by distinction. For most of the novel, she is in touch with nothing beyond herself and cannot in fact bear to be touched by any human being except her mother. Thus Eliot represents the desire for distinction as the absolute disconnection of self from others. It is indistinction, however, that is the greater threat to meaning in the novel; for to see differences indifferently is to lose meaning altogether. And Deronda, in his multiple sympathies, is in danger of becoming indifferent. He has difficulty deciding what to do with his life because he so easily identifies himself with others' sufferings that he sympathizes with all losing causes indiscriminately:

> We fall on the leaning side; and Deronda suspected himself of loving too well the losing causes of the world. Martyrdom changes sides, and he was in danger of changing with it. . . . He wanted some way of keeping emotion . . . strong in the face of a reflectiveness that threatened to nullify all differences. (413-14)

If Gwendolen has no sympathy at all with what lies beyond her, Deronda is so sympathetic that he seems to have no meaning in himself at all and simply assumes an identity with any losing cause.

But in another sense it is Gwendolen who suffers most from indifference even in her desire to distinguish herself. For what Gwendolen discovers is that indifference to everything else is necessary to her own distinction. Indifference thus becomes the surest means of distinction; the surest means of separating herself absolutely from the rest of the world is to be able to claim "that it did not signify what she did; she had only to amuse herself as best she could" (356). Moreover, as long as Deronda is identified as so indiscriminately sympathetic as to be virtually impartial in his sympathies, his reflective capacity is represented as a form of separation from the world. In one of Eliot's most striking relations of incommensurable differences, she recognizes distinction and indifference only as alternative versions of the same loss of meaning. For in Gwendolen and Deronda these two conditions are seen to coexist. Both as psychological and linguistic conditions, distinction and indifference are considered in the novel as conditions that neutralize meaning or empty meaning *of* meaning. In place of these alternatives, the narrative insists on its excesses.

Thus Mordecai's redemptive vision of Judaism is of a phenomenon " 'poised between East and West' " (597). Such Judaism resists its separation from the rest of the world, but the more passionate resistance required in the novel is the resistance to integration or assimilation. The Jews in the novel are not made "acceptable"; they do not fit in, and their redemption consists of their being allowed not to fit in. The social pressure put on the Jews to allow themselves to be assimilated into Christian culture is like the pressure we may put on the novel to resolve its differences: " 'if Jews and Jewesses went on changing their religion,' " as Mrs. Meyrick cheerfully says, " 'and making no difference between themselves and Christians, there would come a time when there would be no Jews to be seen' " (425). Such pressure is resisted by Mordecai, who insists that the Jew would still be a Jew: " 'an alien in spirit, whatever he may be in form' " (587).

Eliot's redemption of meaning resists both separation and indifference by insisting that differences must exist together in an "uneasy" relation. Mirah and Mordecai do not accede to the pressure to be assimilated but maintain their differences, though Mordecai especially thereby gives readers discomfort. Like the "unaccommodating Actual," Mordecai's characterization seems to have "never consulted our taste," and the fact that we cannot see him in our terms tends to make us set him aside, though Eliot insists that he is crucial to the experience of the novel. Knoepflmacher, in the passage quoted earlier, implies that George Eliot's novel is divided because she herself is divided in spirit from the belief she authorizes. But the narrative is an attempt to avoid divisive alienation by representing differing elements—Christians and Jews, believing hero and unbelieving heroine—and insisting that they are related even in their differences. Rather than pretend there is no difference—in her own mind or in what lies outside her— Eliot is thereby true to differences. Her fidelity demands an awkward concept of the relations of differences, which press upon each other without any giving away. And her fidelity thus interferes with the unity and clarity of truth and with the unity and clarity of form. But these are simply not desirable in this narrative; they are identified, as by Mordecai, with the separation of human spirit and form and with indifference to real differences.

To accept the reflective relation of self and world that precludes both individual distinction and identity with others is always a matter of choice, as any relation of self and world, even Gwendolen's realistic ironic relation, is a matter of choice for Eliot. The arbitrary choice to commit oneself to the excesses of self and world is "justified" by Mordecai when Gideon asks him to explain what seems a merely idealistic concept of Judaism:

> "It may seem well enough on one side to make so much of our memories and inheritance as you do, Mordecai," said Gideon; "but there's another side. It isn't all gratitude and harmless glory. Our people have inherited a good deal of hatred. . . . How will you justify keeping one sort of memory and throwing away the other?"
>
> "I justify the choice as all other choice is justified," said Mordecai. "I cherish nothing for the Jewish nation, I seek nothing for them, but the good which promises good to all the nations. . . . But what wonder if there is hatred in the breasts of Jews, . . . since there is hatred in the breasts of Christians? Our national life was a growing light. Let the central fire be kindled again, and the light will reach afar. . . . The sons of Judah have to choose that God may again choose them. . . . The Nile overflowed and rushed onward: the Egyptian could not choose the overflow, but he chose to work and make channels for the fructifying waters, and Egypt became the

land of corn. Shall man, whose soul is set in the royalty
of discernment and resolve, deny his rank and say, I am
an onlooker, ask no choice or purpose of me? That is the
blasphemy of this time." (597-98)

Gideon's demand is for impartiality; he sees another side to
reality and asks that Mordecai justify ignoring it. To justify
the choice would be to provide grounds for it, so that what
appears to be arbitrary and partial would seem to be fair and
impartial. And to some extent this happens, for Mordecai
does suggest moral principle as the grounds of his choice: the
inherited good is better than the inherited hatred. But this is
not really the force of the argument, which does not proceed
as a logical justification of the priority or superiority of what
is chosen. For the argument works by emphasizing similarities
rather than making distinctions, and justification does not in
fact occur.

Hatred is not chosen; it has no significance for Mordecai.
But hatred is not insignificant because it is not Jewish. It is
insignificant because it does not make much difference. It is
something Jews have in common with Christians, for one
thing. But this indistinction does not account for the insignificance of hatred. For the good that Mordecai chooses does
not represent a difference between Jews and Christians either:
it is a good that promises good to Jews and Christians alike.
Thus Mordecai's choices are inclusive rather than exclusive.
His choice of Judaism is not justified by any distinction between Jews and Christians. Mordecai's choice in fact is
"grounded" on only one difference: the difference his partiality makes. If you look at the world impartially, his argument suggests, nothing makes much difference. But if you look
at the world with partiality, you make a difference in it and
to it. Mordecai's choice is to make a difference, though he
acknowledges that choice as absolutely arbitrary and partial.

The argument is difficult to follow, in part because, although Mordecai clearly means to justify the difference he
chooses, he tells us more similarities than differences and thus
clarifies the partiality of his choice. Such statements as " 'I

justify the choice as all other choice is justified' " and " 'The sons of Judah have to choose that God may again choose them' " are redundant: hard to follow because they do not seem to go anywhere. Choice is explained in terms of choice, and these statements seem circular, never logical, progressions. They give no grounds for choice but choice itself and so seem to begin and end in the same place, with the same difference. The justification here includes more than it differentiates, provides no grounds for distinction, and rules out no alternatives.

The example of the Nile, however, illustrates exactly the condition of redundancy we find in Mordecai's justification of choice. There is no choice about the overflow of the river, which remains irreducible. But the Egyptians chose it anyway, and their choice made the excess fruitful. The overflow is superfluous: it does not serve the needs of the people. And so is the choice superfluous, in a sense; for the chosen overflow already exists. The condition requiring choice is a condition of excess: water exceeds the bounds of the Nile, and exceeds the needs of conventional agriculture, just as the Jewish heritage exceeds the bounds of goodness. The water is still "fructifying," though, and so is the heritage capable of being a "growing light." But such differences depend on human choice, and they depend on choices not to deny what is or to start with something new but to find a way of working with the excess that makes a difference with it. To deny the overflow or to deny the mixed heritage as useless would be to give up something that Eliot refuses to lose.

The choice required is a choice of what there is no choice about. Mordecai, for example, is a Jew. That is a condition of his being about which he has no choice, just as the Egyptians have no choice about having been born Egyptian or about the behavior of the Nile. Thus the meaning of one's condition is not due to the self alone but consists of one's parents, for example, and one's natural surroundings. Yet to accept the meaning of the self in excess of the bounds of the self is clearly the reflective equivalent of accepting others in excess of one's own terms. It is in thus committing oneself to the "hard un-

accommodating Actual" of being born a Jew or being born
in Egypt that one can commit oneself to meaning that exceeds
the self. Moreover, to commit yourself to your own partiality
is to commit yourself to that within you which is as hard and
unaccommodating in its arbitrariness as anything that lies
beyond you.

To choose what one has no choice about is thus to make
meaningful what exceeds determination in both self and
world. It is to liberate meaning from the exclusion of irreducible differences and to liberate the self from the exclusion
of its own irreducible differences. Partiality itself is something
we have no choice about; we cannot help loving what we love,
and our tastes thereby are as "unselect" as the world beyond
us which does not consult our tastes. Partiality thus constitutes
an irrational binding of self to others, just as one's parents or
natural surroundings constitute arbitrary and involuntary relations of self to world that lie beyond our control. The choice
that Eliot demands here is the choice of those excesses as
meaningful. It is the choice of acceptance, since it is the choice
of what already is. It is the choice to exceed rationality and
justification, since it is the choice that finds meaning in what
rationality and justification exclude from meaning. But it is
the choice that both accepts differences and makes differences
possible. We can accept the meaningfulness of partiality only
if we accept the differences in ourselves and what lies beyond
us. But once we accept those differences, we are able to take
part in what lies beyond us and make a difference to it.

In a sense, this is to say that the narrative both demands
and precludes choice. For choice is not "free" choice, yet the
excesses of the novel exist side by side with the insistence that
" 'the strongest principle of growth lies in human choice' "
(598). The difficulty, I think, is that George Eliot has chosen
to be redundant and urges the same choice on us. Choice here
is authorized as the choice to *be* redundant or excessive. The
narrative thus re-enacts the situation Mordecai describes
above. George Eliot acknowledges the existence of what exceeds her partiality, just as Mordecai acknowledges the hatred
of the Jews. Although she chooses to commit herself to a hero

who is capable of accepting his birth, for example, as a binding commitment to others, Eliot also recognizes "another side" of the story in Gwendolen, who insists that she is bound to nothing. Deronda is chosen by Eliot, however, as the figure who can make a difference to others. And the difference he can make is reflected in Gwendolen herself as she becomes, under his influence, able to give to others. Thus Eliot's choice does not rule out the "hatred" but commits her to the character who can make a difference even to that hatred in Gwendolen. In this way, Eliot realizes what exceeds her belief but also commits herself to the character who represents the possibility of making a difference to what lies beyond him and differs from him, precisely by his acceptance of it as part of himself.

In the following sections of this chapter I will be considering further the implications of the redemption of meaning that *Daniel Deronda* undertakes. The redemptive suspension of incommensurable differences that precludes both the distinction and the assimilation of differences is reflected in various ways in the narrative, beginning with the narrator's refusal to assume the authority to begin at the beginning and thus distinguish her novel *as* novel. The various versions of redemption in the novel participate in its peculiar sort of redundancy, which Barbara Hardy has called reflective or "mirroring coincidence." This is not, she explains, coincidence imposed by "ordinary narrative conventions of discovery and accident," though such coincidences are present, too. It is more a matter of spatial repetition, or reflection, by which different characters seem to be doing the same thing in different lives in different places. We see the same situations in different characters' lives, and characters see their own situations in other characters' lives. Characters thus "mirror each other," for the reader as well as for themselves.[13] It is in such a relation that I will consider the stories of Deronda and Gwendolen, for their experiences reflect each other in their

[13] Barbara Hardy, *The Novels of George Eliot: A Study in Form* (London: Athlone Press, 1959), pp. 115-16, 124-34.

efforts to avoid the threat of indifference by accepting the indeterminate but binding relation of self and world. Though their lives seem in many ways the reverse of each other, such differences in fact bind them together as do the reversals of image and mirror image. So do various redemptive representations mirror each other in the novel. In Eliot's representation of meaning—the meaning of language, the meaning of freedom, the meaning of human power and authority—we are repeatedly confronted with the reflection and suspension of differing meanings: as when, for instance, she asserts that "the desire to conquer is itself a sort of subjection" (139). Committed to the reflection of differing things in other things, Eliot's narrative complicates and compounds rather than clarifies experience and repeatedly, in its excesses, defies the forms of realism.

Daniel Deronda, like *Middlemarch*, is a novel that finds meaning in bondage rather than freedom. This is explicit in the hero's choice to embrace the traditional "bondage" of the Jews, and it is clear in the heroine's eventual choice to live her " 'life as a debt' " (839). Free to choose, Deronda and Gwendolen do not choose freedom. They choose to submit themselves to others and to bind themselves to the past rather than distinguish themselves from others or create a future that leaves the past behind. George Eliot's refusal to authorize any individual freedom from the constraints of others and the past is reflected in her refusal to authorize this narrative as either novel or complete in itself. She begins, for example, outside the bounds of the fiction with an epigraph, which in form and content denies the independence of her beginning.

> Men can do nothing without the make-believe of a beginning. Even Science, the strict measurer, is obliged to start with a make-believe unit, and must fix on a point in the stars' unceasing journey when his sidereal clock shall pretend that time is at Nought. His less accurate

grandmother Poetry has always been understood to start
in the middle; but on reflection it appears that her proceeding is not very different from his; since Science, too,
reckons backwards as well as forwards, divides his unit
into billions, and with his clock-finger at Nought really
sets off *in medias res*. No retrospect will take us to the
true beginning; and whether our prologue be in heaven
or on earth, it is but a fraction of that all-presupposing
fact with which our story sets out. (35)

Here the narrative insists that it is a beginning that is already
in the middle. A fraction of an "all-presupposing fact," the
beginning not only is a beginning but claims to be arbitrary
and partial. It is this peculiar concept of exchange, in which
what is given by the narrator is already a "given," as part of
an "all-presupposing fact," that also characterizes the relations of human beings in this novel as bound rather than free.

The narrator's desire is to take part in something that exceeds her narrative, to be in the midst of something larger
than she can begin. In light of *Middlemarch*, this is a familiar
desire and a familiar condition of excess. The narrator of
Daniel Deronda here both generates meaning and insists that
there is more to meaning than she generates, like Dorothea
Brooke in the earlier novel, who is both the source of meanings
and dependent on exchanges to reflect or realize her meaning
in others. Dorothea's belief, in a sense, already presupposes
all that her exchanges give her. Yet the exchanges give her
meaning as part of others and give her others as part of her
meaning. She therefore knows herself and others to be only
a part of what she already supposes. The narrator of *Daniel
Deronda*, however, locates presupposition not only in human
belief but in fact; and by so doing she insists on binding human
belief to fact with a rigor missing in the earlier novel.

To identify factuality with presupposition is to insist that
what the narrator gives us is already a "given" in two senses.
It is part of a fact, and therefore knowable. But that fact is
all-presupposing, and therefore it is not knowable but indeterminate. Presupposed by fact, the beginning of the narrative

is thus indistinct from determinate and indeterminate meaning, as is factuality itself here. The epigraph binds the narrative
to factuality: not by claiming its own capacity to realize fact
but by claiming the capacity of fact to presuppose what is not
fact. She thus partializes reality. It is not only representation,
therefore, that exceeds determination here. The given that
precedes language is also indeterminate, as fact makes room
for more meaning than fact.

To recognize the existence of an "all-presupposing fact" is
therefore to insist that we lose nothing with this beginning,
although the recognition of presupposition precludes both the
originality of Eliot's beginning and the self-sufficiency of her
text. It cannot stand on its own; it is neither independent nor
complete. The beginning is only part of something larger, so
it cannot be considered a true beginning. Moreover, since the
fact of which it is a part is an "all-presupposing fact" rather
than a determinant fact, the beginning is partial assumption
as well as partial knowledge. But because this beginning acknowledges that it is a make-believe beginning, it need not
pretend that "time is at Nought." It need not give up meaning
that exceeds its limits in order to begin. In place of beginning
with a lack, this beginning assumes that time can never be at
nought: that we are always in the midst of things, and that
therefore we begin with the assumption of a fact that presupposes everything rather than with nothing.

Eliot's choice to begin with more than a beginning, in inclusive rather than exclusive terms, constitutes a gain of meaning in its resistance to the usual economy of representation.
She insists, later in the novel, that the results of representation
depend on what we start with, and that we can both start
with and gain more than we usually do.

> The driest argument has it hallucinations. . . . Men may
> dream in demonstrations, and cut out an illusory world
> in the shape of axioms, definitions, and propositions, with
> a final exclusion of fact signed Q.E.D. No formulas for
> thinking will save us mortals from mistake in our im-
> perfect apprehension of the matter to be thought about.

And since the unemotional intellect may carry us into a
mathematical dreamland where nothing is but what is
not, perhaps an emotional intellect may have absorbed
into its passionate vision of possibilities some truth of
what will be. . . . (572)

Eliot suggests here that since the intellect that chooses to exclude emotions is capable of arriving at a point "where nothing is but what is not," an emotional intellect may be able to
envision what will be. This is pure hypothesis, of course. But
it is a hypothesis that leaves room for more meaning than do
the hypotheses of unemotional thinking. Even what we call
proof, Eliot insists, always is initially hypothetical and
dreamy, depending on something that is not real or really
known. But the hypotheses on which systematic thought depends are hypothetical reductions of meaning, and Eliot insists
that we can begin with more and end with more.

Axioms are taken for granted or assumed as a given. Although we use language of exchange to identify such phenomena, we use such language to mark the end or the beginning of exchange: the point at which economy is not
functioning. All thinking, then, depends on something being
taken for granted rather than something actually taken from
reality. Outside any economy, what is taken for granted or
assumed as a given can be anything at all; we have a choice
about what we start with. Eliot recognizes that logical thinking
assumes this as the point at which we get nothing for something: a point of exclusion. Proofs "signed Q.E.D." demonstrate what was to be demonstrated on their own grounds but
with an original, as well as a "final exclusion of fact." Or, as
in the epigraph to Chapter One, Science begins with a "pretense of Nought." But it is possible instead to assume the
beginning point as the point at which we get something for
nothing, and this is what Eliot's hypothesis makes possible.
The recognition that there is no meaning possible without
some prior assumption of meaning suggests that we can fill
meaning with the partiality of our emotions rather than reduce
it to terms of lack. Rather than discounting or repressing what

we already have—our feelings—redemptive meaning assumes them in its attempt to find meaning in the world. Thus thinking assumes both the burden of feelings and the burden of facts that impartial thinking excludes from meaning. This is not to say that redemptive meaning gets all the facts. Like the excluded fact of circumcision, facts may still exceed recognition and realization. But the suspension of the terms of representation acknowledges the possibility of what exceeds the representation and allows for the possibility of discovering more meaning than representation gives us.

Thus the narrative begins with an excess rather than a lack, assuming as its "given" that there is more meaning than it can give. More meaning is recognized than can be posited or known, and more meaning is recognized than can be limited to a particular point in time. Beginning with a recognition of its own presupposition in fact rather than with its own originality, the novel reaches backward as well as forward as it begins, conflating past, present, and future in its recognition of that fact. The moment of beginning, or the narrator's present perspective, is not isolated; nor will it limit itself to beginning a development. This is insisted on by beginning at Leubronn, proceeding for fifteen pages, and then going back in time several months to events in England that precede the beginning. Deronda, too, is present at the beginning of the novel, but his story "begins" two hundred pages later with the account of his early life. Beginning *in medias res*, the novel begins again at least twice more, insisting on any beginning as both redundant and partial.

The choice to be redundant, even superfluous, rather than authoritative or original is a choice repeated by Daniel Deronda. For Deronda to choose to bind himself to Mordecai rather than Gwendolen is to choose between two excessive demands. Both Mordecai and Gwendolen believe themselves to be wholly dependent on him. For Gwendolen, Deronda becomes "part of her conscience" (468); " 'You must not forsake me. You must be near,' " she insists (765). And Mordecai's demand is even greater: " 'You must be not only a hand to me, but a soul—believing my belief—being moved by

my reasons—hoping my hope. . . . You will be my life' " (557).
Yet Gwendolen sees Deronda as " 'the beginning' " of her
new self (765), as the determining force of her meaning:
" 'You must tell me . . . what to think and what to do' "
(501). And Mordecai has already presupposed Deronda's
meaning. When Deronda appears on the river (549-51), Mordecai recognizes him, and the text represents him, in the same
terms given us twenty pages earlier in the description of Mordecai's habitual thoughts while standing on Blackfriars Bridge
at sunset. So that when Deronda appears, he appears at "sec-
ond-sight" (527), as a representation of "the figure representative of Mordecai's longing . . . mentally seen darkened
by the excess of light in the aerial background" (531). This
scene, which is the one on which Cynthia Chase focuses in
her consideration of conflicting "modes of identity" in the
novel, suggests that Mordecai functions as a kind of "all-
presupposing fact" of which Deronda can be part; he would
thus give Mordecai another version of what Mordecai already
believes to be a given. Deronda's choice of Mordecai rather
than Gwendolen is, then, precisely a choice not to be a beginning, not to assume authority, but to give something already given and be part of something already presupposed.

This choice, moreover, is represented in explicitly textual
terms; for the appeal of Mordecai for Deronda is the appeal
of a text already written. Mordecai's failed attempt to tutor
the boy Jacob as the inheritor of Mordecai's self is an attempt
to imprint a text on the child. Teaching Jacob to memorize
the words of his own Hebrew poems, Mordecai hopes that
" 'The boy will get them engraved within him . . . ; it is a way
of printing' " (533). And although Deronda resists adopting
Mordecai's "soul" and ideas without being " 'convinced first
of special reasons for it in the writings themselves' " (820),
he chooses, by identifying himself with Mordecai, to receive
or reflect another's meaning rather than initiate meaning on
his own. It is Gwendolen who requires Deronda's authority:
" 'tell me what to think.' " But that authority is exercised by
him only with fear and insecurity. To sympathize with her is
to feel "as if he were putting his name to a blank paper which

might be filled up terribly" (755). To reject Gwendolen's demands is to reject both authority and freedom. For Gwendolen's freedom to be anything—" 'When my blood is fired I
can do daring things—take any leap' " (508)—is exactly what
Deronda cannot commit himself to. Yet the narrator insists
that his "receptiveness is a rare and massive power" (553),
even as it is a power that binds him to what already is rather
than committing him to open possibilities.

To identify the meaning of the hero and the meaning of the
text with meaning presupposed by something that lies beyond
them is to identify authority itself as part of a binding relation
that cannot be grounded in any source. That even characters
in the novel are considered as texts already written suggests
another form of bondage: the intertextual bondage that exists
because all language has already been used. Roland Barthes
is one theorist to insist that there is always a residual meaning
for language and that any use of language is therefore both
a matter of choice, which is momentary, and a matter of
bondage over time:

> True, I can select such and such mode of writing, and in
> so doing assert my freedom, aspire to the freshness of
> novelty or to a tradition; but it is impossible to develop
> it within duration without gradually becoming a prisoner
> of someone else's words and even of my own. A stubborn
> after-image, which comes from all the previous modes of
> writing and even from the past of my own, drowns the
> sense of my present words.[14]

But although Barthes identifies the bondage of present language to past language in terms of loss, such bondage in *Daniel
Deronda* is willfully chosen. For Eliot, this does not result in
imprisonment of one by the other but in a binding relation
in which both are subject to change in meaning as they reflect
each other.

To find an increase of meaning in such bondage and a

[14] Roland Barthes, *Writing Degree Zero*, trans. Annette Lavers and Colin
Smith (New York: Hill and Wang, 1968), p. 17.

disabling loss of meaning in forms of independence is to suggest that Eliot's project resembles more closely Hans-Georg
Gadamer's theory of the inclusion within meaning of presupposition and prejudice. According to Gadamer, we are bound
by our prejudices to assign others' words a meaning different
from any meaning they have on their own. For this reason,
no one can read a text on its own terms. Instead, our understanding of language, and hence of history, is always something that involves prior meanings. Understanding requires
the recognition of presuppositions rather than getting rid of
them:

> A person trying to understand a text is prepared for it to
> tell him something. That is why a hermeneutically trained
> mind must be, from the start, sensitive to the text's quality
> of newness. But this kind of sensitivity involves neither
> "neutrality" in the matter of the object nor the extinction
> of one's self, but the conscious assimilation of one's own
> fore-meanings and prejudices. The important thing is to
> be aware of one's own bias, so that the text may present
> itself in all its newness and thus be able to assert its own
> truth against one's own fore-meanings.[15]

To acknowledge one's own prejudices or partiality when confronted with a text means, for Gadamer, not only an awareness of one's difference from the text but a reciprocal interplay
of these meanings:

> If a prejudice becomes questionable, in view of what an-
> other or a text says to us, this does not mean that it is
> simply set aside and the other writing or the other person
> accepted as valid in its place. . . . In fact our own prejudice
> is properly brought into play through its being at risk.
> Only through its being given full play is it able to ex-
> perience the other's claim to truth and make it possible
> for he himself to have full play.[16]

[15] Hans-Georg Gadamer, *Truth and Method* (New York: Crossroad,
1982), p. 238.
[16] Ibid., p. 266.

Such a relation thus constitutes a fullness, though not a completion of meaning, as it makes meaning mobile and reflexive. The subject seeking to understand will "learn to see in the object the counterpart of itself and hence understand both. The true historical object is not an object at all, but the unity of the one and the other, a relationship."[17]

The relationship that constitutes meaning in this theory of understanding is thus represented as a liberating relationship, even as it binds subject to object, present to past meaning, novelty to presupposition. The prejudice or partiality of the reader is something we usually think of as interfering with meaning, since it prevents the text from being read on its own terms. But by acknowledging our prejudices, we are able to see the text itself as historical, correspondingly "prejudiced" by its own historical context. Thus both subject and object come to include presupposition in their meaning. Meaning occurs as a relation in excess of the means of communication, a relation of the presuppositions that are not objectively clear or clear in the language but that are present in any writer and reader as the biases of any historical situation. This process of understanding interferes with the independence or objectivity of language, as it interferes with the independence or objectivity of any self; but it is in this process of interference that the fullness of meaning is discovered. The fact that such meaning is never neutral is what makes it meaningful. Finding meaning in the biases and prejudices of reader and writer, Gadamer allows both reader and writer to be part of the meaning of a text in the fullness of their partiality as well as their knowledge. To attempt to rule partiality out of meaning is, for Gadamer as for Eliot, a loss of meaning; for meaning always depends on and includes whoever is reading the text.

For Eliot, meaning is similarly suspended in a process that she regards as liberating in its inclusiveness. Her meaning is never free, in that it is never independent of interpretation or partiality. But individuals are freed from exclusion by their recognition that they are committed to any interpretation they

[17] Ibid., p. 267.

make. In this sense, what exceeds the bounds of objective or independent meaning in fact participates in meaning. And this means that meaning cannot be determined according to a particular source or origin but is bound to have no exclusive or singular origin. Meaning is in process, so that her narrative is always in the midst of meaning.

To insist that a narrative begins *in medias res*, Edward Said says, is a convention "that burdens the beginning with a pretense that it is not one."[18] Acknowledging more meaning than she can represent, Eliot does assume a burden of excess meaning. And in doing so, she precludes the possibility of doing "work that compensates us for the tumbling disorder of brute reality that will not settle down."[19] Her excesses, instead of compensating for reality, tend, if we characterize reality in Said's terms, to repeat it. But George Eliot does not want to compensate us for unsettled reality. She attempts instead to give us back what we lose when we use exchange to do that. Refusing to give up the excesses of meaning that order and settlement leave out, she attempts to preclude the need for compensation and also explicitly denies the capacity of forms of compensation to provide satisfaction. For Eliot, the burden of beginning and pretending not to begin, or of meaning which cannot be grounded in its own terms but welcomes the existence of meaning that exceeds its terms, is a burden assumed as part of a different economy of representation.

The economy of redemption is enacted repeatedly not only by the narrator but by the hero. The exchange that preoccupies this narrative is the redemption of pawned valuables. To pawn something, as Gwendolen pawns her necklace at the beginning of the novel, is to give it up in order to secure something else from others. To pawn something is always to give up something that is worth more than the money received in return; so that when one pawns something, one already has something worth more than one needs. What one already has is thus

[18] Edward W. Said, *Beginnings: Intention and Method* (Baltimore: The Johns Hopkins University Press, 1975), p. 43.
[19] Ibid., p. 50.

excessive, though the excess is not identified as useful. But it is this condition of excess which Eliot wishes to restore. Because pawning always entails a loss, it can be said to represent the loss of meaning entailed in conventional concepts of exchange. If, in order to enter into exchange with others, we assume that we must give up what we have or reduce ourselves to common terms, we are essentially always engaged in pawning ourselves. It is the trade-off or trade-in of pawning that characterizes it as the sort of exchange from which Eliot wishes to redeem meaning. Her redemptions are not forms of compensation *for* losses; they are restorations *of* what has been lost when something has been given up in order to gain some sort of security. Eliot allows meáning to exceed both security and common terms in order to allow the fullness of experience to be meaningful.

Daniel Deronda enacts such redemptions for others: "Persons attracted him, as Hans Meyrick had done, in proportion to the possibility of his defending them, rescuing them, telling upon their lives with some sort of redeeming influence . . ." (369). Deronda compensates Hans, Gwendolen, Mirah, and Mordecai, at various times, for what they lack. He spends his time, for example, reading to Hans when Hans temporarily loses his eyesight, so that Hans can win his scholarship; he redeems Gwendolen's necklace from the pawnshop at Leubronn; he saves Mirah's life when she is about to commit suicide; he fulfills Mordecai's wish for a second self. In each case, however, the lack which Deronda fills is a lack of something already or formerly theirs. The redemption gives back what has been possessed already. In this sense, redemption is redundant; what has been given up is given back, and thus the gift is also a return. The redundancy insists that the redemptions Deronda effects reflect back what already exists or has existed rather than providing anything different.

The compensation Deronda provides is thus not a compensation for lacks but a compensation of excess. He does not, that is to say, make up the difference between one thing and another but instead restores differences to their own terms. When the pawnbroker accepts Gwendolen's necklace in exchange for money, he makes up the difference between what she has and what she wants: money for travel. This compensatory exchange involves the loss of all but monetary value. The necklace loses any sentimental or inherent value: it is reduced to the terms that will enable it to be exchanged for a train ticket. For Deronda to redeem the necklace is to return it to its own terms, to restore its incomparability. Deronda thus re-enforces differences rather than resolving or assimilating them.

Redemption, then, refuses to equate differences or to lose the particular meaning of things and thus works against the principle of exchange that demands that things be given meaning in terms of other things. By so doing, it refuses to make up any difference between one thing and another; and it refuses to make up differences in the sense of inventing them, as Said suggests is the responsibility of authority. Redemption thus provides no resolution of the disorder of relations of incommensurable differences. In the case of the necklace, Deronda buys back the jewelry from the order of exchange that determines its meaning in terms of money, insisting that it be valued for its own sake. Rather than giving its value in alien terms, Deronda reflects the value of the thing itself. His authority, then, is reflective; he enables things to revert to themselves rather than be converted into something else. Value is not, therefore, independent when it is redeemed; it depends on reflection. But the reflection does not change the terms of value; it corroborates them.

The redemption thus seems to preclude loss, although it also precludes the security and determination of conventional exchanges. To pawn something is to provide security or grounds for an exchange. The pawned object is put "into hock," confined in order to be held as security for what the pawnbroker gives up. The redemption of the pawn suggests that redemption is a matter of liberating something from having to function as a security; it redeems securities from the obligation to be secure or determinate. For Deronda to redeem is not only to liberate objects from hock, then; it is to liberate exchange from the need for grounds, since his redemptions are themselves always gifts, ungrounded and unsecured. Such gifts do not work as exchanges but seem to defy exchange. Redeeming values from security denies both their security and their priority. They are no longer held in exchange for something else or as grounds for something else. The loss of priority has a historical dimension, too, for redemption unsettles temporal as well as logical priorities. The two objects that are actually redeemed from pawnshops in the novel are both residue of the past: Gwendolen's necklace is made from a chain that belonged to her father, and Deronda's ring belonged to his father. To pawn them is to recognize that the inherited past can be used to secure the present or to determine what one gets in the present. It is also to suggest that the past can be traded in to provide the means of starting anew. To redeem them is to assume "the burden of the past,"[20] just as the narrative's beginning assumes the burden of the past as something that cannot be limited to the terms of the present or gotten rid of. Such redemptions also assume the burden of a present which exceeds rather than is limited to the terms it has in common with the past.

This is, therefore, an unsettling experience. Assuming a burden, such redemptions may give back more than is wanted. For Deronda to redeem Gwendolen's necklace or save Mirah's life is to give them back what they have chosen to give up in order to secure, on the one hand, money and, on the other, peace. In both cases, Deronda burdens these women with something they would rather not have. Gwendolen does not care about her father or about her father's jewels; and she prefers to live without such cares, finding freedom in her independence from others. Mirah is tired of life itself and believes it easier to die. Because Deronda insists that these women be committed to what they would rather give up, his

---

[20] This phrase is taken from Walter Jackson Bate's *The Burden of the Past and the English Poet* (Cambridge: Harvard University Press, 1970). Bate considers the peculiarly modern dilemma of the poet caused by the desire both to imitate past masters and to establish one's difference from them. This is an issue linked to the experience of the sublime, which I will consider briefly toward the end of this chapter.

redemptions do not work as responses to needs; instead they identify a need where none is felt. Both the necklace and the life have been judged to be superfluous or unnecessary, and their restoration thus compensates for no felt lack. The "compensation" of such redemption works to generate or exceed rather than answer need, and in this sense constitutes a demand as well as a gift. Yet it is nevertheless a return. On both counts, redemption is redundant; and the redundancy seems an unnecessary burden. But the burden of the novel—the weight of its meaning and its repeated refrain—is its insistence on redundancy. What Eliot demands is that we value what we already have and what we already are rather than give that up in order to attempt to be secure in ourselves or in the eyes of others.

The relation of one person to another that constitutes the redeeming relation also seems to constitute a burden. Both Gwendolen and Mirah are made uneasy by Deronda's redemptions because he has no business making them. The redemptions put the women in an awkward position, for their relations to him cannot be economized in terms of debt or demand. They have not asked for what he gives them, and he asks no return for what he gives them. Thus Gwendolen at first regards the redemption of her necklace as "an unpardonable liberty" (49), and Deronda, too, is "conscious that . . . he had taken a questionable freedom" (377). The freedom of the redemption is dubious precisely because it is unwarranted: it responds to no demand and is part of no exchange.

Rather than resolving the uncertainty of such relations, Deronda maintains it. With Mirah, "he shrank from what might seem like curiosity, or the assumption of a right to know as much as he pleased of one to whom he had done a service" (267), and "he shrank from appearing to claim the authority of a benefactor" (233). If he has redeemed her life from debt, since she felt the need to give it up in order to secure peace, he maintains the redemption only by denying any indebtedness to him. Thus the redemption generates no exchange to determine the meaning it has rendered indeterminate. What Deronda wants is itself unsettling; he wants to take part in others' lives in ways that cannot be defined by any object or objective. He does not want anything from Mirah or Gwendolen; he wants to make a difference to them. If he does not take, though, the fact that what he gives already belongs to the other suggests that he does not exactly give anything either. He reflects back parts of others. He becomes, by doing so, part of what they are, and he makes what they are dependent on him. For the possessions he redeems can never again be considered quite the others' possessions. They are restored to others through him, and their restoration thereby binds others to him. Deronda does take a liberty, then, because he takes away the liberty of the self-possessed individual.

Thus Deronda's redemptions interfere with the independence and self-sufficiency of characters just as the narrator's redemption of meaning from secure grounds interferes with the self-sufficiency of her narrative. Refusing to begin at the beginning, she refuses to start at "Nought," because she refuses to pretend to have nothing when in fact there is so much there. Thus Eliot gives us back the excess of meaning we are accustomed to giving up in order to make a beginning or end. And this is what Deronda does with others, as he refuses to allow Gwendolen to leave her past behind or Mirah to end her life. The relations in which he takes part are relations in which people are allowed to drop the pretense of "Nought." Assuming a prior excess of value rather than a prior lack, Deronda's behavior, like the narrator's, makes possible relations which are uneconomical but which make room for incommensurable differences. Thus redemption functions on a number of levels to insist that meaning assume the burden of more significance than can be settled. Redemption puts different meanings in suspended and reflective rather than determinate relations and confuses thereby the distinctions that give order to life: distinctions such as past and present, gift and return, self and other. Such differences become part of each other. And in these indistinctions Eliot finds the possibility of making room for value that exceeds the terms of exchange while still maintaining relations among differing values.

To be *in medias res* is the acknowledged condition of the beginning of the narrative of *Daniel Deronda*, as it is the condition of the redeeming hero who repeatedly interferes in others' lives. Precluding any distinct sense of origin, the novel also precludes any distinct sense of end insofar as its hero's desire is to be himself in the midst of things, "an organic part of social life" (413). With Deronda, the novel insists that the subject can both make a difference to objects and be made different by objects. This is an extension of meaning, and it extends meaning beyond the bounds that distinguish subject and object. But such an extension is also a restoration, because it recognizes the meaning that conventional distinctions rule out but that, for Eliot, is in fact present. Meaning in this novel is thus authorized in excess of what we usually regard as meaningful, yet the gift of these excesses is not easy to take.

Gwendolen's resistance to her own redemption makes this evident. Deronda attempts to talk her into taking part in the world around her and so extend her self beyond the limits of her own distinction, as when he insists that she ought to play music even though she is not particularly good at it:

> "A little private imitation of what is good is a sort of private devotion to it, and most of us ought to practise art only in the light of private study—preparation to understand and enjoy what the few can do for us." (491)

Deronda reiterates the need for such an extension of self when he insists that Gwendolen ought to know more:

> "some real knowledge would give you an interest in the world beyond the small drama of personal desires. It is the curse of your life—forgive me—of so many lives, that all passion is spent in that narrow round, for want of ideas and sympathies to make a larger home for it." (507)

For Deronda, such participation in what lies beyond the self is desirable. Yet what he is recommending is imitation rather than originality, secondariness rather than distinction. Gwendolen, therefore, does not " 'feel able to follow your advice of enjoying my own middlingness' " (491). The indistinction of being *in media res* represents for her a loss of meaning.

But if Gwendolen, in her desire for distinction, cannot get outside the bounds of self, Deronda himself, for much of the novel, is so multiple in his identifications with others that his self threatens to disappear altogether. " 'It will not do to give yourself to be melted down for the benefit of the tallow-trade,' " Sir Hugo tells him; " 'you must know where to find yourself' " (224). Eliot insists that the individual find his or her self in between self and others, with each "side" taking part in a relation in which the meaning of each is dependent on and inseparable from the other. The central characters in the novel are initially unable to "find themselves" *in medias res*. With virtually reverse forms of behavior, both Deronda and Gwendolen are uncommitted in their relations to the world around them. The hero seems to have no self to commit to others, to be *only* a reflection of what lies beyond him; and the heroine disregards everything but her own distinction. In this, they reflect each other as alternative versions of neutrality. In order to redeem their meaning, both characters must find themselves in a binding relation of self and world. Yet the redemption offered Deronda, like the redemption offered Gwendolen, seems to constitute a loss of meaning. For if he is too "reflective" to commit himself to anything, it is also clear that his sympathies are what give him value. Yet the critical consideration of his reflectiveness hinges again on the suspension of what lies inside and what lies outside the self. Deronda must suspend the relation between his internal reflections—reflections of his own ideas—and reflection within the self of what lies beyond the self. Thus the redemption of individual meaning is demanding; and in the reflective representation of Deronda and Gwendolen, Eliot clarifies both the demand and the gift of her redemption.

Deronda, who is always, like Dorothea Brooke, taking others' parts, seems to be not so much a self or a subject as a reflection of objects:

His early-wakened sensibility and reflectiveness had developed into a many-sided sympathy, which threatened to hinder any persistent course of action: as soon as he took up any antagonism, though only in thought, he seemed to himself like the Sabine warriors in the memorable story—with nothing to meet his spear but flesh of his flesh, and objects that he loved. His imagination had so wrought itself to the habit of seeing things as they probably appeared to others, that strong partisanship, unless it were against an immediate oppression, had become an insincerity for him. (412)

Like Gideon in the argument with Mordecai, Deronda can always see "another side" to things, and, able to take the part of anyone, he is unable to take a stand. Indiscriminately reflective and sympathetic, Deronda takes multiple parts in identification with others' points of view but does not distinguish himself from others or distinguish between points of view. He is unwilling to take any part that excludes other parts:

With the same innate balance he was fervidly democratic in his feeling for the multitude, and yet, through his affections and imagination, intensely conservative; voracious of speculations on government and religion, yet loath to part with long-sanctioned forms which, for him, were quick with memories and sentiments that no argument could lay dead. (412-413)

In any antagonism, then, Deronda finds himself on both sides, like the Sabine warriors who must fight their "flesh" in order to fight their enemies. His partiality, because it enables him to take the part of anything that is losing, therefore borders on impartiality, since anything at all can be in that condition. Having no consistency, Deronda verges on the "emptiness" of Lovelace, to whom Sir Hugo in fact compares him,[21] be-

[21] Sir Hugo warns Deronda against flirting with Gwendolen: " 'You are always looking tenderly at the women. . . . You are a dangerous young fellow—a kind of Lovelace who will make the Clarissas run after you instead of your running after them' " (409). Deronda's capacity to sympathize with

cause he plays multiple parts but has none of his own. If Lovelace's multiplicity keeps his meaning doubly bound, Deronda's "flexible sympathy"also catches him in repeated double binds. The fact that he cannot choose between different things but can identify, at least potentially, with anything at all means the loss of difference itself. Passion becomes impasse here. His is "a reflectiveness that threatened to nullify all differences" (414), an excess of feeling that has "fallen into a meditative numbness" (414).

Deronda cannot choose for the same reason that he cannot approve of gambling, for to choose one "side" would mean to give up the other.

> "There is something revolting to me in raking a heap of money together . . . when others are feeling the loss of it. . . . There are enough inevitable turns of fortune which force us to see that our gain is another's loss:—that is one of the ugly aspects of life. One would like to reduce it as much as one could. . . ." (383)

Thus Deronda cannot choose anything that means loss to anything else. Yet, as this passage indicates, as long as meaning is left to chance such losses will occur. And Deronda is committed to nothing that might alter chance. The fact that he cannot commit himself to making a particular difference in the world, because he is worried about what such a choice would exclude, means that he is always leaving meaning to chance. He just happens, for example, to see Gwendolen at Leubronn when she loses her money, and he just happens to come along when Mirah is about to commit suicide. These redemptions, then, are due to accident. Deronda's experience thus reflects the very indiscriminacy of chance as he tries to compensate for whatever happens to lose out to something else. And he remains dependent on chance as long as he is

---

others, as if he can enter into their difficulties, makes him particularly attractive to others and suggests also the mobile and partial nature of his own identity.

waiting for something to change his life; all he seems able to do is to wait and see.

What Deronda needs may come from inside or outside him, but it is needed in order to commit his feelings to others with binding force:

> What he most longed for was either some external event, or some inward light, that would urge him into a definite line of action, and compress his wandering energy. . . . But how and whence was the needed event to come?— the influence that would justify partiality, and making him what he longed to be yet was unable to make himself—an organic part of social life. . . . (413)

Here the differentiation the narrator makes between Deronda's predicament and the way to solve it is a difficult one. For if Deronda has no sure sense of himself, the solution to his difficulty seems not to give him one either. The most problematic elements of the difficulty seem to be reflected in its solution, and the solution like the difficulty seems to combine contradictory elements. The need is for both compression and extension, and something must happen "that would justify partiality," itself a groundless and irrational condition. Eliot, too, that is, identifies as desirable two conflicting elements that seem to cancel each other out and thus seems herself to be caught in a double bind. But she is in fact demanding a choice, even though that choice is difficult to identify, given her insistence on the reflective quality of differences.

The narrator recognizes her difficulty here, and Deronda's difficulty, as one of trying to do two different things at once:

> He wanted some way of keeping emotion and its progeny of sentiments . . . substantial and strong in the face of a reflectiveness that threatened to nullify all differences. To pound the objects of sentiments into small dust, yet keep sentiment alive and active, was something like the famous recipe for making cannon—to first take a round hole and then enclose it with iron; whatever you do keeping fast hold of your round hole. (414)

If all differences are nullified, and objects of feeling are as indistinguishable as small dust, how are feelings themselves to be saved from indifference? What is required is a choice, and the choice is needed to separate Deronda's sympathetic feelings from the reflectiveness that neutralizes differences. He has a choice, then, of different kinds of reflection. One of these, reflective analysis, verges on indifference, and this indifference is also reflected in his feelings. The debilitating reflectiveness, therefore, is identified as an internal condition. Deronda's emotions are "faced" with his reflectiveness. He thinks too much to make a choice; and the more he reflects *on* things, the more sides he sees to any question.

The problem, then, is that Deronda is not primarily reflecting what he sees outside him at all. He is reflecting *on* his sympathetic reflections of what lies beyond him and thereby in fact separating his reflective capacity from the outside world. One part of his reflective self thus cancels out another, as his sympathies are assimilated into thought, for "his flexible sympathy had ended by falling into one current with that reflective analysis which tends to neutralise sympathy" (412). This is a self-enclosed experience of reflection, then. And it is because Deronda is enclosed within his *own* reflections that he is necessarily neutralized and impartial in his relations with others. The choice required by Eliot, then, is not only a choice between reflective feelings and reflective analysis but a choice between reflecting what lies inside the self and reflecting what is perceived as lying outside the self. This, then, is the same choice that Deronda demands of Gwendolen. Like her, he must move his energies outside himself rather than consuming them internally.

To pose the problem in terms of the recipe for making cannon does not simplify the difficulty. Eliot clearly means to say that Deronda cannot "pound the objects of sentiment into small dust, yet keep sentiment alive and active," since it is crucial to her concept of reflective relations that objects must be strong if subjects are to be strong. Yet the recipe she cites to support her sense of a double bind in fact works, and it works in the same way that any idea gets realized. You cannot, of course, take a hole and enclose it; a hole is not a hole unless it is already enclosed. In this sense, the recipe begins and ends with the same thing and seems absurd. But the first hole is a "given," an idea that must be held fast within the mind in order to make the hole that is required in a cannon. In this, the recipe resembles any invention. That it is not to be dismissed because of its apparent faulty logic is clearest, perhaps, in the fact that its logic resembles the redemptive determination of Mordecai, "whose yearnings, conceptions—nay, travelled conclusions—continually take the form of images which have a foreshadowing power" (527). For Eliot, a person must have an idea of what is to be done in order to do it, and thus "even strictly-measuring science could hardly have got on without that forecasting ardour which feels the agitations of discovery beforehand" (572). The redundancy of the recipe, therefore, is in fact necessary to creative change, and its apparent logical absurdity is not the problem.

The real question here is not whether the recipe will work but the particular commitment it represents. It represents the idea and the realization of a lack: what is desired is a cannon, and what is needed is a hole. Committed to the nullification of what lies beyond it by the destructiveness of the cannon, the idea is also committed to the lack of anything within. That this project is perfectly capable of being carried through is what Deronda's experience also represents. For, unlike the narrator, Deronda usually "begins at Nought" in his relations to the world. He is as if in the process of enclosing a hole, insofar as he is committed to his own lack of meaning and is behaving in ways that cut him off from any commitment to others. Reflecting on things, he nullifies what lies beyond him. Reflecting on his own sympathies, he nullifies his own feelings. In both cases, he sees at least two sides to things, and he sees these differences in terms of a trade-off: one thing loses if the other wins. Since he cannot choose anything on these terms, he is in effect indifferent to others and indifferent in himself. He is doubly bound not because he is uncommitted or because he is committed to something that is illogical, but because he is committed to a lack of meaning.

Given his commitment to a lack of meaning both within himself and in the world beyond him, the commitment Eliot demands of him is doubled up. Deronda must choose to move beyond his own reflections so that he can perceive the world in terms of its incommensurable differences. But he must also choose to acknowledge his self as an incomparable difference: to be what he is rather than perceive himself as a lack. Because he is nothing to himself, nothing constitutes a "given" for him; what is given in his thinking, that is to say, is a lack of meaning. Deronda's selflessness is thus presented as a lack of meaning that precludes his commitment to the world beyond him. Though he needs compression and definition of his energies, all he has to compress and define is emptiness, as with the cannon. Unlike Mordecai, who is committed to a reflective relation of his ideas and his perception of the world around him, Deronda has nothing to work with; and Eliot gives this as potentially destructive rather than productive of meaning.

In this, Deronda verges on Gwendolen Harleth. The reasons for his selflessness and the means by which he "finds himself" I will consider in the next section of this chapter. Here, however, I want to clarify how Gwendolen characterizes another version of the indifference that paralyzes and neutralizes Deronda. Gwendolen is also locked within the confines of herself and remains noncommittal as long as this is true. She, too, is engaged in neutralizing meaning, moreover, in her efforts to deny any meaningful relation between her self and the world around her.

Described as a "princess" with an "empire" who means "to conquer circumstance by her exceptional cleverness" (69), Gwendolen is committed to her own supremacy. Yet within herself she is ambivalent, always capable of doing two things at once. She, too, then, is committed always to seeing more than one side of things because she does not exceed the bounds of self:

She had the charm, and those who feared her were also fond of her; the fear and the fondness being perhaps both heightened by what may be called the iridescence of her character—the play of various, nay, contrary tendencies. For Macbeth's rhetoric about the impossibility of being many opposite things in the same moment, referred to the clumsy necessities of action and not to the subtler possibilities of feeling. We cannot speak a loyal word and be meanly silent, we cannot kill and not kill in the same moment; but a moment is room wide enough for the loyal and mean desire, for the outlash of a murderous thought and the sharp backward stroke of repentance. (72)

Gwendolen arouses both fear and fondness in others, and this itself seems a reflection of her own capacity for mixed feelings. Unlike Deronda, who is constant in his sympathetic feelings though their objects change, Gwendolen is inconstant in her feelings; and those feelings seem to change here regardless of object. The fact that her feelings are capable of anything, however, represents the potential of Gwendolen's own possibility of being anything. She seldom commits herself to any action that would limit her meaning and remains in fact committed to her own indeterminacy by her desire to distinguish herself. For it is her felt capacity to do anything at all that enables Gwendolen to believe in her distinction; and the fact that she can be anything means that she can always be different.

Thus Gwendolen's indeterminacy gives her the freedom to be anything, and her desire to "lead" commits her to remain indeterminate. When she first appears, reflected in Deronda's eyes at the gambling casino, her concern is only to distinguish herself:

Since she was not winning strikingly, the next best thing was to lose strikingly. . . . There was a smile of irony in his eyes as their glances met; but it was at least better that he should have kept his attention fixed on her than that he should have disregarded her as one of an insect swarm who had no individual physiognomy. (39-40)

Whether Gwendolen wins or loses is insignificant to her compared to whether she is distinguished or undistinguished in
Deronda's eyes. Winning or losing makes little difference, because each constitutes a distinction. Yet this is the only choice
she recognizes, for only in these absolute terms can she be
exceptional. The exclusive difference is necessary to her, and
nothing in between is satisfactory.

Unlike Deronda, who sides with whatever is losing, Gwendolen "sides" with whatever will enable her to win distinction.
Because she finds meaning only in distinction per se, she acts
for the sake of difference itself rather than for the sake of any
particular difference. She is thereby bound, however, to do
and be nothing particular because she is determined to be
different, just as Deronda is bound to do nothing particular
as long as he is impartial. Like Deronda, she is noncommittal,
unable to choose between differences because any difference
will do. Not only is Gwendolen capable of doing anything at
all in order to stand out; she is bound to be able to do anything
at all if she wants always to be distinguished. She is bound,
then, to be noncommittal.

Thus Gwendolen's life is always dependent on chance, since
she takes whatever offers a means of superiority. Gwendolen,
moreover, demands chance and is uneasy unless life remains
chancy. For her, any known quantity is inferior to uncertainty:
" 'There is more in it,' " she says to Grandcourt (184). And
she therefore resists any decision that would rule out any other
possibility. Without his moral "grounds," Gwendolen thereby
comes close again to Deronda as she objects to getting something at the expense of something else and commits herself to
chance by her refusal to commit herself to anything else. "Having come close to accepting Grandcourt, Gwendolen felt this
lot of unhoped-for fulness rounding itself too definitely: when
we take to wishing a great deal for ourselves, whatever we
get soon turns into mere limitation and exclusion" (183). Thus
Gwendolen is limited to possibilities by the fear of loss as well
as by the fact that her ideas are incommensurable with any
realization of them.

In part the static condition of Gwendolen's life is due to

the fact that she can neither lose nor gain anything because she maintains uncertainty. She repeatedly chooses to be in the position of being able to get out of anything she gets into and so hopes to be able to make up for anything she does. This means that her speech and actions tend to resemble her feelings in their indeterminacy, despite Eliot's statement that speech and actions are more definite than feelings. Gwendolen likes to give and take back what she says, either implicitly, as in the sort of ironic repartee that causes Mrs. Arrowpoint to decide that she is " 'double and satirical' " (81), or explicitly, in that "her first impulse often was to say what she afterwards wished to retract" (493). And when she is cruel and "kills"— since she did in fact strangle her sister's canary because it sang when she was trying to sing—she likes to make up for it. She bought her sister a mouse, and she plans to persuade Grandcourt to be generous to Mrs. Glasher, the woman with whom he has had children and whom Gwendolen displaces when she becomes his wife. Thus Gwendolen "had known no compunction that atoning caresses and presents could not lay to rest" (355).

Gwendolen's insistence on seeing things in comparable and compensatory terms is crucial to her noncommittal attitude to the world. She maintains the possibility of doing anything at all and is able to enjoy it as long as she maintains, in one way or another, the possibility of canceling out or compensating for anything she does. She thus commits herself only to things that are unrealized, things that are missing, or things that do not count. Emptying meaning of substance, she recognizes nothing as meaningful in its particularity. Nor does she recognize any relation between herself and meaning except a noncommittal relation. She denies her own choice about meaning by deferring it to chance, and even when she accepts Grandcourt "she seemed to herself to be, after all, only drifted towards the tremendous decision" (348).

Thus, although Gwendolen's inconsistencies give her a sense of power and freedom, Eliot insists that she is always doubly bound. She enacts two forms of subjection: one is her "desire to conquer" and one is her "subjection to a possible self, a

self not to be absolutely predicted about" (173). It is her desire
to conquer and her insistence on keeping possibilities open
that limit and constrain Gwendolen's meaning. And they do
so as they alienate her from her real bonds to others and to
her feelings. For she is truly bound to others, just as she is
truly bound to suffer by the guilt she feels for acts recognized
as incommensurable with any compensation she can make.
Yet both in relation to others and in her self, Gwendolen is
committed to the cancellation of binding meaning: she cancels
out relations to others by always distinguishing herself from
them, and she cancels out her own feelings by experiencing
them as contradictory.

The narrative insists on Gwendolen's dependence even as
she insists on her independence. For no character in this novel
is independent of others. Even Gwendolen's "divinity" is a
dependent quality, something given her by others; and it is
something she cannot maintain on her own. Once her money
has been lost, she is like "one who had been made to believe
in his own divinity finding all homage withdrawn, and himself
unable to perform a miracle that would recall the homage
and restore his own confidence" (334). Like Deronda, Gwendolen finds nothing within herself to provide her with meaning. Yet even Grandcourt, whose mastery of others lies in his
assumption of indifference to others, is dependent on others
to recognize his indifference: his "state of not caring, just as
much as desire, required its related object—namely, a world
of admiring or envying spectators" (646).

The experience of characters who desire mastery, such as
Gwendolen and Grandcourt, confirms that mastery does not
control or determine meaning. Rather than freeing the self
from others, the desire to master confines the self to others'
terms and determines the self according to others. Gwendolen's desire for empire over others, for example, is a desire
that requires the recognition of her superiority by others. She
believes she wants freedom and pleasure, but she wants them
reflected in others' eyes: "She meant to do what was pleasant
to herself in a striking manner; or rather, whatever she could
do so as to strike others with admiration and get in that
reflected way a more ardent sense of living, seemed pleasant

to her fancy" (69). Pleasure itself, as this qualification suggests, comes to represent a double bind for Gwendolen as it becomes an experience of separation from her self. She both recognizes that her pleasure depends on others and wishes to do as she likes, as if that did not depend on others. Her desires are repeatedly represented as in fact binding her to others, though they are desires to differ from others and deny any such bondage:

> She rejoiced to feel herself exceptional; but her horizon was that of the genteel romance where the heroine's soul poured out in her journal is full of vague power, originality, and general rebellion, while her life moves strictly in the sphere of fashion; and if she wanders into a swamp, the pathos lies partly, so to speak, in her having on her satin shoes. Here is a restraint which nature and society have provided on the pursuit of striking adventure; so that a soul burning with a sense of what the universe is not . . . is nevertheless held captive by the ordinary wirework of social forms and does nothing particular. (83)

As long as Gwendolen desires to be exceptional, then, she will be limited, by the nature of her desire and by the conventions of society. For she must be an exception *to* something, and this means that she must always present herself in terms commensurate with convention. In fact constrained by her own determination to differ, she is incapable of acknowledging any incomparable difference in herself. Determined to " 'do what is unlikely,' " she is in fact perfectly predictable in her determination, as Rex points out to her: " 'When once I knew what people in general would be likely to do, I should know you would do the opposite. So you would have come round to a likelihood of your own sort' " (100).

Gwendolen's behavior, then, is determined by her determination to be different, determined as an opposition to others. Her determination makes the binding relation to others a relation of constraint and limitation, binding her doubly by her will to oppose what she depends on and limiting all meaning to distinct forms. Thus Gwendolen rules out the possibility of any exceptional meaning, for she rules out any meaning that exceeds the bounds of convention or distinction. No meaning has any meaning "in particular" for her; instead, all different things are valued for the sake of their difference alone. This both neutralizes meaning of substance and makes any meaning subject to cancellation by a different meaning.[22]

Within herself, moreover, Gwendolen is similarly involved in a double bind as she is "subjected" to possibility. Conscious of her capacity to be anything, Gwendolen is accustomed to seeing this as a sign of her power. But it becomes also a source of terror once she realizes that she is capable of acting in ways that make her guilty of crimes for which there is no compensation: " 'I have thrust out others—I have made my gain out of their loss' " (506). It is as if, once her actions have committed her to an unalterable and incomparable position in her marriage to Grandcourt, she must locate the neutralizing dynamic that has previously characterized her actions within her self. Thus the external commitment is itself neutralized by the noncommittal nature of her doubly bound feelings. Burdened with guilt for having married Grandcourt, Gwendolen is also burdened with the terror that she will murder him:

> "I am frightened at everything. I am frightened at myself.
> When my blood is fired I can do daring things—take any
> leap; but that makes me frightened at myself." (508)

Thus her daring and her terror cancel each other out. Both Gwendolen's guilt and terror are attributed to her conscience, and it seems that conscience is her redeeming characteristic. Conscience, Eliot says in the epigraph to Chapter 35, prevents most people from wickedness (455). But conscience goes no farther than preventing what would contradict it.

Doubly bound by her conflicting feelings, Gwendolen is at

---

[22] Gwendolen's power, then, is limited to the power to oppose or negate something else. Judith Wilt, in *Ghosts of the Gothic: Austen, Eliot, and Lawrence* (Princeton: Princeton University Press, 1980), clarifies this as a sign that Gwendolen is void of meaning. Wilt identifies Grandcourt as the perfect match for Gwendolen and identifies Gwendolen's commitment to Grandcourt not as a "battle of wills" but as a "battle of voids" (p. 217).

first advised by Deronda to move beyond her feelings and interest herself in something else. But everything else, reflecting her feelings, is also " 'all confusion to me' " (507). And because Deronda recognizes that Gwendolen is simply seeing her own " 'inaction' " reflected in the world, he also advises her to activate her feelings:

> "Turn your fear into a safeguard. Keep your dread fixed on the idea of increasing that remorse which is so bitter to you. . . . Take your fear as a safeguard. It is like quickness of hearing. It may make consequences passionately present to you." (509)

Since Gwendolen cannot recognize any object in the world around her that makes a difference to her feelings, Deronda suggests here that she treat her guilt and her fear as objects themselves. She can be afraid of guilt; and she can take hold of her fear and use it to extend her perception beyond the immediacy of her feelings. But for Gwendolen the effect of this advice is another standoff: "In Gwendolen's consciousness Temptation and Dread met and stared like two pale phantoms, each seeing itself in the other—each obstructed by its own image; and all the while her fuller self beheld the apparitions and sobbed for deliverance from them" (738). For Gwendolen, as for Deronda earlier in the novel, passions are at an impasse here. To identify consequences for her feelings does not make any difference to her, because the consequence she most dreads—murder—is also the consequence she most desires. Dread and temptation thus confront each other as reflections *of* each other, and their opposition cancels out the possibility of making any difference. Like Deronda, she is locked within her own reflections, and any attempt to look beyond the immediate limits of her experience makes no difference but remains a vision of mutually exclusive feelings about what lies beyond her.

Gwendolen, too, therefore, is unable to make herself what she longs to be. She is as "impartial" to differences as Deronda is. But, as is clear in the case of Deronda, the internal and external conditions of her life are themselves reflections of the same condition. For George Eliot insists that the emptiness of Gwendolen's life can be located in her relations to others as well as in her self. Gwendolen both denies any meaning in her relations to others by reducing those relations to the terms of opposition and denies any meaning in her self by perceiving her feelings as opposed to each other. In each case, meaning is nullified, as she herself is imprisoned: in the one case by "the ordinary wirework of social forms" to which she is committed and in the other by the mutual obstruction of the feelings by which she is bound. Gwendolen relates to the world, then, as she relates to her self. Like Deronda in this, too, she perceives both world and self as empty of meaning.

The redemption of the meaning of both Deronda and Gwendolen entails a discovery that precludes their own emptiness and enables them to see both self and others in terms of reflective fullness rather than reflected lack. The redemption of meaning, then, maintains the reflective relation of self and world. Deronda discovers that he is a Jew. But this recognition is both one that he shares with others—the Jews who identify him as Jewish before he knows that he is Jewish—and one that gives him meaning in common with others. As Chase has emphasized, it is not clear where such meaning comes from— inside Deronda or outside him. Thus the answer to whether it is "some external event, or some inward light" (413) that will decide Deronda's meaning remains undifferentiated. It is both together, as the fact of his birth and his partiality for the Jews appear together.

A consideration of the redemption of individual meaning thus returns us to a consideration of beginnings. For both Deronda and Gwendolen, there is a question about the source of the meaning they eventually find for themselves. The question about Deronda is "how and whence was the needed event to come?—the influence that would justify partiality, and making him what he longed to be yet was unable to make himself?" (413). This insists that he cannot find himself in himself or begin to make the difference that he wishes to make to others. Gwendolen's question is more explicitly a recognition that she cannot justify making the difference she wishes to make in her life. She wishes to leave Grandcourt. But

> What could she say to justify her flight? Her uncle would tell her to go back. . . . Her husband would have power to compel her. She had absolutely nothing that she could allege against him in judicious or judicial ears. And to "insist on separation!" That was an easy combination of words. . . . How was she to begin? What was she to say that would not be a condemnation of herself? (665)

Gwendolen here recognizes that she cannot justify her partiality: she loathes Grandcourt, but from any impartial point of view he has done nothing wrong. Justice would in fact condemn her rather than Grandcourt, since she chose to marry him knowing what she knew. Gwendolen does not want justice; but neither is she able to act in keeping with her own feelings, because there are no grounds for such action. In the kind of thinking that characterizes her, Gwendolen locates meaning in impartial terms that turn meaning against her and commit her to the loss of meaning.

But although Gwendolen cannot see how to begin to change her life, she has in fact already changed. She attributes this to Deronda: " 'You began it, you know, when you rebuked me' " (509). But the narrator insists that Deronda did not begin to change Gwendolen. Although Gwendolen identifies the beginning of her desire to change in Deronda, the narrative identifies it in Gwendolen: "with what she had felt to be his judgment of her at the gaming table" (833). It is Gwendolen's "first resentment at his critical glance" (377), not anything in Deronda, that moves her to change, for his gaze is one "which Gwendolen chose to call 'dreadful,' though it had really a very mild sort of scrutiny" (226). Rather than being the source of Gwendolen's redemption, Deronda is the projected reflection of her own insecurity about herself. Thus her redemption, like his, originates both in herself and in another's reflection of her own feelings and extends the meaning of what is already within her into a suspension of meaning between herself and what lies beyond her.

Redemption does not lie simply in such suspensions of meaning, however, but demands the commitment of the self to the suspension of meaning. Redemption is binding both because it binds self to others and because it binds self to others in terms of the partial feelings of the self. In both these aspects, redemption occurs as the restoration of a prior meaning which is also an insecure meaning. Both Gwendolen's and Deronda's redemptions restore their "fuller selves" to meaning, but this occurs always as a restoration of meaning to a relative and groundless condition.

Both Gwendolen and Deronda can be considered as characters who have pawned their "fuller selves." It is as if each has put part of the self "into hock," in order to secure meaning in the eyes of others. For each has a fuller self than is evident to others. Gwendolen's "fuller self" that "sobbed for deliverance" from the incapacitating standoff of Temptation and Dread is a self which has little expression in the novel, a self to which she denies both herself and others access:

> What she unwillingly recognised, and would have been glad for others to be unaware of, was that liability of hers to fits of spiritual dread, though this fountain of awe within her had not found its way into connection with the religion taught her or with any human relations. She was ashamed and frightened, as at what might happen again, in remembering her tremor on suddenly feeling herself alone, when, for example, she was walking without companionship and there came some rapid change in the light. Solitude in any wide scene impressed her with an undefined feeling of immeasurable existence aloof from her, in the midst of which she was helplessly incapable of asserting herself. (94-95)

The "fountain of awe" within Gwendolen is a feeling that precludes both self-assertion and any binding connection to what lies beyond her; for it is aroused by a sense of "immeasurable existence aloof from her." Terrified of what exceeds her control and remains indifferent to her, Gwendolen confines her behavior as much as possible to relations with others over whom she can exercise power. For

> always when someone joined her she recovered her in-
> difference to the vastness in which she seemed an exile;
> she found again her usual world in which her will was
> of some avail. . . . With human ears and eyes about her,
> she had always hitherto recovered her confidence, and
> felt the possibility of winning empire. (95)

Rather than being exiled from significance, Gwendolen is able to rule her own meaning by ruling others. Her sense of rule, however, and the sense of her own distinction, require that she rule out her feelings of meaninglessness by assuming in-difference to the part of herself and the part of the world that exceed her control. Thus she secures meaning only with the knowledge that there is more meaning, an excess that threat-ens her security.

Daniel Deronda also has a self that he hides from others and from himself. Not knowing who his parents are, Deronda "immediately shrank into reserve" at any reference by others to his birth, and this "remained a check on his naturally strong bent towards the formation of intimate friendships" (213). Yet he makes no effort to find out about his birth either, for, like Gwendolen, he cannot "deliver" himself from the bond-age of his conflicting feelings: "The desire to know his own mother, or to know about her, was constantly haunted with dread" (246). The haunting dread he feels about his parentage is the fundamental reflection within Deronda of Gwendolen's crippling emotions. Deronda is also terrified of his own in-significance, and he chooses to repress the question of his birth because it threatens him with meaninglessness. When Sir Hugo suggests to him as a child that he might like to be " 'a great singer,' " this

> seemed to Daniel an unmistakable proof that there was
> something about his birth which threw him out from the
> class of gentlemen to which the baronet belonged. Would

it ever be mentioned to him? Would the time come when his uncle would tell him everything? He shrank from the prospect: in his imagination he preferred ignorance. If his father had been wicked . . . , he wished it might never be spoken of to him. . . . (209)

Afraid that he is excluded from "the class of gentlemen," what Deronda fears here, like Gwendolen in the passage quoted above, is being exiled from significance. Rather than confront that, he chooses ignorance of what he is, just as Gwendolen chooses to ignore the "feeling of immeasurable existence aloof from her."

To fear being an exile is to fear being in the condition of the Jews in the novel. Both Gwendolen and Deronda resist such exile by doing what Mordecai refuses to do; they attempt to fit into conventional society, either by obedience to conventional forms of behavior, which Gwendolen practices, or by maintaining identity as a gentleman, as Deronda does. Both attempt thereby to ignore the exile they fear, but in doing so they in fact commit themselves to repeating the insecure relation of self and world that terrifies them. Gwendolen, who dreads the power of an "existence aloof from her" that implies her own humiliation, in fact marries, in Grandcourt, a personification of that aloofness. The indifference that she dreads is also, then, the object of her desire: she is both attracted to Grandcourt's aloofness and attracted to the possibility of being indifferent herself. But the marriage of herself to indifference is also the marriage of herself to humiliation and dread. She can decide to marry Grandcourt only by assuming indifference and "casting away all care for justification." But her choice of "lawlessness" is made "with the shadowy array of possible calamity behind it" because she knows she is guilty of wrongdoing (358). After the marriage,

> Her sense of being blameworthy was exaggerated by a dread both definite and vague. The definite dread was lest the veil of secrecy should fall between her and Grandcourt, and give him the right to taunt her. (479)

Gwendolen is deadlocked by her commitment to the marriage which is also a commitment to her guilt and humiliation, and her life is charged with the dynamic conflict of her power to assert herself and her own humiliation:

> Poor Gwendolen was conscious of an uneasy, transforming process—all the old nature shaken to its depths, its hopes spoiled, its pleasures perturbed, but still showing wholeness and strength in the will to reassert itself. After every new shock of humiliation she tried to adjust herself and seize her old supports—proud concealment, trust in new excitements that would make life go by without much thinking; trust in some deed of reparation to nullify her self-blame and shield her from a vague, ever-visiting dread of some horrible calamity; trust in the hardening effect of use and wont that would make her indifferent to her miseries. (477)

This is an absolutely negative dynamic, for the "supports" for self-assertion are only negations of herself: of her real feelings of guilt and fear of humiliation. The will to reassert herself is a will to recover indifference and is thus limited to nullifying her feelings of humiliation, and she hopes for some means of reparation to nullify her guilt. Indifference is never separable, in Gwendolen's perception, from her own humiliation. Whether perceived in nature, in Grandcourt, or in herself, the recognition of the power of indifference entails a recognition of her own worthlessness.

Deronda is similarly committed to re-enacting his own insecure relation of self and world as he behaves as an English gentleman committed to nothing in particular. Befriending the losing causes of the world with which he identifies because of his own "sense of an entailed disadvantage" (215), Deronda is no more able to commit himself to any particular cause in the world around him than he is able to commit himself to any particular "cause," in the sense of origin, for himself. He prefers a multitude of causes just as he prefers his own indeterminacy to any definite knowledge that might humiliate him.

The meaninglessness of these characters' lives is given us, then, not as an original or necessary condition of being but as their own defense against meaning that exceeds their control and threatens them with insignificance. Both Gwendolen and Deronda maintain the insecurity and indeterminacy of meaning that the one feels most explicitly in relation to nature and the other in relation to his unknown parents. That Gwendolen can do anything at all, once she has internalized the indifference she perceives in nature, and that Deronda may be anything at all are the possibilities that terrify them. But they are the possibilities both characters insist on keeping open in order to ward off insignificance.

This is to identify both Gwendolen and Deronda in reflective relations to an indeterminate and terrifying excess of meaning perceived in the world around them. Gwendolen's confrontation with awe-inspiring nature reads as a traditional sublime moment. And Deronda's relation to his inherited identity can also be seen as an experience of the sublime, according to the correspondences Thomas Weiskel has identified between the natural sublime—the encounter with nature as a power that transcends human power; the rhetorical sublime—the encounter with the literary greatness of prior poets; and the Oedipal crisis—the encounter with the power of parents. To do so, however, is to clarify that George Eliot does not authorize sublimations of experience.[23]

In all of the sublime relations of the human mind to powers that transcend it—the power of nature, the power of past masters in literature, the power of parents to master the self— the individual can identify with the power that exceeds the

[23] Neil Hertz suggests that George Eliot rejects the sublime experience of identification with others because such perception risks cutting the self off from the real world, or from the real differences of self and others. Thus the narrator in *Middlemarch* also withdraws from the identifications with her characters into which she enters. See "Recognizing Casaubon," *Glyph* 6 (1979), pp. 36-40. For Eliot, the dynamics of identity and difference do preclude the emphasis of sublime experience on the internalization of external differences and the transcendence of such differences. Her denial of such identifications, however, does not preclude binding relations of self and others that render the meaning of both indeterminate.

self and thereby allay the anxiety felt because that power lies outside the bounds of the self. In Weiskel's terms, the "sublime moment" occurs when "the habitual relation of mind and object suddenly breaks down. . . . Either mind or object is suddenly in excess—and then both are, since their relation has become radically indeterminate." In reaction to this recognition of the incommensurable relation of subject and object, "the mind recovers the balance of outer and inner by constituting a fresh relation between itself and the object such that the very indeterminacy which erupted . . . is taken as symbolizing the mind's relation to a transcendent order."[24] In Freud's terms, "the super-ego arises . . . from an identification with the father taken as a model."[25] Yet Freudian internalization of the power exercised externally is always ambiguous, since it involves identification with that power at the same time that the self retains its fear or hatred of that power; so that there is an experience of both power and guilt. The Freudian experience corresponds, roughly at least, to Gwendolen's experience; and this suggests why the novel rejects Freudian sublimation as a means of finding the meaning and exercising the power of the self. Gwendolen remains deadlocked by the fact that the very means of power she identifies in the world are means which she feels guilt in exercising.

Yet the more critical aspect of the sublime experience is that it finds meaning in a "relation to a transcendent order." For to identify the experience of indeterminacy with transcendence or order is something George Eliot's fiction resists absolutely. She does not want to "transcend the human,"[26] nor does she locate the power of the individual self in the experience of transcendence. Instead, Eliot insists that any realization of meaning accept both "that hard unaccommo-

[24] Thomas Weiskel, *The Romantic Sublime: Studies in the Structure and Psychology of Transcendence* (Baltimore: The Johns Hopkins University Press, 1976), pp. 23-24.

[25] Quoted in ibid., p. 95, from "The Ego and the Id," in *The Standard Edition of the Complete Psychological Works of Sigmund Freud*, ed. James Strachey et al. (London: 1953-66), XIX, 54-55.

[26] Weiskel, *The Romantic Sublime*, p. 3.

dating Actual" in the world outside the self and the arbitrary partiality of the self as irreducible excesses.

In *Daniel Deronda*, therefore, the experience of the sublime functions as an evasion rather than a recognition of the excesses that render meaning indeterminate. For both Deronda and Gwendolen, the experience that we might call sublime is itself a defense against the real excesses of meaning in the world. The real excesses lie in hard fact and in involuntary feeling, both of which exceed individual control and determination. The indeterminacy of meaning which occurs if these irreducible and incomparable realities are accepted is a matter of the suspension of meaning between world and self: a suspension which moves meaning beyond the confines of self but depends upon and thereby includes both the irreducible world and the irreducible self.

Sublime indeterminacy is itself a fiction in this novel, and it is a fiction authorized by the fear of the reality of incommensurable differences in self and world. This is clearest in Deronda's experience, for he chooses to leave indeterminate what could easily be determined. He is overcome, as a boy, by the possibility that his birth is suspect:

> The ardour which he had given to the imaginary world in his books suddenly rushed towards his own history and spent its pictorial energy there, explaining what he knew, representing the unknown. . . . The impetuous advent of new images took possession of him with the force of fact for the first time told, and left him no immediate power for the reflection that he might be trembling at a fiction of his own. (206)

The sublimity here lies in the expenditure of energy on indeterminate fiction, divorced from reality both in that it transcends reality in its fictitiousness and in that its dynamics are internal, confined to Deronda's mind. The sublime fiction is preferable to knowing the fact because the fact, though it might be anything, would be definite and would exceed Deronda's control. He is terrified here by fictions "with the force of fact." He makes up fearful fictions, as if, as in a process

of Freudian mastery, he might master indeterminacy by creating or "realizing" it himself. But the fact of his birth is
exactly what such fictions protect him from; and the fact is
feared because, beyond his control, it may be incommensurable with what he wants to be.

The sublimity of Gwendolen's "undefined feeling of immeasurable existence aloof from her, in the midst of which
she was helplessly incapable of asserting herself" (94-95), is
likewise a defense against the actual constraints imposed on
her self-assertion. These are constraints imposed by her own
feelings: the feeling of her own insignificance that she projects
onto nature, or the feeling that interferes with her will to marry
Grandcourt. For, "apart from shame, her feeling would have
made her place any deliberate injury of another in the region
of guilt" (342). Gwendolen's re-enactment of sublime indifference seems the internal reflection of the indifference she
perceives in the world around her. But it is this reflective
indifference that saves her from realizing the difference her
own feelings make. For the difference made by her feelings,
like the difference made by Deronda's "fact," is a difference
that lies beyond her control. Her feelings for Deronda, for
example, are something unaccountable and involuntary:

> Why she should suddenly determine not to part with the
> necklace was not much clearer to her than why she should
> sometimes have been frightened to find herself in the fields
> alone: she had a confused state of emotion about De-
> ronda. ... It was something vague and yet mastering,
> which impelled her to this action about the necklace.
> There is a great deal of unmapped country within us
> which would have to be taken into account in an expla-
> nation of our gusts and storms. (321)

For Gwendolen to accept her feelings is to accept her behavior
as mastered: not by external constraints but by internal constraints that bind her to what lies outside her. Eliot's representation of those feelings suggests that they are not themselves to be mastered—either by being defined or repressed—
but are to be accepted as irreducible and incommensurable

with intention or will, like the "hard unaccommodating Actual."

Gwendolen's sublime fiction about Nature, like Deronda's fictions about his birth, is pure fiction. Unlike Eliot's own fiction, their fictions realize ηo binding relation to either arbitrary fact or arbitrary feeling ánd remain thereby absolutely indeterminate. Such fictions transcend the realization of constraints imposed on meaning by what exceeds volition or control. To choose to accept such constraints is to assume the burden of meaning that exceeds volition as it exceeds the bounds of the self. But for Eliot this burden is chosen as a support.[27]

The excesses of meaning in the novel do not provide grounds for meaning, as they exceed any grounds that function as the "given" of secure meaning. But the "givens" of logical thinking are usually denied *as* given: the grounds for exchange, that is, are usually assumed not to be subject to exchanges themselves. Thus the grounds for exchange are separated from the process of exchange, which depends on something that is in fact given and can in fact be taken away. This is what exchanges cannot afford to realize if they are to be secure. Moreover, Eliot suggests, one may deny "givens" as arbitrary because one is unwilling to recognize that the grounds for thinking are a matter of choice. For to see our grounds for meaning as arbitrary choices is to see meaning in ourselves, meaning that thereby risks having no meaning in common with others. What Eliot's redemption offers is a restoration of the real arbitrariness of meaning and thereby a restoration of both the arbitrary nature of what we realize in the world around us and the arbitrary nature of our selves. These restorations occur, however, as the arbitrary excesses of meaning are reflected in both self and others. Other Jews reflect the Judaism in Deronda, just as Deronda reflects the feelings of guilt in Gwendolen. These "burdens"—the Judaism and the

---

[27] Judith Wilt says this, too, of the rectitude that Gwendolen assumes at the end of the novel: it is "not a burden but the only possible support." See *Ghosts of the Gothic*, p. 219.

guilt—thus become supports, as what has been felt to exile and separate the self from meaning becomes the very tie that binds the self to others. Deronda is able to choose his birth as a given, and Gwendolen is able to choose her feelings as givens as they accept them as gifts from others. Rather than assuming a lack as given, they accept excesses of meaning as gifts.

Daniel Deronda thus gives meaning, as do all of the novels I have considered, at the cost of independence. But George Eliot insists that the independence of any meaning is itself a fiction, and a fiction of lack. She thereby identifies her own concept of meaning as achieved at the cost of nothing: as pure gain. What remains more problematic in this novel is the peculiar redundancy of the novel's exchanges. For that redundancy, a matter of restoration, seems regressive rather than progressive in its insistence on finding meaning in what is perceived as already there. To some extent, all of these novels function regressively, since they exceed the terms of historical causality, though Richardson's and Eliot's narratives insist that this revision of experience increases rather than takes away from meaning. One corollary of this in *Daniel Deronda* is the pressure the novel puts on acceptance of what is rather than origination or creation of what is not. This means the acceptance of "givens" that can never be subject to conventional exchange because they exceed the reductive terms of such exchange; and the acceptance itself is part of no exchange but rather a redundant reflection. To identify power in receptiveness rather than in generation is not to preclude change; but it is to preclude the exclusion of differences in self and others from meaning. Eliot emphasizes that the acceptance of what is may be far more difficult than the creation of what is not. In this insistence she is supported by Henry James, who also thereby risks being read as a conservative novelist. In James's *The Golden Bowl*, however, the radical regression from conventional exchange confirms the power that Eliot associates with the gift of acceptance.

CHAPTER SIX
THE GIFT OF ACCEPTANCE:
THE GOLDEN BOWL

The Golden Bowl is a novel about marriage and, therefore, a novel about the union of differences. For Henry James, different people can be "fused" together, and so can the different elements of a narrative. It is the fusion of differences that makes a work of art "true" for him, as it makes the work absolute in its wholeness, so that it cannot be taken apart or figured out. In the Preface to *The Awkward Age*, James writes of the "marriage" of substance and form in a successful work of art:

> They are separate before the fact, but the sacrament of execution indissolubly marries them, and the marriage, like any other marriage, has only to be a "true" one for the scandal of a breach not to show. The thing "done," artistically, is a fusion, or it has not *been* done—in which case of course the artist may be, and all deservedly, pelted with any fragment of his botch the critic shall choose to pick up. But his ground once conquered, in this particular field, he knows nothing of fragments and may say in all security: "Detach one if you can. You can analyse in *your* way, oh yes—to relate, to report, to explain; but you can't disintegrate my synthesis; you can't resolve the elements of my whole into different responsible agents or find your way at all (for your own fell purpose). My mixture has only to be perfect literally to bewilder you— you are lost in the tangle of the forest.[1]

[1] Henry James, *The Art of the Novel: Critical Prefaces*, intro. R. P. Blackmur (New York: Charles Scribner's Sons, 1934), pp. 115-16.

James conceives of marriage here in terms similar to those Maggie Verver uses in *The Golden Bowl* when she describes, in an exchange with Fanny Assingham, what she wants to achieve:

> "I want a happiness without a hole in it big enough for you to poke in your finger."
> "A brilliant, perfect surface—to begin with at least. I see."
> "The golden bowl—as it *was* to have been. . . . The bowl with all happiness in it. The bowl without the crack."

The division between the parts, then, is a breach that must not show:

> "We alone know what's between us—we and you; and haven't you precisely been struck, since you've been here," Maggie asked, "with our making so good a show?" (445)[2]

Maggie Verver works in the novel to consecrate her marriage to the Prince in terms analogous to those James uses to describe the work of the artist in the above passage. Maggie, like James, wants a fusion. In appearance, there is nothing between her and her husband; they are together. Moreover, if we accept James's definition, the show that Maggie and the Prince make—with no "scandal of a breach"—is evidence of a true marriage.

Like George Eliot in *Daniel Deronda*, Henry James is fighting against great odds in this novel. For *The Golden Bowl* works to convince us that experience is more rewarding if we let go of our "realistic" assumptions about the value and meaning of things. If Maggie and the Prince have a "true" marriage, they also have a marriage in which, if truth be told,

---

[2] Henry James, *The Golden Bowl* (Harmondsworth, Mx.: Penguin, 1973). All subsequent references are to this edition, and page numbers are given in the text.

union has been betrayed by adultery. The narrative both tells us that truth and insists that the marriage is nevertheless true. That this is both bewildering and illogical is admitted: in the above description, James even brags about his ability to bewilder us. But truth, for James, is not something to be figured out, and The Golden Bowl demands that we accept truths that cannot be figured out or known. For only such acceptance enables us to have "whole" truths, truths which cannot be taken apart.

The accomplished fusion of form and substance in fiction, James suggests, results in the confusion of critics. Similarly, in order to render her marriage "indissoluble" and herself and the Prince inseparable, Maggie and Adam Verver act in ways that puzzle critics who attempt to figure them out. To figure them out, James suggests above, would be to take apart the fusion they accomplish. For such fusions disable critical procedures for figuring out or determining meaning: identifying "different responsible agents" is one such procedure and "finding your way (for your own fell purpose)" is another. It is not possible to distinguish what causes what if the fusion is successful; nor will any critical purpose be able to give direction or meaning to the work of art.

Two attempts to identify responsibility and purpose in the action of The Golden Bowl, one by a critic and one by a character, result in the kind of confusion James predicts. Frederick Crews gives up determining the moral responsibility of different characters because, although each character feels scrupulously responsible for something, no one feels responsible for what he or she has done wrong:

> Fanny's sin lies not in allowing her motives to be suspected, but in meddling in the first place. She tries to redeem herself only through further meddling. Charlotte has only to tell Maggie of her previous relationship with Amerigo for the marriage to begin on a properly candid basis, but she neglects to do so. Amerigo's conscience does not prevent him from capitalizing on every possible opportunity to deceive the Ververs. And if Maggie and

Adam should do penance, surely it is not for any harm they have inflicted on each other. Each character is concerned with preserving the innocence—that is to say the ignorance—of some other character, but none is really interested in his own guilt.[3]

If James's work defies the identification of responsible agents with responsible purposes, so does Maggie's work in the novel. The Prince, with the purpose of finding out what Adam Verver knows, is unable to find his way either:

He had been trying to find out, and had been seeking, above all, to avoid the appearance of any evasions of such a form of knowledge as might reach him. . . . Nothing, however, had reached him; nothing he could at all conveniently reckon with had disengaged itself for him even from the announcement, sufficiently sudden, of the final secession of their companions. Charlotte was in pain, Charlotte was in torment, but he himself had given her reason enough for that; and, in respect to the rest of the whole matter of her obligation to follow her husband, that person and she, Maggie, had so shuffled away every link between consequence and cause, that the intention remained, like some famous poetic line in a dead language, subject to varieties of interpretation. (531)

Here the Prince, like the critics addressed by James, cannot find out what he purposes to know and instead is faced with a "tangle" of meanings. Nothing is distinguishable. No element "disengages itself" from other elements; nothing appears "between consequence and cause"; and the resultant fusion means that the Prince cannot see through the Ververs' behavior to what lies behind it. In fact, if the Prince, as a critic, is faced with the problem of getting to their meaning by getting to their intention, the intention, instead of appearing as an underlying ground for definitive interpretation, comes itself to appear as a line of poetry. What should lie behind remains

[3] Frederick C. Crews, *The Tragedy of Manners: Moral Drama in the Later Novels of Henry James* (Hamden, Conn.: Archon Books, 1971), p. 97.

itself only a sign, and that in a dead language. So not only can the Prince not go behind or see beneath what he is trying to interpret; he cannot get around it by referring to other sources or contexts either. The line of his search, then, leads him only to another line, one "subject to varieties of interpretation."

Readers who attempt to decide the meaning of *The Golden Bowl* are frustrated, like the Prince, by the fact that the narrative provides no grounds for a knowledgeable and decisive interpretation. The novel precludes knowledge, and this occurs both in the heroine's refusal to acknowledge reality as determining meaning and in the narrative's refusal to let us see through Maggie's fiction. There is not clearly an underlying reality in the novel that distinguishes her fiction as a fiction. Critics may provide their own grounds, such as moral grounds, for determining the meaning of the novel; but this in itself is to deny the givens of the novel and necessarily leads to its dismissal.[4] Critics who attempt to deal with the novel on its own terms assume that it means to be ambiguous or indeterminate. Some have recognized the narrative's refusal to determine meaning as a sign of its moral complexity and, more recently, as a formal representation of James's interest in meaning as a process rather than a matter of knowledge or determination. Dorothea Krook accepts the ambiguity of *The Golden Bowl* as indicative of James's "total vision," in which "the sense of the grimness and bitterness of human life is inseparably fused with the sense of its beauty and blessedness."[5] And Nicola Bradbury suggests that, as James's fiction "gradually diverts our curiosity from a search for answers towards an interest in the process by which questions arise,"

[4] Among such critics is F. O. Matthiessen, for whom *The Golden Bowl* is "finally a decadent book." See *Henry James: The Major Phase* (New York: Oxford University Press, 1944), p. 102. F. R. Leavis suggests that with this novel James "let his moral taste slip into abeyance" in *The Great Tradition: George Eliot, Henry James, Joseph Conrad* (New York: George W. Stewart, 1950), p. 161.
[5] Dorothea Krook, *The Ordeal of Consciousness in Henry James* (Cambridge: Cambridge University Press, 1962), p. 324.

the reader's understanding is "bound up with the novelist's understanding: and it is the elasticity, variety, and expressive power, but also the ultimate limitations of the novel form itself (which must finally rely on suggesting what cannot be put into words), that represent in the reading process the reach and the inevitable boundaries of understanding."[6] Such readings shift attention from knowledge to conditions in James's fiction that preclude or precede knowledge.

Such mixed feelings as Krook and Bradbury acknowledge as readers of *The Golden Bowl*—grimness and beauty, power and limitation—are mixtures of generative and restrictive values. And the acceptance of James's refusal to determine meaning usually leads critics to identify conflations of gain and loss in his fiction. If, as Tzvetan Todorov says, James's narratives identify an end—a "figure in the carpet"—that they proceed toward but never reach, then the power of his fiction depends on withholding.[7] We are suspended between what is given and what is withheld; both presence and absence are crucial, and the suspension of meaning is also a frustration of meaning. Ruth Yeazell describes a similar experience when reading *The Golden Bowl*:

What the characters refuse to talk about, what they refuse even to think, becomes for us—especially in retrospect—

[6] Nicola Bradbury, *Henry James: The Later Novels* (Oxford: Oxford University Press, 1979), p. 2.

Richard Hocks, in *Henry James and Pragmatistic Thought: A Study in the Relationship between the Philosophy of William James and the Literary Art of Henry James* (Chapel Hill: University of North Carolina Press, 1974), also considers the indeterminate or "open-ended" quality of James's prose, in the illuminating context of his brother's philosophy. The relationship of the brothers that Hocks recreates shares, moreover, the intricate complexity of human relations in Henry James's novels. It is a relation of "confluence" rather than influence, of conscious pragmatistic thought in William and unconscious pragmatism in Henry, a relation that clearly exceeds, as Hocks insists, any simple structure of antagonism or agreement or priority. See especially "Part Two: The Brothers 'Confluent,' 'Conjoined,' 'Concatenated': A Letter to Henry Adams," pp. 49-112.

[7] Tzvetan Todorov, *The Poetics of Prose*, trans. Richard Howard (Ithaca: Cornell University Press, 1977), p. 145.

the real substance of James's fiction. But the actual experience of reading the late James is still less emotionally
tidy than we usually recall. . . . Few novels demand more
persistently that we translate them, yet few novels feel so
relentlessly verbal, even so untranslatable.[8]

To identify the indeterminacy of meaning in the novel in these
terms is to insist that the substance of the novel is lacking or,
according to Todorov, that lack is part of its "substance."
The acceptance of indeterminate meaning in *The Golden
Bowl* thus entails a "divided response" from most critics.[9] But
both James and Maggie Verver insist on the absolute quality
of their fictions, which are both secure and substantial. James's
insistence that "the thing 'done' " is a fusion suggests stability
and solidity; and Maggie's hope that the golden bowl can be
"reconstituted" so that it will hold happiness (445) also suggests that what she works to achieve is a solid support. Di-

---

[8] Ruth Bernard Yeazell, *Language and Knowledge in the Late Novels of
Henry James* (Chicago: University of Chicago Press, 1976), p. 129.

[9] Ralf Norrman, in *The Insecure World of Henry James's Fiction: Intensity
and Ambiguity* (New York: St. Martin's Press, 1982), states that "the divided
response is precisely the right reaction to the novel" (p. 175). Norrman insists
that distinctions are so indeterminate in the novel that differences "come to
the same thing" (p. 164): "Maggie (like Charlotte) is 'both—and'—both a
saint and a witch in the sense that the material for either reading is present
in James's text" (p. 175). The equivalence of differences, to the extent that
no choice makes a difference either, seems to me to be something that James
works against and something that *The Golden Bowl* rejects absolutely.

Mark Seltzer, recognizing the divided response of most criticism of James's
novel, locates the principal division as one of love and power. Critics needing
to distinguish between practices of love and power, he argues, cannot reach
a recognition of "the perverse entanglement of love and power in the novel."
See *Henry James and the Art of Power* (Ithaca: Cornell University Press,
1984), p. 95. This entanglement Seltzer identifies with the complexes of power
Michel Foucault elaborates in his social theory. Seltzer's work is particularly
valuable for his insistence that art and power cannot be distinguished in
James's fiction and that aesthetics' attempts to separate the two are themselves
a sign of the way art and its adherents cover up art's exercise of power in
our society. It seems to me unquestionable that practices of love and power
and art coincide in *The Golden Bowl*. But I am arguing that their interrelation,
like the interrelations of the characters, works for something more than
control.

vision is precisely what such language denies. Though the meaning of the novel is never knowable, and thus the solidity of James's and Maggie's achievements does not rest on solid grounds, the meaning they create is supposed to "hold," both because it resists penetration and because it supports happiness.

I want to consider here how *The Golden Bowl* is both indeterminate and absolute. The novel represents a fiction whose fusions preclude divided responses as they preclude the distinction of differences. The fusions are accomplished by a process of acceptance that occurs in place of economical exchange, a process that, instead of relating what is gained to what is lost in terms of an exchange, *accepts* both gains and losses on their own terms. Losses do not, therefore, affect the meaning of gains. Gains do not make up for losses, and gain is thereby freed from determination by loss. Losses are taken *as* losses, of which nothing can be made. This narrative does not *deal* in lack, which is to say that it makes no exchanges with lack, because lacks are empty and therefore have no generative potential, unless one would generate loss. Only gain provides any substance, and therefore only gains are made more of. If we sense what is missing in the narrative, we sense what is irrelevant to James's and Maggie's fictions. It is irrelevant precisely because it constitutes in itself kinds of lack. What Maggie finally excludes from meaning, that is, are divisions, losses, lapses, breaks. She lets go of losses in order to hold on to gains undiminished by losses. The refusal to make anything of losses is not a denial of loss but an acceptance of loss, and it is acceptance that constitutes the power of this fiction.

Acceptance in *The Golden Bowl* is an absolute phenomenon. As in the "sublime economy" James describes in the Preface to *The Spoils of Poynton*, such acceptance exceeds the terms of even exchange:

Life has no direct sense whatever for the subject and is capable, luckily for us, of nothing but splendid waste. Hence the opportunity for the sublime economy of art,

which rescues, which saves, and hoards and "banks,"
investing and reinvesting these fruits of toil in wondrous
useful "works" and thus making up for us, desperate
spendthrifts that we all naturally are, the most princely
of incomes.[10]

James's economy is sublime because it deals in excess, in far
more than life needs or makes use of. Fusing together two
concepts that do not logically fit together, the sublime economy unites indeterminate excess with a system of exchange.
Like George Eliot, James insists that the sublime excesses of
experience are not transcendent but practical and useful. But
his economy is also identified with waste, for art is altogether
outside the realm of conventional economical exchange. It
accepts what life throws out as useless and provides what is
also wasteful: an income for us "spendthrifts." To identify
art with what life wastes rather than with profit is to insist
that art has no exchange value, or that its value always exceeds
need, as do Eliot's redemptions. Whereas the conventional
exchanges of society either are defined by or define need, the
lack that constitutes need has no place in James's economy.
His economy deals in excess.

One element of this excessive representation is James's acceptance of differences on their own terms. Here again he
resembles Eliot. Because, in his "sublime economy," he does
not use what he accepts to fill a lack, James need not limit
the dimensions of what he takes in to fit the dimensions of a
lack. The elements of fiction may be felt by some critics as an
attempt to make up for the lack of reality. But James does
not acknowledge this economy. Fiction exceeds reality altogether and deals strictly on its own terms; it "makes up" a
princely income, but it does not make up for the loss of anything. It makes more of what life already acknowledges as
too much. There is no exchange between life and art in common terms that would reduce either or identify either as lacking what the other has.

Yet fiction is nevertheless generated by the acceptance of

10 James, *The Art of the Novel*, p. 120.

life's excesses. It is therefore inseparably fused with life in its sublimely economical relation to life. This is characteristic of James's sense of difference, which renders differences both absolute in themselves and inseparable from each other. He represents differences without representing the difference *between* them: life is wasteful, and art is wasteful, and the difference between them is not determined. To make a distinction between differences requires some sort of equation. Either one different element must be represented in terms of another element in order to be compared or contrasted; or both elements must be represented in terms common to both. But either way, the terms of distinction are not wholly representative of both differences: something is left out in order to reduce differences to comparable terms. James therefore leaves differences absolute and incomparable in order not to lose anything of them. He does not give us the differences between differences, for that in itself constitutes an exchange by which we lose something in order to gain a relation. He thus accomplishes a fusion by refusing to tell differences apart or reduce them to comparable terms.

The acceptance of life's excesses by art is not a relation determined as an exchange; nor is the relation between what is accepted and what is made of it. In the Preface to *The Golden Bowl*, James describes how art "makes up" wealth by describing another process of acceptance. He remembers confronting "the accumulated good stuff" of the novel when he came to revise it. With the good stuff "seeming insistently to give and give," except for "certain lapses,"

> the sense of receiving has borne me company without a break. . . .The blest good stuff . . . seemed to pass with me a delightful bargain, and in the fewest possible words. "Actively believe in us and then you'll see!"[11]

The responsibility of acceptance in *The Golden Bowl* is, similarly, the responsibility of active belief. Such belief entails not only the acceptance of things on their own terms but the active

[11] Ibid., p. 341.

appreciation of them. It is more a matter of taking than of passive acceptance, and it is in this sense that the Ververs' acquisitive powers are clearly generative powers. The Ververs' "rare power of purchase" (541) is the power to "buy" the Prince and Charlotte. They can buy anything because of their excessive wealth, and this excess is signaled by the fact that it disables fair exchange, as when Mr. Verver's "easy way with his millions" during the marriage settlement "taxed to such small purpose . . . the principle of reciprocity" (30). To "deal" with the Ververs is to be outside the realm of economical exchange. But this is not the only sign of their excesses. For the Ververs buy the Prince and Charlotte not only in the sense that they "take" them but also in the sense that they believe in them: the sense in which they are taken in by them. The Ververs' acquisitiveness, then, represents their capacity both to be taken and to take: their capacity to believe in as well as accept things as they are. Their "sublime economy" thus disables fair exchange in another way, for it, like James's, is a process of taking and being taken rather than of give and take. Their belief cannot be structured as an exchange. The acceptance of the Prince and Charlotte as they are, moreover, is an acceptance of what most economies would identify as too much to take: betrayal and adultery. Those characters are accepted in excess of the terms of a fair deal, and this acceptance marks the recognition of the narrative that excess characterizes everyone. Everyone is, or has, more than the economical exchanges of society can deal with. Because the Ververs accept the excesses of others, they, like the artist with his "splendid waste," are able to generate a fiction that realizes excessive value. The Ververs' work is the work of art. They achieve the fusion of fiction and reality by realizing the value of what they believe in.

Adam Verver is the most accomplished economist in the novel. The process by which he "makes up" his world is a process of fusion, and it is in such terms that he decides to marry Charlotte Stant:

He had as to so many of the matters in hand a divided view, and this was exactly what made him reach out, in his unrest, for some idea, lurking in the vast freshness of the night, at the breath of which disparities would submit to fusion, and so, spreading beneath him, make him feel that he floated. What he kept finding himself return to, disturbingly enough, was the reflection, deeper than anything else, that in forming a new and intimate tie he should in a manner abandon, or at the best signally relegate, his daughter. He should reduce to definite form the idea that he had lost her—as was indeed inevitable—by her own marriage; he should reduce to definite form the idea of his having incurred an injury, or at the best an inconvenience, that required some makeweight and deserved some amends. And he should do this the more, which was the great point, that he should appear to adopt, in doing it, the sentiment, in fact the very conviction, entertained, and quite sufficiently expressed, by Maggie herself, in her beautiful generosity, as to what he had suffered—putting it with extravagance—at her hands. . . . She had sacrificed a parent, the pearl of parents, no older than herself: it wouldn't so much have mattered if he had been of common parental age. That he wasn't, that he was just her extraordinary equal and contemporary, this was what added to her act the long train of its effect. Light broke for him at last, indeed, quite as a consequence of the fear of breathing a chill upon this luxuriance of her spiritual garden. . . .

Once he had recognized it there everything became coherent. The sharp point to which all his light converged was that the whole call of his future to him, as a father, would be in his so managing that Maggie would less and less appear to herself to have forsaken him. . . . The way in which it might be met was by putting his child at peace, and the way to put her at peace was to provide for his future—that is for hers—by marriage, by a marriage as good, speaking proportionately, as hers had been. (166-68)

Mr. Verver's wish to see disparities "submit to fusion" prevails here. The chief disparity that he would see fused is the disparity between himself and Maggie. For he has lost her; their separation is "inevitable." The disparity first at issue here, however, is his "divided view" of marriage to Charlotte. The view is divided between gain and loss: if he gains Charlotte, he will lose Maggie. The marriage would "reduce to definite form" Maggie's loss because it would appear to be a compensation for Maggie's loss. Thus, by making up for her loss, it would appear as proof of her loss.

Everything becomes coherent, though, when Mr. Verver recognizes that his marriage to Charlotte can appear as something else: not as the corroboration of the real division between father and daughter but as the corroboration of the fictitious sameness that Maggie believes characterizes them. Maggie likes to think of her father as "her extraordinary equal and contemporary," and Mr. Verver can confirm this belief by behaving like her—by marrying just as she has married, doing the same thing she has done rather than doing another thing to compensate for what she has done. Having recognized, in the previous paragraph, the similarity of the Prince and Charlotte, Mr. Verver has prepared his way to appear, by marrying Charlotte, to meet or fuse himself with Maggie even as he accepts her loss.

One economy that is avoided here is the economy of reparation. Marriage to Charlotte is unsatisfactory as long as it looks like a means of amends. Rather than repair the break between himself and Maggie, Mr. Verver wants to make it appear that they are inseparable, two of a kind. Thus, rather than make up for the loss of Maggie by the gain of Charlotte, he will manage what appears to be a double gain, or gain on both sides: he will gain proportionately as Maggie has gained. The break is not repaired, then. What would repair it, in reparation, is seen instead as a pure gain, disconnected from any loss. Like Maggie in her desire to have the golden bowl "as it *was* to have been . . . without the crack," Mr. Verver wants to make it appear that there is no breach.

This requires something different from a realistic premise to start with, just as it requires something different from logical reasoning to complete. The break, of course, is really there, inevitably. But the grounds of Mr. Verver's solution are not real. He reaches his fusion of disparities on the basis of Maggie's make-believe. If he acknowledges the real division, the marriage can appear only as a reparation that confirms the loss. If he can act according to her belief, however, he can use the marriage to sustain their fusion. That his future is the same as hers, that marriage for himself is also marriage for her, are confusions of the two characters that mark the fusion Mr. Verver accomplishes here.

Other confusions mark the progression of his thoughts. What first seems the necessary effect of marriage to Charlotte is that Mr. Verver will give definite form to his loss of Maggie. But eventually in the passage his desire not to give form to that loss becomes precisely the reason for marriage to Charlotte. It is at first difficult to see much difference between the problem and the solution, since the same act is first one and then the other. Such confusions are crucial to the project of fusion undertaken here, though. For the project demands that even differences be subject to fusion; differences must also be able to appear with no difference between them. Thus, although there is a real difference between the first view of the marriage and the second view of the marriage, it is also true that the marriage that is the problem is the same as the marriage that is the solution. Causality, then, or the distinction between cause and effect, is another economy that is unsettled in this passage, which begins and ends, in one sense, with the same thing. The marriage to Charlotte both generates and solves the problem in Mr. Verver's mind. But in James's economy, this redundancy is effective; for the effect of the solution is to make it appear that no solution is needed. The effect of the solution is to erase the cause for the solution, or to fuse them together.

Such thinking does not deal with the real problem, then. Mr. Verver takes a passing glance at the real problem, "that he had lost her," recognizes it as inevitable, and, with that, dismisses it from further consideration. For to deal with the loss would be to deal with something that can provide no support, and he wishes to "feel that he floated," supported by the fusion of disparities. Mr. Verver is, of course, engaged in these thoughts because of the loss, but the loss is not what concerns him. And this is what makes the Ververs' behavior so extraordinary. Maggie, too, when confronted with the fact that her husband has had an affair with Charlotte, never addresses the problem, per se, at all. What is most striking in the scene in which she informs the Prince that she knows about the affair is what is missing from it. She never asks why, how, or how could you? This refusal to talk about the problem is shocking not only in its moral but in its epistemological negligence. For we assume that problems can be solved only if the problems themselves are understood. But Maggie, once the fact is evident, requires and receives no explanations for it whatever. She does not even look into it, let alone get to the bottom of it.

> What it came to was that seeing herself finally sure, knowing everything, having the fact, in all its abomination, so utterly before her that there was nothing else to add— what it came to was that, merely by being *with* him there in silence, she felt, within her, the sudden split between conviction and action. They had begun to cease, on the spot, surprisingly, to be connected; conviction, that is, budged no inch, only planting its feet the more firmly in the soil—but action began to hover like some lighter and larger, but easier form, excited by its very power to keep above ground. (426).

Like Mr. Verver's thoughts in the earlier passage, Maggie's response here is imaged as a kind of floating. Her action will float free, so that what she does will be disconnected from what she knows, unrelated to its grounded certainty. And this occurs, moreover, because she is *"with* him." She could not identify herself with the Prince if she acted according to her knowledge, for if her behavior were tied to or motivated by his adultery, their relation would be grounded on their division.

The image of floating is repeated in another crucial scene

late in the novel, when father and daughter are together in the park at Fawns and Maggie declares,

> "My idea is this, that when you only love a little you're naturally not jealous. . . . But when you love in a deeper and intenser way, then you are, in the same proportion, jealous; your jealousy has intensity and, no doubt, ferocity. When, however, you love in the most abysmal and unutterable way of all—why then you're beyond everything, and nothing can pull you down."
>
> ". . . I do *feel* . . . beyond everything—and as a consequence of that, I daresay," she added with a turn to gaiety, "seem often not to know quite *where* I am." (476)

In this statement, Mr. Verver recognizes

> The mere fine pulse of passion . . . , the suggestion as of a creature consciously floating and shining in a warm summer sea, some element of dazzling sapphire and silver, a creature cradled upon depths, buoyant among dangers, in which fear or folly, or sinking otherwise than in play, was impossible. . . . (477)

The image of floating is perhaps less surprising here than in the earlier passages cited, since it represents passionate rather than rational behavior. We are accustomed to figuring passion as something that carries us away, and so the irrational implications of floating—the loss of bearings and the loss of direction—are familiar as implications of passion. But the image not only represents feelings, like knowledge, as something not to be gone into but insists that passion is a matter of surface rather than depth. So that not only do the Ververs seem to deny the depths of passion, but they seem to deny, or reverse, crucial assumptions about human behavior. The whole notion of the unconscious as a realm of feeling lying beneath the surface of rational consciousness assumes that the most "unutterable" feelings, for example, are inexpressible because they exist at a deeper level than that of utterance, a rationalizing process. Yet Maggie's description of love in three stages confuses such distinctions. While she represents the stages at increasing depths, she finally conflates the "most abysmal and unutterable" depths with height—so that when you are deepest "nothing can pull you down." Heights and depths are fused together.

Moreover, because the image of passion floating on the surface constitutes the same refusal to look into things as the floating and fusion of Adam's thoughts, the narrative seems to refuse to look into just the matters with which it is most concerned: the emotional relationships of its characters. Either Maggie is lying when she says she is not jealous, or the fact that she is "beyond" jealousy seems a sign of the shallowness of her passion. Like the questions she does not ask the Prince when she knows what he has done, the absent element in this scene—jealousy—seems precisely what ought to be present if passion were deep. Given the Prince's affair with Charlotte, Maggie's lack of jealousy seems a lack of passion. Of course, she may be lying, since she has recognized in her previous walk in the park with her father that, with him, she must never "so much as indirectly point" at the truth (357). But the fact that we cannot know whether she is lying or not, and the fact that we understand by this point in the novel that that is not really an issue, may be seen as indications of a shallowness similar to that which characterizes passion here.

Thus F. O. Matthiessen criticized the novel as both unrealistic, almost "hollow of real life," and morally shallow. James, he says, can use "strangely ambiguous images" such as Charlotte held on a leash by Mr. Verver and ignore their cruelty because he "seems to want to keep uppermost . . . the unobtrusive smoothness of his 'dear man's' dealings."[12] Leo Bersani, too, who is sympathetic to James's attention to the surface of behavior as a means of liberating his characters' desires from "a crippling notion of truth," nevertheless sees the liberation occurring at the cost of psychological depth. For Bersani, the language through which desire is experienced constitutes a process that takes the place of a desiring subject

[12] Matthiessen, *Henry James*, pp. 104, 100.

as *the* subject of the novel. All experience is free to change if represented differently.

> This is the profound justification of James's refusal "to go behind": because experience is never without design, it's impossible to locate an original design, that is, an absolute fact or motive which could not itself be recomposed, whose nature would not be changed by changes in its relations.[13]

If for Matthiessen some substantial or fundamental element of real experience is missing from the novel, for Bersani it is not the fact that anything per se is missing but the fact that nothing is more substantial or fundamental than anything else that means that there are no depths to experience in this narrative. It is not the lack of experience but the indistinction of such differences as those which priority, causality, and history impose on experience that characterizes the novel for Bersani. Like other critics considered earlier, Bersani sees in *The Golden Bowl* a mobility of values, with none privileged as absolute.

It is my contention that there are absolute facts and absolute differences in the narrative but that, like the inevitable loss of Maggie that Mr. Verver virtually ignores in the earlier passage, they are left alone. The "depths" are present in the above description of a "creature cradled upon depths," for example. But they are not gone into. Although the novel indeed suggests that everything can be changed or "recomposed," its pressure consists precisely in its insistence that freedom entails leaving certain things alone. Thus Maggie's and the Prince's behavior after he knows that she knows of his adultery consists of " 'I let him alone' " and " 'He lets me alone' " (444). This is not a form of separation, for it is the ways of "going into" things that the narrative recognizes as ways of separation.

What I have identified as missing, for example, in the above passages—the questions about the reasons for the Prince's

---

[13] Leo Bersani, *A Future for Astyanax: Character and Desire in Literature* (Boston: Little, Brown, 1976), pp. 130, 148.

adultery, in the one, and Maggie's jealousy, in the other—
would in fact function, if present, to confirm his and her
separation. Like Mr. Verver avoiding his loss of Maggie in
his consideration of marriage to Charlotte, Maggie avoids
looking into the fact of adultery. She presents her evidence,
is confirmed in her knowledge, and then lets it alone. Her
action will not be connected to the division of herself and the
Prince at all; thus she will not repair the breach, for that would
be to act in ways determined by the breach. Similarly, to go
beyond jealousy is to go beyond separation from the Prince,
for jealousy is also an experience of a lack of love. Moreover,
to get beyond jealousy is to get beyond a particular economy
of reparation similar to that which Mr. Verver and Maggie
avoid in the earlier passages cited. For to "look into" jealousy
leads theorists to conclude that it arises from a lack of commitment in the subject and functions as a projection of and
compensation for one's own inability to commit oneself.
" 'Projected jealousy' keeps the patient's own impulses to unfaithfulness out of conciousness," Otto Fenichel writes, having
asserted "the fact that it is people who are, in a sense, incapable of love who become most readily and most intensely
jealous."[14] According to this economy of jealousy, others'
unfaithfulness is assumed in place of and in order to compensate for or justify one's own unfaithfulness.

Maggie does experience jealousy. She feels jealous both before the Prince begins again his affair with Charlotte (138-
39) and after she begins to suspect something. And in fact her
initial reaction to her own suspicions is to wonder " 'What if
I've abandoned *them*, you know?' " (316). If we chose to go
into it, then, we might recognize an economy at work in which
the equivalence and exchangeability of characters prevail. If
Maggie chose to go into it, she would almost certainly recognize an exchange determined by reparation. For not only
would the expression of jealousy demand reparation, but the

[14] Otto Fenichel, "A Contribution to the Psychology of Jealousy," in *The
Collected Papers of Otto Fenichel, First Series*, ed. Hanna Fenichel and David
Rapaport (New York: W. W. Norton, 1953), pp. 351, 350.

experience of jealousy itself seems to be an experience of compensation, once we look into it. But the fact that Maggie does
not go into it or admit her jealousy to others, and the fact
that she goes "beyond" it, suggest that what she manages to
avoid is the compensatory economical character both of such
feelings and of the ways we think about them.[15]

Thus the narrative and its heroine choose to leave certain
things alone because to go into them is in fact a form of
separation. Although the novel works for freedom, therefore,
its freedom is in part, as Bersani suggests, freedom *from* meaning; though this is true only insofar as to say what something
means is to provide an explanation or grounds for it. This is
to locate significance as a fusion of indeterminacy and determination. For although the narrative recognizes the interchangeability or indeterminancy of meaning, it does not represent this as a phenomenon of liberation. On the other hand,
although it recognizes absolutes, it does not recognize absolute
values as the grounds for determination. Neither indeterminacy nor determination is quite available in this text. Meaning
is free in the novel because it depends on choice, and meaning
is absolute because it is provided by absolute commitment.
Thus, as in *Pamela* or *Middlemarch*, freedom is a matter of
the commitment of the self to meaning. The "responsibility
of freedom" (426) is to keep above grounds, but the very
concept of responsibility here suggests that there must be pressure exerted in order to do so, or that freedom is not "free"

---

[15] Mark Seltzer looks into the experience of jealousy in the novel and finds
something different from these economies in *Henry James and the Art of
Power*. Seltzer does not separate love and jealousy but insists on the very
dependence of Maggie's love on jealousy, to the extent that her love requires
jealousy. He suggests, too, as he reads in the context of Foucault's relations
of power, that marriage in the novel depends on adultery. In fact, he says,
"adultery, in *The Golden Bowl* at least, *constitutes* marriage" (p. 80), as acts
of transgression against the limits of conventional forms are seen to constitute
their boundaries. Though the complicity of theoretically opposed elements
of experience is crucial to James's fiction, it seems to me that James is nevertheless able to identify absolute differences, made by choice. Although it is
true that James's fiction and Maggie's fiction too "look like" repression, it
is their difference that I am trying to clarify in this chapter.

but bound by responsibility. This is not the freedom to make free with all values interchangeably, then. Bersani recognizes James's conflation of freedom and pressure when he qualifies the assertion that "his subject is freedom" with the demand that we "understand that word in the sense of inventions so coercive that they resist any attempt to enrich—or reduce— them with meaning."[16] The freedom to invent is also coercive, in his reading, and the coerciveness, moreover, lies precisely in the refusal to go behind that also constitutes the freedom to recompose all experience. Freedom is thus bound up with coercion, and the recomposition rather than determination of meaning is as much a command as a freedom.

To recognize this conflation of freedom and coercion is to recognize just the fusion of differences that James works for. Freedom is experienced inseparably from coercion; it includes its difference and disables us from identifying exactly the difference *between* them. Moreover, to be confronted with such a confusion, as in the phrase "what would condemn it, so to speak, to the responsibility of freedom" (426) or in the Prince's recognition that Mr. Verver "was as bad—that is as good—" as Maggie (35), is to be faced with meaning that cannot be figured out. Terms that must be different are put together so that they cannot be separated. As Bersani says, the meaning of such statements cannot be enriched or reduced; there is nothing to add or take away. In a sense, there is no choice but to accept the statement's absoluteness at face value, for we can make no even exchange with it or for it. The possibility of such exchange has been ruled out by the representation of differences without difference. Moreover, the act of represen-

---

[16] Bersani, *A Future for Astyanax*, p. 132. For Bersani, the freedom of the narrative works against itself and against the narrative. For Maggie, he says, after re-forming the relations of the four central characters, finds herself not in fact representable by any form. "As part of the very energy of their social representations, Stendhal and James thus designate privileged, non-representable areas where their heroes transcend, or die to, the novels which seem to exist so that these heroes may escape from them" (p. 153). But if, as I am arguing, the narrative acknowledges throughout the absolute and unrepresentable nature of meaning, then the ending does not constitute a "break" with the narrative.

tation that fuses differences together in this way is itself an act of absolute acceptance, since it represents differences indiscriminately. The burden of such representation, its responsibility, is the excess of reality; it bears this excess by representing an excess of meaning. This is not a recognition of the freedom of representation to call anything anything and thus change meaning by representation. It is a recognition of the "responsibility of freedom" to the absolute and irreducible nature of reality and the responsibility of freedom to accept the irreducible nature of things even though nothing can be made of it.

So that if representation assumes a certain absolute value that cannot be gone into, it assumes this both in the nature of what it represents and in its own form. It is the form of acceptance that does not make a difference. The pressure of the narrative is thus the pressure to accept rather than change by exchange. In the passages quoted above, Adam accepts his loss of Maggie and Maggie accepts the Prince's adultery. They do not do anything with these facts or make anything of them. Instead, they make up and give form to fictions that share the absoluteness of those facts: the fiction that Maggie has not forsaken Adam, the fiction that there is no break between the Prince and Maggie. These fictions are believed in without grounds: there can be no grounds for sheer belief, which can be accepted, therefore, only if *not* gone into.

Thus the Ververs treat fiction no differently from fact. But this is not a denial of reality. It makes possible precisely the acceptance of reality, once we see that good faith can apply to real things as well as to fictions, or that a trade-off can be avoided in both cases. If we recall Edward Said's insistence that fiction is "molested" by its recognition that it is not real, we can see that James's work insists that even our nonfictive relations to reality are molested by the same recognition. Because in real life, too, we enter into exchanges with the world of objects and others, making them different for us—or, in human relations, more often wishing they were different for us—than they are in themselves. To do this is implicitly also to recognize that we, too, are always something different for others than we are for ourselves. Although other writers have found freedom in the flexibility of these very differences, James's concept of freedom in *The Golden Bowl* entails a different reversal of values. What he suggests is not that all values are subject to change and exchange and so free of determination, but that all values, both in reality and in fiction, can be both absolute *and* free of determination.

Rather than enter into exchanges which free things from determination in order to avoid alienation and which represent the indeterminacy of reality with representations of indeterminate meaning, James and the Ververs defeat the alienation of conventional exchange by accepting reality as absolute and irreducible and offering for our acceptance an absolute and irreducible representation. The most important difference between an indeterminate representation and James's representations, I think, is that his work for total rather than partial acceptance. The Ververs accept the absoluteness of things. Their capacity for "the extraordinary American good faith" (34), a capacity shared by James, is precisely their capacity for acceptance of things—whether real or fictive—without making them different.

Such acceptance constitutes a terrific pressure not to go into things, the pressure required to remain on the surface without sinking into the depths. The narrative keeps us above ground by its fusions, which allow no gaps to open up. If we, like the Prince, want to know exactly what is going on in this novel, we will either be frustrated in our desire or stop reading: not because the narrative does not give us enough but because it gives us too much, more than we need if we need to know. Thus, we are given condemned freedom and the Ververs' bad goodness. This can be exhausting, for the prose is relentless in its refusal to let us "get it." But if the pressure results in our recognition that there is, in fact, nothing to get—that we are not supposed to figure things out or get to the bottom of them—then the pressure has, in James's terms, kept us afloat.

But there is little relief. For just as Mr. Verver appreciates the Prince's form as "inveterately round," without "the sharp corners and hard edges, all the stony pointedness" of architecture (119-20), James takes pleasure in making no points. Any possible point seems to get smoothed over. James prefers the form of roundness, without the relief provided, as physical relief would be provided in a building's surface, by straight lines and sharp angles. Thus, not only is it difficult to get the point in passages such as Adam's consideration of marriage to Charlotte, but other conventional "points," especially turning points in the development of the story, get smoothed over too. The evening that Maggie waits for the Prince to come back from Matcham is a turning point, in a sense. It comes, too, at the point in the narrative where we switch to Maggie's point of view. But although it is the point at which she recognizes "that she had made . . . a difference in the situation" (301), exactly what that difference is remains unclear. The narrative proceeds for pages and pages, and Maggie's thoughts go at first in the "wrong" direction—thinking she has abandoned the Prince and Charlotte rather than the other way around—before we see any difference she has made. And if we try to pinpoint that difference as her recognition that Charlotte and the Prince are together, that can seem only an inadequate representation of thirty pages of James's narrative. Taking thirty pages to describe a turning point is in itself enough to smooth that point over, to make us stop seeing it *as* the point.

In this passage as in others, James's prose moves us around the point for so long that it no longer stands as the point. In its roundness, the narrative circulates. Relief would come if we got to a point or if some point came out. But we do not get the point, because it really is not there. If we name the point of that turning point, for example, we do what James does not do. For James, to come out with a point would be to let us down.

Yet we tend to experience this, again, as a lack. We feel what is missing. Both the language and the silences in the text can be seen as lacks: the language is evasive itself, and things are otherwise evaded by being left unsaid. The Ververs, similarly, can be said to skirt the issues when they do talk and otherwise to avoid the issues by keeping quiet. But for James,

both language and silence are full, not empty; both are excesses rather than lacks. If they were lacks, they would constitute breaks in the surface of his form. Nicola Bradbury has
written of "The Development of Silence as a Means of Expression" in James's novels, emphasizing its double nature as a
lack of signs and a sign in itself: "The simplest unit of expression, serving to divide up other units and make them com-
prehensible, silence is also a tribute to what lies beyond the
bounds of form, and observes decorum with respect to the
inexpressible." But in each case silence is or signifies a lack,
and Bradbury's conclusion about the golden bowl is therefore
that "the crack, like the bowl, is precious, and inevitable."[17]
But James's novel works to get rid of cracks, and one sign of
this is the change that occurs in Maggie's treatment of silence.

Maggie herself, particularly earlier in Book Second, often
fills in silences or replaces silence with imagined dialogue.
Then having imagined the unspoken dialogue, she recognizes
why the silence must be maintained. So that she imagines but
does not speak the speech that declares her concern to Amerigo when she has waited for his return from Matcham:

> Some such words as those were what *didn't* ring out, yet
> it was as if even the unuttered sound had been quenched
> here in its own quaver. It was where utterance would
> have broken down by its very weight if he had let it get
> so far. (312)

Maggie both hears the admission of fear and hears it break
down in the silence. Similarly, she later imagines a speech
about Charlotte that remains unspoken because "she
couldn't—and he knew it—say what was true. ... She
couldn't challenge him, because it would have been—and
there she was paralysed—the *note*. It would have translated
itself on the spot, for his ear, into jealousy" (351-52). And
any admission of jealousy, she has already realized, would
"end the game" (322).

In such cases, speeches are both given and withheld, and
the silence is therefore a lack of something we know might

[17] Bradbury, *Henry James*, pp. 13, 196.

be there. These passages are about breaking things. Maggie imagines breaking the silence, and breaking the silence with speech that would itself break down, in the one case, or constitute a break between her and the Prince, in the other. In other cases, however, silences are not lacks, and breaks are not imagined. Such is the silence between Maggie and the Prince when they are leaving each other alone:

> She never, at present, thought of what Amerigo might be intending, without the reflection, by the same stroke, that, whatever this quantity, he was leaving still more to her own ingenuity. . . . She had hours of exaltation indeed when the meaning of all this pressed in upon her as a tacit vow from him to abide without question by whatever she should be able to achieve or think fit to prescribe. Then it was that, even while holding her breath for the awe of it, she truly felt almost able enough for anything. It was as if she had passed, in a time incredibly short, from being nothing for him to being all. . . . (453)

Here, although Maggie "interprets" the silence, she interprets it as a sign of absolute confidence and agreement. Thus what she imagines is not a breakdown; she does not even think, here, of breaking the silence either. The breaks that would constitute lacks are themselves missing. What she imagines is a pressure, and a pressure sufficient to keep up her strength. Moreover, silence here represents for Maggie exactly the move from "being nothing for him to being all," exactly the conversion from lack to fullness which silence itself undergoes in the novel.

If what Maggie puts into the silences she experiences is doubt or fear, or any expression of insecurity, the result is a break; for such insecurities are already breakdowns. If silence is filled with confidence, however, the silence is not a break at all; it is solid enough to support her. So with her father later in the narrative:

> Nothing, truly, *was* at present between them save that they were looking at each other in infinite trust; it fairly wanted no more words, and when they met . . . a pair of

birds in the upper air could scarce have appeared less to invite each other to sit down and worry afresh. (492)

Here, though there is "nothing" between Maggie and her father except "infinite trust," that trust fills the emptiness with something on which, again, they can remain afloat.

In a sense, this may seem to beg the question of silence, because it is confidence or trust that makes the difference. It *is* confidence that makes the difference; and, most importantly, this difference is absolute. The relation of the interpreter and the silence becomes a relation *of* absolutes. Confidence is always, necessarily, absolute, or it is not confidence. And its effect is to fill all gaps, even the "nothing" of silence. Although we are accustomed to regarding the insecurity of language or silence—the spaces they leave open to different interpretations—as what makes possible the relation between the medium and its interpreter, here it is exactly an eventual security that characterizes both the medium and its interpreter. Both language and silence are full of meaning if the interpreter is full of confidence. Yet this does not at all deny the indeterminacy of meaning. In fact, once confidence begins to function, the mobility and indeterminacy of meaning can increase, because no difference can make a difference to confidence.

Belief, trust, good faith, and confidence are the conditions that enable meaning to be secured in *The Golden Bowl*. "The extraordinary American good faith" precludes knowledge: "they knew, it might have appeared in these lights, absolutely nothing on earth worth speaking of" (252). It consists, instead, of innocence and imagination (34), and Maggie's "imagination was clearly never ruffled by the sense of any anomaly" (252). Innocent and imaginative, faith generates security as it precludes anomalies: things fit together. The "infinite trust" that holds Maggie and her father together after their expressions of belief in each other (485) is also innocent and imaginative rather than knowledgeable; they never define or prove the terms of their trust. Yet Maggie's good faith is "trying" to the Prince, who wishes she would admit that she doesn't know anything. And " 'the way she believes in one' " is trying to Charlotte, who says that " 'It takes stuff, within one, . . . to stand it' " (97). Maggie's faith and belief constitute an acceptance so *un*demanding that, for the Prince and Charlotte, it constitutes a demand. "Taking stuff," that demand is felt, however, as a demand that disables exchange, both because it does not take anything away and because it acknowledges no lack or need. " 'There's nothing, absolutely, that one *need* do for her,' " as Charlotte says, because " 'she doesn't miss things' " (96-97). Nor does Maggie's belief in others allow her to recognize anything missing in them. Her acceptance, then, constitutes a demand that is also a gift, a demand that exceeds need, a demand that others be related to her uneconomically.

To believe in or trust someone is to accept him or her absolutely. The economic implications of good faith, belief, and trust are thus "sublime," as exchange becomes redundant: an acceptance of others that precludes lack. To be confident is another form of belief, belief in oneself, and confidence also functions in absolute terms and as a gain that is the "grounds" for more gain. For Maggie to be "confident" is for Maggie "to be right" (303); and it is Adam Verver's confidence that makes his "boldness of acquisition" as a collector:

> He had gained confidence only with time, but when he had taken real possession of the place it had been never again to come away. . . . The right ground for elation was difficulty mastered, and his difficulty—thanks to his modesty—had been to believe in his facility. (127)

The gain of confidence is the gain that enables Mr. Verver to "buy" art. But to insist on confidence as the most important form of faith is to move faith outside the bounds of propriety and suggest another reason that the Ververs are hard to take. For "confidence" straddles the line that distinguishes independence and self-reliance from boldness and obtrusiveness, as it also straddles the distinction between modesty and a peculiarly American form of self-assurance.[18] If belief enables Maggie to accept, confidence enables Mr. Verver to take, and the conflation of belief and confidence, like the conflation of accepting and taking, indicates that belief is necessary to gain or aggrandizement even as it functions outside the terms of any but a sublime economy.

Belief thus seems to take more than it gives. For James, however, taking is not an easy form of gain, precisely because the taking he advocates is redundant and uneconomical. Such taking does not satisfy needs or lacks, and such taking occurs independently of giving. Only to take, in any relationship, is thus to risk feeling left out, as the Prince and Charlotte feel with the Ververs. Yet it is precisely because belief enables acceptance, or taking, to occur in excess of the limits usually imposed by exchange that enormous gain is possible.

To accept what exceeds need, even to the extent that such a gift constitutes a demand, is a difficulty James considers in the Preface to *The Portrait of a Lady*. James's prose always gives too much, putting the burden on his readers to accept more than enough:

> So early was to begin my tendency to *overtreat*, rather than undertreat (where there was choice or danger) my subject. (Many members of my craft, I gather, are far from agreeing with me, but I have always held overtreating the minor disservice.)[19]

If his prose is always overdoing it, James himself is also, at another point in the Preface, in the position of receiving more than he needs. He cannot work well in Venice; the place does not serve his purposes.

> How can places that speak in general so to the imagination not give it, at the moment, the particular thing it

---

[18] Gary Lindberg, in *The Confidence Man in American Literature* (New York: Oxford University Press, 1982), identifies the peculiarly American character of the con man. In his Introduction, Lindberg links the confidence of the con man to the imitative as well as innovative quality of the New World; to the "prevailing promissory tone" of migration in America; and to the creation of faith—"a confidence man *makes* belief" (pp. 6-7).

[19] James, *The Art of the Novel*, p. 57.

wants? . . . The real truth is, I think, that they express, under this appeal, only too much—more than, in the given case, one has use for; so that one finds one's self working less congruously . . . than in presence of the moderate and the neutral, to which we may lend something of the light of our vision. Such a place as Venice is too proud for such charities; Venice doesn't borrow, she but all magnificently gives. We profit by that enormously, but to do so we must either be quite off duty or be on it in her service alone. . . . Strangely fertilizing, in the long run, does a wasted effort of attention often prove.[20]

The incommensurability of what Venice gives and what James wants is identified first here as a lack—in negative terms—and then realized as an excess. But the excess is demanding.

Venice gives so much that exchange is virtually precluded, for the writer lends nothing himself to the effects she produces. She also gives so much that he can't use it. Yet there is enormous profit possible if he wants nothing for his own purposes; the waste is eventually "fertilizing." This is an uneconomical relation because all the giving is on one side and all the taking on the other. Such is the relation of James to his readers, too, in the passage about the fusion of form and substance quoted at the beginning of this chapter. For the fusion that constitutes art also disables its readers from finding "your way at all (for your own fell purpose)." Though there is profit in the "magnificent" gift, a gift that also constitutes an absolute demand, the recipient only profits "strangely," since getting a profit is indistinguishable from giving up any need or purpose of his own: you gain by total surrender.

Taking becomes indistinguishable here from being taken or taken in. A similar fusion of gain and surrender characterizes giving, too, in the Preface to *The Golden Bowl*, where James says that "the essential property" of "any literary form conceived in the light of 'poetry' " is "to give out its finest and most numerous secrets, and to give them out most gratefully."[21] Here the fact that giving coincides with gratitude

[20] Ibid., p. 41.
[21] Ibid., p. 346.

suggests again that to be accepted is what we might be most grateful for. The two passages together suggest, on the one hand, that to accept the most magnificent gifts is to be taken but, on the other hand, that to be taken, with all one's secrets, is in fact something to be grateful for. For then one is totally accepted, and this is true no matter which side of the "exchange" one is on. There is no equivalence in such a relation, although there is absolute acceptance on both sides.

Giving is not a difficulty in these passages. In other works of James, giving is similarly represented as the safer or easier act. The "fair exchange" is also evaded in earlier novels, but it is evaded by the refusal to take. Thus, in *The Ambassadors*, Mme. de Vionnet exclaims, " 'What it comes to is that it's not, that it's never, a happiness, any happiness at all, to *take*. The only safe thing is to give. It's what plays you least false.' " And Strether seems to echo this when he declares his " 'only logic. Not, out of the whole affair, to have got anything for myself.' "[22] Milly Theale, too, the redemptive heroine of *The Wings of the Dove*, declares, " 'I give and give and give. . . . Only I can't listen or receive or accept—I can't *agree*. I can't make a bargain.' "[23] If, in Mme. de Vionnet's terms, such characters are safe, the characters of *The Golden Bowl* are engaged in a dangerous enterprise.

"Giving" appears seldom in this novel, and when it does it is usually in the form of "giving up" or "giving away." This is virtually to continue the identification of generosity and renunciation that is clear in the earlier novels. "Taking," however, recurs over and over again, even as the form of Maggie's redemption of others: "They thus tacitly put it upon her to be disposed of, the whole complexity of their peril, and she promptly saw why: because she was there, and there just *as* she was, to lift it off them and take it; to charge herself with it as the scapegoat of old. . . ." (457). Maggie's behavior is seldom represented as a form of payment; but when it is, even paying is a form of taking, as when she buys the golden bowl:

[22] Henry James, *The Ambassadors*, ed. R. W. Stallman (New York: New American Library, 1960), pp. 349, 375.

[23] Henry James, *The Wings of the Dove*, afterword F. W. Dupee (New York: New American Library, 1964), p. 330.

"I did 'believe in it,' you see—must have believed in it somehow instinctively; for I took it as soon as I saw it. Though I didn't know at all then," she added, "what I was taking *with* it." (432)

If someone "buys" something in this novel, the act is seen as an act of belief. Only faith, which is absolute but indeterminate and groundless, makes possible the acceptance of an object as it comes to differ from what it was first taken to be. For to believe in something is to give it a value as indeterminate and groundless as the belief on which it rests. That neither in the "purchase" of the Prince or in the purchase of the bowl does Maggie get what she or her father has paid for emphasizes that taking in the novel, like Milly Theale's giving, is never part of a fair exchange. For if acceptance were limited to the terms of such exchange, these objects would be returned, being more than was bargained for. When the Prince and Charlotte find that they have taken something different in their marriages than they bargained for, their response is to return; they return themselves to their past relationship. But though the Ververs have been "taken" when they take the Prince and Charlotte, it is exactly this reciprocal acceptance that will constitute their strange and enormous profit.

If the emphasis on taking in the novel seems to preclude the act of giving, it does so because the two in fact get fused together, as they are in the above quotations from the Prefaces. Acceptance becomes the act of generosity in the novel. This is increasingly clear in the forms of behavior that are called taking. Thus Mr. Verver refuses to accept Maggie's statement that she is selfish (" 'I won't take it from you' ") because

"When a person's of the nature you speak of there are always other persons to suffer. But you've just been describing to me what you'd take, if you had once a good chance, from your husband." (478)

This follows the discussion in which Maggie says she is " 'beyond everything,' " and the only referent for " 'what you'd take' " is behavior on the part of the Prince that might otherwise cause jealousy. Taking, however, is specifically here what precludes selfishness and what seems itself a form of suffering. What Maggie takes, that is, is what she must bear.

A more confusing use of the term comes at the end of the narrative when Maggie declares to Fanny that the Prince must be willing to see Charlotte again:

> "He ought to wish to see her. . . . That," said Maggie with the courage of her conviction, "he ought to be ready, he ought to be happy . . . to take from her. It's as if he wished to get off without taking anything." (522)

Taking here, too, assumes the meaning of a burden. Yet, at the same time, the last line constitutes such a complete reversal of our assumptions about what we avoid when we get off without doing something that it insists on the conflation of giving and taking in the narrative. Thus taking cannot be distinguished from generosity as it becomes a form of belief, a form of being taken in. Taking is a burden, but taking, as common sense and Adam Verver tell us, is also a form of gain. It remains true in this novel that the more one can take, the more one can get; though it remains true in sublime terms that fuse differences together. Giving and taking can be conflated because the relation they constitute is an absolute relation. There is no difference between giving and taking in such a relation because the acceptance of differences is absolute, and thus no difference in another can determine a difference in the terms of relation to another.

Acceptance, therefore, is no bargain. The Prince is bothered at the beginning of the novel because he wants to understand his marriage as an exchange and cannot do so. He sees that exchange is precluded by the Ververs' consideration of him as a " 'morceau de musée' ":

> It was as if he had been some old embossed coin, of a purity of gold no longer used, . . . of which the "worth" in mere modern change, sovereigns and half-crowns, would be great enough, but as to which, since there were finer ways of using it, such taking to pieces was superfluous. That was the image for the security in which it was open to him to rest; he was to constitute a possession,

yet was to escape being reduced to his component parts.
. . . What would it mean but that, if they didn't "change"
him, they really wouldn't know—he wouldn't know himself—how many pounds, shillings and pence he had to
give? These at any rate, for the present, were unanswer-
able questions; all that *was* before him was that he was
invested with attributes. (43)

Having been "invested with attributes," the Prince would like
to know what they are, since he is sure some return will be
expected on them. But their estimate is incalculable, and so
is the return he assumes he will have to make. For "Who but
a billionaire could say what was fair exchange for a billion?
That measure was the shrouded object" (44).

There are two shrouded objects, however, when the Prince
tries to look into his relation to the Ververs. One is his value
for them—a "large, bland, blank assumption of merits" (43)—
and the other is the Ververs themselves, or Americans in general. Trying to get to know them, the Prince is confronted,
like Poe's Gordon Pym, with "a thickness of white air that
was like a dazzling curtain of light, concealing as darkness
conceals, yet of the colour of milk or of snow" (42). The
Prince deals with this by trying to get to know his father-in-
law, and to do this he starts a collection. "Liking explanations,
liking them almost as if he collected them" (135), he "wanted
first to make sure of the *whole* of the subject . . . ; after which
the innumerable facts he had collected would find their use"
(137).

This project is doomed to failure, for the Prince never does
figure the Ververs out. For in order to know their value, he
must be able, as we are told in the above passage about figuring
out his own value, to take them to pieces. Unable to take to
pieces a "large, bland, blank assumption" or a white cloud,
the Prince tries to start at the opposite end, to collect pieces
and put them together. Yet his procedure, at least when applied to Adam Verver, will never *get* the whole.

It was as if the grandpapa's special show of the character
were but another side for the observer to study, another
item for him to note. It came back, this latter personage

knew, to his own previous perception—that of the
Prince's inability, in any matter in which he was concerned, to *conclude*. The idiosyncracy, for him, at each
stage, had to be demonstrated—on which, however, he
admirably accepted it. This last was, after all, the point;
he really worked, poor young man, for acceptance, since
he worked so constantly for comprehension. And how,
when you came to that, *could* you know that a horse
wouldn't shy at a brass band, in a country road, because
it didn't shy at a traction-engine? It might have been
brought up to traction-engines without having been
brought up to brass bands. Little by little, thus, from
month to month, the Prince was learning what his wife's
father had been brought up to; and now it could be
checked off—he had been brought up to the romantic
view of *principini*. Who would have thought it, and where
would it all stop? The only fear somewhat sharp for Mr.
Verver was a certain fear of disappointing him for
strangeness. . . . He didn't know—he was learning, and
it was funny for him—to how many things he *had* been
brought up. (133-34)

For Mr. Verver, the evidence of variety in his character is a
pleasant discovery, and the indeterminate nature of the discovery is not disturbing. He seems to work backwards, since
he moves from present to past. But there is no determinate
relation between them; what occurs is the recognition of their
mutual indeterminacy. The variety of present evidence means
that the past itself, which if considered historically ought to
be seen as the grounds for the present, opens up to include
more possibilities of meaning. Mr. Verver's "freedom to see"
(128) requires no grounds for what is seen and instead allows
what is seen to open up more things to view. The Prince,
however, because he would like to comprehend, which means
to reach a sense of wholeness, is frustrated by the fact that
the pieces do not fit together to form a whole. Each fact
remains an idiosyncracy, and no one fact rules out other possibilities. Experience is various, as Mr. Verver recognizes.

There is a difference between a brass band and a traction-engine. And it makes a difference which particular horse is confronted with them, because horses are brought up differently. Differences generate differences here, and no difference can take the place of other differences. The Prince is accumulating more and more, as he accepts everything he sees in Mr. Verver, but he is faced with his familiar difficulty. There is no clear form or figure for what he sees, and he would like to know what it all comes to.

But the Prince remains—after almost two years of marriage—both unknowing and unknown, related to the Ververs as Mr. Verver sees his present related to his past: there is indeterminacy on both sides.

> He was never even yet sure of how, at this, that or the other point, he would strike them; they felt remarkably, so often, things he hadn't meant, and missed not less remarkably, and not less often, things he had. He had fallen back on his general explanation—"We haven't the same *values*"; by which he understood the same measure of importance. (120-21)

Confronted with endless differences, the Prince feels the abundance as a lack. Because he wants a "fair exchange," which secures rather than "misses" meaning, he feels differences as a lack of the common terms or common ground that would make exchange valuable.

James himself does not figure out Adam Verver either. We, that is, do not *know* more about him than the Prince does. James does not provide the kinds of connections that the Prince misses. He does not put together the parts of Mr. Verver's character on any logical or comprehensive grounds; and the presentation of the character does not come to a clear figure. Mr. Verver, for example, seems too easygoing and too easily distracted to have been such a successful businessman.

> Variety of imagination—what is that but fatal, in the world of affairs, unless so disciplined as not to be distinguished from monotony? Mr. Verver then, for a fresh,

full period, a period betraying, extraordinarily, no wasted year, had been inscrutably monotonous behind an iridescent cloud. (113)

Mr. Verver has variety of imagination; but, since he is a successful businessman, he can have it only if it is indistinguishable from monotony. Therefore, the second sentence tells us, James will simply put the one in place of the other. It is not, of course, a fair exchange, for there are no grounds whatever for the exchange of monotony for variety. It is an irrational confusion. But, having fused together Mr. Verver's contradictory characteristics, James puts the whole confusion behind a cloud, where it remains, unclarified. So that we, like the Prince, are confronted with one of those clouds that preclude explanation and knowledge.

The Prince can be seen again as like some readers of James's text in his reaction to the Ververs, whom he finds "trying" as he reaches a "strange final irritation" midway through the narrative (252; 251). For if we accept such a representation as the above passage gives us, we do so without knowing exactly what it is talking about. If we can take it, we can do so only without knowledge or grounds for acceptance. For the Prince, the acceptance of unknown quantities is frustrating. But such acceptance is what James describes in the Preface as his relation to his own collection: the "accumulated good stuff" that is the material of the novel. The "bargain" that the stuff makes with him is " 'Actively believe in us and then you'll see!' " (19). This is the bargain of the novel, too, and the bargain the Ververs make with the Prince, although he, understandably, does not recognize it as a bargain.

The Prince, the narrative insists, cannot know the Ververs, and any attempt at knowledge is an attempt that separates or reduces things to "component parts." James works consistently to defeat or preclude such separations. This can be seen in the various fusions in his language, and it can be seen in his choice of absolute acceptance as the most satisfactory relation of characters. If absolute acceptance characterizes human relations, however, another crucial and conventional sep-

aration is defeated: that is the separation of our primitive
selves, whose behavior is unacceptable to others, from our
conscious and mature selves. This is the separation that brings
security and independence to the ego in the Freudian scheme
of development. The concept of fusion rather than division,
if applied to a single self or to the relation of self and others,
is both unrealistic, since two or more people cannot really be
fused together, and primitive. That James manages to represent fusion not as primitive but as idealistic is typical of just
the fusions of contraries he accomplishes repeatedly. But the
ability to believe is not a cultivated but a primitive capacity;
for belief cannot recognize the distinctions and separations
that both knowledge and safety require. Belief must be absolute and indivisible. Belief, therefore, is the very means necessary for acceptance of the absolute and indivisible selves
James represents.

   If for James what matter most are belief and feelings—as I
am arguing—and if *The Golden Bowl* is a novel about belief
and love, then we are in primitive territory. But for James this
is territory where crudeness and refinement merge. James is
like Maggie, whose "place" is

> that improvised "post"—a post of the kind spoken of as
> advanced—with which she was to have found herself
> connected in the fashion of a settler or a trader in a new
> country; in the likeness even of some Indian squaw with
> a papoose on her back and barbarous bead work to sell.
> Maggie's own in short would have been sought in vain
> in the most rudimentary map of the social relations as
> such. The only geography marking it would be doubtless
> that of the fundamental passions. . . . (516-17)

It is not clear here whether Maggie is a settler advancing into
new territory or a barbaric native: someone who has always
been there, like the barbaric unconscious, but has been displaced by someone else. She is both at once and thus has no
place on the map. To speak of James as crude seems ludicrous
perhaps. Traditionally we think of James as refined, as refining
experience in fiction that is contemptuous of commonness.

But this is not exactly right; for he is both refined and crude. What drives his fiction beyond the common is James's insistence that what people have in common is a paltry and impoverished basis for human relations. He represents conventionally unacceptable excesses, allowing the human being to be too much to take in any even exchange, too much to be mapped or planned. That such excesses are not represented exactly is precisely part of his insistence that the exchange of language for such excesses would reduce them to "common" terms.

Adam Verver stands in the novel as the alternative to the Prince, partly because of his commonness. But Mr. Verver is common only in the sense that he is crude; he is not at all translatable into common terms. Like his namesake, he is both primitive and unique. The fact that his capacity for acceptance is represented as a "boldness of acquisition"; that his "extraordinary American good faith" entails an extraordinary self-confidence; and that his capacity to believe in things is represented as a capacity to buy them all suggest that he is a fusion of refined and crude characteristics. The only "possession" Mr. Verver is really proud of is his "confidence" (127). He does not doubt himself; he "knew, by this time, knew thoroughly" the "high authenticities," both in works of art and in people (121).

> Nothing perhaps might affect us as queerer, had we time to look into it, than this application of the same measure of value to such different pieces of property as old Persian carpets, say, and new human acquisitions; all the more indeed that the amiable man was not without an inkling, on his own side, that he was, as a taster of life, economically constructed. He put into his one little glass everything he raised to his lips. . . . (159-60)

Here again, James does not "look into" the matter, but the confusion of people and carpets is in fact queer, at least on the grounds of any economic or aesthetic principle. But Adam Verver's "aesthetic principle" cannot be identified as a principle at all. He has learned, but he has "learnt the lesson of the senses" (160). Mr. Verver's taste is neither exactly refined nor aesthetic, as the passage insists by applying it to what he puts into his mouth.[24] To treat the art collector's taste as a physical sensation is not only to fuse together refinement and crudeness but to insist that looking into it would be as absurd as looking into his "knowledge," which is a matter of confidence. Both characteristics, like those the Prince observes in him, are idiosyncratic.

We do not look into Mr. Verver, then, nor does he look into things. His life has been a life of acquisition, but his art collection is a sacred thing to him, "treasures sifted to positive sanctity" (125). His acquisitions seem, moreover, as their sanctity suggests, to be believed in and taken without knowledge of them. The only works of art we see him acquire are the Damascene tiles, and in this case he is "distracted" by Charlotte's presence; but he does not bargain for them, and he simply seems to accept the seller's word and price after having seen the tiles. This is not merely a matter of confidence or good faith, though. That is, Mr. Verver does not trust himself to recognize a fake, nor does he trust the appearance of the work to mean that it is really what it is said to be. For his sense of authenticity does not rule out fakes. "He cared that a work of art of price should 'look like' the master to whom it might perhaps be deceitfully attributed" (126). The fact that a painting called a Raphael looks like a Raphael, then, is what Mr. Verver cares about. Thus his senses are sufficient to recognize what he calls the "high authenticities" (121).

What Mr. Verver himself looks like, we are told, is a "financial 'backer' " of plays, "watching his interests from the wing, but in rather confessed ignorance of the mysteries of

---

[24] Dorothea Krook suggests that "taste" is Maggie's enemy. "The destructive element that the Prince and Charlotte embody in the aesthetic principle, their 'touchstone of taste,' " is what "Maggie must annihilate in order to accomplish her task." See *The Ordeal of Consciousness*, pp. 267-68. But instead of annihilating taste, James turns it, in his representation of Adam Verver, from an objective and impartial principle into a matter of personal sensation and personal confidence.

mimicry" (141). Though he does not understand mimicry, it is imitation that Adam Verver backs in this narrative; or, more exactly, it is the indistinction of good imitations and the real thing. He does not care about the difference if it cannot be seen. He believes in and "consecrates" the pieces of his collection; and this involves neither knowing nor caring what origin or past lies behind their surfaces.

The Prince, however, believes in history. He thinks himself "somehow full of his race":

> The effect was nowhere in particular, yet he constantly felt himself at the mercy of the cause. He knew his antenatal history, knew it in every detail, and it was a thing to keep causes well before him. . . . What was this so important step he had just taken [signing the marriage contract] but the desire for some new history that should, so far as possible, contradict, and even if need be flatly dishonour, the old? (38)

The Prince seems to think that history determines what one is, though he also believes that histories are interchangeable, since he wants to be given a new one. The Prince's hope is that he will be changed. This is echoed again in his wish to know his worth in "modern change" and his fear that "if they didn't 'change' him, they really wouldn't know—he wouldn't know himself—how many pounds, shillings and pence he had to give" (43). The Ververs do not want to change him, though. The Prince is for them like their works of art, and this means that they accept him as a "thing visibly perfect in its kind" (160) rather than evaluate him in their own terms. The Prince expects the terms of acceptance to be specified so that he can know his own worth, but the Ververs clarify no grounds for his value and give him no exchange value. And this means that he cannot be changed.

Yet he has no terms of his own and finds himself located somewhere between his history and the Ververs. Wanting always to know where he stands, he finds himself in a "false position":

The difficulty was, for the nerves of daily intercourse with Maggie in particular, that her imagination was clearly never ruffled by the sense of any anomaly. The great anomaly would have been that her husband, or even that her father's wife, should prove to have been made, for the long-run, after the pattern set from so far back to the Ververs. If one *was* so made one had certainly no business, on any terms, at Matcham; whereas if one wasn't one had no business there on the particular terms—terms of conformity with the principles of Eaton Square—under which one had been so absurdly dedicated. (252)

Here the Prince arrives at the sense of his own anomalous position, thereby separating himself emphatically from Maggie, who is incompatible with anomaly. Every point he recognizes, moreover, *is* an anomaly: a disparity that helps him break apart the situation. He is not like the Ververs, for one thing; he has just described them as "children." But for another, if he were he should not have been sent to Matcham. And for another, if he is not, then he should not be sent to Matcham and be expected to behave like the Ververs.

His solution to the breakdown is, logically, the separation of himself from the Ververs. Having recognized from the beginning of the novel that what is extraordinary about Maggie " 'is the way she believes in one' " (97), the Prince and Charlotte use precisely the lack of knowledge that such belief entails to justify separation from her:

"... It represents for us a conscious care—"
"Of every hour, literally," said Charlotte. ... "And for which we must trust each other—"
"Oh, as we trust the saints in glory. ... It's all too wonderful."
... "It's too beautiful."
... "It's sacred," he said at last. (236-37)

Here the Prince and Charlotte invoke the sacred as the means of separating themselves from the Ververs and keeping themselves together. The Ververs remain sacred, because innocent and simple; and the relationship of Charlotte and the Prince is a sacred trust, because they have undertaken to preserve that sacred innocence from knowledge of what is really going on. The sacred here becomes what is not real and must be kept separate from reality, whereas for the Ververs the sacred is constituted by their own belief in a thing, which for them is as good as or the same as the real thing.

Here Charlotte and the Prince manage to break apart the most crucial fusion of the novel: that of belief and reality. They also, however, do so with the same language that the Ververs use to maintain it: "trust," the "beautiful," and the "sacred." R. P. Blackmur has suggested that Fanny Assingham functions in the novel as a "degraded" form of Maggie in her purposeless lies and manipulation of characters.[25] And clearly here, too, the Prince and Charlotte may be said to be a form of the Ververs. The novel itself, in this sense, is full of bad imitations as well as imitations that are indistinguishable from, or are, the real thing. The Prince and Charlotte also have an economy of acceptance that employs the same language as the Ververs' acceptance. But their acceptance is not absolute; and it effects separations rather than fusions.

The Prince's acceptance of history is an example of this. He seems to believe in history, but he accepts his history only until a better one comes along. Then, he assumes, he can trade one for the other. Moreover, his concept of history is always of a phenomenon separate from himself, imposed by external circumstances. Thus he can tell Maggie that " 'There are two parts of me' ": the history of " 'other people' " and his " 'single self,' " which she knows nothing about (33). Like the exchange value he expects the Ververs to give him, his historical meaning is not really his. The Prince is already, then, a divided consciousness, in a "false position" even before he marries. It is difficult to identify any "single self" for the Prince

---

[25] R. P. Blackmur, *Studies in Henry James* (New York: New Directions, 1983), p. 155. Blackmur distinguishes two kinds of lying in the two characters: "Mrs. Assingham would lie to create a false truth, Maggie would lie and does—to everyone but her husband—to preserve her vision of the real truth."

at all, for he does little in the novel except repeat the futility he recognizes in his family's history (39). As with his collection of facts about the Ververs, or his affair with Charlotte, his behavior is futile; though it is not clear, because James renders indistinguishable what the Prince would distinguish, whether this results from the way he has been brought up or from his " 'single self.' " The Prince's futility, that is to say, has no clear origin, though it is recognizable most clearly in his insistence on knowing where he stands and getting to the point.

It is with Charlotte that he is able to do both. For Charlotte, until the Prince stops talking to her, knows how things stand. Having accepted Adam Verver as a husband, for example, she performs "the duties of a remunerated office" (241). Unlike the Prince, whose marriage contract leaves him in a false position, Charlotte knows what return is required of her. Having signed the " 'contract' " and accepted the situation, she has only " 'to act as it demands of me' " (202). But Charlotte, faced with the demands of her marriage, is not taken in. She is careful to limit her actions to exactly what is required. Even what is not required—her affair with the Prince—is interpreted by her as in fact determined by the exchange. When she claims her freedom, she says to Fanny, " 'how can I not see it as it is? You'd see your own quickly enough if the Colonel gave you the same liberty. . . . Your husband doesn't treat you as of less importance to him than some other woman' " (202). Here freedom itself is grounded in exchange, determined as the remuneration for what Mr. Verver does *not* demand of her.

Charlotte identifies everything she does as an exact return for something given or an exact acceptance of something given. Thus her affair with the Prince is not a matter of choice. They are, for her, a "perfectly passive pair" who do nothing. " 'There has been plenty of "doing," ' . . . but it's all theirs, every inch of it; it's all a matter of what they've done *to* us' " (221). Charlotte can justify everything as part of an exchange and thus is able to provide what the Prince feels the lack of: "a discerned relation between a given appearance and a taken meaning" (266). As she says to him, " 'you can't *not* know

... where you are' " (230), given her ability to provide a definitive meaning for everything.

The Prince, however, knows where he is by different means. He separates himself from the Ververs by recognizing that there are no common terms shared by him and them. Since fair exchange only works on common terms, it follows that they are unfair and he can justifiably keep separate from them. Once he arrives at this sense of a clear-cut situation at Matcham, he, too, has his freedom:

> He knew why he, at any rate, had gone in, on the basis of all forms, on the basis of his having, in a manner, sold himself, for a *situation nette*. It had all been just in order that his—well, what on earth should he call it but his freedom?—should at present be as perfect and rounded and lustrous as some huge precious pearl. (268)

The Prince defines his position "on the basis" of having been true to form, or true to the terms of the sale. His freedom, like Charlotte's, is thus determined by an exchange; but his freedom is determined on the grounds of a completed exchange. He claims his freedom as what is left, for himself, once the forms are conformed to. The Prince is in very good form in the society at Matcham, but he is uncomfortable because "something of him, he often felt at these times, was left out" (248). His discomfort is resolved by his recognition that he is free to do as he likes with the part the good form does not include. As he has done before, the Prince here divides himself into two parts, the one determined by others—the formal meaning—and his own free meaning. Thus he also divides his good form from his own richest part—the free, huge, and precious part of him.

Adam Verver is true to form, and this commitment renders form indistinguishable from reality. Moreover, Mr. Verver necessarily commits himself to form when he appreciates it, because his means of recognizing its value is a personal matter, a matter of his own taste. The Prince and Charlotte are not committed to form at all. They practice form noncommittally and use form as a means of separating themselves from others or even of separating, in the Prince's case, parts of the self from other parts of the self. Both Charlotte's identification of everything as determined by an exchange and the Prince's division of what is covered by exchange and what remains, as a profit, when exchanges are completed accomplish a non-committal freedom. The very "form" in which the Prince pictures his freedom suggests that it is something he might turn around and sell. Like the history that can be traded for another, or the self that is sold for a profit, the Prince's freedom is exchangeable.

Thus there is no personal commitment in these characters; there are only forms of personal disconnection. The Prince, like Charlotte, simply "accepts" his pearl of freedom: "he was taking but what had been given him; the pearl dropped itself . . . straight into his hand" (268). But their claimed passivity is the mark of their difference from the Ververs, for the Ververs' acceptance is not passive. Like James's "good stuff" that demands that he " 'Actively believe in us and then you'll see!,' " the good stuff in the novel demands active commitment to it. This is what the Ververs' acceptance consists of. Mr. Verver sees things and appreciates them. He is committed to their value not only by his belief in them but by his appreciation of them. For appreciation is not a passive receptivity; it is an activity.

Mr. Verver's appreciation increases, or "appreciates," the value of what he sees.[26] His acceptance makes a difference to the meaning of the object, though it does not change the object itself. This appreciating relation of the "seer" to the object is the relation to which his art collection is dedicated. The works

[26] Carolyn Porter, in *Seeing and Being: The Plight of the Participant Observer in Emerson, James, Adams, and Faulkner* (Middletown, Conn.: Wesleyan University Press, 1981), views the Prince's "appreciation" by the Ververs in exclusively monetary terms, as part of a capitalistic enterprise in which he, as capital, is "hoarded" (pp. 140-46). James's use of financial terms seems to me significant as part of his attempt to make economy "sublime" by using its language for uneconomical relations. Porter's reading, however, identifies the "reification" of human values in the novel, whose exchanges she views as absolutely, and inhumanly, economical.

of art in the museum will be subject to endless appreciation. The relation of the appreciator to the objects is not, of course, discernible; it is not the sort of relation the Prince wants. For the Prince, the fact that his marriage identifies him as a museum piece means that he will be taken off the market and thus have no value; whereas for Mr. Verver, the removal of objects from the marketplace makes possible their greater appreciation. The Prince's capacity to "see" is correspondingly limited. Like his namesake, he is, at the beginning of the novel, as he says to Fanny, " 'starting on a great voyage' " (45). But what he wants to accomplish is what the earlier "discoverer" accomplished: he wants to know where things are and be able to put the Americas on the map. Having looked at the Americas, Vespucci turned around, leaving their appreciation to others. Prince Amerigo, too, not seeing and appreciating the worth of the Ververs, returns to where he was before.

It is Maggie's action that I want to consider now, as action that fuses together the divisions between the characters. The love that Maggie works for is an absolute value, and it is a matter of absolute acceptance. It involves the acceptance of another on his or her own terms rather than on any common terms, and it therefore involves appreciation rather than understanding or knowledge. Maggie reaches this condition first with her father, in their last conversation alone together, when she realizes that he and Charlotte are leaving. As he stands before her, in a posture of "assurance,"

> It had the effect, for her, of a reminder . . . of all he was, of all he had done, of all, above and beyond his being her perfect little father, she might take him as representing, take him as having, quite eminently, in the eyes of two hemispheres, been capable of, and as therefore wishing not—was it?—illegitimately, to call her attention to. . . . There was a long moment, absolutely, during which

her impression rose and rose, even as that of the typical charmed gazer, in the still museum, before the named and dated object, the pride of the catalogue, that time had polished and consecrated. . . . Before she knew it she was lifted aloft by the consciousness that he was simply a great and deep and high little man, and that to love him with tenderness was not to be distinguished, a whit, from loving him with pride. (483-84)

Mr. Verver demands that Maggie take him as more than she knows him to be, as representing more than her "perfect little father." She does this by taking him as a work of art, "polished and consecrated" by time, inexplicable and unknowable and absolute in himself. As she accepts this, she recognizes that her tenderness cannot be distinguished from pride. For if she takes care of and protects the diminutive father who is also a "great citizen," she must be both tender toward and proud of him. And this confusion of tenderness and pride takes the ground out from under her love of him. Maggie is "lifted aloft" by her recognition that her relation to him cannot be grounded or defined, since he cannot be grounded or defined. Unless she would divide the "little father" from the "great citizen," Maggie cannot feel that she must take care of him. Mr. Verver has succeeded here in making it impossible for her to feel that she has forsaken him, for she cannot feel that he is dependent on her. He is absolute and indivisible in himself and greater than she knows him to be.

If Maggie accepts this, however, she must herself be transformed, in response to his transformation, into a reproduction of his success.

The sense that he wasn't a failure, and could never be, purged their predicament of every meanness—made it as if they had really emerged, in their transmitted union, to smile almost without pain. . . . Oh, then, if she wasn't with her little conscious passion, the child of any weakness, what was she but strong enough too? . . . his strength was her strength, her pride was his, and they

were decent and competent together. This was all in the
answer she finally made him.

"I believe in you more than anyone." (484-85)

Maggie is taken in here. She is made to believe more about
herself than she knows herself to be because she can accept
her father as more than she knows him to be. To accept the
strength and capacity in him that exceed her tenderness and
that make her tenderness indistinguishable from pride is also
to be strong and capable herself and to make him, therefore,
also proud. These are more fusions than exchanges, effected
as a process of "transmitted union." They are indistinctions
made possible by the indistinction of his absolute difference
and her absolute acceptance of it.

To reach such fusion, Maggie must remove her relations to
others from any grounds whatever and deny their determination by, or as, an exchange. In the above passage, when
Maggie is asked to accept Mr. Verver as more than the "little
father" she has protected, she is asked to accept the fact that
she owes him nothing. Acceptance thus exceeds and precludes
fair exchanges in this narrative, and so does love. Like taste,
love is idiosyncratic; there is no reason or justification or
definition for it. It is to be accepted, by characters and readers,
as itself inexplicable and unknowable, just as it is seen to
involve the acceptance of others as inexplicable and unknowable. To attempt to look into a relationship is, for James, to
deny it or reduce it, as is clear in Charlotte's and the Prince's
analyses of their relations to the Ververs which always justify
separation from them. When Maggie stops trying to see
through the Prince's behavior and concentrates instead on
"seeing him through" (515), she makes the difference that
constitutes love; for she is, in the first case, distinct from him
and, in the second, with him.

The history that Fanny Assingham provides as a summary
of the first half of the narrative represents what Maggie eventually works to preclude:

"Maggie had in the first place to make up to her father
for her having suffered herself to become . . . so intensely

married. Then she had to make up to her husband for
taking so much of the time they might otherwise have
spent together to make this reparation to Mr. Verver
perfect. And her way to do this, precisely, was by allowing
the Prince the use . . . of Charlotte to cheer his path . . .
in proportion as she herself . . . might be missed from his
side. By so much, at the same time, however, . . . as she
took her young stepmother, for this purpose, away from
Mr. Verver, by just so much did this too strike her as
something again to be made up for. It has saddled her,
you will easily see, with a positively new obligation to
her father, an obligation created and aggravated by her
unfortunate, even if quite heroic little sense of justice."
(293)

Here the form of reparation that Fanny identifies in Maggie's
behavior is the same form of exchange that Mr. Verver resisted
earlier in the novel in his consideration of marriage to Charlotte. It is the form of justice, too, in its equitable treatment
of different loved objects; no one is to have more than another.
As long as she is bound to justify her feelings, however, Maggie's behavior is a matter both of taking away and giving. She
can justify the difference between her love for the Prince and
her love for her father only by equating them, and in order
to do this she initiates an economy of reparation that opens
up as many gaps as it attempts to close. The inconclusiveness
of the " 'vicious circle' " Fanny identifies is generated by the
initial lack Maggie identifies: the difference she wants to make
up. Like the Prince's attempt to put together the different
aspects of Mr. Verver's character, this attempt cannot be concluded. For the differences are always different in this narrative: absolute and inequitable. And the difference between
one love and another is in part the difference between the
people loved, since love involves the acceptance of others as
absolutely different.

The turning point of the novel—the evening when Maggie
waits at home for the Prince—does not, however, mark a
turning away from but a repetition of the economy Fanny

describes above. Maggie's attempt to find out what is going on is, like the Prince's searches for knowledge, constructed as a series of breaks that take the world around her to pieces. She begins with a "small breach with custom" (310), waiting at their house instead of her father's, and then decides to look into the Prince's reaction:

> It had made for him some difference that she couldn't measure . . . , and back and back it kept coming to her that the blankness he showed her before he was able to *see* might, should she choose to insist on it, have a meaning—have, as who should say, a historic value beyond the importance of momentary impressions in general. (310)

Trying, like the Prince, to look into a "blankness" (his surprise), Maggie speculates on possible ways to confront him and then arrives at her "plan" for dealing with it: to make up for having " 'abandoned' " Charlotte and the Prince (316). Her attentions to the Prince are "unmistakably met" (319), as are her attentions to Charlotte, because of which the Prince spends more time with Mr. Verver, having been "prompted . . . to meet and match the difference" Maggie has made (326). With the couples rearranged, however, Maggie realizes that the Prince and Charlotte have met her too exactly for it to be all her own doing and that they must have "a plan that was the exact counterpart of her own" (328).

Maggie's attempt to fill in the gaps, in this case too, creates another gap. But this is filled by the Prince, and Maggie recognizes then that she has not really made a difference: Charlotte and the Prince have prevented it by compensating for her compensations. That is, they are also making a difference, one equal to hers. But if they are repairing her reparations, Maggie is not responsible for what is happening. And this recognition enables her to go back and revise the meaning of the historic moment. Then she recognizes that the Prince's surprise on that evening was not a sign of his lack of her but a sign of his relation to Charlotte: not a difference that Maggie can make up for, but a positive difference, an unknown quantity that she must account for.

Maggie now knows what she is looking for: evidence of their togetherness. Unlike the Prince, who is inconclusive in his searches, Maggie has a chance of reaching a conclusion because she already knows what she expects to find out.

> Ah, when she began to recover, piece by piece, the process became lively; she might have been picking small shining diamonds out of the sweepings of her ordered house. . . . Then it was that the dismissed vision of Amerigo, that evening, . . . gave out its full power. (328)

Like a historian or critic discovering new meaning, Maggie recovers her past, finding what previously seemed insignificant or ambiguous to be facts of great value. Picking through "the refuse of her innocent economy," she picks up the pieces required by the economy of knowledge: pieces that can be fitted to the assumption she starts with. "It fitted immensely together, the whole thing, as soon as she could give them a motive" (330).

But because Maggie cannot come up with a motive herself, she gets no farther. Unlike James with his "splendid waste," Maggie does not believe in what she collects. She is constructing a history of distrust and bad faith, and therefore the waste she picks up remains useless. James's representation of both reparation and knowledge is a representation of forms of futility that lead nowhere but back to what they begin with. Reparation makes up for something. Its practice therefore entails an equivalence of differences as the good makes up for the bad. But because such an exchange is artificial, the repair always shows the difference that remains between what is done and what is done to make up for it. There is always some difference left to make up for, once the practice begins. Knowledge, too, gets no more than it begins with; to know anything is to find grounds or reasons for it. But what is to be known must be known in order to begin.

Maggie is faced at this point in the novel with the futility of both reparation and her search for knowledge.

Knowledge, knowledge, was a fascination as well as a
fear; . . . her apprehension that he would break out to
her with some merely general profession was mixed with
her dire need to forgive him, to reassure him, to respond
to him, on no ground that she didn't fully measure. To
do these things it must be clear to her what they were
for; but to act in that light was, by the same effect, to
learn, horribly, what the other things had been. He might
tell her only what he wanted. . . . (395)

What might repair the break with the Prince—his profession
and her forgiveness—is exactly what must also clarify reasons
for the break. Yet if he "breaks out" with a profession of
something, that *will* only constitute another break, for she
will not know if it is true, and she can forgive him only if she
knows what he has done. A "profession" would be unreliable:
a statement that she could accept only as a belief. And she
wants knowledge, with firm grounds. Maggie cannot, at this
point in the novel, believe in, or accept absolutely, what she
can be given.

There are only breaks, therefore, in this passage; there is
little consistency. Maggie's feelings are inconsistent, for one
thing, and that means that knowledge is two conflicting things
at once. Knowledge is a mixture of fascination and fear, and
Maggie's fear that the Prince will speak is mixed with her
need to forgive him. But her need to forgive him is qualified
by her need to know the grounds for forgiveness; it is this
that accounts for her apprehension about his "general profession." This recognition might be conclusive if *it* were allowed
to stand unqualified, but at this point the mixed feelings about
knowledge reappear: she needs to know what he has done,
but it would be horrible to find out. Thus Maggie is committed
neither to knowledge nor to reparation. Each is broken apart.
And the fact that he might lie just increases, again, the inconclusiveness of the whole consideration. But it is not only
the subject matter that is coming apart and breaking down
here. The passage is in pieces that are not linked together.
Each sentence takes apart the grounds of the previous sen-

tence, and each sentence stands separate, without conjunctions or transitions to tie it to the last sentence. Moreover, what breaks apart the conclusiveness of the first sentence is a repetition of the first part of that sentence: the mixed feelings about knowledge. And what breaks apart the assumptions of the second sentence—that she must deal with knowledge—is a repetition of the earlier apprehension that the Prince will not give her knowledge. The passage keeps covering the same ground but never puts the pieces together.

Although Maggie can recover facts to fit a preconception in the passage quoted earlier, she recovers nothing but the uncertainty she starts with in this passage. Thus James is not simply insisting on the futility of knowledge and reparation here. If both knowledge and reparation return to what they begin with, so does uncertainty. The only way to get anywhere in this novel is to have faith. Faith, too, is both the beginning and the end of the meaning of what is believed in. But meanings that rest on faith cannot be undermined or taken apart unless faith itself ceases to exist. Faith, that is, provides "grounds" for meaning that preclude the determination of meaning as lack or loss.

Maggie's relation to knowledge here is strikingly like Daniel Deronda's mixed feelings of desire and dread about his birth. What is at issue in both cases is not simply the construction of knowledge as a mental process; what is at issue is recognition of a fact. Like Deronda, Maggie Verver cannot commit herself to the loss of meaning that the unknown fact might represent. To know that fact would be to have grounds for meaning that would preclude binding relations to others: Deronda would be cut off from the world of gentlemen, as Maggie would be cut off from the Prince. For both Eliot and James, such knowledge is not to be repressed; both insist that reality can be accepted. But such knowledge is not allowed to determine separations and reparations. It is faith in others that enables both Deronda and Maggie to accept the facts without losing meaning or losing others because of them.

It seems crucial to both novelists' concepts of exchange that reparation is the *cause* of such knowledge but is precluded as its effect. Knowledge comes to Maggie by accident; it can come only by accident, since she cannot come up with a motive herself and cannot trust the Prince to tell her the truth. But the accident is not exactly an accident. The purchase of the bowl also constitutes a repetition. For Maggie has been taken again; she has bought damaged goods. Thus she learns the truth about the marriage as she learns about another bad bargain she has made in good faith. But she also learns the truth in the form of a reparation. The way she knows she has been cheated by the Prince is by the efforts of another man who has cheated her to make up for what he has done. Thus it is reparation, again, that uncovers another break, as it does in *Daniel Deronda*. For Deronda's mother also discovers herself to her son in order to make reparation: to the memory of her father, whom she abandoned and rejected as she abandoned and rejected Judaism. *Daniel Deronda* redeems the losses of reparation by representing Judaism not as a break but as a binding relation to others. The vicious circle of reparation in *The Golden Bowl* is redeemed by Maggie's acceptance of the Prince's infidelity as a loss that nothing can make up for. The knowledge of a fact that for others represents separation and requires reparation is accepted on other terms by both heroic characters.

The threat of knowledge to separate belief and reality is the threat posed by Fanny Assingham. If reparation uncovers the break in *The Golden Bowl*, it is Fanny's knowledge that breaks to pieces all that Maggie believes in. Fanny, the most "knowing" character in the novel, smashes the bowl, hoping to destroy its symbolic value. " 'Whatever you meant by it— and I don't want to know *now*—has ceased to exist' " (421). Fanny has seen that "Maggie herself saw the truth" (414). But Fanny denies the truth. She asks Maggie to believe, whatever the truth of the matter, in the good faith of all concerned and to be determined now not by the truth but by her own faith in her father:

"Rest on it."
"On his ignorance?"

Fanny met it again. "On whatever he may offer you.
Take that."
"Take it—?"
Mrs. Assingham held up her head. "And be grateful."
(419)

This is what Maggie will do. Her strength will depend on how
much she can take, no questions asked. Yet this means that
she must take her real losses as well as accept her father's gift
of confidence and faith. She will not reject reality.

Yet not only is the reality hard to take. What Mr. Verver
has to offer Maggie is difficult to accept because what he offers
looks to her like an imitation rather than the real thing. When
she begins to treat him "hypocritically" in their walk together
in the park, Maggie sees that he too is "pretending" with her:
"he had begun to *imitate*—oh, as never yet!—the ancient tone
of gold" (358). Maggie has gone on this walk determined to
deceive her father,

> setting herself the difficult task of making their relation
> . . . not fall below the standard of that other hour, in the
> treasured past, which hung there behind them like a
> framed picture in a museum, a high watermark for the
> history of their old fortune; the summer evening, in the
> park at Fawns, when . . . they had let their happy con-
> fidence lull them with its most golden tone. (357)

It is her father's imitation of the golden tone of confidence
that Maggie decides to "take," for it is, as Fanny suggests,
only confidence that will carry her through, only high water
on which she can float.

But confidence, during this second walk in the park, is
faked; it is a reproduction of the museum piece. If Maggie
accepts her father's imitation of "the ancient tone of gold,"
this is no different from accepting the bowl itself—which is
also an imitation of ancient gold—and all it represents. It is
no different from accepting the Prince, the other museum piece
that has turned out to be a fake. Maggie picks up the pieces
of the bowl that Fanny has broken because if she is to recon-

stitute her faith she must reconstitute reality, too. The truth, for Maggie, is not something that must cease to exist in order for faith to exist. For Maggie, what is believed *is* reality; there can be no distinguishable difference. Fanny, by breaking the cracked bowl to pieces, wants to insist that Maggie's " 'whole idea' " (420) can be smashed to pieces and gotten rid of. But she also leaves Maggie with the evidence that the whole idea is in fact the reality of the situation. For Maggie's idea, of course, is precisely that her marriage and her father's marriage have come apart. Thus Fanny's act, an act of knowledge, realizes the division of the characters and also confirms the separation of reality and belief. Reality has come apart in Fanny's hands, and Maggie's faith, therefore, according to Fanny, can hold only if reality ceases to exist for her. Fanny makes the bowl into refuse and refuses to believe in it; but this splendid waste is not something that Maggie can throw away. For her faith is not separable from the reality of the golden bowl. The golden bowl is the symbol both of the reality and of Maggie's faith. Her faith, too, has been cracked; it, too, has been broken to pieces by Fanny's attempt to deny the truth; and it has, as Fanny means the truth to do, ceased to exist.

It is the bowl, therefore, that Maggie insists must be put together again in order to have happiness: " 'the golden bowl—as it *was* to have been' " (445). And this is so despite the fact that the golden bowl, even " 'as it *was* to have been,' " is an imitation, not real gold. Like the imitation of old gold that her father offers her, the bowl Maggie works to "reconstitute" is not really what it seems to be. But it is really, thereby, the same as reality and the same as faith. For there are only two ways to tell the difference between the golden bowl and real gold. Either one has to ask, as Charlotte asks the shopkeeper. Or one has to " '*want* to smash it' " (106), as Fanny does. Faith, too, can be seen to be invalid only if it is doubted in the first place or if someone wishes to break it. And like the golden bowl, faith has no grounds for its appearance. To want to discover its grounds is already to have begun to break the faith. Maggie, then, can recognize her father's behavior as an imitation of confidence only because she has lost her own. But she will accept his faith, after she knows the truth about the Prince, without asking any more questions about it: not as an imitation but as the real thing. For the essential similarity of the bowl and of faith is that, as long as one believes in them, one cannot tell whether they are imitations or real.

Maggie's faith reappears out of nowhere, without grounds and precisely as the recognition that her action must be freed from her knowledge. In place of knowledge as grounds for action, the belief that the Prince needs her will commit her action to freedom: "What would condemn it, so to speak, to the responsibility of freedom . . . was the possibility, richer with every lapsing moment, that her husband would have, on the whole question, a new need of her, a need which was in fact being born between them in these very seconds" (426). Maggie makes up this need as a possibility, which, as long as she believes in it, will demand that she be committed to him again, no matter what she knows. It is from here on to the end of the narrative that Maggie fuses together the pieces of her reality by making up representations that put pieces together. Thus she sees herself as with the Prince, having "got into his labyrinth with him" (427). And she represents his behavior, too, even when he says nothing in reply to her accusations, by signs that he is with her, making up words on his part to fill in the gap: "she *had* to represent to herself that she had spiritually heard them, had to listen to them still again, to explain her particular patience in face of his particular failure" (448). Maggie puts herself into the breaks between herself and others, providing what is needed to fuse them together, "being herself left, for any occasion, in the breach. She was essentially there to bear the burden, in the last resort, of surrounding omissions and evasions . . ." (503). Thus, Maggie not only "reconstitutes" reality but constitutes, herself, the difference between lack and fullness; she fills in the differences.

This does not mean, however, that Maggie's representations suit others or that she gives according to the needs others feel.

Maggie imagines that both the Prince and Charlotte are caged or tied up by their ignorance about what Mr. Verver or Maggie knows. But Maggie does not free them from their ignorance, because knowledge, for her, constitutes neither freedom nor reality. Nor is freedom an exchange value for Maggie, as it is for Charlotte and the Prince; it is not something she can give. Maggie understands freedom as commitment. And she does give both the Prince and Charlotte the chance to free themselves by giving them the chance to commit themselves. Her challenge to the Prince to " 'Find out for yourself!' " (438) is a challenge to him to commit himself. It is for this reason that his suffering "must be relieved by his act alone" (489). Charlotte, too, is given no help by Maggie until she decides to act for herself.

Commitment is what Maggie works for, and commitment requires active acceptance of others without the common grounds required by economical exchange. The process of fusion is a process that works only if such exchanges do not occur with their reductions of differences to common terms. The common terms which make differences comparable, moreover, imply that what is given and what is taken are values determined by the exchange. Thus Charlotte and the Prince can insist that exchange takes responsibility out of their hands. If, on the other hand, one practices exchange "responsibly," as Maggie does, it may work to effect justice and reparation. But these exchanges are also reductive of differences and therefore inconclusive in their attempts to make up for any difference. The assumption that differences are comparable is necessary to knowledge: only common terms of some sort make possible "a discerned relation between a given appearance and a taken meaning" (266). Knowledge—as a mode of thought rather than as the acceptance of facts—works economically in such a relation, to account for the difference between appearance and reality, what is given and what is taken. But such an account of difference is always inconclusive too, as something is always left out. All of these exchanges preclude total acceptance or the fusion of differences, because they acknowledge unacceptable values as well as exchange values, leaving things out as well as putting things together.

Knowledge is an inadequate relation for James and for the Ververs because it cannot "grasp" the relation of faith. Maggie knows about the Prince's adultery, but she does not settle for this knowledge as the "discerned relation" between what the Prince appears to be and what she takes him to be. For the discerned relation would constitute an enormous gap: the difference between his apparent worthlessness and the fact that he nevertheless means the world to her. Knowing the Prince to be false, Maggie does not believe him to be worthless. Her love commits her to him; and this is not a discernible relation. It exceeds understanding and knowledge. If we choose to make relations discernible, James insists, we are going to lose a lot; for to discern a relation between things is to discern lacks.

The Prince wants to discern relations. He wants to figure out a relation between Mr. Verver's apparent unruffled confidence and what that appearance means: is Mr. Verver "faking it" or does he not know? Now whether Mr. Verver knows or not is irrelevant to his relation to the Prince, as Maggie's experience makes clear: for knowledge would not account for his relations to others, just as knowledge does not account for Maggie's faith and love. But the Prince, by discerning the relation as a relation of knowledge, would be able to tell exactly where he stands in relation to Mr. Verver. If he knew that Mr. Verver knew about the affair, he would know that Mr. Verver knows him to be a fake. Then he would have an exact relation: one of clear debt, which is what he has always wanted. Such a relation would be a reductive misrepresentation of the relation, but the Prince, unlike the Ververs, would probably "settle" for it. It would have the advantages of being clear and distinct; but it would lose the advantages of both love and faith.

Fusion can be effected only by the commitment of the self to others and by the separation of what is given from what is taken in order to avoid the loss of meaning that fair exchange entails. This means, in effect, that relations per se disappear: the relation between differences is not a difference that one can tell or discern, as differences are bound together indiscernibly. If differences are absolute, and different people are absolutely different, their acceptance cannot occur on any common terms. What is given can be accepted, but it cannot be accepted *for* anything else. Reparation, therefore, becomes impossible, and debt becomes impossible. Maggie loses her father; but this loss in incomparable, as is Charlotte's loss of the Prince. The losses are therefore to be accepted as final.

> The note was struck indeed; the note of that strange accepted finality of relation, as from couple to couple, which almost escaped an awkwardness only by not attempting a gloss. Yes, this was the wonder, that the occasion defied insistence precisely because of the vast quantities with which it dealt—so that separation was on a scale beyond any compass of parting. (542)

The fact that the note of acceptance attempts no gloss here does not constitute an escape from reality or awkwardness. But the awkwardness would be increased if a gloss were attempted. For no gloss would encompass the scale of the loss; it cannot be adequately represented, explained, or glossed over. The loss must simply be accepted, without even the compensation that a relation of interpretation would provide. For compensation entails the reduction of what we have to the terms of what we don't have: a lack determines meaning as tied to loss. James will not use language like this. The acceptance of loss as loss is necessary to both his and Maggie's freedom. Only when she realizes that nothing will make up for the loss of anything else can she be free to let go of what is lost and hold on absolutely to what she has, for its own sake. To insist that no gain makes up for any loss is to insist again on the incomparability and irreducibility of differences. It is James's insistence that if losses are, as Mr. Verver knows from the beginning, inevitable, they nevertheless do not require the loss or reduction of anything else in return. If one can simply *take* losses, then one is free also to take gains.

The separation of loss and gain, like the separation of a given appearance and a taken meaning, implies that more can be given and more taken than in conventional exchanges. It also implies that by giving, one can take others in and that by taking, one can be taken in. Maggie is taken in by her acceptance of the Prince in marriage, as she is taken in by the golden bowl; in this sense, she is fooled by the difference between her idea of something and its reality. But she is taken in again by the Prince at the end of the narrative because of her active and voluntary acceptance of his difference from her:

> She was seeing him through—he had engaged to come out at the right end if she *would* see him: this understanding . . . had fairly received, with the procession of the weeks, the consecration of time; but it scarce needed to be insisted on that she was seeing him on *his* terms, not hers, or that, in other words, she must allow his unexplained and uncharted, his own practicably workable way. If that way . . . happened handsomely to show him as more bored than boring (with advantages of his own freely to surrender, but none to be persuadedly indebted to others for), what did such a false face of the matter represent but the fact itself that she was pledged? If she had questioned or challenged or interfered . . . she wouldn't have been pledged. . . . (515-16)

As in the earlier scene with her father, Maggie is *with* the Prince here because she accepts him as more than she knows him to be and accepts his terms of representation. The Prince, with his clear sense of indebted relations, may still happen to be false, but Maggie allows him a false face as she allows him an unexplained way of being. His false face is precisely the sign of her commitment because it represents the difference she accepts between the appearance he offers and what he means to her. Moreover, she can see him through only if she sees him on his terms; for only if she accepts what he gives her will he see that she believes in him. Maggie is taken in here by her own volition. Her commitment requires that she be taken in.

Maggie's eventual belief in the Prince is an active belief,

therefore, and it is active both because she intends to accept him on his own terms and because such acceptance precludes any settlement. For absolute acceptance can occur only with mixed feelings. It is precisely when Maggie accepts her father as more than she knows him to be that she cannot distinguish her tenderness from her pride. Nor can she at the end of the novel settle or define her feelings for the Prince: she feels both "pity and dread" in the final scene. But such reactions are also fused together; she feels both at once. Thus, to accept others' indeterminacy is to feel herself indeterminate. And this also unites her to them, as what she feels becomes inseparable from what they are.

The Golden Bowl is a trial. What is being tried is faith. The trial, therefore, is never a matter of justice, for faith cannot be reduced to "just" terms. Moreover, justification would involve "looking into it" and would thereby break faith. As James says of the final scene, in which loss is accepted but not glossed, "To do such an hour justice would have been in some degree to question its grounds" (542). Faith is tried, rather, in the sense that its strength is tested to see what it will bear, as the crystal bowl, reconstituted, would be tried, under pressure, to see whether it would hold. The narrative tries its readers, too. Both trying and demanding, it presses us to accept more than a "just" representation and something quite different from a "just" conclusion.

To be tried in this sense is to be proven, not in the sense of logical proof, on external grounds, but in the sense of being oneself proof against doubt. The trial does not, therefore, result in strength; but the trial proves strength. Faith, too, is not gotten as the end or goal of experience; it comes with and is proven by experience. This is why the narrative is not a history. The Prince has a history: "as fixed in his place as some statue of one of his forefathers" (516). What he is is determined by his past. But for the Ververs and for James, the passage of time is a process of consecration: a process that renders the meaning of things both indeterminate and sacred as meaning comes to be taken on faith alone. Justice would demand a history. But the trial of *The Golden Bowl* is precisely whether we and the characters can bear it if they are *not* brought to justice.

The Prince wants to be "tried and tested" at the beginning of the narrative. "Invested with attributes" by the Ververs, he wants those attributes put to "the practical proof," for only then will he be changed (43). Such a trial would be a trial by others whose actions would decide his value. The Prince's insistence to Maggie that she has "found out nothing" about his " 'unknown, unimportant—unimportant save to *you*— personal quantity' " similarly puts the charge on her to discover what he is (33). The Prince's own sense of his "personal quantity" is not exactly missing in the novel; but that quantity can appear only if others demand it. He has a definite idea of his capacity for "personal loyalty," for example; but what is missing is any "call" for it.

> That was what it all came back to again with these people among whom he was married—that one found one used one's imagination mainly for wondering how they contrived so little to appeal to it. He felt at moments as if there were never anything to do for them that was worthy—to call worthy—of the personal relation. . . . He might vulgarly have put it that one had never to plot or to lie for them. . . . (238)

The difficulty for the Prince is that in order to escape the futility of his past he has to do something. Yet all that he knows how to do is what he has done in the past. The fact that the Ververs do not require him to do anything at all leaves him nothing to do. Yet if they were to put him to the proof, he would prove to be only what he has been in the past.

The Prince's trial with the Ververs is just that he is not tried; they neither prove nor decide his worth. What is most trying for him is the fact that, ignorant as they are, they nevertheless assume that they know him (252). He thus feels "left out" on two counts: they neither know anything about him, nor do they miss knowing anything about him. Nor, in their acceptance of him, do they make any demands that might change what he is or bring out his "personal quantity."

The Prince gets temporary relief from this trial in his affair with Charlotte. She comes after him, makes her demands, and demands, moreover, that he do only what he has done before. Not only does the Prince resume the affair, but he is able to experience again his capacity for personal loyalty: he now has something to plot and lie for, both in his relations with Charlotte and in his relations with the Ververs. But his trial resumes when Maggie finds out and refuses to try him *for* what he has done; she accepts that and thereby precludes any reparation on his part. But she tries him *with* the burden of commitment. Not her commitment: for she withholds that, suspending any declaration of her own and thereby giving him nothing, on a second count, to which he can respond or by which he can know where he stands with her. The burden is on him, and the outcome of his trial—whether he will be committed or not—is for him to decide.

Maggie tries him by trumping up a false charge—" 'Find out for yourself!' " And the Prince tries. The charge is not an accusation but a challenge; he is charged with a burden. And it is phony not because it is a crime he did not commit but because it does not constitute a real burden. Maggie herself does not know what he wants to know, and she counts on him not being able to find it out either. As long as he bears the charge, then, he will be "given over, without a break, to the grey medium in which he helplessly groped" (489). Yet in this sort of trial it is up to the victim to drop the charges; and the Prince does not choose to do so. He chooses to stay in his prison:

> He struck her as caged. . . . There was a difference none the less, between his captivity and Charlotte's—the difference, as it might be, of his lurking there by his own act and his own choice; the admission of which had indeed virtually been in his starting, on her entrance, as if

even this were in its degree an interference. That was what betrayed for her, practically, his fear of her fifty ideas, and what had begun, after a minute, to make her wish to repudiate or explain. . . . She had, for these instants, the sense that he exaggerated, that the imputation of purpose had fairly risen too high in him. She had begun, a year ago, by asking herself how she could make him think more of her; but what was it, after all, he was thinking now? (526-27)

The Prince has committed himself. But he has commited himself to Maggie as someone she does not know. He attributes "fifty ideas" to her, whereas she has, as she feels, "nothing but her old idea, the old one he knew" (527). It is he who has invested *her*, at this point, with attributes whose value *she* doesn't know.

But if he commits himself to the false charge, it is up to Maggie to be true to the false charge. This is her gift to him: another imitation, but a fake that he takes for real and that he is taken in by. Whereas the Prince at the beginning of the novel wanted his attributes put to the proof of explanation and clarification, Maggie must allow him to believe what he wants to believe about her, recognizing that her attributes "hold" because they are held by his belief. She cannot repudiate the phoniness or explain the truth unless she would break faith.

Maggie has met the Prince "on *his* terms," even as she has met him on her own terms, the terms that render fake and real indistinguishable. She has met his terms not only because she has waited for him to commit himself but because she has acknowledged his plotting and lying and has, moveover, plotted and lied herself. " 'It's you, *cara*, who are deep,' " the Prince tells her in the scene with the broken bowl (436). And Maggie does discover her depths, to herself and to him, while discovering his depths. It is on these "depths" that the Prince now "floats," for they are what sustain his interest in her. The Prince, then, loves Maggie on terms completely different from her terms. For he is bound to her by the sense that he will never stop trying but will never see to the bottom of her. To commit himself to Maggie is not to accept her as she is, no questions asked. It is, as his continuous questions in Chapter 41 insist, to be bound to someone because she continues to challenge his desire to know. What Maggie wants, she discovers at the end of the novel, is "his presence alone" (546-47). But for the Prince, Maggie's presence is not enough; in the above passage, her presence even threatens his commitment. He is committed to the "fifty ideas" that he can fear and wonder about; he is committed, as in fact he has always been, to trying for something he cannot get.

Because Maggie accepts the Prince, he is *not* changed. She recognizes "her having had . . . to 'do all,' to go the whole way over, to move, indefatigably, while he stood as fixed in his place as some statue of one of his forefathers" (516). But though he is what he has always been, her love makes an extraordinary difference. For the Prince is no longer, at the end of the novel, a being divided from himself. At the beginning of the narrative, he is divided between two conceptions of himself: he is what his past has made him, but he wants to be changed, too, in order to escape from the futility of that past. This itself, however, is a futile desire, for the only way he sees to change is if the Ververs change him. He cannot commit himself to change. What Maggie offers the Prince, with her demanding gift, is a chance *not* to change, but to find, in loving her, commitment to what he is. He is allowed to love her not as someone who will deny his past but as someone right out of that past: a fearful kind of Borgia figure. Even more extraordinarily, she allows him, as long as she does not explain herself to him, to be committed to rather than divided from his own futility. He is bound to her by his very need always to try for more than he has: the need which has previously separated him from himself. He is committed to both Maggie and himself through her allowance. She allows him to take her as whatever he needs her to be in order to be both inseparable from her and indivisible from himself.

Charlotte is also tried by Maggie, though her trial is to be charged with nothing at all. Rather than giving her a false

charge, Maggie gives Charlotte a false exemption, in the scene
on the terrace at Fawns:

"I accuse you—I accuse you of nothing." (468)

"You must take it from me that your anxiety rests quite
on a misconception. . . . You must take it from me that
I've never thought of you but as beautiful, wonderful and
good." (469)

As the construction of these exemptions suggests, what Maggie offers is ambiguous: a gift that is a demand; a release that
is a double bind. Charlotte is accustomed to being in a secure
position. Throughout the first half of the novel, she is always
justified in her actions: not because the narrative does her
justice but because she is able to justify her behavior as part
of a fair exchange. Although Maggie's lies let her off, therefore, by exempting her from any obligation whatever, Charlotte is now, for the first time in her own eyes, in a false
position. For the exemption itself is groundless: she must take
here what she cannot justify taking. And, furthermore, to be
exempted is to be offered no grounds whatever on which she
can justify herself: she is given nothing to answer for and has
no debt to pay. Charlotte is left to carry on her "false repose":

The falsity of it had laid traps compared to which the
imputation of treachery even accepted might have seemed
a path of roses. The acceptance, strangely, would have
left her nothing to do—she could have remained, had she
liked, all insolently passive: whereas the failure to proceed
against her, as it might have been called, left her everything, and all the more that it was wrapped so in confidence. (502)

The real trap for Charlotte is that, with nothing to accept or
answer for, she herself must provide the grounds for her position. It is all left to her.

Charlotte must commit herself: either to her "real" banish-
ment or to the false exemption Maggie has offered her. "To
be doomed was, in her situation, to have extravagantly in-

curred a doom" (511), for, as long as she is charged with
nothing, to act doomed is to give the only signal that she
deserves to be doomed. So Charlotte comes up with "something else that would give colour to her having burst her
bonds" (511) in her second scene with Maggie. " 'What I ask
for,' " Charlotte tells Maggie, " 'is the definite break.' "

> . . . "You want to take my father *from* me?"
> . . . "I want really to possess him," said Mrs. Verver.
> "I happen also to feel that he's worth it."
> Maggie rose as if to receive her. "Oh—worth it!" she
> wonderfully threw off.
> The tone, she instantly saw, again had its effect: Char-
> lotte flamed aloft—might truly have been believing in her
> passionate parade. (513-14)

What Maggie allows Charlotte to do here is to take. And this
occurs on Charlotte's terms—the terms of a fair exchange:
Charlotte takes Mr. Verver in return for Maggie taking the
Prince. Charlotte lives up to the false exemption, because she
uses it to create a fiction in which she can believe: the fiction
of getting her own back, or the fiction of justice. This is the
only act of commitment Charlotte has made since she got the
Prince alone for a few hours before his marriage at the beginning of the novel. In one sense, it does not make much
difference, if Mr. Verver is taking her back to America anyway. But it makes all the difference, too, for it makes the
difference of commitment which Maggie wants to create: "the
great thing was to allow her, was fairly to produce in her, the
sense of highly choosing" (509).

Charlotte, then, remains, like the Prince, unchanged. She
remains with her principal need for justification and, rather
than changing, returns to the security that characterizes her
at the beginning of the narrative, when she states to the Prince,
" 'This is what I wanted. This is what I've got' " (93). In these
two instances only, Charlotte takes what she can get and
justifies it on the grounds of her own desire. These are the
only terms on which she can commit herself, and they are the
terms on which Maggie accepts her.

The false charge and the false exemption that Maggie offers the Prince and Charlotte are not, therefore, exactly fakes. They are, on the one hand, feints of Maggie's: misrepresentations that mislead. But the Prince and Charlotte are taken in by them, enabled to believe in themselves because Maggie has allowed them to take the fakes as real. But for Maggie, this means that the misrepresentations *are* real or are indistinguishable from real. For if the others believe in them, that realizes them and constitutes their reality. To deny their reality would be to deny to the Prince and Charlotte the only "grounds" for existence that Maggie recognizes: the grounds of confidence. It would take them apart.

Maggie's own trial consists of accepting such differences: the differences between what she is and what others whom she loves are. Her faith must bear these differences without allowing them to make any difference to it. Divisions and breaks occur; but breaks do not count. They are accepted as such, and that is that. For to make something of them would be to allow them to determine the meaning of other things. Maggie precludes such exchanges. She takes her losses. She is thereby let off from a just trial too, as Mr. Verver hopes will happen early in the narrative.

"I let him go," said Maggie.
"You let him, but you don't make him."
"I take it from him," she answered.
"But what else can you do?"
"I take it from him . . . I get off by giving him up." (524)

This is her father's gift to her: the gift of freedom from guilt and reparation. And this is the redemption the Ververs offer.

For Henry James as for George Eliot, redemption has nothing to do with reparation: it constitutes the absolute denial of reparation as it constitutes the absolute acceptance of differences that are themselves absolute and incomparable. For the individual self, this is the only way James sees to be free from either the negation of what one has or the negation of what one is. Maggie can be free to appreciate what she has only if she can accept the loss of her father as something that nothing else will make up for. Similarly, Charlotte and the Prince can be free to appreciate what they are only if they are accepted on their own terms, with nothing missed and nothing missing. Charlotte and the Prince are redeemed in this narrative insofar as they are enabled to believe in what they are. This can occur because Maggie does not ask them to be what they are not or to make up for what they may be seen to lack.

The redemption occurs as redemption must occur in order to bring freedom: on no grounds whatever. It occurs because Maggie loves them and believes in herself. Both indeterminate and absolute, like self-confidence, love is the beginning and the end of the experience of the novel. The fact that neither its beginning nor its end is represented means that we are not really given a beginning or an end for the experience of the novel. Those "points" are missing, and in part this is because there is no point to love. There is no saying why, or to what end, unless we would break it to pieces or finish it off. Love makes the difference that cannot be told. It is the "large, bland, blank assumption of merits" (43) that the Prince cannot figure out and that James refuses to account for. Maggie simply loves the Prince. For no reason ever given, the feeling remains, unchanging and inexplicable, "the hard little passion which nothing he had done could smother" (489). There is nothing to do about love. Like the presumption of Pamela's love, the assumption of Maggie's love takes as it gives. It is as if part of no exchange at all, an excess of gift and acceptance. To know that about love is to know that love can redeem experience from the reductions and losses of conventional exchange.

This does not mean that there is nothing more to be done, in life or in fiction. But it means a radical revision of our sense of action and accomplishment. Nothing much happens in *The Golden Bowl* if we see it in terms of plot, as the brevity of any critic's plot summary suggests. Maggie and Mr. Verver do not seem to do much; they seem to wait for more things to happen than they do themselves. Nor do the Ververs, in their wealth and ease, feel the need to do many things that others do. Their contentment and inactivity are part of what the Prince finds so trying. Moreover, the redemption that structures the narrative suggests that what happens is a repetition of what has happened before. The marriages that are saved at the end of the novel occur at its beginning. And one sign that the Prince and Charlotte are redeemed is the fact that they are allowed to be what they already have been.

Mr. Verver recognizes the problem but knows what he is doing:

> " 'Let us then be up and doing'—what is it Longfellow says? That seems to ring out. . . . But the beauty of it is, at the same time, that we *are* doing. . . . We're working it, our life, our chance. . . . We *have* worked it, and what more can you do than that?" (362)

To work a life is not a clear proposition: it gives us no plot at all, by leaving out what is worked for and what is worked with. What the Ververs do is to take what life offers and make it work. This means refusing to impose on life a goal, a means, or a purpose; for those would reduce the possibilities of what could be taken. To work life, moreover, means not doing anything that will make a new difference; it means instead doing something that will fuse together the old differences, going back and getting rid of any breaks that interfere with its working. The Ververs go over material that has been gone over before because they move back into primitive territory— emotional territory—in order to fuse together the divisions within and between characters: divisions caused by loss, separation, guilt, reparation. Rather than progress toward something they feel the lack of, they regress toward a fullness that would reconstitute the emotional being as a whole. This effectively would get rid of the initial impetus of desire if desire were motivated by lack. But the Ververs' desire to reconstitute those whom they love into whole and undivided beings is generated by a fullness: the fullness of their self-confidence and the fullness of their acceptance of others.

What James himself wants to do is suggested in the quotation at the beginning of this chapter from the Preface to *The Awkward Age*: "the thing 'done,' artistically, is a fusion, or it has not *been* done." But if the Ververs have to go over things in order to fuse differences together, James, too, proceeds by working the same material over. The repetitions in the novel are always repetitions with a difference. But the repetitions insist on something crucial in James's vision. Things are what they are, for one thing, and to "work" them is to appreciate what they are rather than imagine what they might be otherwise. This is not to preclude change; for as James says in the Preface to *The Golden Bowl*, "the whole conduct of life consists of things done, which do other things in their turn."[27] But the most difficult and fully rewarding work is to make the most of things: the work of appreciation. And this work is always a matter of both vision and revision. For things may nòt work the first time; and if they do not work for all they are worth, you have to rework them. In James's art as in the Ververs' life as art, value does not lie in originality but in a sublime usefulness. The "original" may be only a first draft. If the earlier version—of a work of art, of a self—is one you cannot believe in, it must be "worked" until you can believe in it.

Crucial scenes in the novel are replayed and revised until they are "done." The scenes between Maggie and her father are as much repetitions as developments. The first is remembered as a picture in a museum that sets a "standard" for the second (357); in the second, Maggie identifies Mr. Verver as imitating the "golden tone" of the first (357); in the third, Maggie identifies him again with a picture in a museum, "polished and consecrated" by time (484), and herself as his imitation, "the child of his blood" (485). Mr. Verver never "breaks" in these scenes: he always seems confident. But he must replay and represent his confidence over and over in order for Maggie to accept what has seemed an imitation as

[27] James, *The Art of the Novel*, p. 347.

the real thing. At the same time, she accepts herself as indistinguishable from him, as capable and confident a reproduction as he is himself.

Maggie's second scene with Charlotte, in the garden at Fawns, is also a replay of her first, on the terrace:

> Charlotte was seeing her come, through patches of lingering noon, quite as she had watched Charlotte menace her through the starless dark. . . . The point, however, was that they had changed places. . . . (499)

But if they have really changed places, so that Maggie is now the victor and Charlotte the victim, Maggie returns them to their "original" places in the original scene, although that scene was itself a fake, the scene of the false exemption. Maggie, like her father before her, believes in what she did the first time: lying and letting Charlotte have her way. She reproduces that scene here, forcing Charlotte to recognize that, if at first it looks different, this scene will reconstitute the previous scene: Maggie will repeat her "abjection" and Charlotte will seem to triumph (511). In the second version, however, if Charlotte's triumph rests on a misconception, it is not clear what the false grounds are. Accepting Maggie's humility again, Charlotte claims the confidence in herself that Maggie's own confident faking allows. The acknowledgment of what Charlotte has done is left out; but what is spoken are not clearly lies.

Imitation or reproduction becomes indistinguishable from originals in these repetitions. Mr. Verver and Maggie replay earlier scenes in order to consecrate their fictions. These are not exactly ritualistic repetitions that secure belief by denying unstable reality. They are more ritual than history; and what is left out is what would preclude belief. But what is left out, therefore, is what belief cannot realize; it is the reality of loss. What these scenes ignore are losses, lacks, lapses of belief itself, all of which must be accepted simply as losses—as nothing—and made nothing more of. To work loss is to get loss. Loss is accepted in the novel, but it is not made to work, to generate reparation and regret. The Ververs' make-believe thus accomplishes the fusion of meaning that James says in the Preface is possible in fiction, whose " 'connexions' are employable for finer purposes than mere gaping contrition."[28] The fusion of the fake and the real makes possible the generation of confidence rather than contrition. For the recognition that what has seemed fake can be believed in also enables characters to have confidence in other things they have not been able to believe in—themselves. First Maggie, then Charlotte, realizes her own confidence with the realization of another's earlier imitation of confidence in her.

This realization is a realization of both dependence and difference. Charlotte is absolutely different from Maggie; so is the Prince; so is her father, though she believes he is young, like her. The differences, moreover, are absolute. They are absolute because they are idiosyncratic and unique, and they are absolute in that they do not make a difference to Maggie's capacity to accept others. Her relation to others is a relation of absolute acceptance, and it is a relation that allows and even generates difference. But it is a relation that opens up no gaps. The differences are positive rather than negative. This means that the differences generated are not differences between characters; nor are they anomalous differences. They are differences that are accepted and are therefore differences in agreement with another character. Thus Maggie becomes strong when she accepts and believes in her father's strength. Charlotte becomes confident when she accepts Maggie's abjection. And the Prince becomes committed in relation to Maggie's mysteriousness. In the latter two relations, we assume that Maggie is faking. But, just as Mr. Verver plans at the beginning of the novel to make it look as though Maggie has not abandoned him, Maggie acts in accordance with what the Prince and Charlotte need in order to believe in themselves.

This means, on the one hand, that characters become different in relation to others. But it is a specific difference that

[28] Ibid., p. 348.

is made in these relations: the change from insecurity to confidence. It is the transmission of belief that occurs, a transmission made possible by the acceptance of differences and by the imitation of those differences. The Prince and Charlotte must choose, as Maggie must choose, to lose and to gain. But the choice is to give up something to which they are not committed and to take others to whom they can commit themselves. This is the extraordinary difference made by Maggie's acceptance. It is the difference of "active belief" that will realize, from the "splendid waste" of life, the extraordinary gains of fiction. For the Prince and Charlotte are both identified as potentially wasted or futile characters in the novel. Yet they come to take satisfaction in themselves. And Maggie and her father can take satisfaction in them too, when they accept them as " 'incomparable' " (543) and uncompromising in their differences from the Ververs.

Thus acceptance replaces need in *The Golden Bowl* as the generative element of relations among different characters. Or we can say that the need to be accepted, as one is, is the sole need that James's novel recognizes in order to gain happiness. In order to feel confidence, one must make believe, and one must make believe that the self is not lacking. That belief can enable one to accept others rather than either demand that they meet needs in oneself or regret that they cannot meet needs in oneself. And thus confidence can generate confidence. The fact that Maggie's "fusion" with the Prince and with Charlotte is fake is irrelevant if the fusion generates belief. Some fusion with another, some relation with another that takes the other in, is clearly necessary to these characters in order to believe in themselves.

These beliefs "originate" in belief. There are no grounds for confidence, and there is no origin for belief but belief. The presence in the narrative of the earlier versions of scenes that "work" insists, moreover, that imitation or secondariness is irrelevant to value. If a reproduction generates belief, it constitutes the only sort of origin James values. For life works in the novel as art works for James—only when it compels belief.

This is to recognize the essential redundancy of James's vision and his representation: a redundancy that constitutes his defeat of reductive exchange. James believes in redundancy. He believes in the excesses of life, and he believes in doing things over until they are "done." His excessive acceptance is James's gift, as it is the gift of the Ververs to the Prince and Charlotte in *The Golden Bowl*.

AFTERWORD

When Pamela, early in Richardson's novel, writes to her parents, "your *poverty* is my *pride*, as your integrity shall be my imitation" (87), we can recognize that we are in the hands of a narrator who subscribes to something like James's "sublime economy." Like Clarissa, and like the heroic characters and narrators of *Middlemarch, Daniel Deronda*, and *The Golden Bowl*, Pamela uses language that is both indeterminate and practical and represents with such language human relations that are both unaccountable and profitable.

It is just the practical effects of such an economy, or just the fact that indeterminate, "artful" representation *has* practical effects in these novels, that is unsettling, for characters as for many readers. If Pamela were using paradox in the above quotation only as a figure of speech, we might rest comfortably with the recognition of epigrammatic wit. But the exchanges among characters, in *Pamela* and all of these novels, put into practice relations as indeterminate as those of her language. Indeterminate relations become practical relations.

If language does not establish truth as a total or objective phenomenon, language presents us with a choice: the choice between trying to gain possession of such truth even though we do not have the means to do so and accepting the indeterminacy of truth that language implies. Richardson, Eliot, and James have authorized the latter choice. And in doing so they have discovered that language is, in the very indeterminacy of its meaning, true to the partial and indeterminate nature of human beings and offers us the possibility of being true to ourselves rather than divided from ourselves by a concept of truth that rules out partiality and indeterminacy.

Practically, we cannot resolve the differences that language represents. Language can be used to provide such a resolution, of course; but any such resolution, as deconstruction has demonstrated, can also be represented as irresolute. As George Eliot reminds us, if we begin with certain axioms, we can arrive at axiomatic truth; but the choice of axioms is arbitrary, and truth remains arbitrary and partial. We are left with the paradox of partial truth, then; or with validity rather than truth, as the idea of truth is defeated in the practice of language. In the novels I have considered in this book, language is used not to provide such resolutions of differences but to bind differences together without resolving them. Paradoxes abound in such relations, and all meaning is partial and arbitrary. But indeterminacy and arbitrariness do not defeat the principle of meaning; they are always meaningful even as they are means of meaning. Meaning does not work against itself, nor does the practice of language work against the idea of meaning.

The recognition of Richardson, Eliot, and James that partiality is binding rather than divisive is what enables them to represent alien differences in committed relations with each other. Put into practice, the paradoxical possibilities of committed alienation are realized in human relations that liberate human beings not only from the constraints of trying to distinguish ourselves from true meaning but also from the constraints of trying to distinguish ourselves from each other. We can commit ourselves to others in relations that leave room for differences but preclude division, just as we can commit ourselves to the differences inherent in the relations of language.

The gaps in language, then, may work for us rather than against us. The undecidable nature of the meaning of language leaves us room for choice and insists that our choices of meaning are purely arbitrary and partial. The gaps are where we come in. We may enter into language to wish for something else; we may miss something because of the gaps. Or we may enter into language to commit ourselves, in our partiality, to the partiality of language. And if the relations of words always leave open spaces, we may find ourselves, as parts of relations, in those spaces. Relative and partial, language thus offers us the opportunity *not* to make up for something missing.

Henry James wrote at the end of the Preface to *The Golden Bowl* that, "as art is nothing if not exemplary, care nothing if not active, finish nothing if not consistent, the proved error is the base apologetic deed, the helpless regret is the barren commentary, and 'connexions' are employable for finer purposes than mere gaping contrition" (348). If we took advantage of representation, James suggests here, we would not be sorry. Language need not represent losses, and human beings need not be lacking, if the very partial and relative nature of the one empowers the partial and relative nature of the other to find meaning not in differences themselves but in the relations among them. This is an excess of meaning that inheres in human relations, and it is insofar as meaning inheres in the very excesses of human relations that meaning can be meaningful.

INDEX

alienation: and commitment, 31-34, 187-88; in *Daniel Deronda*, 222-23; of the Freudian self, 23-24, 32-33n, 39; in *The Golden Bowl*, 292; Marx's theory of, 29-30; and realism, 30-31, 151-52, 187, 211
Austen, Jane, 4

Barthes, Roland, 234
Bataille, Georges, 28n
Bate, Walter Jackson, 240n
Bateson, Gregory, 32-33n
belief: as confidence, 295-96, 297-98; in *Daniel Deronda*, 43-45, 216-17, 219-20; as faith, 297, 307, 326-27, 345-46; in *The Golden Bowl*, 279-80; in James's fiction, 47-48, 279; William James on, 43-45. *See also* partiality
Bersani, Leo, 41, 168; on freedom in James, 42n, 286-87, 289-90; on realistic fiction, 18, 162, 172, 187-88; theory of deconstructed self, 35, 36-37
Blackmur, R. P., 312
Bové, Paul, 6, 193n
Bradbury, Nicola, 274-75, 294
Braudy, Leo, 98, 99, 129, 130-31
Brooks, Cleanth, 6-7
Brooks, Peter, 19, 77-78
Brown, Homer O., 65

Cameron, Sharon, 78-79
Castle, Terry, 99, 102, 146
Chase, Cynthia, 32n, 209-11, 233, 258
Chodorow, Nancy, 25-26
Crews, Frederick C., 272-73

deconstruction: in *Clarissa*, 134-40; critical assumptions of, 5, 7-8,

11-12; of *Daniel Deronda*, 32-33n, 209-12; Eliot's evasion of, 175, 209-13; and irresolution, 347; and mastery, 34-37, 39; and nothingness, 36, 37; in *Pamela*, 36, 65-66
de Man, Paul, 36, 142-43, 144
Derrida, Jacques, 5, 7-8, 10
Dickens, Charles, 4
Donovan, Robert Alan, 55n
Duruz, Nicholas, 23n

Eagleton, Terry, 52-53n, 98, 102, 148-49
Eliot, George: concept of authority, 42-45; concept of meaning, 3-4, 15-16, 17, 34, 47
——— *Daniel Deronda*, 15-16, 43, 208-69, 323-24; authority in, 43-45, 233-34; exchange in, 238-42; privilege in, 10; sexual differences in, 26n
——— *Middlemarch*, 15-16, 43, 150-207, 289; authority in, 155, 161, 188-207; exchange in, 166, 186; power in, 155, 167, 184-87, 196, 198-99
——— *The Mill on the Floss*, 26n

Fenichel, Otto, 288
Fielding, Henry, 56, 73
Forster, E. M., 20-21
Foucault, Michel, 39-41, 42n, 46n, 187
freedom: and commitment, 32, 42, 186-87, 328; in *Daniel Deronda*, 228; in *The Golden Bowl*, 289-91; in *Pamela*, 58-59
Freud, Sigmund, 25n; and narrative structure, 19, 191; reality principle, 17, 22-23, 152; on repression, 22-23, 39-40, 211, 307; super-ego, 22-23, 265

Gadamer, Hans-Georg, 235-36
Gardiner, Judith Kegan, 26n

Haight, Gordon S., 206n
Hardy, Barbara, 163n, 208, 217,
    227
Hartman, Geoffrey H.: on interpre-
    tation, 63-64; on literary lan-
    guage, 12-13, 16, 17, 147n; "re-
    dundancy principle," 69, 156
Heidegger, Martin, 193n
Hertz, Neil, 177n, 264n
Hocks, Richard, 275n
Hulcoop, John F., 168n

imitation: in Daniel Deronda, 243;
    in The Golden Bowl, 309-10,
    312, 325-27, 342-44
individualism, 51-52

James, Henry: on art, 5-6, 11, 270,
    347, 348-49; concept of author-
    ity, 47-48; concept of meaning,
    3-4, 16-17, 34, 47; "sublime
    economy," 47-48, 277-79, 298-
    300, 347
—— The Ambassadors, 300
—— The Golden Bowl, 16, 17, 47-
    48, 269, 270-346; exchange in,
    297-98, 300-303, 313-15
—— The Portrait of a Lady, 49
—— The Wings of the Dove, 300
James, William, 43-45, 48
Johnson, Barbara, 8, 34, 134-35
Joplin, Patricia Klindienst, 147n
justice, 136-41, 332-33

Kinkead-Weekes, Mark, 55n, 100n
Knoepflmacher, U. C., 151n, 163n,
    188n, 216-17, 222
knowledge: in Clarissa, 143-44; in
    Daniel Deronda, 210, 323-24; in
    The Golden Bowl, 273-74, 296,
    302-306, 321-27, 328-29; inde-
    terminate nature of, 45-47; in

Middlemarch, 154-55, 159-60,
    167, 180-84
Krieger, Murray, 54
Krook, Dorothea, 274-75, 309n

Lacan, Jacques, 30-31, 211, 213
Leavis, F. R., 206, 217-18, 274n
Lentricchia, Frank, 40
Levine, George, 18, 188n, 209
Lindberg, Gary, 298n
Lukács, Georg, 152

MacCannell, Juliet Flower, 65-66
Mauss, Marcel, 27-29, 30, 49
Marx, Karl, 27, 29-30
Matthiessen, F. O., 274n, 286-87
Michaels, Walter Benn, 45n
Miller, J. Hillis, 161, 163n, 168,
    181, 188, 202

New Criticism, 5-7, 9-11
Nietzsche, Friedrich, 42n, 46
Norrman, Ralf, 276n

Ollman, Bertrell, 29

partiality: 37-38, 45, 235-36;
    Eliot's use of, 43-45, 47, 174-76,
    182-83, 198-200, 207, 226, 236.
    See also belief
plot, 20-21; in Clarissa, 102-103,
    123-29, 132; in Daniel Deronda,
    214-16; and Freudian thought,
    19-20, 77-78; in The Golden
    Bowl, 340-42; in Middlemarch,
    162-63, 190-92, 205; in Pamela,
    55-56, 70-76
Pope, Alexander, 54
Porter, Carolyn, 315n
poststructuralism, 5, 7-8, 9-10, 31.
    See also deconstruction
Price, Martin, 53-54

realism, 17-18, 161-62; in Clarissa,
    102-103; in Daniel Deronda,

209-16; in *Middlemarch*, 151-52,
201-203
redundancy, 14-16, 32, 49, 69,
156; in *Daniel Deronda*, 227,
232-33, 238-42; in *The Golden
Bowl*, 16, 297-98, 346; in *Middlemarch*, 156, 207; in *Pamela*,
55-56, 69
repression, 39-41, 73-74, 145-48,
260-62; in Freudian thought, 22-
23, 39-40, 182, 211
Richardson, Samuel: concept of art,
5-6; concept of authority, 42-43;
concept of meaning, 3-4, 15-16,
17, 34, 47
—— *Clarissa*, 14-15, 24, 97-149;
exchange in, 105-10, 112-15;
and *Pamela*, 49, 97-98, 100,
146-47; power in, 42-43, 101-
104; sexual differences in, 26n,
119, 133-35
—— *Pamela*, 14-15, 31, 36-37, 51-
96, 289, 347; art in, 11, 54, 60-
62; and *Clarissa*, 49, 97-98, 100,
146-47; exchange in, 14, 59, 67-
68, 82-96; power in, 41, 42-43;
privilege in, 10, 11; sexual differences in, 26n
Roussel, Roy, 52, 53

Said, Edward, 22, 237, 291; on authority, 200-201, 203, 239
Schafer, Roy, 65n
Schorer, Mark, 151n, 163n
self: in *Clarissa*, 115-19; deconstructed, 35, 65-66; in feminist
theory, 25-26; in Freudian theory, 19-25; in *Middlemarch*,
176-79; in *Pamela*, 77-85
Seltzer, Mark, 276n, 289n
Spacks, Patricia Meyer, 66n
Stevenson, John Allen, 113n

Thackeray, William, 4
Todorov, Tzvetan, 21, 275, 276
Tristram Shandy, 5
truth, 45-47, 49; in *Clarissa*, 100,
143-45; in *The Golden Bowl*,
271-72; in *Middlemarch*, 155,
190-94; in *Pamela*, 57, 60-65,
73-74

Warner, William Beatty, 98, 99,
101n, 132-33, 148n
Warren, Robert Penn, 6-7
Watt, Ian, 51, 52, 77, 100n
Weiskel, Thomas, 264-65
Wilt, Judith, 135n, 256n, 268n
Wolff, Cynthia Griffin, 99

Yeazell, Ruth Bernard, 275-76

LIBRARY OF CONGRESS CATALOGING-IN-PUBLICATION DATA

MCKEE, PATRICIA, 1945-
HEROIC COMMITMENT IN RICHARDSON, ELIOT, AND JAMES.

INCLUDES INDEX.
1. ENGLISH FICTION—HISTORY AND CRITICISM. 2. COMMITMENT
(PSYCHOLOGY) IN LITERATURE. 3. ALIENATION (SOCIAL
PSYCHOLOGY) IN LITERATURE. 4. SOCIAL VALUES IN
LITERATURE. 5. RICHARDSON, SAMUEL, 1689-1761—CRITICISM AND
INTERPRETATION. 6. ELIOT, GEORGE, 1819-1880—CRITICISM AND
INTERPRETATION. 7. JAMES, HENRY, 1843-1916. GOLDEN BOWL.
I. TITLE.
PR830.C634M35 1986 823'.009'353 85-17018
ISBN 0-691-06666-3